Who Ruled Tudor England

Who Ruled Tudor England

An Essay in the Paradoxes of Power

G.W. Bernard

BLOOMSBURY ACADEMIC
LONDON • NEW YORK • OXFORD • NEW DELHI • SYDNEY

BLOOMSBURY ACADEMIC
Bloomsbury Publishing Plc
50 Bedford Square, London, WC1B 3DP, UK
1385 Broadway, New York, NY 10018, USA
29 Earlsfort Terrace, Dublin 2, Ireland

BLOOMSBURY, BLOOMSBURY ACADEMIC and the Diana logo are trademarks
of Bloomsbury Publishing Plc

First published in Great Britain 2022
Paperback edition published in 2023

Copyright © G.W. Bernard, 2022

G.W. Bernard has asserted his right under the Copyright, Designs and Patents Act,
1988, to be identified as Author of this work.

For legal purposes the Acknowledgements on p. vii constitute an extension of this
copyright page.

Cover design: Terry Woodley
Cover image: An Allegory of the Tudor Succession: The Family of Henry VIII, unknown artist,
16th century, (Photo by: Sepia Times/Universal Images Group via Getty Images)

All rights reserved. No part of this publication may be reproduced or transmitted in
any form or by any means, electronic or mechanical, including photocopying, recording,
or any information storage or retrieval system, without prior permission in writing
from the publishers.

Bloomsbury Publishing Plc does not have any control over, or responsibility for, any
third-party websites referred to or in this book. All internet addresses given in this
book were correct at the time of going to press. The author and publisher regret any
inconvenience caused if addresses have changed or sites have ceased to exist, but
can accept no responsibility for any such changes.

A catalogue record for this book is available from the British Library.

Library of Congress Cataloging-in-Publication Data
Names: Bernard, G. W., author.
Title: Who ruled Tudor England: an essay in the paradoxes of power / G.W. Bernard.
Description: First edition. | London ; New York: Bloomsbury Academic, 2021. |
Includes bibliographical references and index. |
Identifiers: LCCN 2021006753 (print) | LCCN 2021006754 (ebook) | ISBN 9781350176898
(hardback) | ISBN 9781350176928 (ebook) | ISBN 9781350176911 (epub)
Subjects: LCSH: Great Britain–Politics and government–1485-1603. | Power (Social
sciences)–England–History–16th century. | Great Britain–History–Tudors, 1485-1603. | Great
Britain–History–Tudors, 1485-1603–Historiography. | Tudor, House of.
Classification: LCC DA315 .B385 2021 (print) | LCC DA315 (ebook) | DDC 942.05–dc23
LC record available at https://lccn.loc.gov/2021006753
LC ebook record available at https://lccn.loc.gov/2021006754

ISBN: HB: 978-1-3501-7689-8
PB: 978-1-3502-2981-5
ePDF: 978-1-3501-7692-8
eBook: 978-1-3501-7691-1

Typeset by Deanta Global Publishing Services, Chennai, India

To find out more about our authors and books visit www.bloomsbury.com and
sign up for our newsletters.

To my students and colleagues over many years

Contents

Preface	viii
Introduction	1
Part I Historians: Historians of Tudor government	
Sir Geoffrey Elton	3
R.B. Wernham	11
Penry Williams	16
Gerald Harriss	16
C.S.L. Davies	18
Jennifer Loach	23
Peter Gwyn	24
Part II History	
1a Monarchy: Legitimacy and personality	31
1b Monarchy: Ceremony, the arts, tyranny?	40
2 The power of the nobility	49
3 Parliament: The political nation	66
4 Finance	89
5 Military organisation	99
6 A 'Tudor Revolution in Government'?	113
7 The personal	128
8 Enforcement, dissent and rebellion	138
9a Poverty and policy	157
9b The crown and religion in Tudor England	160
9c The exception of Ireland	174
Conclusion: Paradoxes of power	176
Epilogue: The influence and legacy of Sir Geoffrey Elton	185
Notes	193
Bibliography	211
Index	222

Preface

It was reading Anthony King's *Who Governs Britain?*, published in 2015, that made me wonder whether a comparable study could be written about the government and politics of Tudor England. This book is my answer. I have long been intrigued by the nature of power. I have often touched on that when focusing on other aspects of the period. But here consideration of power is central. I seek to show where power lay—and where it did not lie. I am alert to the paradoxes of power: at moments rulers could appear all-powerful, a short time later almost impotent. But I am also conscious of how profoundly our understanding is affected by the claims of historians, and so I have begun this book with a series of biographical sketches of those scholars who over the last six decades have set the agenda for the study of how Tudor England was governed. I aim here to add a fresh dimension to the study of these themes.

Several friends guided my steps. Simon Payling and Nicholas Evans read my text and gave useful advice. Peter Gwyn, Cliff Davies, Anne Curry, Alastair Duke and Alan Thacker offered shrewd suggestions. I thank Anne Borg warmly for reading the proofs. And I must especially thank Mark Stoyle and Greg Walker for reading and commenting most helpfully on drafts and for their invaluable encouragement.

Introduction

Who ruled Tudor England? How effective was that rule? Those are the questions that this book seeks to answer. It is a study of government, that is to say, in the words of the *Oxford English Dictionary*, the conduct of matters of state. Any settled society requires some authority to defend itself against enemies from outside, to deal with disturbances within, to regulate its affairs, to provide laws, to secure compliance with them, to resolve disputes, to administer justice, to solve or at least to alleviate problems. A country must be governed. How a society is governed tells you a great deal about its character.

And government matters. In the past twenty years there has been something of a shift in the priorities of historians from the public to the private: from the history of states and constitutional documents and international diplomacy to the history of the social conditions of the people and the history of private life, of sexuality, gender and identity. Certainly such subjects are important, but so too is government. Those who rule can profoundly affect the lives of those whom they govern, in ways good and bad. We live in an age of increased scepticism, even cynicism, about politicians and civil servants—men, still usually men, men in suits who in often infuriating ways seem to interfere with our lives, telling us what is good and bad for us, while being on the make and on the take themselves as they fail to provide surgeries and hospitals, schools and universities, of world-class quality, or to manage the economy so that housing to rent or buy is readily available. But even if you do not think much of those who govern—perhaps especially if you do not think much of those who govern—it is nonetheless important to understand how a country is or was governed, because, for good or ill, it matters now and it mattered in the past, very much. And it is helpful to ask if all government is much of a muchness, or if styles of government change, whether cyclically, or in a definite direction such as from primitive to complex systems of government.

Studying the nature of government in sixteenth-century England has a very special quality since anyone attempting to do so researches and writes under the shadow of one of the greatest and most influential historians of all time, Sir Geoffrey Elton (1921–1994). His claims were bold, controversial and influential in surprising ways. In this book I shall look not just at the sources available for an understanding of Tudor government, not just at the contested interpretations historians have put forward but also at the lives and experiences of those historians themselves, in the belief that knowing the historian enriches our understanding of the history they wrote. In *What is History?* E.H. Carr famously told his readers that they must seek to know the historian whose words they are reading: 'when we take up a work of history, our first concern should be not with the facts which it contains but with the historian who wrote it.'[1] I follow his dictum here. When we in the twenty-first century ask 'Who ruled Tudor England?' we could reply that it is historians who rule—in the sense that it is to historians that we look to understand the past and it is from historians that we absorb views of the past. Consequently, knowing where historians were coming from is invaluable. It is for that reason that this book, unusually for an academic history monograph, begins with the lives of scholars who have dominated the study of Tudor government.

Part I

Historians
Historians of Tudor government

Sir Geoffrey Elton

Sir Geoffrey Elton (1921-1994) must be counted among the greatest of English historians. His book *The Tudor Revolution in Government* has made a lasting impact. He won fame and honours. He was knighted in 1986. On his death in 1994 *The Times* devoted a leading article to his work. On 1 December 2005, the *TLS* published a two-page commentary (by the historian of Elizabethan Catholicism, the late John Bossy) on the life and work of Elton. In 2011 as editor of the *English Historical Review*, I accepted and saw into print Ian Harris's article on Elton's interpretation, 'Some Origins of a Tudor Revolution', an article that, most remarkably, treated his book as a historical source in its own right. Harris is a specialist in the religious thought of the later seventeenth century: it is a mark of Elton's importance and influence that Harris should have been stimulated to make his intervention, to which we shall soon return.[1]

Let us especially reflect on the fact that the man we knew as Geoffrey Elton was a refugee from Nazi persecution.[2] Gottfried Ehrenberg—the future Geoffrey Elton—was born in 1921. His family were thoroughly assimilated German Jews. Most remarkably, his maternal grandfather, Siegfried Sommer (d. 1925), was at school in Kassel with the future Kaiser Wilhelm II and evidently struck up a close friendship: when Sommer died in 1925, the by-then exiled Kaiser sent a wreath.[3] Elton's father, Victor Ehrenberg (1891-1960), was a professor of Classics, holding the position of chair at the German University in Prague. Gottfried went to the German Gymnasium in Prague. He was due to take the equivalent of A-levels in summer 1939. But in September 1938 the Munich agreement partitioned Czechoslovakia. Worse still, Nazi animosity towards Jews, even such thoroughly assimilated Jews as the Ehrenbergs, intensified: Victor Ehrenberg feared that he would be excluded from the German University and lose his post and livelihood, simply because he was Jewish, and that his sons would be excluded from the German Gymnasium for the same reason. Victor Ehrenberg consequently applied for and received a year's fellowship to come to England and also secured a visa. But that was just a temporary arrangement: he came in 1938 but left his wife and sons behind.⁴ What happened next depended on an extraordinary coincidence. Ehrenberg's wife Eva had long before shared an English governess with her friend Netty, a vivid detail that reveals the upper-middle-class world in which the Ehrenbergs lived. Sometime later that English governess had returned home to marry a Methodist minister called Charmley. Later still, as fears of Nazi persecution grew, Eva's friend Netty and her husband fled and settled in England. One day in 1938 they were travelling on a train in Wales and, making polite conversation, asked a fellow passenger whether he knew Mr Charmley, a Methodist minister. Astonishingly, he did know him and even knew his address, in Colwyn Bay, North Wales: Charmley was chaplain there at Rydal School. Netty subsequently wrote to Eva about this extraordinary encounter.⁵ Eva, as the Nazi threats intensified, then wrote to Charmley, pleading for help. The headmaster of Rydal School responded by offering a scholarship for her younger son Ludwig—on the assumption that Gottfried, the elder, would remain in Prague as he was so close to taking the equivalent of A-levels. But Eva insisted that both sons were accepted. And so the boys abandoned their studies and the Ehrenbergs left Prague in February 1939, travelling through Germany, visiting their relatives there, before arriving in England. Asked by immigration officials about the linguistic proficiency of her sons, Gottfried and Ludwig, in English, Eva lied, saying they spoke English well; and they were allowed in.⁶

The Ehrenbergs were safe. But they lived apart. Victor was first in London and then in Cambridge until his grant ran out. In the war years he would teach first in a school in Carlisle, then as a lecturer in King's College, Newcastle, substituting for a lecturer serving in the war, then as a schoolteacher again and finally at Bedford College, University of London, as professor of ancient history for the rest of his career.⁷ Eva, Gottfried and Ludwig went to Colwyn Bay, and the boys attended Rydal School.⁸ Despite what their mother had confidently told immigration officials, neither of them could speak English, but they quickly mastered it—Gottfried won a school prize in English language within four months, astonishing the headmaster—and resumed their studies.⁹ Gottfried wrote historical dramas about the Spanish Armada and about assassination through the ages, as well as a skit on Hitler. Most of his historical reading was recent.¹⁰ And he did well enough at Rydal School to be encouraged to apply for a scholarship at Oxford in late 1939 and in early 1940, on that occasion interviewed by H.A.L. Fisher, politician and historian, author of a volume first published in 1913 and dealing with the period 1485 and 1547 in a series, *The Political History of England*. Intriguingly, given what was to come, Gottfried did not answer questions on the entrance paper dealing with Henry VII or Henry VIII. He was rejected—maybe because his knowledge of English history, while remarkable given his circumstances, was not yet at the highest level.¹¹

What next? He considered applying to the University of Manchester. But once the war began, many schoolteachers were called up for military service. That created vacancies in schools. And Gottfried was soon gainfully employed teaching History and German at Rydal School, where he had so recently been a pupil. At the same time he studied for an external degree of University of London. There were far fewer universities then than there are now. The University of London offered what were called external degrees, what we would call a correspondence course. It was pretty basic. Tutors set assignments; students wrote them and sent them to their tutors by post and received feedback. It was much cheaper for the student than living away from home but there were no lectures or classes, no summer schools in the vacations, no websites of course and no interaction with other students. All the same, Gottfried seized the opportunity. Among his options was one in Roman history, his father's subject; it led to what became his first academic article in print, on Caesar's Gallic Proconsulate, in the *Journal of Roman Studies* in 1946.[12]

Before Gottfried completed his external degree, he was called up by the British Army. He was instructed to change his name—he would be in great danger if he were ever to become a prisoner of war in Germany as his German name would identify him as a traitor fighting with the English against Germany—and so he chose the name Elton, anglicising his first name Gottfried as Geoffrey.[13] Called up and trained, Sergeant Geoffrey Elton saw action at Anzio and ended his military service serving in intelligence in Graz in Austria. In the army Geoffrey Elton learned to smoke and to drink, and turned into an Englishman: later he would say that he should have been born English in the first place. He did not directly speak of such things, but as an exiled victim of Nazi tyranny, he manifestly appreciated the constitutional monarchy and parliamentary democracy he found in Britain and it is not surprising that he would choose to study them. What he especially valued was what R.B. Wernham called 'the peculiar English blend of freedom with order'.[14]

When he resumed his studies after military service, he took a first-class degree. He also won the Derby scholarship given annually to the top history student: it funded three years' full-time study leading to a doctorate. By this point Elton's father Victor Ehrenberg had, as we have seen, finally got a permanent academic post. With an academic as father, and with other academics in the family, it is not surprising that Geoffrey Elton decided to follow that road, as did his younger brother Ludwig, anglicised as Lewis Elton (1923–2018), who became professor of physics and then professor of education in the University of Surrey.

Geoffrey Elton approached a number of historians about exactly what he might study, contacts facilitated by his father. Elton had earlier met J.E. Neale, Astor professor of history at University College, London, biographer of Queen Elizabeth and student of Elizabethan parliaments, when Neale and the History Department at University College London had been evacuated to Bangor, North Wales, during the war years. And Neale's nephew, a pupil at Rydal School, was taught by Elton. It was Elton's parents who urged him to contact Neale and they met in 1943 or 1944. Neale suggested Henry VIII's parliaments as a topic for a PhD and agreed to act as his supervisor.[15] On his discharge from the army, Elton went to see Neale, in July 1946. Elton told me a story about this. It's a nice story, but given that in a letter to his parents at that time Elton informed them that he was writing to Neale to ask whether the subject Neale had offered him in Bangor—in late 1943 and 1944—was still available, the story is not to be wholly trusted. What Elton told me was that two of Neale's female students, whom he met in the corridor while waiting to see Neale, advised him not to touch Queen

Elizabeth or parliamentary history, since Neale would not want a younger rival on his home territory. Accordingly Elton told Neale that he would 'do Henry VIII, Sir'. So Neale instructed him to read through the *Letters and Papers of the Reign of Henry VIII*. Between 1856 and the 1930s three scholars, J.S. Brewer, J. Gairdner and R.H. Brodie, read through the surviving documents in the Public Record Office (now called The National Archives, then in Chancery Lane, London, now at Kew), the British Museum, London (the documents then held there are now in the British Library), and many private archives relating to the reign of Henry VIII. They summarised and sometimes quoted directly a huge number of documents. And they then arranged them chronologically. The fruits of their labours were published in a series of huge tomes, the *Letters and Papers, Foreign and Domestic, of the Reign of Henry VIII*, thirty-six all told. J.S. Brewer (1809–1879) was responsible for the first ten going down to 1529 (and he also prepared substantial introductions which were republished as a separate book). On his death James Gairdner (1828–1910) then took over and prepared a further twenty-six volumes, assisted by R.H. Brodie for the last eight.[16]

And according to Elton, it was as he read through *LP* that he came to the view that Thomas Cromwell, Henry VIII's leading minister in the 1530s, was the crucial figure in Tudor government and that Cromwell's decade saw a fundamental transformation of English government.[17] If Neale had earlier advised him to study Henry VIII's parliaments, then perhaps Elton did indeed come to shift his focus away from Parliament and on to Cromwell during his researches. Parliament is not the central topic in Elton's dissertation. Instead Elton very much deals with Cromwell. He finished his PhD thesis, which bears the title 'Thomas Cromwell: Aspects of His Administrative Work', by September 1948, just two years after he began.[18] That was an astonishing feat. Elton was clearly a brilliant student. He was also immensely diligent. He studied hard in the Public Record Office by day reading manuscripts and he then spent evenings sorting through his notes and writing. He confessed to having taken Christmas Day and Boxing Day off.[19] Maybe the experience of exile had driven him on; maybe, as a refugee and outsider, he had few friends in an age when there were in any case fewer social opportunities and distractions for young people. He may also have been acutely aware that he had lost time. He was beginning his graduate studies at the age of twenty-five, four years older than undergraduates at Oxford and Cambridge who would typically take their final examinations aged twenty-one. The sooner he could finish his doctorate the better if he was hoping to make an academic career. Who can say? Perhaps important too was that he had absorbed from his general reading (as we shall see) an interpretative framework into which he could place his detailed material. He was living with his parents in London (so I would guess that he did not need to go shopping or cook his meals or do his laundry or deal with water hammers or leaking taps). And his parents lived within easy reach of the Public Record Office, British Museum and Institute of Historical Research. It was also in these years that he met and married Sheila Lambert, a formidable scholar in her own right.[20]

Elton quickly thought about applying for university lecturerships. He seems to have turned down an offer of one at Liverpool in 1947 and pulled out from a competition at Bangor. He then had the good fortune to be appointed to a university post as an assistant lecturer at Glasgow and, even more remarkably, soon to move on to an assistant lecturership at Cambridge.[21] At Cambridge he succeeded Kenneth Pickthorn, an historian who had published a study of Tudor government in two volumes. Until 1948, the universities elected members of Parliament sitting in the House of Commons. It was Pickthorn who sat for the University of Cambridge from 1935 and continued while serving as an MP to undertake his duties as a lecturer. But Attlee's government abolished the university seats. That confronted Pickthorn with awkward choices. He could have simply given up his political interests and continued as a lecturer at Cambridge. There would then have been no vacancy for Elton to fill. But Pickthorn opted instead for politics, securing election as a Conservative MP for the Carlton division of Nottinghamshire in 1950. Well before then he had resigned his lecturership.[22] It was to that lecturership, though at the level of a junior assistant lecturer, that Elton was appointed in 1949. He quickly took on a great deal of teaching, becoming a fellow at Clare. In 1953 he secured appointment to a permanent university lecturership and remained in Cambridge for the rest of his career, being promoted to professor in 1967 and ultimately to Regius Professor in 1983 till he retired in 1988. By any standards it was a stellar academic career.

It was built upon his early researches. Elton's PhD thesis, submitted in 1948, was, as we have seen, entitled 'Thomas Cromwell: Aspects of His Administrative Work'. The book of the thesis, published in 1953, was rather more sensationally called *The Tudor Revolution in Government*. That phrase was, of course, not a sixteenth-century term.[23] Where had it come from? One answer is that it may have been coined by one of the examiners of Elton's PhD thesis, C.H. Williams, professor of history at King's College London, who, the story goes, said 'it seems to me, Mr Elton, that what you have stumbled across is—what shall I call it—a kind of Tudor Revolution in Government'. Unfortunately, this may be no more than *ben trovato*. R.B. Wernham, then at Trinity College, Oxford, and later professor of modern history at Oxford, one of the other examiners, told me that he had no such recollection—and that he suspected rather the influence of Elton's supervisor Neale.[24]

So where had the notion of 'revolution' come from? What is remarkable is that there is nothing of revolution in Elton's PhD thesis itself, only a brief reference to the Reformation as a revolution but nothing on administrative changes as revolutionary.[25] Evidently the phrase 'Tudor Revolution in Government' must have occurred to Elton later.

Elton once claimed to me, as I have already noted, that he found Thomas Cromwell when he read through the *Letters and Papers of Henry VIII*.[26] More than that, in his book *The Practice of History*, Elton asserted that 'the theories . . . concerning Tudor government which I have proposed . . . came to my mind . . . because the evidence called them forth'.[27] Yet can 'the evidence' explain the use of the term 'revolution'? 'The very conception of revolution', Ian Harris insisted, 'is itself an interpretative conception, not a matter of irreducible fact, a comparative term.'[28] 'That some changes constitute a revolution, whereas others do not, is a comparative assessment, in other words the work of someone's mind as it assesses evidence.'[29] Undoubtedly, Elton read through the *Letters and Papers of Henry VIII* and certainly he then went to the archives, the Public Record Office and the British Library, but, Harris continued, 'he did not find a file containing documents labelled "revolution" because that was not how men at the time thought. Of course they may have been living through a revolution without realising it, but that pushes us away from the evidence and back to Elton's use of the term "revolution". 'No revolution ever stepped forward fully recognisable from administrative files in the Public Record Office in Chancery Lane.'[30]

It was, Harris shows, the demands of turning the thesis into a book that led Elton on to the revolution in government. He embarked on some revisions—a chapter on Cromwell's fall and more on Cromwell's life—and approached W.D. Hogarth, secretary of the Athlone Press. Hogarth responded that Elton's proposed book suffered from being neither a rounded biography of Cromwell nor a general study of Tudor administration.[31] In response, Neale urged Elton to turn his work into a biography of Cromwell.[32] That would have required a good deal more work. Elton would have had to undertake the laborious research that one of my students, Mike Everett, later carried out for his PhD, now published as *The Rise of Thomas Cromwell* (2015), research which took Mike three years and which took the story no further than 1534. It would have taken several more years of research to cover the whole of Cromwell's life.[33] And Elton was never very keen on biographies of sixteenth-century people, on the grounds that we lack the personal sources that can throw light on character and motivations. 'I don't see much point in writing the life of a man of whom we know virtually nothing before he was 35, and nothing except the official persona thereafter.'[34] So Elton ruled out developing his thesis into a biography of Cromwell. Nor was he keen on writing a general history of Tudor administration. We can only guess why. Elton was a young man in a hurry and such a project could again have taken years. And perhaps Elton believed that it was not necessary since in the researches he had already undertaken he had established that key changes in the central administration occurred in the 1530s and that Thomas Cromwell was their author.

What could he do? Between 26 and 29 January 1951, Elton, Ian Harris claims, wrestled with the challenge of getting more or less what he had already written accepted by a publisher as a book. He needed to offer plausible reasons why he had not written a biography of Cromwell and why he had focussed on financial institutions in the 1530s rather than writing a rounded study of Tudor administration over the century as a whole. What he came up with was a revolution—the claim that in the 1530s Thomas Cromwell had masterminded and accomplished a revolutionary transformation of the way England was governed. That dealt with the objections he had encountered and also had the advantage of making his findings seem very important. And so the 'Tudor Revolution in Government' was born.[35]

Harris has claimed that if Elton's latching on to the notion of a revolution in government was very much a tactical and pragmatic response to the challenge of persuading a publisher to take on his manuscript and publish it as the book that Elton needed to consolidate his academic career, nonetheless Elton was researching and thinking within a long-established tradition of administrative and constitutional history. Harris showed that Elton's use of the term 'revolution' was not in itself a novelty. Nor was his conviction that administrative institutions were very important in the government of a country. And nor was the belief that transformations in the administration could be revolutionary. Elton, Harris argues, would have been reading such claims as part of his undergraduate degree in history.

That is no longer the case. In the two generations since Elton began his studies in the late 1940s, the history curriculum has been transformed. In his day, and indeed still in many ways in mine, a typical history undergraduate degree concentrated on the constitutional and administrative history of England. Essentially history degrees explored how by the mid-nineteenth century England/Britain had evolved its unique system of constitutional, or limited, monarchy and parliamentary sovereignty. Now, as we have already noted, history students are as likely to study the personal as the public, to study identity, ethnicity and gender rather than government. History students no longer study the continuous history of the development of the English/British nation but rather study various aspects of the histories of countries all over the world.

That was not what Elton experienced. He studied English constitutional and administrative history. And Ian Harris has from Elton's footnotes identified in detail what Elton read and the influence it had on him. Harris claims that Elton was drawing on interpretations of administrative developments put forward by earlier scholars, all of them keen to emphasise the significance of the central administration of the English monarchy and to assess changes over the centuries.[36] James Anthony Froude (1818–1894), cited by Elton, had written about the supreme influence of Thomas Cromwell, 'the universal authority to whom all officials looked for instruction', and about a period of revolution.[37] Similar claims were made by J.R. Green (1837–1883), referring to Thomas Cromwell as the author of 'this great revolution'.[38] What they had in mind was not exactly what Elton claimed. They were more concerned to assert Cromwell's part in the break with Rome and associated religious changes; Elton would initially emphasise his administrative reforms, though later he would also make claims for Cromwell's religious policies. But all the same, Froude and Green highlighted Cromwell and wrote about him in terms of revolution. A.P. Newton (1873–1942), writing in 1924, referred to 'the administrative reforms that mark the Tudor period as the turning-point of English history'.[39] In a monograph published in 1923 M. Greir Evans had seen Cromwell as transforming the office of king's secretary.[40] On the importance of administration itself, Elton learned much from T.F. Tout (1855–1929), professor of medieval history in the University of Manchester, who wrote a six-volume history entitled *Chapters in the Administrative History of Medieval England: The Wardrobe, The Chambers and the Small Seals* (1920–33). It was from Tout, Ian Harris argues, that Elton learned the distinction between government by the royal household and government by bureaucratic departments, the former medieval, the latter modern, a formulation central to Elton's claims.[41] Tout's pupil V.H.H. Galbraith (1889–1976), director of the Institute of Historical Research, University of London, while Elton was a graduate student, asserted that a series of administrative changes together revolutionised the working of central government between 1450 and 1550. But Galbraith specialised in the eleventh and twelfth centuries and did not develop that claim relating to the fifteenth and sixteenth centuries further. We know, though, that Elton discussed his own researches with Galbraith.[42]

In no sense was the young Geoffrey Elton plagiarising the work of these scholars. It is easy to see, though, when a scholar as acute as Ian Harris points it out, just how much there was—just how coherent an interpretative framework there was—for Elton to draw on and to refashion in his own way. The importance of administrative institutions, the significance of changes in the early sixteenth century and the leading role of Thomas Cromwell were all themes Elton would have found in various guises in the writings of those who came before him, notably Froude, Green, Tout, Galbraith and Evans. Elton's footnote references show that he had indeed read their works. And in his very first footnote he declared that 'acknowledgement and full reference to all these and others, is, of course, made in the proper places'.[43]

It is very common for scholars to highlight, indeed to exaggerate, the significance of what they have found. Calling Cromwell's administrative work 'a revolution in government' was a very effective way of proclaiming the importance of what Elton felt he had discovered. If Elton came up with the label 'a Tudor Revolution in Government' over a weekend when he was puzzling over how to make the text of his PhD thesis acceptable to a publisher, that explains a curious feature of his book, that the concept of 'revolution' is never closely defined and never does much explanatory work. There is, for example, no careful comparison with other periods or other administrative reformers, judged by explicit criteria of what a revolution would amount to. It reads more like a label stuck over something already there. And when the text of his PhD thesis is compared with the subsequent book, the abiding impression is that 'revolution' was just added in places, with little or no further revision. By contrast, my sometime tutor Peter Dickson, who was to publish an immensely important study *The Financial Revolution: A Study in the Development of Public Credit 1688-1756* (1967), explicitly confronted, as we shall see, just what he saw as a revolution and how what he had been studying amply justified that term.

The title of Elton's book published in 1953—*The Tudor Revolution in Government*—made the boldest claims possible for Cromwell's administrative changes. Just two years later, in 1955, Elton published his *England under the Tudors*, a textbook for sixth-form students and undergraduates, summarising his case for a Tudor Revolution in Government in a chapter and, importantly, extending the case for a revolution to cover the break with Rome and the royal supremacy, both confidently attributed to Thomas Cromwell. The textbook proved very successful, and his claims were thus spread far and wide in sixth-forms and universities.

Not everyone agreed. But one of the curious features of the discipline of history is that the most eminent and publicly recognised historians are also those whose arguments are most vigorously debated and opposed. And Elton's *Tudor Revolution in Government* certainly provoked many. We shall later look in detail at the substance of Elton's claims and of the counterclaims of his critics. And there is more to be said about Elton's methods. But before that I want to offer similar sketches of the lives of Elton's most significant critics.

R.B. Wernham

R.B. (Bruce) Wernham (1906–1999) was the external examiner of Elton's PhD thesis, and he then wrote a devastating review of Elton's book in the *English Historical Review* in January 1956, questioning some points of detail but above all rejecting the whole framework on which Elton had erected his case. We shall come back to that, but now we shall look at Wernham's long life.[44]

The son of a tenant farmer near Newbury, Berkshire, Wernham went from St Bartholomew's Grammar School to Exeter College, Oxford, taking a first in 1928 and then studying for a DPhil on English foreign policy in the 1590s. He did not find a congenial supervisor in Oxford. After a year he moved to London to work on the State Papers in the Public Record Office. He was assigned a supervisor in London— J.E. Neale, the same scholar who would nearly two decades later supervise Geoffrey Elton. Wernham would thank Neale as 'the kindest and most stimulating counsellor and friend since my earliest ventures in Tudor history'.[45] Wernham quickly acquired a mastery of Tudor handwriting and in 1930 he was appointed to a new post in the Public Record Office, a two-year assistantship to edit manuscripts. He spent his time sampling a wide range of manuscripts and abandoned his planned doctoral dissertation. He did make some remarkable discoveries, on the treatment of William Davison, diplomat and secretary of state, tried and committed to the Tower of London as the public scapegoat for the execution of Mary Queen of Scots in 1587, but paid his salary as secretary of state for the rest of his life.[46] And Wernham was also invited, remarkably for a young scholar, to address the Royal Historical Society on 'Queen Elizabeth and the Siege of Rouen, 1591'.[47] Quarrels and tensions in the Public Record Office led to the resignation of the editor of the Elizabethan *Calendar of State Papers, Spanish*, and the subsequent appointment of Wernham, at the unusually young age of twenty-six.

At this time Wernham also prepared, together with J.C. Walker, *England under Elizabeth* (1558–1603), a volume of sources designed for undergraduates. Wernham was very happy working in the Public Record Office, but that collection suggests that he had university teaching in mind. And in October 1933 Wernham was appointed to a lectureship at University College, London, Neale's college. But remarkably, just a few months later, Wernham was elected fellow of Trinity College, Oxford. Trinity allowed him to spend a day a week in the Public Record Office, where he was appointed an external editor, paid at hourly rates, of the Foreign Calendars. Wernham would produce several volumes of *Calendars of State Papers, Foreign*. Volume xxii dealing with diplomatic correspondence relating above all to the Netherlands in summer and autumn 1588 appeared in 1936, including full and detailed summaries of several hundred letters and a magisterial survey of Queen Elizabeth's policy towards the United Provinces. Volume xxiii, with summaries and often full transcripts of some 743 documents covering the first seven months of 1589, was complete by September 1939, but it would not be published till 1950.

The war intervened. Wernham was deemed unfit for active service and joined the Photographic Interpretation Unit at Medmenham, Buckinghamshire, where he studied aerial reconnaissance photographs and advised Special Operations Executive on suitable landing sites for its agents. In October 1943, he was transferred to the Historical Branch of the Air Ministry in London and, alongside fire-watching duties, was commissioned to prepare a history of Bomber Command since 1914. In just over a year he produced a text of some 140,000 words, 'elegantly written and impeccably scholarly', according to Noble Frankland, on *The Pre-war Evolution of Bomber Command* which went up to 1938. After the war, and indeed as late as 1949, Wernham was put under pressure to take his account further and produce a full history of Bomber Command during the war. But Wernham wanted to return to teaching and to the sixteenth century. Maybe he was also aware just how tricky it would be to write an official history that was both honestly critical and acceptable to politicians and air chiefs. Remarkably, however, Wernham was to become involved in a different way. One of his pupils at Trinity, Noble Frankland, who returned to Oxford after serving for two years as a navigator in Bomber Command, went on to secure a post in the Historical Branch of the Air Ministry, and from January 1949 prepared an Oxford DPhil thesis under Wernham's supervision on Bomber Command in the Second World War. A year later Frankland was commissioned with Sir Charles Webster to produce the official history of what was termed the Strategic Air Offensive. Wernham would review the ensuing four volumes, published in 1961, in the *Oxford Magazine*.

His influence had been considerable. His style of teaching—regular meetings, a succession of encouraging and probing questions—allowed students to feel that they had worked out their ideas for themselves without quite grasping how far their tutor had sent them on their way. In his own typescript prepared in 1945, Wernham had declared how 'Bomber Command was the supreme expression, and its operations were the first test, of an official established British belief that, for an unmilitary island power closely neighboured by great continental military states, an "independent" Air Force is an essential weapon of defence', before going on to note that 'how difficult an operation effective long range bombing on the grand scale was in fact to prove, few people had yet realised'. That was in miniature the conclusion that Webster and Frankland would reach in *The Strategic Air Offensive against Germany, 1939-45*.

Wernham explained in his review how the received view was that Bomber Command had been starved of money before the war and was consequently too small to achieve effective results: as it gradually expanded it became more effective, sapped German strength and ultimately played a decisive part in the allied victory. Frankland and Webster showed that, far from being a revolutionary innovation, air power was subject to the same general principles as those governing the conduct of armies and navies. For the most part the results of bombing were disappointing; not till the German fighter force was confronted and air superiority established did bombing make a decisive contribution. The conviction that by destroying industries, communications and morale, bomber aircraft might cripple enemy armies and fleets grew out of, though it was not really tested by, the experiences of 1914–18; in 1944–5 bomber aircraft did indeed come close to doing just that. But in the early 1940s, the belief that 'the bomber will always get through' proved misguided: German fighters prevented daytime bombing; night-time bombing was wildly inaccurate; poor weather and industrial haze made navigation difficult. All that could be attempted was systematic obliteration of Germany's major cities, and even that proved challenging. But once Bomber Command with the help of the Americans had established air superiority, which they did in 1944, they were more successful. Yet instead of concentrating on focussed attacks on oil targets, transport and communications, Bomber Command continued to see general area bombing as the most decisive action that it could take. With victory in sight, such destruction and terror 'became an embarrassment to the conscience', Wernham noted, concluding that Bomber Command 'for most of the time fought the way it did, not from choice, but because that was the only way it could fight at all when it alone could fight'.[48]

Back in Oxford after the war, Wernham continued to work on his calendars of the *State Papers, Foreign*. But in 1950, the new Deputy Keeper of the Public Record Office, Sir Hilary Jenkinson, terminated the series on grounds of their cost and the time they took to produce. Instead of detailed summaries, there would be descriptive lists and indexes of names, places and subjects. Wernham found a way of subverting Jenkinson's scheme. He did indeed prepare lists. But he also prepared what he called an Analysis, a consolidated summary in more or less narrative form, arranged geographically. Wernham's *Analyses* were lengthy. The first volume, dealing with 1,344 documents, appeared in 1964, the second in 1970, the third in 1980, the fourth in 1984, the fifth in 1989, the sixth in 1993, the seventh posthumously in 2000. What would now be done—if it were done at all—by a team of researchers was here done by one man amid the varied duties of a full-time academic. Hugh Trevor-Roper jibed that Wernham was 'an archivist not an historian'.[49] Certainly Wernham was deeply committed to the archives and was a great and ultimately prolific editor. And there was an antiquarian streak to his interests, not least his acute sense of place. His diaries were not reflective but nor were they simply appointment diaries, though they did record each day the number of tutorials he had taken, the number of lectures given, committee meetings attended, the number of essays marked, the number of letters he had written together with the names of their recipients, what he had read, the number of hours he had worked on the *Lists and Analyses*, the number of words of his next book that he had written—together with the maximum and minimum temperature and a brief characterisation of the day's weather, as well as matters small ('stray cat had two kittens in middle of lawn') and large ('serious trouble in Korea').

The best justification of Wernham's painstaking approach is that all his calendaring proved to be the groundwork for his eventual books. *Before the Armada: The Growth of Tudor Foreign Policy 1485-1588* (1966) did not quite clinch the point as it was less a monograph and more a very decent superior textbook, redolent of those older school manuals that had summaries in bold type indented in the text. It is best seen as a necessary contextualisation of his core interests, England's relations with France, Spain and the Low Countries from the late 1580s to the late 1590s. In 1975, already in retirement, he was invited to give Una's Lectures in the University of Berkeley, California, published as *The Making of Elizabethan Foreign Policy 1558-1603* (1980). Here Wernham polemically took issue with Charles Wilson, professor of economic history at Cambridge, who had argued that Queen Elizabeth's failure to intervene in the Netherlands in the later 1570s was dangerously mistaken. Wernham insisted that

Queen Elizabeth did have a policy, more hers than anyone else's, even if shaped by circumstances. He believed that Wilson underestimated very seriously 'the depth of the divisions, religious, social and political, within the United Netherlands and the strength of the particularist motivation of the movement' while overestimating William of Orange's control over the radical Calvinists in Flanders. Wernham had in successive years written and then comprehensively rewritten a set of lectures, never published but delivered to undergraduates at Oxford, 'The Netherlands 1559-1750', showing a remarkably detailed command of their history. And against Wilson, Wernham argued that Elizabeth was right not to intervene in 1577–8. Her interventions from 1585 on were far more justifiable: quite unexpectedly the French monarchy was close to collapse and France in danger of falling under Spanish control, with incalculable risks for England.

In his retirement Wernham completed his study, published as *After the Armada: Elizabethan England and the Struggle for Western Europe 1588-1595* in 1984 when he was seventy-eight. His central aim was to show the importance of the continental and military side of the war against Spain as against the more fashionable emphasis on its naval and oceanic aspects: the soldiers who served in Normandy, the Netherlands and Brittany achieved more than the exploits of Drake and Hawkins. Wernham's narrative brings home forcefully the multiplicity of the concerns of Elizabeth and her advisers; the hectic press of events; the limitations on her freedom of action ('the trouble in the sea war was that a sixteenth-century government lacked the power to harness this private enterprise, operating primarily for profit, to a national strategic purpose'); the difficulties of obtaining reliable information, not least on the intentions of allies, as well as those of enemies ('one of the greatest difficulties that faced all sixteenth-century governments was the difficulty of assessing accurately their intelligences about their neighbours and enemies'); the war-weariness, induced by years of heavy financial demands and impressment of men for no immediately obvious victories, seen in parliamentary reluctance to grant taxation in 1593. Queen Elizabeth emerges as the dominant force in these years, willing to embark on aggressive actions, notably the ill-fated attempt on Portugal in 1589, Willoughby's expedition in support of Henry IV later that year (which 'did more than a little to make possible Henry IV's famous victory at Ivry in March 1590') and the despatch of the earl of Essex in support of Henry IV's siege of Rouen in 1591, until from late 1591 Elizabeth returned to a more defensive policy, in particular to prevent Spanish dominance of Brittany. 'Although her more ambitious offensive plans and enterprises came to nothing', Wernham wrote, 'she and her Dutch and French allies did prevent Spain from establishing its control over the whole of western Europe, from acquiring the crown of France and destroying the Dutch republic. In this defensive achievement Elizabethan England had played a very considerable part.'

Penry Williams's verdict when reviewing *After the Armada* was heart-felt:

> to comprehend fully the achievement of Mr Wernham in the research and writing that went to produce this splendid book, one must work . . . on the period after 1596, when we no longer have his guidance. To do that is like walking in hill country where no ordnance survey maps are available. The sense of deprivation is severe, even alarming. One can only ask, selfishly, for more.

And that is what Wernham gave. On 28 October 1985, when he was seventy-nine, he began the sequel; he completed it on 25 June 1992 when he was eighty-six. *The Return of the Armadas: The Last Years of the Elizabethan War against Spain 1595-1603* was published in 1994 when he was eighty-eight. As C.S.L. Davies noted, it is 'a carefully crafted and superbly integrated narrative which illuminated the relationship between strategic debate, diplomacy and naval operations'. *After the Armada* and *The Return of the Armadas* are monographs impressive at any age; to produce them long in retirement is a staggering achievement.

Asked in 1995 to give a talk to the Senior Historians on 'how and why we study history', he denied that he had a method other than working carefully through as many of the main sources of whatever he was going to write about as he could cope with, taking very full notes of all that seemed relevant and then going over and over them to piece the story together till he began to get some ideas of it in its wholeness. His credo is revealing:

> What has always fascinated me has been the enormous complexity and multiplicity of the subject, what Thomas Hardy rather lugubriously called 'the mournful many-sidedness of things'—the way in which over a particular period of time and a particular area (in my case it has been predominantly the 16th century and West Europe), how in that period, that region a multitude of influences criss-cross, interweave, interact, clash and conflict to produce a movement of change, to produce tensions that eventually burst out, often as the result of some comparatively trivial accident—that Henry III of France had a wrist that was just not strong enough to deflect the assassin's dagger. . . . Some comparatively small accident that makes an eruption possible and causes the whole process to lurch off on a somewhat different course. The attraction and the challenge of history to me is to try to see all that as a whole, and to see also not only what people of the time saw in the main area of their vision but also what they saw out of the tail of their eye, in their peripheral vision—to see all that in its wholeness, 'to grasp the scheme of things entire'—that is for me the appeal and challenge of history.

In an unpublished talk, Wernham reflected on 'Elizabethan Sea Power and 20th century Air Power', noting how 'the rulers of the realm faced similar revolutions on matters of national defence, showed similar foresight in planning novel ways of dealing with them, but also similar lack of foresight in applying novel methods and in realistically assessing their effectiveness'. In Wernham's hands, what he had learned from studying Elizabeth's foreign policy and military strategy informed his understanding of Bomber Command; what he learned from studying Bomber Command in turn enriched his treatment of how Elizabeth dealt with the Armadas. Wernham's was an eminently practical wisdom. We shall return to this when we examine his critique of Elton's *Tudor Revolution in Government* a little later in this book. But next we shall look at the lives of two historians, Penry Williams and Gerald Harriss, a few years younger than Elton, who in 1963 published articles in *Past & Present* assessing and rejecting Elton's Tudor Revolution in Government. Elton replied; Williams and Harriss countered; Elton answered back. It was an epic historians' controversy.[50]

Penry Williams

Penry Williams (1925–2013) came from a Welsh family from Breconshire. Both his father's and his mother's families could be traced back to a vicar of a parish near Brecon in the 1570s. His father was for a time handicapper to the Calcutta Turf Club. Williams was born in Calcutta. His father then became a bloodstock agent, dealing in the breeding and selling of racehorses. The family was affluent enough to send Penry to prep-school and then to Marlborough from 1938 to 1943. In 1943 he joined the Royal Artillery. In 1945 he was sent to India and Java. In 1947 he went up to New College, Oxford. As he had lost time in war service, he opted to study for just seven terms, not nine, but that proved a mistake and he felt under academic pressure most of the time. To his great disappointment he took a second, not a first. But by then he was determined to become an historian and the 'further education and training grant' he had been given by the government when he was demobilised was renewed allowing him to continue his studies. New College appointed him a junior lecturer which brought in a small fee per tutorial and allowed him to dine on high table with the Fellows. In 1951 he was appointed to an assistant lecturership in the University of Manchester. That year he met June, a South African student then studying at Oxford, and they married; they had two children. In these years he was working on his doctorate, on 'The Council in the Marches of Wales under Elizabeth I'. In 1955 he completed it; in 1959 it was published by the University of Wales Press. He then collaborated with Gerald Harriss, briefly his colleague at Manchester, to write the critique of Elton's Tudor Revolution in Government for *Past & Present*. Penry told me, if I recall aright, that it had been the editor of the journal, Trevor Aston, fellow of Corpus Christi College, Oxford, who invited them to submit a joint-essay. Penry thought that that article got him the fellowship at New College, Oxford, to which he was appointed in 1964. Writing it stimulated him to prepare a wide-ranging book published as *The Tudor Regime* (1979), still the most useful single book to read on the subject. It is a classic of modern historical writing. But it is also a powerful critique of Elton's Revolution. Williams's key insight was that 'the strength of Tudor government lay in a skilful combination of the formal and the informal, the official and the personal', a formulation to which we shall return.[51]

Gerald Harriss

Gerald Harriss (1925–2014), son of an east London clerk, was awarded an exhibition at Magdalen College, Oxford. He came up in autumn 1943. But war service intervened. He was placed on a six-months' officer training course. And he was to serve in naval intelligence, including learning Japanese. He did not return to Oxford till 1946. He won prizes as an undergraduate—the Stanhope Prize for an essay on Margaret of Anjou and the Gibbs Scholarship—and he took a first in 1949. The formidable K.B. McFarlane, who we shall encounter on several occasions in this book, was one of his tutors. Never an easy man to deal with, as Harriss noted, he was brilliantly revising accepted views of the later middle ages and Harriss greatly valued being taught by a scholar at the height of his powers and the cutting edge of scholarship, 'the most vital and stimulating experience any student can hope for'. But Harriss, while greatly influenced by McFarlane, as were several other young historians at this time, was always his own man, writing that dealing with 'so complex and sophisticated a character, who combined shyness with sociability, a prickly sensitivity with acerbic comment on his colleagues, a tolerance of undergraduate gaucheness and folly with abrupt dismissal of any pretentiousness or pomposity', was challenging and formative. Along with many other young men from relatively humble backgrounds, he was determined that having been through war he would win the peace. As his long-term colleague Angus Macintyre put it, he shared and remained true 'to the values of that post-war generation as they were epitomised in the promises and legislative achievements of Attlee's Labour government: the wish to create a more egalitarian and juster society; an unchauvinistic patriotism; a belief in self-discipline; a certain measure of austerity, a moral radicalism which condemned greed and materialism'.[52]

He completed his doctorate, in support of which he was awarded the Bryce Research Scholarship, in 1953. That year he was appointed to a two-year research fellowship in the University of Durham. In 1955-6 he was an assistant lecturer in the University of Manchester, where Penry Williams was one of his colleagues. He then went back to Durham as a lecturer. In 1965 he was promoted first to a senior lecturership and then to a readership. In 1967 he was elected fellow and tutor in history at Magdalen College, Oxford, succeeding McFarlane. He remained in Oxford for the rest of his career, being appointed reader in 1990 and retiring in 1992.

His DPhil thesis was an intensive study of administrative history, 'The Finances of the Royal Household, 1437-1460', completed in 1953. Harriss not only dealt with the intricacies of the subject but saw it as a key to understanding political and constitutional history more widely. In a substantial monograph, *King, Parliament and Public Finance in Medieval England to 1369* (Oxford, 1975), Harriss revealed an emerging system of national taxation dependent on parliamentary consent. In emergency, in necessity, monarchs were entitled to ask their subjects for assistance, and their subjects could not refuse to help their monarch in times of need, but they could plead poverty and bargain over the timing of taxation and the rates at which it was levied, a theme to which we shall return. In *Cardinal Beaufort: A Study of Lancastrian Ascendancy and Decline* (Oxford, 1988), Harriss returned to the period he had focussed on while preparing his DPhil and produced a remarkably subtle account of English politics and government finance. With his friend and colleague Maurice Keen he taught a well-subscribed Special Subject on Henry V and edited an important collection of essays, *Henry V: The Practice of Kingship* (1985). In retirement Harriss wrote a work of magisterial and independent synthesis, *Shaping the Nation: England 1360-1461* (2005).

Harriss had, as we have noted, been taught by K.B. McFarlane, one of the most influential historians of the mid-twentieth century, several of whose pupils became Oxford tutors. McFarlane's perfectionism and ill-health meant that when he died aged sixty-three in 1966, he left many drafts that a more thrusting scholar would long before have published. Gerald Harriss played a leading part in seeing into print McFarlane's

Lancastrian Kings and Lollard Knights (1972) and collecting together McFarlane's published articles with a valuable introduction of his own, in a single volume, *England in the Fifteenth Century*. Harriss also edited a volume of McFarlane's *Letters to Friends, 1940-66* (1997). Those letters included McFarlane's biting criticism of Elton's *Tudor Revolution in Government*, to which we shall return. Harriss's deep interest in the financial administration of late medieval England made him ideally placed to assess Elton's far-reaching claims.

C.S.L. Davies

In his seventies, C.S.L. Davies (1936–2016), known to all as Cliff, whose life-long historical interests had centred on what he, like other scholars, called 'Tudor England', suddenly realised that the so-called Tudor monarchs never called themselves, and never saw themselves, as 'Tudor'. Everyone, historians and members of the public alike, assumed that 'Tudor' was a contemporary term, but it was not. Henry's claim to the throne did not come from his Tudor ancestry, which was embarrassing. A century earlier, his grandfather, Owen Tudor (*c.* 1400–1461), a low-born Welsh adventurer and courtier, rather sensationally secretly married Henry V's widowed queen, the French princess, Catherine de Valois. Their son Edmund was ennobled as earl of Richmond. Edmund married Lady Margaret Beaufort. Their eldest son was the future Henry VII. After his father's death, Henry naturally styled himself earl of Richmond. Why would he have called himself Henry Tudor? His claim to the throne, which was not straightforward, depended on various links back to John of Gaunt, third son of Edward III. It was Richard III who referred, disparagingly, to him as Henry Tudor. Henry's claim was not that he was founding a new dynasty of his own but rather that he healed the divisions which had beset the royal family from the death of Edward III: Henry reunited the Lancastrians and Yorkists, not least by marrying Edward IV's daughter, Elizabeth. Referring to his Tudor ancestry would not have helped him here at all.[53] It is intriguing that when—after it burnt down in 1496—Henry rebuilt the royal palace on the Thames south-west of London known as Sheen Palace, he gave the new palace a new name. But he did not call it Tudor Palace. Instead, remembering his title before he became king, he called it Richmond Palace, after the earldom of Richmond—Richmond, Yorkshire—that he had inherited.

In a series of forceful articles Cliff drew out the conclusions of his epiphany, namely that Tudor rule should not be treated as a unity or as somehow distinct from what came before and after, and that there was no special identification between Tudor monarchs and Tudor people. 'If the use of anachronistic terms is unavoidable, the greater, surely, is the obligation on historians to warn their readers that they are doing so.'[54]

All that was wholly characteristic of Cliff's approach. He would be provoked to look searchingly at a cliché unthinkingly repeated by a lazy historian, and then, much thorough study later, he would offer a wide-ranging re-interpretation. Here Cliff went on fascinatingly to argue that powerful people *c.* 1500 were not, and could not be, well informed about the recent past. While sons of noblemen and gentry might know of the exploits of their fathers and grandfathers, the chronicles (the main source of information) were full of inaccuracies and chronological impossibilities, and the details they contained were not fashioned into a coherent narrative.[55]

Cliff's concerns over misleading labels had been voiced earlier when he expressed his unease about dividing up the past into periods. He was especially wary of neat formulations such as 'the age of this', 'the century of that'. 'Medieval' was a term to be avoided because it assumed that the years between 1000 (or earlier) and 1500 formed a distinct unity. Certainly such terms were convenient, he agreed, but added that 'words have a subtle way of determining one's cast of thought; and this is a dangerous proceeding'.[56]

How had he become interested in Tudor history—if I dare call it that—in the first place? It was, he told me, when he was fifteen and on a family holiday in Wales that he bought S.T. Bindoff's *Tudor England*, in a bookshop in Lampeter and was at once captivated. Born in 1936, the son of a dairyman in Hammersmith, London, Cliff went to St Paul's School and then to Wadham College, Oxford, where he took a first and embarked on a DPhil supervised by Lawrence Stone in the years that Stone was writing his *Crisis of the Aristocracy*. In 1963 he married Kathleen, another history student; they had two children. That year he took up an assistant lecturership—in nineteenth- and twentieth-century European economic history—in the University of Glasgow. A year later Lawrence Stone moved to Princeton and Cliff was elected fellow and tutor at Wadham where he remained as tutor till 2001 and as archivist till the final months of his life. It was the reign of Henry VIII that he chose for his DPhil thesis. Working in a period dominated by Sir Geoffrey Elton—under the shadow, as he chose to put it in the speech he gave at his retirement dinner—of Elton's claim that so important were the administrative reforms imposed by Thomas Cromwell in the 1530s that they amounted to a Tudor Revolution in Government—Cliff avoided direct polemic but presented a richly nuanced study of how armed forces were supplied, showing both that bureaucratic forms of organisation did not in themselves guarantee effectiveness and that informal ad hoc methods could be surprisingly successful, a point to which we shall return.

Cliff's approach was intellectual and cerebral but there was surely here a personal dimension too. His interest in armies and not least the detailed administration of war owed much to his experience of National Service in Germany before going up to Oxford. He had opted to get it done before coming up to get it over with (though perhaps he was responding to the convention in Oxbridge). Ironically, had he deferred and embarked on a DPhil he would have been exempted as the criteria changed. He was made company pay-clerk and then transferred to battalion orderly office, where he was made Part II Orders Clerk, keeping the battalion records, noting arrivals, promotions, departures and the award of stars that could increase your pay, which he quite enjoyed, as he was excused parades and boots and came to know what was going on as he illegally looked at the personal files of senior officers and NCOs, which he suspected 'pre-shadowed an obsession with Namierite biographical history'. He was based in Brunswick, near the East German border, so right up against the Iron Curtain. He read reports in the *Guardian* of large-scale Soviet and East German exercises. Had war broken out they would have had no hope. Only later did he puzzle over the nearby camp for displaced persons. They were under strict instructions to have nothing to do with them. More than that, they were seen as somehow dirty, sub-human. That led Cliff to muse when later reading about ordinary German soldiers who shot Jews and gypsies when ordered to do so that there would have been no difficulty in getting British volunteers for something similar, especially among the remaining veterans who had just seen service in Egypt. And it was typical of Cliff that he should have taken up the invitation to spend Christmas with a German family: he would remain in touch for many years. There was time to read in the English Institute and to travel at the army's expense: in Cliff's case to Vienna.[57]

He never turned his DPhil into a monograph. A rich article in the *Economic History Review* and a paper on the Navy Board in the *English Historical Review* sufficed.[58] That reticence was a pity, not least since his chapters on the campaigns of Henry's and Edward VI's reigns show Cliff's remarkable talent for the lucid exposition of complex detail. A decade and more later, Cliff would return to military themes, arguing powerfully that through the experience of war Queen Mary reunited a divided ruling class in the late 1550s.[59] Cliff also wrote movingly about the experiences of the common soldier in war and its aftermath.[60]

Cliff was in many ways a reactive historian whose writings responded to distortions, errors and glib assumptions. Given his parents' Welsh background, it would not have been surprising if Cliff had studied Welsh history, as Penry Williams, whose Welsh ancestors could be traced back to the sixteenth century, did. But against Colin Richmond's nostalgia for local and democratic community in the England of his boyhood, Cliff remembered the chilling stories of Caradoc Evans, particularly *My People* (1915), about West Wales in *c.* 1900: 'the chapels run by poor tenant-farmers who could hire and fire the minister, creating a spiritual and economic tyranny over mere labourers; the poor ill-treating the poor just as badly as the landlord or bourgeois employer may have done', concluding that 'small-scale rural communities could be cradles of cruelty and intolerance, in Ireland and America perhaps as much as in West Wales'.[61]

On completing his thesis, in the mid-1960s Cliff's interests turned to popular rebellions. When A.G. Dickens presented the rebellions in the north of England in 1536 as essentially economic and material in their motivation, Cliff was provoked into writing a classic article in *Past & Present*, 'The Pilgrimage of Grace Reconsidered', showing against the tide of Marxist fashion that religious convictions underlay and legitimated the rebellion.[62] That led on to studies of other rebellions—I remember a stunning seminar paper on Ket's rebellion—and much European comparison. A paper in *Annales* might well have grown into the book it was originally planned to become.[63] A decade later an unlikely intervention by Geoffrey Elton into the world of rebellions provoked Cliff into writing a vigorous and subtly argued response.[64]

But the principal challenge Cliff accepted in the early 1970s was to write a volume in a new series, the Paladin History of England. *Peace, Print and Protestantism: English History 1471-1558*, published in 1976, was much more than a textbook, demonstrating Cliff's gift for the lucid exposition of where current scholarship stood and of complex situations such as the state of international relations, before launching on his own original and brilliant reinterpretations. Not surprisingly, he was seen as the obvious scholar to prepare a volume for the New Oxford History of England but Cliff increasingly felt that he had had his say in that form.

Instead it was his teaching a new Special Subject in the 1980s on the Wars of the Roses that inspired a stream of papers: on the early experiences in exile of the future Henry VII; on John Morton, who would serve as Henry VII's Lord Chancellor and archbishop of Canterbury; on the ways in which the Wars of the Roses were not just a series of English civil wars but a vital part of European power politics; on Yorkist resistance to Henry VII; on the anomalous position of the Channel Islands; on the supposed Breton sack of Bristol of 1484. All these themes were explored in meticulous detail and quickly written up in lucid prose.

A dedicated college man, Cliff joined with his colleague Jane Garnett in writing its history, published as *Wadham College* in 1994 and updated in 2009. He had already written on a Warden in *Somerset and Dorset Notes and Queries* in 1975, and, especially in retirement, tracing the lives of those associated with Wadham in the seventeenth and eighteenth centuries became something of a passion. Cliff loved Namierite biographical inquiry, the fun of the chase, enjoying nailing down the precise details of relationships. Getting things right was the first duty of the historian. But in Cliff's hands such an approach led to substantial articles such as that on the young Christopher Wren in the 1640s and 1650s (provoked by another writer's insufficiently researched and inaccurate biography).

Cliff once remarked that 'what most historians claim to do is, I take it, to try to reconstruct "what really happened" and then try to explain why things turned out as they did. That is, and is bound to be, our major preoccupation'. Cliff, however, contrasted that generously with his friend Colin Richmond's concern[65]

> to illuminate shared human experience across barriers of time and space, as an aesthetic—even . . . quasi-sacramental exercise. The sudden glimpse of a common humanity, like a bright interval on a misty day, is part of the historical experience . . . it reminds us of the point . . . that the future is always a mystery. . . . Pondering the particular at leisure within a wide-ranging general framework, grappling with uncertainty and ambiguity, is a useful antidote in a discipline where an emphasis on production is in danger of mechanising, of dehumanising the whole historical enterprise.

The wide range of Cliff's historical interests is remarkable. What is striking is how original, and how much against the consensus, much of what Cliff wrote was at the time he wrote it, and how often when his views became fashionable, he moved on. Unconvinced by structural explanations, he once devoted a whole lecture to contingencies, to moments when the course of history might have been permanently changed. But when that way of looking at the past became prevalent, Cliff came to question the new orthodoxy, not denying the place of contingency but offering a spirited defence of Lawrence Stone's more structural approach to the English Civil

War. In conversation in the last months of his life he had been taking an increasingly 'whiggish' view of the constitutional claims being articulated by parliamentary leaders in the early seventeenth century, seeing serious and increasing divisions rather than consensus. The outspoken Elizabethan MP Peter Wentworth may have been put in the Tower by his colleagues but, he wrote, 'I cannot but see his assertions about free speech feeding into the seventeenth century and helping to transform the tenor of debates.'

Earlier, at a time when Edward Seymour, Protector Somerset, who ruled in the minority of Edward VI after Henry VIII's death, was seen as a liberal statesman unusually sympathetic to the plight of the poor commons, Cliff published a paper highlighting the Vagrancy Act of 1547—and its provisions that vagabonds should be treated as slaves.[66]

When the late medieval church was seen as doomed because full of abuses, Cliff was offering a much more positive view, notably taking religious concerns seriously in that classic paper on the Pilgrimage of Grace. But he applied the same rigorous scrutiny to his own interpretations. At a conference in 1982 he memorably wondered whether revisionist historians of the late medieval church were becoming too pietistic. While he continued to admire John Morton, archbishop of Canterbury and Lord Chancellor under Henry VII, he came to take a resoundingly critical view of Thomas Wolsey, archbishop of York and Lord Chancellor under Henry VIII, not least for introducing into England a degree of episcopal pluralism and ostentation until then found only on the continent.

Studying rebellions, Cliff undermined dominant explanations in terms of class conflict, but he was as critical of conservative interpretations that denied the existence of any tensions between the landed classes and the commons. Cliff had long taken a benign view of the nobility, seeing them as purposeful servants of the crown, overseers of the localities in the monarch's interest, rather than as disruptive. But in the 1980s as he taught the Wars of the Roses, he came to offer a less sympathetic view, notably seeing chivalry 'as privileging a small proportion of medieval society at the expense of the rest', 'a fig leaf for, indeed a precipitant of, noble violence'. And he came especially to question the idealisation of Henry V whose claims to the French throne he thought specious and spurious. While no pacifist, increasingly he came to see war as an abomination, sometimes necessary, but never to be entered into lightly.

Visiting Temple Newsam, Yorkshire, Cliff was provoked by the sheer scale of the house to ask why historians of the early seventeenth century were no longer placing the corruption of courtier-administrators at the centre of their inquiries.

When scholars increasingly interpreted politics in terms of what they called propaganda, seeing monarchs as exploiting the arts and creating images of their authority in order to increase it, Cliff was unconvinced. 'Who was taken in?', he subversively asked at a seminar. Who would actually see and understand works of art executed in a complex symbolic style? Would not those a monarch was supposedly seeking to impress know all too well when that proclaimed image was at odds with the reality? Cultural historians, he wrote, 'so often assume that an idea only has to be enunciated to be (a) widely known and (b) accepted', 'a view of the reader as like submissive puppies, rolling on their backs and accepting what was being handed down and behaving accordingly'.

Cliff wanted to feel how things worked in practice. The injunctions at the beginning of Elizabeth's reign declared that the communion table must be moved from the east wall of the church into the body of the chancel for services. Together Cliff and Kenneth Fincham, historian of altars, tried moving the communion table in Wadham College Chapel accordingly: if official policy was observed, Cliff wryly noted, there must have been lots of sprained backs among churchwardens.

Cliff was fascinated by the lives of historians, especially those caught up in the Second World War, and was intrigued by how much their experiences contributed to the history they later wrote. Historians, like politicians, should, he urged, have some experiences outside the professional. He would have welcomed, I feel sure, the approach I have taken in this book.

Jennifer Loach

Jennifer Loach succumbed to cancer on 29 April 1995, a week short of her fiftieth birthday which she was bent on celebrating in Prague; we had discussed hotels, restaurants and sights to see. She combined a rapier-sharp mind with rigorous and deep scholarship. Educated at King Edward VI School for Girls, Birmingham, she was awarded an Open Scholarship by St Hilda's College, Oxford, where she became president of the Junior Common Room, won the H.W.C. Davis Prize and in 1967 took the best first of her year, reputedly scoring alphas in all ten of the three-hour examination papers on which at that time final degree classification was based. Her outstanding ability was recognised by the award of a senior scholarship at St Hilda's College followed by a junior research fellowship at Somerville College. Somerville then appointed her a lecturer—which meant bearing a heavy teaching load but with no security of tenure. It was in 1970 that I was fortunate to be sent to her for a term's tutorials in sixteenth-century European history. She was formidably well-read and clearly prepared very hard for her teaching. She was very generous with her time—tutorials timetabled for an hour often lasted two. She was skilled in posing deceptively simple questions, never imposing her superior knowledge, shrewd in the practicalities of essay writing and examination techniques. In 1974 she was elected fellow and tutor in history, a permanent position, and she remained at Somerville for the rest of her life. She became a prominent figure in the Faculty of History and from 1989 served as an elected member of Hebdomadal Council, the ruling body of the university. Although still young for such a post, she was actively considered when another college was electing its head of house. Had she lived, that is an ambition she could very well have achieved.

An original and thoughtful undergraduate essay on what other scholars called the mid-Tudor crisis shows her already exploring themes she would study for her doctoral research. Her specific topic was parliaments in Mary's reign. This was a little-explored area for which sources are scanty and often tantalisingly obscure in meaning. In so far as there was an orthodoxy on that subject, it was the portrayal by Sir John Neale of Parliament as essentially engaged in conflict with the crown, ultimately leading to civil war in the 1640s. Mary's parliaments were troublesome precursors, not yet grown to full maturity. Loach began with such assumptions but quickly realised that they were unfounded. Instead Loach insisted that the ruling classes represented in parliaments were engaged in a common enterprise in which the monarch was the managing director and MPs the shareholders, working in partnership. And Loach would insist on the importance, within parliaments, of the House of Lords. Her findings and arguments were published in a monograph, *Parliament and the Crown in the Reign of Mary Tudor* (1986), and a survey, *Parliament under the Tudors* (1991). She then turned to researching and writing a biography of Edward VI. This was incomplete when she died but there was sufficient to allow Penry Williams, who had supervised her DPhil thesis, and me to turn it into a book, *Edward VI*, published in 1999.

Peter Gwyn

It was the bedtime stories that his father told him that first aroused Peter Gwyn's interest in history and made the past for him 'such an exciting world to inhabit'—so he wrote in the preface to his book and many times repeated to me. That led him on to study history in the University of Bristol, where he much admired Patrick (Paddy) McGrath, author of *Papists and Puritans in the Reign of Elizabeth I* (1967), highlighting (in the preface of his biography of *Wolsey*) his 'combination of scepticism and commitment'. It is worth noting that, in *his* preface, McGrath had thanked 'Mr P.J. Gwyn', remarkable since Gwyn was then only in his mid-twenties.

Many years later, when I was lamenting yet another bureaucratic form to complete, this one asking what kind of historian I was, Gwyn took the conversational challenge seriously and declared that he would say of himself that he was a very professional historian, meaning by that that the archives held no terrors, that he was alert to the technical problems involved in studying documents and that he had mastered Tudor handwriting and Tudor Latin abbreviations. He had read through all the relevant sources, and while making good use of the summaries in the *Letters and Papers of Henry VIII*, he had read the original documents in the Public Record Office, now The National Archives, and the British Library, rather than relying on the summaries alone. He was a great believer in office hours, in regular application to the task in hand. He may have been on the fringes of academe but he was no dilettante amateur.

His years at Winchester College honed his talents as archivist and as charismatic teacher of history. His resignation—provoked by the college's decision to sell its Malory manuscript—brought that to an end. But looking back, he told me that he had already been wanting to move on from teaching, especially at the level of commitment a school such as Winchester College demanded. Why? Because he wanted to be a participant, not just a spectator, in the study and writing of history. Initially it was Thomas More who attracted him, but by 1980 he had settled in Oxford and focussed on Thomas Wolsey, Henry VIII's leading minister, Lord Chancellor, archbishop of York, Cardinal and Papal Legate. Wolsey, he noted, had long had 'a bad press': Catholics blamed him for not preventing the Reformation, Protestants saw him as an embodiment of the abuses of the Catholic Church. Jack Scarisbrick, professor of history at Warwick, had written a marvellous life of *Henry VIII* (published in 1968) in which he had in part rehabilitated Wolsey, presenting him as pursuing a policy of peace and restraining Henry VIII's bellicose ambitions. Peter greatly admired Jack's imagination and verve but argued in a paper published in the *Historical Journal* in 1980 that Wolsey was always the king's servant and that what he sought was not peace but always the king's honour, sometimes best achieved through peace but sometimes through war.[67] With characteristic grace, Jack Scarisbrick conceded that Gwyn was right. Meanwhile Longman, urged on by David Palliser, gave him a contract for a *short* book on Wolsey. And so Gwyn embarked on what was to become his magnum opus. In 1982 Sussex Tapes, a company producing educational materials, invited Gwyn and Scarisbrick to take part in a ninety-minute discussion about Wolsey. I still play that tape to my students each year—and every year's new cohorts encourage me to continue doing so. That discussion, in many ways more an interview in which Scarisbrick asked Gwyn about his research, showed that by 1982 Gwyn had essentially worked out the grand lines of interpretation and the approach he would follow (and could present them lucidly and briefly and so offer successive generations of my students an invaluable guide to the book's 666 pages).

Against the thrust of claims by the young David Starkey, by Eric Ives, by Geoffrey Elton, by John Guy and many more, that Henry VIII was an essentially weak, lazy and manipulable king, Gwyn argued that policy was made by Henry VIII, who chose, elevated and rewarded Wolsey because he was extraordinarily talented, hard-working and totally loyal. Wolsey, as the title Gwyn gave his book insists, was *The King's Cardinal*. And large parts of Gwyn's book are given over to showing that the sources, rightly read, do not support the then fashionable interpretations of Henry VIII's reign as a cockpit of factional rivalries.

For Gwyn, Wolsey was—after serving the king—a great activist, well aware that much was amiss in the commonwealth and needed reform. One wonders in passing how far Gwyn was influenced here by the state of Britain in the late 1970s and by Margaret Thatcher in the 1980s as a reformer facing self-interested opposition—he was always an admirer. However that may be, Wolsey was undoubtedly interested in social reform. Landowners were reminded of their obligations to the poor commons. Noblemen were not to see themselves as above the law. Wolsey, Gwyn maintains, was also a reformer of the church. He was one of many within the church in the early sixteenth century who felt that monasteries were not living up to their ideals and ought to be reformed. Some of the smaller monasteries should be dissolved and their revenues used to create new dioceses allowing more efficient administration than was possible in England's unusually large dioceses.

So active a minister could not but provoke criticism, even opposition, as he cut through vested interests. Polydore Vergil, a papal tax-collector in England since 1502, briefly imprisoned after a dispute with Wolsey, offered a critical view in his *Anglica Historia*, the edition published in 1555 covering Wolsey's career.[68] It has too often been taken as reliable, not least by the young David Starkey. In his *Chronicle* Edward Hall offered an unflattering and conspiratorial view of Wolsey's activity. The priest and poet John Skelton wrote biting satires (although he then switched to panegyrics of Wolsey).[69] The linguist John Palsgrave mocked Wolsey's action as Lord Chancellor in Parliament in 1523.[70] In 1529 Thomas Lord Darcy drew up detailed complaints against Wolsey.[71]

Modern historians have tended to rely on these often vivid and colourful sources when presenting Wolsey. Gwyn instead subjected these criticisms of Wolsey to close and critical scrutiny, giving primacy to letters and administrative documents written at the time, and a very different picture emerged. In many ways his book is a sustained rebuttal of all the contemporary charges against Wolsey. It is not a biography in the modern sense—Gwyn noted how little evidence there was for Wolsey's inner life. Nor is it a study of Wolsey as builder and patron of the arts. Gwyn begins his book by noting Wolsey's building, his purchase of tapestries, his choir, but despatched them briskly because he doubted that studying Wolsey's artistic patronage brought us any closer to Wolsey the man. It was not till 1988 that he visited Hampton Court Palace. There has been more writing on Wolsey and art, but Gwyn, I suspect, would only have found his doubts about its evidential value confirmed. Nor is Gwyn's book (like so many recent publications on Tudor history) simply a pleasant and evocative narrative of events and actions. It is rather a powerful submission on Wolsey's behalf by Gwyn acting as a kind of defence counsel. Within a broadly chronological framework, chapters and sub-chapters are arranged by theme, rebutting one by one criticisms made of Wolsey in his lifetime and often repeated by modern historians. Again and again Gwyn questioned what too many historians before him had lazily accepted and retold. Wolsey, it becomes clear, has been misunderstood and unfairly maligned. No, he did not scheme to bring down Edward Stafford, third duke of Buckingham: Buckingham destroyed himself by listening to the prophecies of a monk that Buckingham should one day be king. No, Wolsey did not mishandle parliaments: in 1523 he secured an unprecedentedly high grant of taxation. And much more could be said in that vein. Gwyn thus transformed our understanding of Wolsey, a great achievement.[72] Moreover how he did it offers a model for historians. He takes you by the hand and goes through the evidence piece by piece, offering you sufficient detail to judge for yourself and in particular to judge whether he himself is right. Gwyn saw his book as 'something akin to a detective story, in which all the evidence will be treated as clues to be shared with the reader'. And unlike historians who just give their answers, Gwyn insisted in putting in his main text—not buried in footnotes or simply left out—his detailed reasons for the conclusions he reached, even if that made his book more combative and argumentative, more detailed and longer, than some would like. But 'there is this advantage, that by allowing the reader to follow my reasoning so closely, by presenting alternatives . . . he or she will be in a much better position to spot the mistakes, or just to make up his or her own mind'.[73]

Gwyn undoubtedly hoped to make an impact—and he certainly has. But he recognised the challenges. He was all too aware that 'a few lines of poetry can be more destructive than any amount of prose'. Skelton's description of Wolsey as *alter rex* would, Gwyn assured us, 'be strenuously resisted in this study . . . but one has a suspicion that in the end Skelton will win out'.[74] Gwyn, I think, would have seen himself as throwing a pebble—no: a rock—into the historical pond, hoping to make a splash, and trying to avoid getting wet from the backwash himself. But when the waters settled, Gwyn did not insist but moved on to the next pond.

That in some ways diminished his academic impact. Suppose Peter had become a conventional academic—but he was the first to say that if he had been undertaking the teaching and administrative duties of a university historian in the 1980s he would never have completed his book. Jack Scarisbrick invited him to take on some part-time teaching in the University of Warwick. He was tempted, but moving to France seemed a better long-term proposition. I can't help wondering, though, what might have happened at Warwick, not least supposing Gwyn had succeeded Scarisbrick on his retirement and if he had supervised young PhD students. Gwyn, I fear, was too free a spirit to thrive in a modern university. Still, Peter's withdrawal from active historical research, from going to seminars and conferences, did limit his direct influence. I urged him to write an epitome of *The King's Cardinal* to make his findings more accessible to students, but he did not want to go over the ground again. As he was completing his *Wolsey* he became involved with Nikolai Tolstoy and was pursuing historical research in a very different field. Perhaps he might have written a book on that, but in the Creuse far from any academic library, that was always going to be difficult. Ian Mitchell, whose research Peter much admired, went on to write that book.[75] Moreover, Peter had other plans for himself as historian. He set off to France with many volumes on India and Pakistan after the Second World War; he planned a book on the partition. But the challenges of settling down in the Creuse made that unrealistic. Gwyn's historian's eye saw clearly: several scholars have since then written studies of the kind that he had in mind. In his years in France Gwyn did write the occasional incisive review for the *Times Higher* and the *English Historical Review*,[76] and he commented astutely on drafts of my own work that I sent him, but commitment to his gardens took over. The urge to write remained, as his gardening blog (http://gersoisgardening.blogspot.com/2018/?m=0) shows, but he wrote no more Tudor history. And there is no story to be told of how his thinking evolved. Gwyn has left just one book. It is throughout very critical of Elton's approach and claims. Gwyn's portrayal of Wolsey as a great activist makes Thomas Cromwell's contributions in the 1530s look much less revolutionary than Elton would have them be. But Gwyn was not in the academic mainstream, holding no university post, and from 1990 living in France far away from the libraries and seminars in London and Oxford he used to frequent.

But it is time to move on from the lives of these Tudor historians. We shall return to the grand claims of Elton, as well as to his influence, and we shall consider more deeply the insights of his critics. But now I want more directly to pose the broad question, 'Who ruled Tudor England?'

Part II

History

1a

Monarchy

Legitimacy and personality

My short initial answer to the question 'Who ruled Tudor England?' is that the monarchs did. I agree with Sir Thomas Smith, the Elizabethan lawyer, who declared that 'the prince is the life, the head and the authority of all things that be done in the realm of England'.[1] For England was a monarchy and the government of the country was above all influenced by the character and abilities of its monarchs. If the monarch was strong, so was the government. Thus, any discussion of Tudor government must begin with an assessment of the Tudor kings and queens. But first, we should consider who was the rightful monarch during the Tudor period. It was not always obvious and undisputed. The rules of primogeniture did not always provide a clear-cut monarch. A weakness of the system of hereditary monarchy was that difficulties arose when a monarch had several children but his immediate successors had none. Monarchs with an unquestioned title to the throne were by that fact alone powerful, but an existing or would-be monarch whose legitimacy was challenged could quickly lose power.

Henry, earl of Richmond, the future Henry VII (born 1457, ruled from 1485 to 1509) was a usurper who won the crown in 1485 as a puppet installed by a French king, who had supported him with arms and money in the hope of weakening the power of Richard III by plunging England into civil war. But no such lasting civil war developed because Henry won an overwhelming victory at Bosworth Field in which Richard III was killed. Even so, Henry faced several subsequent challenges. There was Ricardian resistance in Yorkshire, Wales and Jersey. It took a major battle to defeat Lambert Simnel, who claimed he was Edward, earl of Warwick, son of George, duke of Clarence, and thus a nephew of Edward IV, at Stoke in 1487, when Henry was actively supported by only a few noblemen. Perkin Warbeck, pretending to be Richard, duke of York, Edward IV's younger son, dominated Henry's foreign policy in the 1490s, gaining a good deal of support from French and Scottish kings, from Margaret, duchess of Burgundy, Edward IV's sister, and even (secretly) from some members of Henry's court. Eventually Warbeck was captured and imprisoned, and in the second half of the reign Henry's crown was more secure.[2]

No doubt when Henry then married his children to the children of foreign monarchs—Arthur was married to Catherine of Aragon, Margaret to James IV of Scotland—what he intended was to bind his family to foreign powers and secure implicit international recognition that he was rightful king of England. But he still faced challenges. Two de la Pole brothers claimed the English throne. Their father was John de la Pole (1442–1492), second duke of Suffolk, who married Elizabeth Plantagenet (1444–1503/4), sister of Edward IV, and who avoided commitment in the disputed successions and rebellions of the 1480s. His eldest son, John de la Pole (1460–1487), earl of Lincoln, died on the battlefield at Stoke in 1487, supporting Lambert Simnel. His younger brother Edmund de la Pole (?1472–1513), earl of Suffolk, was initially loyal to Henry VII. But the king did not allow him to inherit all his father's lands and, following an indictment for committing murder in 1498, he fled abroad. He returned the following year but fled again in 1501, this time with his younger brother Richard de la Pole (d. 1525), arriving at the court of Maximilian, who he hoped would support his claim to the crown. But Maximilian found it more lucrative to accept huge loans from Henry VII and to send Edmund back to England. Edmund was promised that his life would be spared and was lodged in the Tower. His younger brother Richard remained abroad. Henry VII then died in 1509. He had lived long enough for his surviving son Henry to succeed unchallenged to the throne at the age of seventeen. Adult male heirs have the best chances. But when Louis XII, king of France, provocatively recognised Edmund de la Pole as king of England in 1512, the young Henry VIII was incensed. Before embarking on an invasion of France in 1513, he had Edmund executed on 4 May 1513, even though Edmund had himself done very little against the king. In response Richard de la Pole at once assumed the title of earl of Suffolk and openly claimed the crown. From then on he was the focus of a handful of discontented exiled Englishmen, but he never attracted a substantial following, and the vicissitudes of his family over the previous generation meant that while he had followers in East Anglia, he had not inherited great ancestral estates that could serve as a springboard for rebellion in England. And he became a pawn in the conflict between Francis I, king of France, and first Emperor Maximilian and then Emperor Charles V in the 1510s and early 1520s. In 1523 Francis I sent both de la Pole and John Stewart, duke of Albany, to stir the Scots to invade England, but the campaign was not co-ordinated and petered out. Ultimately de la Pole would die serving the French king against Charles V in the battle of Pavia in 1525. It is quite thinkable that in some circumstances de la Pole could have turned into a serious claimant to the throne, but such circumstances never arose.[3]

Edward Stafford (d. 1521), third duke of Buckingham, was executed for treason in 1521 because it had recently been revealed by discontented former servants that over a period of almost ten years he had been listening to the prophecies of a Carthusian monk in Somerset that Henry VIII would have no male heir and that Buckingham would be his successor as king. Buckingham knew that what he was doing was wrong, telling the monk that if the king got any knowledge of it, he, the duke, would be utterly destroyed. But he secured little support, as he himself recognised (and as we shall see further).[4]

It is also significant that the later rebels of 1536 who were hostile to religious changes, especially the dissolution of the monasteries, never directly challenged the king's title to the throne. There was no obvious alternative monarch. Thomas Tempest, offering the leaders of the rebellion advice, pointedly referred to the depositions of Edward II and Richard II but placed his emphasis on Thomas Cromwell as evil councillor and concluded by praying for the king's honour.[5]

Was Henry VIII worried about the future? Did his lack of a legitimate male child explain his disenchantment with his first wife Catherine of Aragon—or was concern about the succession the public excuse justifying his private passion for Anne Boleyn? In the event Henry would have a son by his third wife Jane Seymour—she died shortly after giving birth—and that child Edward succeeded his father unchallenged in 1547. But political disputes arose over who should rule during Edward's reign. There were serious quarrels between the young king's uncles, Edward Seymour (1500-1552), created duke of Somerset and Protector of the Realm, and Thomas Seymour (c. 1508-1549), who wanted recognition as Governor of the king's person and who was even prepared to try to kidnap the young king—not surprisingly, he was executed for treason in 1549.[6] Somerset's mismanagement, notably revealed in the popular rebellions of 1549, provoked his critical fellow councillors into joining together to arrest him. John Dudley (1503-1553), earl of Warwick and later duke of Northumberland, emerged as the leading councillor against the background of continuing plotting by Somerset was eventually executed for treason in 1552. Political instability was an inescapable feature of any royal minority: who could unquestionably claim to be the supreme authority?

Worse followed since Edward's death in 1553 led to a disputed succession. Northumberland, and very likely Edward himself, wished to exclude Mary, Henry VIII's daughter by Catherine of Aragon, from the throne in favour of Lady Jane Grey (eldest granddaughter of Mary, Henry VIII's younger sister) to whom he had married one of his sons, Guildford. Jane was proclaimed queen in London. But Mary vigorously set about raising the nobility and gentry resident in East Anglia (especially the earls of Sussex and Oxford, Lord Wentworth, Sir Richard Southwell, Sir Thomas Cornwallis) and their armed forces. Sir John Williams rallied men for Mary in Oxfordshire; there was mutiny on royal ships off Ipswich. All that reinforced divisions on the council; many had gone along reluctantly with Northumberland's plans and were now being wooed on Mary's behalf by the imperial ambassadors. Religion was the key dividing force in 1553. Catholics who wanted to reverse Henry VIII's break with Rome and the religious changes introduced in Edward's reign supported Mary, while some (though significantly not all) of those who welcomed the Protestantism of the new English prayer book and the removal of images from churches supported Northumberland. Both sides raised armed force; Northumberland set out to attack Mary, but then suddenly gave up, and so after Lady Jane Grey's nine-day reign, Mary became Queen. Yet it was only narrowly that England avoided a civil, international and religious war in 1553 on the lines of those that were to rage in France and in the Low Countries in the second half of the sixteenth century. That was not because of any significant differences, let alone superiority, in political structure but largely a matter of luck. Within months Mary faced a serious rebellion in early 1554. Known as Wyatt's rebellion after its leader in Kent, Thomas Wyatt, it was for a brief period a very serious threat: the rebels got as near to the heart of royal power as Southwark, just across the Thames from the Tower of London. They were probably prepared to depose Mary in favour of her sister Elizabeth (daughter of Henry VIII's second wife, Anne Boleyn), and it is likely that

Elizabeth knew of their plan and agreed with it. But leading noblemen, notably the earls of Shrewsbury, Pembroke and Arundel, stood loyal to Mary, and the rebellion was defeated. In many ways the rebellion was a re-run of the disputed succession of 1553, with the additional grievance that Mary wished to marry Philip of Spain. Yet to call England a de facto 'elective monarchy' on the grounds that in 1553 the political nation chose the monarch is to exaggerate. An elective monarchy would have established procedures of choosing the monarch. And the key point is that in 1553 the political nation was divided.[7]

Mary's intended Spanish marriage continued to provoke misgivings, even after the match was celebrated in 1554. What would Philip's rights be if Mary died before him? In July 1554 it was agreed that if she died childless, he would lay no claim to the throne of England, but it is clear that he had hopes of increasing his influence. There were plans to have Philip crowned and draft bills to exclude Elizabeth from the succession, but none of these were realised. The sudden death of Mary from influenza in 1558 ended Philip's English ambitions.

Elizabeth succeeded untroubled. What would bulk large during her reign would be her leading subjects' fears for the succession should Elizabeth die childless. Mary Queen of Scots, her most obvious successor, was regarded as unacceptable, both for her association with Catholicism and for her personal irresponsibility. The later sixteenth century was an age of political assassination, and fears that Elizabeth would be murdered influenced politics in her reign. In 1584 leading councillors formed the Bond of Association, signed by members of the Privy Council, senior clergy and leading gentry and townsmen, intended to frustrate any Catholic seeking to take advantage of an assassination. But it was not needed. Elizabeth died in her bed at the age of seventy in 1603.

* * *

Did these monarchs rule as well as reign? How able were they? How skilfully did they rule? Henry VII was intensely suspicious, reflecting his long years in exile during which he absorbed a pessimistic view of the realities of politics from the fringes of court politics in Brittany.[8] His awareness of just how much his victory at Bosworth Field in 1485 owed to the unpredictable defection from Richard III of Thomas Stanley (c. 1435–1504), first earl of Derby, no doubt explained his constant preoccupation with pretenders day and night. He was ruthless, possibly neurotic, after the death of his elder son Arthur in 1502. He was a very skilful political operator, very good at bargaining the maximum gains for the minimum of concessions. His character may well have deteriorated in his later years. Polydore Vergil, a papal tax-collector resident in England from 1502, suggested that his virtues had become obscured by avarice. We shall return to the question of how far his rule turned into something approaching tyranny. The lack of personal sources means much of Henry's reign will always be seen in a dim sepia light. But there is little doubt that Henry was in command and that he was an effective king. It has often been claimed that Henry meticulously initialled every page of accounts of expenditure and that that showed him as a committed 'hands-on' ruler, the first king of England who was a business man, a tag that inspired the fifteen-year-old Richard Southern and contributed to his awakening as an historian.[9] And the chapel at the east end of Westminster Abbey which he intended for Henry VI but which turned into his own memorial chapel demonstrates his power as well as his piety.

Henry VIII, Henry VII's son, born 1491, succeeding in 1509 and reigning till his death in 1547, is surely the most famous of English monarchs. That owes much to the wonderful portraits by Hans Holbein the younger. It also owes a good deal to Henry's six wives. These were satirised in Sellar and Yeatman's *1066 and All That*, where it is remarked that Henry VIII, a 'strong king with lots of wives, invited his ministers to play a game called Bluff King Hal: blindfolded, they knelt with their heads on a block, and guessed whom the king would marry next'.[10] That was not just the perception of modern wits. A rhyme circulating during the rebellions of 1536 declared that 'as for the king, an apple and a fair wench to dally withall would please him very well'.[11] But there was much more to Henry than wenching. We have just noted how Henry VII initialled accounts. Much less well known is the fact that Henry VIII did the same, as Sybil Jack has shown.[12] Henry's personal desires largely determined the course of policy in his reign. The wars of 1513, 1522–3 and the 1540s against the French and the Scots required money. One of the attempts to raise it provoked a short-lived rising in 1525. And the heavy financial demands in the mid-1540s bequeathed a difficult inheritance to Henry's young heir. Henry's desire for an annulment of his first marriage, to Catherine of Aragon, in order to marry Anne Boleyn, with whom he had fallen deeply in love, led to the repudiation of papal authority and a series of religious changes, notably the dissolution of the monasteries in the late 1530s, which in turn produced a threatening, if ultimately unsuccessful, rebellion, the Pilgrimage of Grace in 1536.

Yet if Henry embarked upon large actions, he was nonetheless cautious. In his foreign policy he was always careful, reluctant to embark on military campaigns except with in alliance with foreign powers, with no extravagant individual thrusts, not even in 1525 when Francis I, king of France, had been shatteringly defeated at the battle of Pavia and France lay seemingly defenceless, with its king now Charles V's captive. Did Henry seriously believe that he might one day realise his claim to be rightful king of France? All that went back to the Norman Conquest and what we see as the twelfth-century Angevin Empire, with kings of England claiming and sometimes ruling Normandy and Gascony. In the fourteenth century Edward III claimed to be king of France. In 1431 Henry VI was crowned king of France, but by the mid-fifteenth century all had been lost, Calais apart. Henry VIII nonetheless inherited that claim. Sometimes he pursued it with vigour, at other times he at once seemed willing to settle for much less—for example the duchies of Aquitaine and Normandy—or even to forget about it altogether.

Henry was also a skilful politician capable of shrewd reflections worthy of Machiavelli. He saw 'the common manner and fashion of the world to be such as benefits to be done and hoped [for] [i.e. in the future] be more effectual in the containing and preservation of good will and earnest friendship than those [benefits] which be already perceived and taken which [men] lightly pass over and be forgotten'.

Henry warned his diplomats negotiating with Francis, king of France, they were to take care not to offer too much but equally not to leave the French despairing that no concessions would be made.[13] Similarly after the rebellion in the north in 1536, Henry gave Thomas Howard, third duke of Norfolk, his lieutenant, instructions on how to respond when those who had remained loyal to the king during the rebellion and had consequently suffered spoils and robberies at the hands of the rebels petitioned for redress. Norfolk was to accept all bills, supplications and complaints, but he was not to make any final settlement, but rather wait till the king came north, as he planned to do. Norfolk should entreat 'the parties aggrieved till that time to satisfy and content themselves with patience, putting them in such indifferent comfort that they neither utterly despair in their suits nor gather such courage as they might thereupon report they should have undoubted restitution which might cause the offenders to enter in to despair and so attempt further inconvenience'.[14] A shrewd monarch indeed. We cannot know whether Henry had read Machiavelli. On this evidence he did not need to. But the paradoxes of power are to be noted here too. Henry, as we shall see, imposed his vision of the church after the break with Rome. But he could not commit those who ruled after him. Henry laid down elaborate provisions in his will, but these were ignored by his executors in his son's reign. As Shakespeare cynically observed, 'if a man do not erect in this age his own tomb ere he dies, he shall live no longer in monument than the bell rings and the widow weeps'.[15] And Henry's widow, Katherine Parr, did not wait long before marrying Thomas Seymour.

Edward VI, Henry VIII's son, was born in 1537, succeeded in 1547 and died young in 1553. He was scarcely able to rule himself, certainly not at the beginning. It is plausible to suppose that he became more involved in government as he grew into his teens. This turns on whether quite sophisticated treatises, for example on the coinage, that survive in his handwriting were his own work or whether he was simply doing a sort of homework, copying in his own hand texts that his tutors had devised. Should he be seen as a precocious godly imp, committed at the age of fifteen to a full-blown protestant reformation; or was his real interest, as that of so many aristocratic youths, in hunting, tournaments and war? Edward never reached adulthood, dying most likely of respiratory disease that modern antibiotics might readily quell but against which even Tudor kings were helpless. We have already noted that Edward's death was followed by a disputed succession reflecting religious divisions. Edward's part is controversial. By 1553 he was old enough to have some grasp of the issues and the way in which the crown was settled on Lady Jane Grey was just the kind of scheme an adolescent might devise.[16]

Mary, Henry's elder daughter, born in 1516, has long been treated as a failure, and worse, but more sympathetic approaches are now common. She showed courage and political flair in the disputed succession of 1553 and against Wyatt's rebellion in 1554, on that occasion making an impressive speech in the London Guildhall. Against the background of the worst harvests and devastating influenza epidemics of the century, she succeeded in establishing and strengthening her government, notably in successfully enforcing outward conformity to her religious policy of restoring Catholicism. Elizabeth Russell brilliantly showed how the view of Mary as a failure, as inexperienced, as politically inept, as weak and under pressure, derived from the despatches of Simon Renard, the Spanish ambassador. And Renard, Russell claimed, acquired that impression of Mary not because it was true but because it was the view of herself that Mary put forward when dealing with him. In dealing with the papacy and in negotiating over her marriage to Philip of Spain, Mary was cautious, aware that some in the political nation had been won over to Protestantism and rather more were uneasy at a Spanish marriage. By emphasising such concerns, not least in her regular meetings with Renard, telling him that she spent her days shouting at her Council, but with no result, she succeeded in obtaining advantageous terms, as Russell noted. 'She was . . . adept in using her perceived principal weaknesses as her prime strengths in negotiation.' There would be no demand that those who had acquired ex-monastic lands in her father's reign should return them. And the marriage treaty was very favourable to English interests. Russell concluded that 'it would seem that where Mary led Renard by the nose, the empire, Spain and the papacy followed, and the policy which worked on him was equally effective when used directly on Pole, Charles, Philip and the pope'.[17]

Elizabeth was born in 1533, succeeded in 1558 and died in 1603. She was a determined ruler, well aware of the limitations on the power of any monarch. She has often been unfairly misinterpreted as weak or indecisive when she was more realistically being cautious, not least in her foreign policy, where she was reluctant to become too involved in the religious conflicts in France and the Low Countries. Often the politics of her reign saw her resisting pressure from her own councillors—to marry, to name a successor, to intervene on behalf of beleaguered Protestants abroad.[18] Yet right at the beginning of her reign, the Spanish ambassador, the count of Feria, declared that 'she is determined to be governed by no one' and that Mary's councillors were 'extremely frightened of what Madam Elizabeth will do with them'.[19]

Despite that, one eminent historian of Elizabeth's reign, Patrick Collinson, has gone so far as to claim that Elizabethan England was really a republic that happened to be a monarchy. Those who administered the country locally did so, he claimed, with little reference to the queen or council, a matter we shall return to when considering the question of enforcement. More importantly still, Collinson argued that the queen's councillors saw themselves as holding a position almost independent of the queen. Collinson urged that the experience of ruling in the boy king Edward's name right up to the final months of his life left a vivid memory of conciliar—in Collinson's view, republican—rule. And for Collinson, as we have seen, the disputed succession in 1553 showed that England was an elective monarchy.[20]

All that is extravagant. That disputed succession was not a contest in which the political nation chose the candidate best qualified to rule. Had there been a clear and indisputable successor there would not have been a disputed succession. And religious allegiance was crucial, with Catholics supporting Mary and Protestants Lady Jane Grey and John Dudley, duke of Northumberland. No one thought of abandoning monarchy and introducing a republic. People did not overtly see themselves as members of a commonwealth with the right to depose monarchs who did not meet their expectations.

Nor did Elizabeth's councillors ever seek to replace the queen or to transform a monarchy into a republic. In 1563—soon after Elizabeth nearly died of smallpox—William Cecil (1523-1598) planned an interregnum council which would call Parliament to determine to whom of right the imperial crown of this realm belonged. But that was not republicanism: that was maintaining monarchy at a point at which the succession was uncertain. The Bond of Association in 1584 was intended to disqualify anyone from benefitting from Elizabeth's putative assassination, above all Mary Queen of Scots, after William the Silent, the Dutch hero, had been assassinated, and revelations were made of plots against the queen's life. Burghley and the Privy Council sponsored the Bond of Association, with the explicit aims of 'pursuing to the uttermost extermination anyone attempting harm to the queen's person' and blocking the succession of anyone on whose behalf such acts were attempted. Much has been made of the way that this Bond was drawn up as a covenant, with no one given overall control. Burghley again planned for a Great Council to summon Parliament to hear claims to the throne and 'to accept such a person to the crown of the realm as shall to them upon their peaceable deliberations and trials appear to have best right to the same in blood'. The question in 1563 and in 1584, as throughout Elizabeth's long reign, was who should succeed her as monarch, not whether a republic ruled by a group of councillors was better than a monarchy. Was this republican discourse? Was England, as Collinson put it, really a republic that happened to be a monarchy? That is surely misplaced. None of all this was directed against the institution of monarchy. England's enemies were international Catholics, not Queen Elizabeth, not monarchy. All these schemes provided for the continuation of monarchy. It is worth noting that few in sixteenth-century England wrote about, or advocated, a republican constitution, as we have noted. The word 'republic' was used to mean *res publica*—the common weal—not rule without a monarch.

The mid-seventeenth-century Civil Wars would result in the execution of Charles I and the abolition of the monarchy, but that was emphatically not what the parliamentary critics of the king had set out to achieve in 1641-2. It was the course of the war and the determination of Charles who refused to compromise over religion, and especially over episcopacy, that led to the parliamentary critics of the king who remained in 1649—a much smaller grouping than those who had raised armed force against Charles in 1641-2—and the leaders of the parliamentary army stumbling into what was de facto a republic. The emergence of Oliver Cromwell, the most important of those army leaders, as quasi-monarch in 1653 and recipient of an invitation to assume kingship in 1657, eloquently illustrates the lack of enthusiasm and preparedness for any lasting republican settlement. The restoration of the monarchy in 1660 clinches the point.

Much has, all the same, been made of the spread of classical learning and with it the study of ancient writers who wrote about republican Rome. No doubt in the fifteenth and early sixteenth centuries scholars were influenced, and maybe, over time, in the long sixteenth century, so were sons of gentry who began going in increasing numbers to the universities. But it is hard to offer any specific documentation for such claims. It would take rather longer for classical learning to dominate.

But it is vital to emphasise that in the sixteenth century, and long before, the English monarchy was what we would call a constitutional monarchy and what contemporaries would have seen as mixed monarchy. In 1215 King John had been compelled to agree in principle to various restrictions on his previously untrammelled power. Intriguingly, Magna Carta, the Great Charter, was not much invoked in the sixteenth century—it would take the lawyer Sir Edward Coke to reassert its topical relevance in James I's reign. But, crucially, a convention had evolved in the thirteenth century and been maintained ever since that taxation could not be raised by a monarch unless the House of Commons in Parliament had given its consent. That made the English constitution very different from that of France: not *dominium regale* but *dominium politicum et regale* in the words of the fifteenth-century lawyer Sir John Fortescue. The monarch enjoying *dominium regale* 'may rule his people by such laws as he makes himself, without their assent, and therefore he may set upon them impositions such as he will himself, without their assent'. The monarch exercising *dominium politicum et regale* by contrast 'may not rule his people by other laws than such as they assent to. And therefore he may set upon them none impositions without their assent'.[21] And in as much as Collinson's claims for a monarchical republic have anything worthwhile to add, it is in reminding us of Fortescue's dictum.[22]

Thus the strength of the Tudor monarchy, and the strength of Tudor government, varied according to political circumstances—above all, was there an uncontested adult monarch or was there uncertainty, or worse dispute, over who should rule—and more generally according to the political skills displayed by kings and queens and the success or failure of their policies, especially their foreign policies and, from the 1530s, their religious policies? What also mattered greatly was monarchs' choice of counsellors and especially leading ministers. Monarchs were expected to choose men of virtue and learning and political skill to serve them. And they did. It is sufficient here to mention Thomas Wolsey, Thomas Cromwell and William Cecil to demonstrate how much monarchs could gain from securing such able men. Queen Elizabeth chose Cecil, declaring[23]:

> I give you this charge, that you shall be of my privy council and content yourself to take pains for me and my realm. This judgment I have of you, that you will not be corrupted with any manner of gift, and that you will be faithful to the state, and that without respect of my private will you will give me that counsel you think best.

But what became of that duty when, as often, the queen refused to hear that counsel? Her councillors responded by trying to control the presentation of information to the queen, by emphasising and exaggerating Catholic plots, by using Parliament as an arena to put pressure on her, by using court entertainments, plays and poems to reinforce their message, all in the hope of getting Elizabeth to do what she did not want to do. But Elizabeth, as the skilful tactician that she was, countered by rarely attending her Privy Council—where councillors en bloc could cajole or object—by talking to her councillors in ones or twos and by consulting men whose opinion she valued such as William Paget, the third earl of Sussex, or Walter Ralegh, whether at the time they were formally councillors or not.

1b

Monarchy

Ceremony, the arts, tyranny?

Monarchs derived great authority from the universally accepted belief in monarchy. Contemporary political theorists stressed the powers of the crown. Monarchy was seen as the only thinkable form of government: hardly anyone in Tudor England toyed with any republican ideas, even though, as we have just noted, increasing familiarity with classical literature would have by the end of our period made educated readers aware of the history of ancient Rome. But in the sixteenth century the words 'res publica' meant 'commonweal' or 'commonwealth', not rule without a monarch. More generally, opposition to the monarch was seen as unsettling because it would lead to rebellion, which in turn was seen as dangerous and wicked because it would lead to anarchy and economic ruin. Priests and preachers were called upon to declare the necessity of obedience to the monarch. Up to 1534 the parish priest would pronounce a solemn curse four times a year on a list of wrongdoers. The *Homily on Obedience* (1547), read out in church four times a year, instructed parishioners that 'the high power and authority of kings, with their making of laws, judgments and officers, are the ordinances not of man but of God. . . . We may not resist, nor in any wise hurt, an anointed king which is God's lieutenant, vicegerent and highest minister in that country where he is king'.[1]

Monarchs enjoyed wide powers, what were called 'prerogatives'. They had the right to wage war and make peace. They could choose their wives or husbands, their councillors, the judges in the courts of law and officials in church and state. They alone had the power to issue coins. They could set the rates at which customs' dues were levied on goods imported or exported. They could ask their subjects to grant them gifts of money, 'benevolences'. They were legally protected by capacious laws of treason. To rebel against a monarch was treason. To plot and conspire the death of a monarch was treason. To talk about rebelling or conspiring against a monarch was increasingly seen as treason. To join an enemy of the monarch such as the monarch of another country was treason. To reveal secret information to an enemy was treason. To interfere in the succession and transfer of power after a monarch died was treason. Defeated rebels were often charged with treason, an assertion of power restored after the shock of rebellion. Treason was punishable by death and by confiscation of property: bringing charges of treason against vanquished enemies facilitated their punishment and humiliation. But sometimes it was an act of weakness to invoke treason. The problem was that bringing charges of treason against your enemies and rivals was an attempt to seize a moral advantage, a search for an absolute that conferred certainty, an attempt to find firm ground in a marsh. If everyone agreed that treason against the monarch was wicked then traitors were not just criminals but wicked—but those charged with treason would not so readily agree. As Sir John Harington's epigraph has it, 'Treason doth never prosper/what's the reason?/Why—if it prosper, none dare call it treason'.[2]

Monarchs could not themselves be tried at law for any crimes they had committed. Equally, however, they could not interfere directly with the courts of law, for example by suspending a judge, though they could instruct their legal officers to accept pleas of not guilty (as was done for William Horsey, chancellor of the bishop of London, indicted for the murder of the London merchant and suspected heretic Richard Hunne). Monarchs could also exercise the prerogative of mercy by granting pardons. That is to say that they could waive the punishment imposed by the courts on someone found guilty of a crime. Pardons have been misunderstood. Anyone granted a pardon was not thereby declared to be innocent or to have been the victim of an unjust law. It was simply that for reasons thought good, the monarch believed that carrying out the standard punishment on this occasion would be wrong. Monarchs were deeply involved in making laws, but they made them in and through Parliament, as we shall see. Monarchs could also issue proclamations on their own authority, but these orders that their subjects should, or should not, do something usually emphasised an existing law. How far such orders could lead to prosecution in the law courts was moot.

* * *

Did the arts reinforce the claims of monarchs to power? Both Henry VII and Henry VIII were builders and rebuilders of royal palaces, Henry VIII especially so. At one level this was personal extravagance and self-indulgence, but did it at another level have serious political purposes? When Henry VII built Richmond Palace, when Henry VIII built or improved palaces at Bridewell, Eltham, Greenwich, Hampton Court, St James's, Nonsuch, Oatlands, Richmond, Westminster, Windsor and Woking, when they were building or rebuilding the grandest, the largest, the tallest, the most luxuriously and fashionably decorated and furnished buildings in their realm, were they making a declaration of their power?[3] Holbein's portraits show Henry VIII as a huge, broad-shouldered king, a ruler before whom men would kneel in respect and in fear, a king who would be obeyed. Holbein's iconic portrait-image of Henry VIII now in the Thyssen Gallery in Madrid is unflattering, suggesting a cruel and arrogant man, an image of 'power without pity', as Susan Foister has put it.[4] To present that portrait as part of a deliberate plan of propaganda works only if one supposes that Henry wanted to frighten people into submission. And those broad padded-shoulders reflect contemporary fashions rather than anything specially designed by and for the king, who may simply have had the good fortune to be painted by Holbein, an artist of genius. Nor was Henry VIII consistently portrayed, for example on coins, in the manner Holbein devised. The most likely intended audience of Holbein's portrait was not his subjects but Francis I, king of France, to whom the pictorial message was that Henry was not to be trifled with.

Portraits of Elizabeth—who (judging from a draft proclamation of 1563) was very anxious that 'debased images' of her should not circulate—were icons: they were not meant to be likenesses. Elizabeth was shown more as 'a serene goddess, timeless and perennially beautiful', 'made to seem younger as she got older' (as in the flattering Rainbow portrait, 'round-faced, radiant and rejuvenated', possibly painted in 1602 when she was seventy) than as a real, ageing and therefore mortal woman (only the Ditchley portrait of 1592 shows her as an old woman with sunken cheeks) in paintings full of symbolism: she is standing on a map of England, bearing the sword of justice, holding the olive of peace, pointing to the Bible of true religion. 'Who really understood the symbolism of renaissance art?' Theodore Rabb has asked.[5] The arcane iconography that some modern scholars have teased out was most likely largely incomprehensible to most viewers, as Sydney Anglo suspected. The assumption of some art-historians that those who commissioned or even viewed works of art possessed erudite knowledge to a depth that would earn them a doctorate from the Warburg Institute today is, as Cliff Davies insisted, a leap of faith.[6]

More revealing are the flatteries of monarchs in ceremonies such as royal pageants, visits by foreign monarchs, progresses and entries. Geoffrey Elton, who we have seen as the advocate of administrative reform worthy of being labelled the Tudor Revolution in Government, was very dismissive of the arts: 'we need no more reveries on accession tilts and symbolism, no more pretty pictures of gallants and galliards'.[7] But the lawyer Edward Hall who wrote a *Chronicle* that is one of the main sources for the history of Henry VIII's reign was clearly impressed, as his loving retailing of the details of tournaments and pageants shows. Monarchs were presented as truly regal figures, comparable with legendary, classical and Biblical heroes. Richard Rich, speaker in parliament in 1536, presented Henry VIII thus: as prudent and just as Solomon, as strong and brave as Samson, as handsome as Absalom. How far was all this deliberate policy designed to cover up monarchical weakness by good public relations? How far were people taken in by such rhetoric, as Cliff Davies wondered? What if the reality did not match the rhetoric? But perhaps the key is not that monarchs were using the arts to enhance their power but that contemporary expectations of how monarchs should live included magnificent display. Monarchs who failed to live up to such demanding ideals risked losing face.

And was panegyric itself double-edged? To praise is to endorse certain values. To praise a monarch for being wise, just and merciful is to set out a programme and criteria by which that monarch should be judged. And it is also to hint at the possibility of blame, of criticism if a monarch does not live up to the ideals expressed in panegyric. And anyone who praises implicitly claims the authority to criticise as well. As G. Dodd has put it,[8]

> such terms were used not so much to flatter the king as to express what was looked for in his kingship. They articulated a rhetoric of expectation. They exposed the

emptiness and inadequacies of the current regime when there was nothing to celebrate except monarchy itself, and the hopes and aspirations that it embodied.

Progresses allowed Tudor monarchs to be seen by their leading subjects and by the common people. But monarchs did not visit every part of their realm. Henry VII went north in 1486–7, confronting Lambert Simnel the pretender and later he went regularly to central England, but he went just once to Wales and never to Ireland. Henry VIII's progresses revolved around hunting. Not till 1541 did he visit York. Elizabeth famously went on summer progresses, twenty-three in her forty-four-year reign, staying in the houses of her noblemen, courtiers and counsellors. But she never went further west than Bristol or further north than Stafford. Elizabeth never went to the south-west or the catholic north but always to relatively populous, wealthy, protected areas. She did not use progresses as a way of pacifying troubled regions.[9] Unmarried and childless, perhaps she simply enjoyed travelling within defined and familiar limits and staying with those courtiers and counsellors who were the nearest she had to friends.

Scholars may then have been too quick to read political significance into ceremonies, art and architecture. Much of the pageantry and display at court may have been no more than an exuberant enjoyment of wealth, with no explicit political intentions, though clearly building palaces and taking part in opulent ceremonies undoubtedly conveyed an impression of power. But there is one clear exception. Roy Strong long ago asked whether Henry VIII's patronage of Holbein was 'part of an attempt to promote a triumphant image of sacred kinship in support of his goals'. On the frontispieces of the English translations of the Bible authorised by Henry VIII, and especially on that of the Great Bible, Henry is presented as in direct communication with God, literally a prophet to his people, bringing the word of God in English to his bishops who in turn bring it to his people who cry out 'vivat rex'. That was a powerful image that made the boldest of claims. This was what Henry meant by the royal supremacy. As Strong pointed out, 'the idiosyncratic nature of the whole programme suggests that it may have been dictated by the king himself'. The title page of the Coverdale Bible in 1535 was certainly executed by Hans Holbein, the king's painter; on grounds of style a case can be made that Holbein did the frontispiece of the Great Bible as well.[10] And since copies of the Great Bible were to be placed in every parish church, the image would be widely seen. How far onlookers understood and accepted the message is, of course, unknowable. But if propaganda is sought, this is a very vivid example.

The religious aspects of monarchy were significant in further ways. Coronations were especially grand occasions. Henry VIII's coronation in 1509 'presented the king as a link in a chain that stretched back to the time of Edward the Confessor', the saint-king whose crown he briefly wore. Kings were anointed with holy oil on the hands, the breast, the back, the shoulders, the elbows and the head. Then they were anointed again on the head with chrism (a mixture of oil and balsam, with perfume added). They were consequently seen as super-human, semi-divine figures. They touched for the king's evil: at a special service, conducted by the leading clergy, the monarch laid his hands upon each person in a long queue of sufferers from scrofula (a tubercular inflammation of the lymph glands of the neck, caused by drinking infected milk). The king's miraculous healing powers were seen as stemming from his consecration at his coronation and from the very nature of monarchy. Henry VII formalised the ritual: was it part of a usurper's assertion that he was the rightful king? Nineteen times between 1529 and 1532—years for which accounts survive—Henry VIII exercised these royal thaumaturgic powers: sums of 7s 6d were paid to those who declared themselves healed.[11] Kings and queens also claimed the power of hallowing rings: in ceremonies they rubbed rings between their fingers and distributed them to sufferers. Miraculous cures were attributed to earlier kings: Henry VII attempted, inconclusively, to have Henry VI declared a saint, and over a hundred cures were reported as having been worked by him. In the long run monarchy would undergo a process of de-sacralisation, or 'disenchantment': religious divisions, intellectual scepticism, scientific rationalism and economic change would unsettle monarchical authority derived from God. One can imagine Elton arguing that the need to integrate society through symbolic acts and rituals diminished as administrative structures became more efficient and the coercive power of the state grew. But all that was true only in the very long run. At various points in our period the sacral nature of monarchy was remodelled and reasserted and the close link between church and state endured.[12] Elton's emphasis on the Tudor Revolution in Government as a key stage on the way to modernity leaves important aspects of the past untouched.

And were such semi-divine Tudor monarchs despots, tyrants? There was undoubtedly a despotic flavour to the later years of Henry VII. The use of suspended financial agreements—bonds and obligations by which people bound themselves to pay set large sums of money if they misbehaved in the future—went beyond contemporary norms after 1502. Edmund Dudley, Henry VII's minister, set out in a petition after the king's death a list of some eighty persons 'as I think were hardly entreated and much more sorer than the causes required', adding that 'the mind of the king's grace ... was much set to have many persons in his danger at his pleasure'. There was a marked increase in such bonds and obligations from around 1500.[13]

Can such methods be defended? James Ross has studied a lawsuit brought by Sir William Clopton of Long Melford, Suffolk, accusing Edmund Dudley of fraud. Dudley had allegedly interfered in Clopton's process in the exchequer of pleas—intervening in a common-law case in which crown interests were not directly at stake and then defrauding of Clopton. It was a clear-cut case of a leading minister manipulating the common law for the king's financial gain. Dudley may have been acting to please the king without Henry being directly involved, but Henry must bear ultimate responsibility for the actions of his leading councillors, especially when these were part of a pattern.[14] Henry VII's policy was one of political misanthropy. It was not directed against particular groups but at anyone and everyone. After Henry's death, so vigorously voiced were complaints against his ways of ruling that a nationwide inquiry to redress grievances was quickly established, with many members of the political nation sitting on commissions to cancel bonds. The best defence of Henry VII would be that he went beyond contemporary norms only to a small extent and that his practices, including the use of bonds and recognisances, had been anticipated by Edward IV when he faced similar challenges.

Henry VIII expected to be obeyed. In a circular letter sent to his bishops during the Pilgrimage of Grace in November 1536, the king ordered them to declare to the people the obedience due by God's law to the sovereign against whose commandments they were in no wise to use violence '*though they were unjust*' (my italics).[15] In January 1539 Castillon, the French ambassador, begged to be allowed to return home since he feared that Henry, the most dangerous and cruel man in the world, would do him some ill turn.[16] Henry VIII's methods turned increasingly tyrannical. His actions were not indiscriminate: they were directed against those suspected of certain actions or beliefs. The way he brought down Thomas Wolsey, for a decade and a half his tireless leading minister, is revealing. He had come increasingly, but unfairly, to doubt Wolsey's commitment to the king's pursuit of an annulment of his marriage to Catherine of Aragon. Threatening Wolsey was an ingenious way of putting pressure both on the pope and on churchmen in England. What Wolsey was brought down for were supposed offences against the fourteenth-century statute of praemunire, which sought to limit foreign interference in the English church. Technically by exercising the powers of his office as papal legate, Wolsey was seen as breaking that law. This was ridiculous, indeed monstrous, since Wolsey had accepted the legateship with Henry's approval. Moreover, if Wolsey were guilty then so were all other churchmen and especially church court officials. And Wolsey's admitted guilt was then used against churchmen generally, as part of political manoeuvres to deter them from opposing the king's policies.

Such pressures became more general once Henry secured his annulment, married Anne Boleyn and broke from Rome. Anyone who then spoke in defence of the pope or in defence of Catherine of Aragon or who criticised Henry's new queen Anne Boleyn or criticised the newly declared royal supremacy over the church risked finding himself (Elton's phrasing) in custody after the words spoken had been reported, undergoing interrogation by local justices of the peace and even, sometimes, by Henry VIII's chief minister, Thomas Cromwell. 'This is precisely what is meant by a policy of *in terrorem*: out of a hundred men, one man finds himself in prison, another gets himself executed, the other ninety eight read the lessons correctly, and conform', Joel Hurstfield wryly observed.[17] 'If there was terror it existed in the mind only', countered Elton,[18] but that is exactly where terror would take root. John Husee, Lord Lisle's tireless servant in London, vividly testified to the prevailing atmosphere when he warned Lady Lisle 'not to speak when she heard things spoken which she liked not: although ceremonies, such as offering candles to images, were right good, yet she might do a very good deed to conform herself partly to the thing that is used and to the world as it goeth now'.[19] Christopher Chaitour, a servant of the bishop of Durham, was asked 'is there none that grudgeth with such pulling down of abbeys in your country'; 'no', he replied, 'for if there be any such, they keep it secret, for there hath been so sore punishment.'[20]

True, most of those accused and convicted of treason in the 1530s were dealt with according to the due process of law. But relevant laws were extended: the Treason Act of 1534 notably widened the definition of treason. As Sir Geoffrey Elton once revealingly put it, in a chilling sentence which shows exactly the opposite of what he was claiming, 'I had to consider whether the government twisted the law in its political trials: the answer was that it did not because the law was made sufficient for the purpose'.[21] Was Henry VIII 'more careful of law than of justice'? Much of what he did was scrupulously legalistic, but that is not necessarily incompatible with tyranny. An official account of Henry VIII's reformation robustly declared how the king never caused any man to be put to death by absolute authority but by ordinary process. No one had been condemned but by twelve of his peers and no lord without the sentence of twenty-four lords at least. Who can find in his heart to think the king that so hath judgements ministered by the law and by ordinary jurisdiction to be a tyrant?[22] But that was disingenuous. That was not least because the definition of treason was extended to include accusing the king's councillors of being 'false varlets in devising of false laws', as Robert Yule, the old and blind rector of Sotby, had done.[23]

In treason cases the crown exploited the period between arrest and trial to inflict what amounted to a trial by inquisition on the suspect. The ostensible purpose of such a procedure was to investigate the ramifications of the alleged crime, to secure information about accomplices. But it also gave the government the opportunity to conduct what amounted to a private trial, to put pressure on the suspect, perhaps by leading him on to incriminate himself, and to prepare its own case. The most notorious aspect of these pre-trial procedures was the use of torture on victims of special notoriety and recalcitrance to secure confessions, especially in Elizabeth's reign. 'According to the king's highness pleasure' referred to in a letter from Thomas Cromwell just received, Gilbert Talbot and John Russell 'at sundry times as well by way of advertisement [warning] as after *by pinching with pain* [my italics]' examined James Pratt, vicar of Crowle, Worcestershire. Just what did 'pinching with pain' involve?[24] Torture was not legal but it was routinely used by the Elizabethan Privy Council against catholic priests and, sometimes, those suspected of treason. Under Henry VIII torture was not common. Perhaps physical or psychological deprivation—being held in cold, damp, dark isolation—was sufficient. Arrested and sent to the Tower, Sir Geoffrey Pole was interrogated about his and his relations' suspected treason, and then tried to kill himself, going on in effect to turn king's evidence against his relatives.[25] Trials could be influenced. Bishop Rowland Lee, president of the council in the marches, informed Cromwell in 1538 that he had put some of the JPs on a jury in a treason case, implying that that would make sure that the right verdict was delivered.[26] A circular letter dated 25 June 1535 from the king to assize judges asked them to declare the treasons of the late Bishop John Fisher (executed on 22 June) and Sir Thomas More—yet More was not to be tried until 1 July.[27] There is a notorious entry in Cromwell's memoranda about 'the abbot [of] Reading to be sent down to be tried *and executed* [my italics] at Reading with his accomplices. Similarly the abbot of Glaston[bury] at Glaston[bury]'.[28] The antiquary John Leland described Richard Whiting, the abbot of Glastonbury, as 'homo sane candidissimus et amicus meus singularis'—'a most honest man and my great friend'—but these words in Leland's manuscript are crossed out, presumably after Whiting's execution. Was he motivated by conviction, prudence or fear?[29]

In the 1530s governments developed the use of parliamentary bills of attainder which simply asserted that the accused was guilty of treason and condemned him to execution but cited no evidence whatsoever. Traditionally, such bills had been used against fugitives or against those already convicted of treason so that all their lands could be seized by the crown. Now this procedure was used more widely, not least when conviction at common law may have seemed unlikely. Some sixty-eight individuals were condemned in this way between 1531 and 1547 and thirty-four were executed. That is enough, as Stacy has written, 'to challenge the assertion that the period was a triumphant age of legalism. Far from respecting the common law, Henry and his ministers cynically used it to destroy their enemies when possible and unashamedly evaded it to destroy their enemies when necessary.'[30]

Marillac, the French ambassador, was shocked by the executions of three papists—Thomas Abel, Richard Fetherstone and Edward Powell—and three Lutheran preachers—Robert Barnes, William Jerome and Thomas Garret—on the same day. None of them had been told the reasons for which they were condemned, something that was possible only in England, he claimed.[31] Parliament, he alleged, had entirely transferred its authority to the king, allowing his opinion alone to have the force of law.[32] In early 1537, martial law was used against the rebels who had unsuccessfully besieged Carlisle Castle: the duke of Norfolk said that if he had proceeded trial by jury, not a fifth of those he had condemned would have been found guilty.[33]

In 1534 the Act of Succession compelled every adult man (and possibly woman) to swear an oath to the succession, that is, in effect, in support of the break with Rome. To refuse was to be guilty of misprision of treason. Everyone was being compelled publicly and under the threat of divine penalties to accept royal policy. It had the appearance of free choice and consent but in fact it was imposed under pressure. There are overtones here of modern totalitarian governments claiming the support of 99 per cent of their people. And Henry VIII was in effect asserting the right to say what their subjects should and should not believe: the Act of Six Articles was boldly entitled 'An Act for the abolishing of diversity of opinions in religion'. By twentieth-century standards, when untold millions perished in concentration camps, labour camps or gas chambers under Nazi or Soviet barbarity, and when thought and even poetry was tightly monitored and controlled, any tyranny in Henry VIII's reign may seem small; apart from those involved in rebellions, 883 were accused of treason in the 1530s, of whom 308 were executed. But tyranny is not essentially a matter of numbers, and it is imperative to avoid slipping into saying things like '*only* 308 were executed', as if a single judicial murder were not wicked enough. It is a better defence to point out that the figures do suggest some attempt to establish the facts, rather than just an unthinking machine of destruction. Even noblemen could sometimes be acquitted, as William, Lord Dacre, was in 1534. More significantly, many, if not all, of those condemned in the 1530s, including Sir Thomas More, Bishop John Fisher, the Charterhouse monks or the religious radicals Barnes, Jerome and Lambert, were 'guilty' by contemporary standards in the sense that they had disagreed with, disobeyed and finally resisted the will of the king, if only (for example) in refusing to agree that he was justified in breaking with Rome: they were not in that sense 'innocent' victims of a tyrannical whim; they were, or perhaps more accurately, they could, from the king's point of view, be seen and feared as political or religious opponents.

* * *

What has been offered so far is a kind of maximum statement of kingship, and of royal power, arguing that the adult monarchs who ruled England from 1509 to 1603 were, in different ways, skilful, determined and ruthless, even at times tyrannical, rulers who made an impact and who largely accomplished their aims. The characters of monarchs were, I have suggested, crucial.

But I am not arguing that monarchs could achieve anything they wanted. Having here sketched a maximum case, I shall go on in this book to consider as much the limitations and constraints on royal power. I wish to explore the paradoxes of power, to consider how power is everywhere but also nowhere. I want to ask whether monarchs had no choice but to work with their nobility, men whose ownership of large tracts of land gave them considerable influence. I want to consider how parliament—which I see as the representative of the political nation—limited the powers of monarchs. Already in my discussion of the ways—perhaps the tyrannical ways—that Henry VIII imposed the break with Rome, I have been raising the question of how far England was a constitutional monarchy. That is to say, were there conventions, was there a sense of the right and wrong ways of doing things and did they deter a monarch from doing just as he or she pleased? I want to reflect on the relationship of monarchs to the law and consider how far judges could restrict royal power. I want to assess the power of monarchs more generally. How far were monarchs confined by what the modern political commentator Robert Mackenzie called 'the hard facts of the situation'? Monarchs, as we shall see, could raise taxes, but they could not raise unlimited sums. They could try to raise large armies but they could not always prevent armies from melting away in the course of a poorly planned and inadequately equipped campaign. Monarchs were dependent on institutions and conventions for the enforcement and implementation of their policies. How often were monarchs' wishes in practice thwarted? And yet, even if the powers of monarchs were more limited than they might at first seem, how far, nonetheless, could skilful monarchs could get much of what they most wanted done? In short, in what follows in this book I aim specially to reflect on what I see as the paradoxes of power.

2

The power of the nobility

In 1521 Sir William Compton, Henry VIII's closest personal servant, in effect arrested Edward Stafford, third duke of Buckingham, inviting him to join Compton and travel to London. Buckingham was then tried for treason and executed, as we have already noted. Buckingham's fate has often been taken as evidence of a weakened nobility, not least since the charges against him have been seen as flimsy. A nobleman, it would seem, simply had to criticise the king and down he went. But Buckingham's behaviour had been more than merely imprudent. He had over several years made visits to a monk in Hinton Charterhouse and had listened to his prophecies that Henry VIII would have no male heir and that Buckingham or his son would one day be king. Buckingham's descent made him a possible candidate for the throne. In visiting the monk, Buckingham could be seen as questioning the legitimacy of Henry VIII as king of England. Moreover he—according to the testimony of disaffected servants—had voiced forceful criticisms of the king and of his leading minister Thomas Wolsey, and even declared that if he had been imprisoned for retaining, he would, when kneeling before the king, have suddenly risen and stabbed him.[1] On the face of it Buckingham was behaving like the caricature of a rebellious nobleman and Henry, by treating that behaviour as treasonable, was behaving like a would-be absolute ruler, tolerating no dissent. Yet there are paradoxes of power here. Buckingham may have spoken out against the king and Wolsey, but he did so privately, in the hearing of servants whom he expected would keep what he said to themselves. Buckingham never *did* anything that could be seen as political action against the king. And, crucially, Buckingham was on his own. He himself lamented that other noblemen would not join him:[2] 'it would do well enough', he testified, 'if the noblemen durst break their minds together, but some of them mistrusteth, and feareth to break their minds to other, and that marreth all'. And so he secured little support, as he himself recognised (and as we shall see further). Indeed the satirical poet John Skelton would jibe that noblemen were cowards for not restraining Cardinal Wolsey—but that jibe cannot be taken at face value, since accusing noblemen of cowardice is just what you would do when they do not do what you would want them to do.[3] So what seem markers of the power or of the weakness of the nobility turn out to be much more complicated. Buckingham was powerful enough, as a large landowner and a descendant of monarchs, to appear in the eyes of Henry VIII as a potential threat. Henry, son of a usurper, was wary. And in 1521 he acted decisively. But all this is best read in terms of a relationship between a monarch and a leading nobleman that had been uneasy and never warm. It shows neither that noblemen were dangerously powerful nor that noblemen were no longer very powerful at all. It shows neither that kings were weakened by potential threats nor that kings were all-powerful. Rather it illustrates the paradoxes of power in Tudor England.

That is also the most fitting way to consider the actions, at the end of Elizabeth's reign, of Robert Devereux, second earl of Essex, too often presented as exemplifying a rebellious but weakened nobility. Yet Essex was no Buckingham. He was a courtier-magnate who lacked a landed endowment. He succeeded for a while in building a nationwide following held together by little more than his influence over royal patronage, but once that influence was removed by Queen Elizabeth, he found he had no solid resources of his own to assert himself, let alone mount a credible rebellion. And whether what he attempted in 1601 was a rebellion is fiercely disputed.

It has been argued that Essex and his circle had been influenced by reading Tacitus, historian of ancient Rome, who depicted the evils of tyranny, especially that of the Emperor Nero. Essex and his friends allegedly came to see Elizabeth as a modern Nero—or a Richard II, deposed for tyranny in the late fourteenth century. As a nobleman, Essex had the duty of restraining the tyrannical queen and her evil councillors. There is no doubt that some of those associated with Essex would write about him and events in these terms, though the evidence of that tyranny seems to have been no more than the queen's no longer—and for good reason—showing Essex exceptional favour. But perhaps all this exaggerates the force of ideas as instigators of political action. Just as Buckingham's fate in 1521 is best seen in terms of a difficult relationship over several years between king and nobleman, so Essex is best understood in terms of his relationship with the queen. Elizabeth indulged Essex for many years when he ignored instructions and acted impetuously and independently. For all his enthusiasm and interest in the science of war, Essex was never as effective a military commander as he believed he was, and his conduct in the military campaigns in Ireland was palpably open to question, not least when he disobeyed the queen's instructions. By 1600 Elizabeth was no longer willing to entrust him with high responsibilities. That was the queen's prerogative.

When Essex assembled his friends and tried to force access to the queen in February 1601, was that an act of principled resistance to a tyrant? Was it an act of peevish folly, rather like the way he had earlier burst into the queen's bedchamber on returning from Ireland? Or was it an act of suicidal despair? What did Essex expect? Did he hope that Elizabeth would once again yield to his charm and entreaties, forgive his importunity and restore him to political influence? Did Essex, so used to getting his way and emerging from scrapes relatively unscathed, sincerely believe that that would be the outcome and that once more all would be well? Was Essex really thinking of deposing Elizabeth, were not his actions much too shambolic to be seen as an intended coup d'etat? To pose those questions is not to deny that Essex and his followers may have sincerely believed in the political theories that offered them intellectual justification for their actions. Such theories may have included Tacitean concepts of limited monarchy. But the ideas and values that had influenced Essex also included notions of chivalry, especially those involving devoted personal loyalty and service to the monarch. And Essex's actions in 1601 seem more instinctive than principled. If when Essex rhetorically asked 'What, cannot princes err? Cannot subjects receive wrong? Is an earthly power or authority infinite?', and if, when Elizabeth insisted that 'a prince was not to be contested withal by a subject', matters of political or constitutional principle were certainly present, the formulations show that both were driven by personal rather than ideological considerations. When Elizabeth remarked 'By God's son, I am no queen; that man is above me', she was being sarcastic: her remark is not evidence of Essex's power. And she insisted that she was no tyrant: 'Let tyrants fear; I have always so behaved myself that, under God, I have placed my chiefest strength and safeguard in the loyal heart and good will of my subjects.' And the actions of Essex, an emotional man, are best read in the context of an often turbulent relationship with Elizabeth over many years.[4]

Such paradoxes of power as shown by the fates of Buckingham and Essex characterise the situation of the Tudor nobility. On the one hand some historians have projected an image of noblemen as men of power, but the most perceptive scholars have grasped that they were never all-powerful. On the other hand many historians—and certainly Sir Geoffrey Elton—have seen the nobility as of diminished importance in the government of Tudor England, pointing rather to a decline in their power; again the most perceptive scholars have offered a much more nuanced account in which noblemen were crucially important.[5]

It has been too easy and too simple to see the dynastic and personal conflicts we know as the fifteenth-century Wars of the Roses as the malign work and all but last gasp of a selfish and scheming nobility, rather than as a consequence of the complex weaknesses and legacies of Henry VI. And it has been correspondingly straightforward then to present the Tudor century as an age of firm and stable royal government in which determined monarchs and leading councillors established first a 'new monarchy' and then a 'Tudor Revolution in Government'. Often all that is seen as at the expense of the nobility, with noblemen reduced to the status of ornaments in an enhanced royal court while the Tudors relied on new men, drawn from social categories below the nobility, to rule the localities. Such notions have been expressed more subtly. The sixteenth century has been seen as a time of a fundamental shift from a culture based on honour, lineage and locality to one based on obedience, civil society and the nation, or in other words, from values associated with noble power in a decentralised society to those associated with royal power in a centralised state. And in that transformation noblemen allegedly lost their long-held right to influence the king's government. The development of a small Privy Council staffed largely by professional administrators allegedly deprived noblemen of 'access to the decision-making machinery of government'. Some scholars have seen the power of noblemen in the localities declining and their financial fortunes of noblemen ever more precarious as they allegedly spent recklessly to reassure themselves of their status and more directly to continue to command the allegiance of their inferiors. Noble households allegedly declined in significance and the crown interfered more and more in noblemen's relations with their tenantry. Changes in military technology allegedly diminished the role of noblemen in war.[6]

It sounds a formidable catalogue. Yet, however tenacious the notion of a declining nobility in Tudor England has proved to be, it is nonetheless seriously misleading. Its first fault, as has already been hinted, is the assumptions it makes about previous centuries. It usually implies a romantically exaggerated view of all-powerful medieval barons and takes as typical of medieval England the worst disruption of the mid-twelfth-century anarchy and the mid-fifteenth-century Wars of the Roses. But the nobility were never as dominant as this model supposes. For example, it was never true that the north knew no prince but a Percy: the Percies, earls of Northumberland, were both matched in the north by other noble families and considerably dependant on the crown for local office, notably the wardenship of the east marches.[7] Historians who make claims that the power of the Tudor nobility was declining often fail to compare their Tudor evidence with evidence such as this for an earlier period: the comparison is all too often with an idealised, nostalgic and schematic vision of the middle ages. Yet it was never the case that tenants unthinkingly followed their noble leaders into the field: for example, there were many fifteenth-century instances of tenants' reluctance. The nobility cannot then be seen as weakened, as is sometimes claimed, because it was supposedly losing control over lesser men.

But, it might be countered, Tudor nobles did lose their influence in central government. That suggestion again mistakes the nature of the earlier role of the nobility. Noblemen, as K.B. McFarlane insisted, were not aspirants to office, they were counsellors. As such they were involved in the most important decisions that governments took, for example over war or royal marriage plans, but they were not, except for a few individuals, much interested in taking part in the day-by-day work of executive government, not least since they would have no difficulty in responding in more informal ways to any decisions that directly affected their interests.[8]

Nor were noblemen somehow diminished by the royal court. The royal court was not, as is often supposed, the creation of Henry VIII, however splendid his palaces may have been. Historians may have been misled by the sudden abundance of new sources notably ambassadors' letters, full of gossip about who was in or out of favour. Occasional scraps of evidence suggest that something very similar had been happening before. Kings had always had courts or households. At a most basic level, kings had to be housed, clothed and fed in a style appropriate to their position and that meant buildings and staff on a large scale. Courtiers could do well for themselves. Studies of the royal household in the century after the Norman Conquest of 1066 show that it was the 'mainspring of government' and the centre of display, while household knights played an important part in war and more generally benefitted from their proximity to the king. The complaint that the king raised up new men from the dust was eloquently made by the chronicler Orderic Vitalis about Henry I in the early twelfth century. Literary satires of the hell of the court and the miseries of the life of the courtier first date from the reign of Henry II. Chaucer would write how 'at the king's court' it was 'each man for himself'.[9]

There is little to show that the royal court, and in particular its alleged development under Henry VIII, was intended to reduce the power of the nobility. That monarchs summoned noblemen to court with the aim of preventing them from doing mischief locally by cutting them off from their landed estates and turning them into tamed ornaments of the court is a long-lasting historiographical myth: the evidence of correspondence and accounts shows that noblemen spent most of their time on their estates. Mythical too is the somewhat contradictory claim that noblemen wanted to be at court but were excluded and consequently lost influence. Attendance at court was assuredly very important for men on the make, for courtiers and councillors who came from relatively humbler backgrounds and rose through royal favour. But for established noblemen it was sufficient to attend court on grand occasions. The most important royal ceremonies—the coronation and the funeral of Henry VIII— did continue prominently to involve the nobility, in various ceremonial roles, from which they drew substantial material rewards. Such ceremonies have rightly been seen as binding together monarchs and their most important subjects. When significant issues arose, noblemen were consulted formally—for example in meetings of a great council—as well as informally. And noblemen were directly involved in parliaments, sitting as members of the House of Lords.

Looking for noblemen active daily in the central administration or at court is thus to look in the wrong place. The strict definition of a nobleman was a man summoned personally to attend as a member of the House of Lords whenever the monarch called a parliament. Noblemen held titles: in order of precedence dukes, viscounts, marquesses, earls or barons. The ancestors of the Tudor nobility had at some point been raised to the peerage by the monarch of the day. Noblemen's titles passed by inheritance. Thus at any given time, the nobility would be a mixed group, a few whose forebears had been ennobled centuries before and some recently promoted by the reigning king. A major characteristic of noblemen who inherited their title was that usually they also inherited substantial holdings of land. Moreover those holdings of land were usually concentrated around their principal residences. And the key role that such noblemen played in the government of Tudor England was to oversee the regions in which their landholding gave them sway. In the 1510s there were the Percies earls of Northumberland in Northumberland and Yorkshire, the Cliffords earls of Cumberland in the north-west, the Nevills earls of Westmorland in the Lakes and Yorkshire, the Stanleys earls of Derby in Lancashire and Cheshire (confusingly, the geographical titles of noblemen did not always correspond to the actual location of their estates), the Talbots earls of Shrewsbury in south Yorkshire and Derbyshire, the Greys marquesses of Dorset in Leicestershire, the Howards dukes of Norfolk in Norfolk, the Staffords dukes of Buckingham (we have already encountered the third duke) in Gloucestershire, the Herberts earls of Worcester in the marches, the Courtenays marquesses of Exeter in the south-west, the Fitzalans earls of Arundel in Sussex, the Bouchiers earls of Essex in Essex, the de Veres earls of Oxford in Essex, the Greys earls of Kent in Bedfordshire. In some ways England was a federation of noble fiefdoms. In effect England was divided into spheres of influence. From the mid-sixteenth century, maps began to be drawn demonstrating noble influence. Thomas Seymour, ennobled as Lord Seymour of Sudeley, discontented brother of Edward Seymour, Lord Protector in the first years of Edward VI's minority, 'would divers times', according to Sir William Sharington, 'look upon a chart [map] of England which he hath and declare . . . how far his lands and dominions did stretch . . . when he came to Bristol, he would say, this is my Lord Protector's, and of other, that is my Lord of Warwicks'.[10] In Elizabeth's reign, Burghley also had such maps prepared.

Was such a pattern of noble overlordship over the regions of England, based on the possession of landed patrimonies, simply an inheritance from the past which Tudor monarchs and their leading ministers sought to diminish and to replace? Nothing was further from their actions. Monarchs recognised that they could never rule alone. They always needed others to serve them, to give advice and to implement policies. Clearly some of those involved in such duties would be well rewarded. Monarchs allowed their leading councillors and courtiers not only to enrich themselves in royal service but also to build up holdings of land that would serve as the basis of a family patrimony and eventually of promotion into and within the peerage. What the most successful courtiers and councillors were doing was to convert the possibly ephemeral royal favour which they enjoyed into something more lasting—a landed patrimony which their family would enjoy for generations. Many of them, especially principal ministers and the most trusted close servants, achieved ennoblement.

Courtiers such as Sir William Compton—whom we have already seen arresting the third duke of Buckingham in 1521—amassed a fortune in royal service and turned it into land. Compton's landholdings in Warwickshire, where he built a picture-book early-sixteenth-century house at Compton Wynyates, allowed his grandson Henry Compton to be ennobled by Elizabeth as Lord Compton. In time the Lords Compton became marquesses of Northampton, residing in Compton Wynyates to this day.[11] Thomas Cromwell, Henry VIII's leading minister in the 1530s, built up holdings of land in Sussex, was ennobled as Lord Cromwell and then as earl of Essex: had he not fallen in 1540 his family would have become established as landed magnates. William Cecil, Lord Burghley, Elizabeth's long-serving principal minister, enriched himself and built spectacular residences, notably at Burghley, Lincolnshire. The enrichment and ennoblement of courtiers and councillors were thus renewing the nobility which would have otherwise dwindled as peers died without male heirs.

What is remarkable is that Tudor monarchs went along with all this. A vivid example makes the point. John Russell (d. 1555), courtier and diplomat, was ennobled as Lord Russell (and later was promoted earl of Bedford) and was endowed with concentrations of land, offering him the scope to build up comparable local dominance. It is misleading to suggest that the Russells were advanced 'with the firm understanding that they were to be the crown's agents, never an independent territorial power': the massive grants of former monastic land that Russell received in the late 1530s were made in perpetuity and were regionally concentrated in the south-west.[12] Moreover the timing of Russell's elevation is significant. It occurred after the fall of Henry Courtenay (c. 1498–1538), marquess of Exeter, till then the leading landowner in Somerset and Devon. Why did he fall? Not because Henry VIII or his ministers sought to destroy the nobility. Henry had showed significant favour to him, promoting him marquess of Exeter in 1525. But the king's break with Rome and dissolution of the monasteries clouded the relationship between the king and the marquess. Exeter had been one of many noblemen who served the king loyally against the rebels during the Pilgrimage of Grace in 1536. But then Henry learned how Exeter had privately voiced sympathetic understanding of the Pilgrims of Grace, denounced newly appointed bishops as heretics for their support of the break with Rome, criticised the enhanced treason laws and complained of the knaves that ruled about the king, hoping to give them a buffet one day. Such private grumbling was in no sense a conspiracy, much less a rebellion, but, fearing foreign invasion, Henry VIII treated it as treason. Whether Henry was justified is debatable.[13] My principal claim here is rather that the downfall of Exeter could have served as an opportunity for Henry and Thomas Cromwell to have replaced a nobleman who dominated the area in which he held land by a different way of overseeing the regions. Exeter could have been replaced by a non-noble legally trained administrator given the kinds of powers that French monarchs were giving to what would be called *intendants* in the seventeenth century, men appointed by the king with no independent standing in the areas they oversaw. Nothing of the kind took place in Tudor England. As we have seen, Henry replaced Exeter by Sir John Russell, ennobling him and endowing him with lands formerly held by Exeter and by the dissolved Tavistock Abbey. Exeter was treated as a bad apple which had to be removed, but he was replaced by a new nobleman. That is eloquent testimony to the continuing role of the nobility in ruling England. Such new nobles readily identified with noblemen of ancient lineage: their long-run interests were similar. And there was a Tudor twist to this tale. Quite a few Tudor courtiers and councillors proved to be comparable founders of lasting landed families. That was in part because from the 1530s (with a brief exception in Mary's reign) royal councillors were no longer men making their way up the hierarchy of the church and rewarded by the monarch with senior positions—notably bishoprics and deaneries—in the church. Now councillors were almost all laymen. Churchmen had not been able to found landed dynasties: laymen could—and often did. But such new nobles should not be seen as 'a new style of service aristocracy'. These men were preoccupied by service at court and in council. What they were doing was not in itself new.

Did this system of noble supervision of the regions of England work? In 1549 rebellion broke out in Devon and Cornwall. Russell, the new overlord in the south-west, led the government's resistance and ultimately crushed the rebels in a series of pitched battles. Another vivid example may be found earlier. In 1536 the Pilgrimage of Grace, a large rebellion involving as many as 30,000 men in the north of England protesting against Henry VIII's religious policies, especially the dissolution of the monasteries, threatened Henry's throne. The Pilgrims succeeded in occupying York. If the rebels had then moved southwards in large numbers—as Cornishmen had moved eastwards in a tax rebellion in 1497—and if they had secured greater support along the way, then the pressure on Henry VIII might have become overwhelming. But the Pilgrims did not succeed in moving further south than Doncaster. That was not because they were so attached to their own regions that they did not think of leaving them. It was rather because they faced the formidable opposition of George Talbot (1468–1538), fourth earl of Shrewsbury. It was his loyalty to Henry VIII that was crucial in the failure, in the end, of the Pilgrimage of Grace. Shrewsbury's estates were centred on Sheffield and extended southwards through Derbyshire to Nottinghamshire. If the Pilgrims were to move south, they would have to move through Shrewsbury's area of influence. But Shrewsbury was wholly loyal.

He mobilised his servants, tenants and friends at once, raising 3,654 men within a week.[14] He deterred John Hussey, Lord Hussey, whose principal residence was at

Sleaford, from joining the rebels in Lincolnshire. He marched north to Doncaster to save that town from the rebels. He halted the momentum of the rebels' advance. Outnumbered, he (and the duke of Norfolk) twice made a deal with the rebels, making promises in exchange for their dispersing, and worked to divide the rebels' leaders, trying to win over Lord Darcy.

In short, Shrewsbury held a firm base in the north Midlands and south Yorkshire for the king. That may have been in spite of his own preferences: he does not seem to have been very sympathetic to Anne Boleyn, and his will and elaborate chantry chapel in what is now Sheffield Cathedral show that he remained a conservative in religion. But he and his family had owed a great deal to royal favour, he held many offices on crown lands and he displayed an instinctive loyalty to the crown that characterises the service nobility of late medieval and early modern England. Shrewsbury's loyalty, firmly and boldly displayed, kept his own area free from rebellion. It stiffened the commitment of other noblemen—Thomas Stanley, third earl of Derby in Lancashire, George Hastings, earl of Huntingdon, and Thomas Manners, earl of Rutland, in adjacent areas in the east Midlands and Thomas Howard, third duke of Norfolk, whom Henry VIII sent northwards to join Shrewsbury. Shrewsbury's action moreover deprived the Pilgrims of the hope that they would receive support from great nobles and weakened their claim that such great men were not being consulted by the government in the making of policy. If the rebels pressed on and resorted to military force, they would now find themselves fighting the very noblemen whom they were urging should be heeded by the king. Shrewsbury's role was thus crucial: which way he was inclined, it was thought 'verily the game were likely to go'.[15] It is scarcely an exaggeration to say that in October 1536 the fate of Henry VIII and of the break with Rome lay in the hands of the fourth earl of Shrewsbury.

Once again we shall note the paradoxes of power. What made Shrewsbury's action possible was his ability to raise armed force quickly. Within a week he had assembled 3,654 men. That is hard to square with any sense of the nobility in decline, of noblemen less and less able to mobilise their tenants, neighbours and friends, a matter to which we shall return. As we shall see in Chapter 5, it was noblemen and greater gentlemen who supplied the bulk of the armed forces sent by Henry VIII on large-scale campaigns in France in 1513 and 1544. Noble commanders on such occasions were not figureheads but were thoroughly involved in making tactical decisions. Shrewsbury's instinctive loyalty to the crown in 1536 casts grave doubt on claims that noblemen saw themselves as having a duty of rebellion against overweening monarchs. And Tudor monarchs had little difficulty in mobilising the armed power of their nobility. There were again paradoxes of power here. On the face of it, the nobility possessed the means to have challenged royal power by force, and many historians have written as if that is what nobles did or were always on the point of doing. But in practice they used their military power against the crown very rarely. Loyalty to monarchs was very strong. Despite immediate appearances, noblemen were not a threat. And for that reason monarchs and leading ministers did not see any imperative reason to change the system they ran. Indeed, after popular rebellions broke out in 1549, the government's response, after the rebellions had been defeated, was to appoint lords lieutenants in every county, not least to look out for any further rebellions. In mid-Elizabethan England the lords lieutenancy was revived, with the threat of Spanish invasion in mind. Lords lieutenants were appointed by the crown. But in practice it was the leading nobleman in a county who was appointed. The lord lieutenancy was not some kind of nationalisation of the powers of noblemen. Rather than a transformation, the lord lieutenancy, to repeat, was a formalisation of the existing responsibilities and powers of noblemen in the regions.

The nobility very much continued to rule Tudor England. Of course, much of the detailed donkey work of local government (to which we shall return in a later chapter) was done by the gentry, serving as JPs and on commissions, but that was not a novelty of the Tudor age and went back to at least the fourteenth century. More delicate tasks, however, such as the great military survey of 1522, were often entrusted to special commissions including leading noblemen. County studies, practically convenient approaches for graduate students in search of a PhD topic, may give a disproportionate weight to gentry families compared to noblemen whose estates in a single county may not have been that great, but whose influence may have stretched across several counties. Relations between noblemen and gentry remained various: they did not undergo a sea change. Noblemen might no longer issue indentures and pay retainers fees, but they continued to employ significant numbers in their service. Noble households were being rivalled by the universities and the Inns of Court as centres of gentry education, but the greatest noble families continued to maintain them. Nobles continued to exercise patronage on their estates and to spend much of their time on their patrimonies. Noblemen did not habitually use force locally in pursuit of their interests or to impose their authority on neighbouring gentry, but in so far as they did, they were still well capable of doing so at the end of the sixteenth century.

Problems could arise when, as we have seen, there was disagreement over the legitimacy of a monarch. It had taken a while for Henry VII to deal with what he saw as the disloyalty of those who did not accept his rule. Still, only a few nobles joined the pretenders Lambert Simnel in 1487 or Perkin Warbeck in the 1490s. Religious division would complicate matters. In 1553 the dying king Edward and his leading minister minister John Dudley, duke of Northumberland, attempted to divert the crown from Mary in favour of Lady Jane Grey, to whom Northumberland had married his son Guildford. Revealingly, the makers of that coup were men like Northumberland, courtier-administrators. They were defeated, as we have seen, by provincial nobles and gentry, especially Thomas, Lord Wentworth, Henry Radcliffe, earl of Sussex, and John Bourchier, earl of Bath, whom Mary rallied to her cause, not least as they shared her continuing commitment to Catholicism.[16]

Were the regions bordering on Scotland and Wales different? There is a tendency for historians studying the marches and marcher lords to assume that the greatest problem and concern for English kings was the threat that the power of such lords allegedly posed to their tenure of the throne. Of course, that could be a reality at certain moments, especially at times of a disputed succession or civil war, but it seems mistaken to suppose that when, say, Henry VIII considered the north of England, his first concern was whether the Percies would launch a rebellion against him. That was not likely. Much more immediate a threat was the possibility of Scottish invasion and much more urgent was the need to strengthen border defences to withstand the Scots. Disunity would weaken those defences, so the crown tried hard to minimise disputes between northern lords. Above all, the crown was anxious that key posts were held by able and hard-working noblemen. At that personal level there might be doubts about the suitability of particular individuals, and noblemen might sometimes be criticised for incompetence or even arrested for treason. But when a nobleman was passed over or dismissed, what happened next was usually not some fundamental reform of the system of military administration in the borders, but rather the appointment of another nobleman or at least substantial landowner whom the monarch hoped would prove more competent and more reliable. After William, Lord Dacre, was arrested and tried in 1534 for supposedly treasonable dealings with the Scots, and dismissed as warden of the west marches even after he had been acquitted of charges of treason, he was simply replaced by the first earl of Cumberland, in much the same way that his Dacre ancestor had been built up by the crown in the 1460s. Dacre's trial was puzzling since, while Tudor monarchs did indeed face or fear Scottish invasions in 1513, 1523, 1532 and 1542, it was never likely that they would also face the defection to the Scots of border noblemen.

And when Tudor monarchs did embark on institutional reform, it was when they could find no suitable capable noblemen with whom to work. The development of regional councils—the council of the north, the council of the marches—in the sixteenth century illustrates that well. Regional councils were as much an administrative convenience for local litigants as an instrument of royal government, and their introduction and development can often be linked to the chance absence of a suitable adult nobleman to supervise a region. The considerable development of the council in the north from 1537 reflects the lack of competent adult noblemen, untainted by involvement, however unwilling, in the Pilgrimage of Grace.

At first glance the complex rising in the north in 1569 can be more plausibly seen as a textbook noble rebellion, but such an impression does not survive closer analysis. Queen Elizabeth and her leading ministers were increasingly uneasy about the northern counties. What made them stop giving important responsibilities to the seventh earl of Northumberland and to William Lord Dacre (d. 1563) was not any hostility to magnates as such but rather well-founded doubts about their competence (in the case of Northumberland) and fears about their lack of enthusiasm for the new religious settlement. If Northumberland, Dacre, Cumberland, the fifth earl of Westmorland (succ. 1549), and other northern nobles were unhappy, it was not because they were excluded from court but because they wanted the queen and her ministers to follow different religious policies. In 1567 Northumberland became a catholic again. Increasingly these discontented northern nobles looked to the succession to resolve their discontents: the arrival in England of Mary Queen of Scots in May 1568 was a catalyst of intrigues, also involving the fourth duke of Norfolk. The government mishandled the situation, summoning Northumberland and Westmorland to London: their rebellion began more as a means of resisting arrest than as a carefully planned conspiracy.

The rebellion was, it has been argued, what emerged from weeks of vacillation and dissension, not from careful planning. Its roots lay in alienation from the government, especially over religion. It was also a hurried, ill-prepared, above all defensive rebellion. Northern gentry were associated from the start, indeed often took the initiative. It was not a 'feudal' revolt—tenants, servants and friends of the earls were only a small proportion of those who took part and only a small proportion of the earls' tenants were mobilised. But there was much popular support, and in many ways what happened was more a popular rebellion against religious change, comparable to those in 1536 in the north and in 1549 in the south-west, than a noble revolt. Some 6,000 well-equipped yeomen assembled. But in the end the rebellion failed. If the northern earls did take part, the rebellion did not win the support of the nobility of the realm more generally. The loyalist commander, Thomas Radcliffe (c. 1525–1583), third earl of Sussex, was able to bring the rebellion to an end.[17]

Over the Tudor century, relatively few noblemen were ever rebels. That strongly suggests that nobles were not keen on disorder. They were reluctant to jeopardise the agrarian economy on which their wealth was based. Far from seeing their status as noblemen as imposing a duty of revolt, far from subscribing to some clearly defined aggressive theory of 'aristocratic conciliarism', they joined in rebellions only in desperate self-defence, often provoked by some personal injustice. Disputed successions and civil wars appalled noblemen. And overwhelmingly they rallied behind monarchs when rebellions broke out. Noblemen and gentry gave overwhelming support to Henry VII against a small-scale popular rebellion in Yorkshire in 1489. When the Cornish rebelled against taxation in 1497, only one nobleman, James Tuchet, Lord Audley, attempted to exploit the troubles. When there was widespread refusal of the Amicable Grant, a provocative financial demand, in 1525, noblemen, far from fanning the flames of revolt, instead did what they could, at some personal risk, to persuade men to agree to make a grant and, in East Anglia, to put down a small-scale rising against it. In 1536 the fourth earl of Shrewsbury's actions against the Pilgrims of Grace show, as we have already seen, his detestation of rebellion. Noblemen who felt discontented might grumble privately, as did Edward Stafford, third duke of Buckingham, and Henry Courtenay, marquess of Exeter, but they did not raise rebellion; indeed in 1536 Exeter mobilised his forces in support of Henry VIII. It does not seem that noblemen were driven by ideology. Their political actions were somewhat rough and ready efforts to deal with urgent political problems. In so far as they drew on any ideas, it was not some sophisticated political theory, but rather a much less tangible, though undoubtedly real, sense of what was right and what was wrong. Theories, in so far as they were invoked at all, tended to be used retrospectively to validate decisions taken and actions done in the heat of the moment, instinctively, to deal with immediate challenges. There are paradoxes of power here too. In theory, noblemen could have joined together and mounted effective rebellions. But over the Tudor century they did not use their power in this way.

Another long-held belief about the nobility in sixteenth-century England was that its financial position declined, a belief elaborated in grandiose theories of the 'crisis of the aristocracy' (according to which noblemen's incomes fell as their expenditure rose) or of the 'rise of the gentry' (according to which the gentry acquired wealth and status at the expense of the nobility). But there are serious flaws in such arguments and attempts to demonstrate them statistically ran into the sand.

Such approaches begin with the selection of a sample. That seems at first straightforward. Why not follow Lawrence Stone in *The Crisis of the Aristocracy* and define the nobility as the parliamentary peers? Yet that was not a fixed category. Not all of them married and had sons who succeeded them. Without new creations, the total of peers would inescapably fall. The prerogatives of monarchs included the power to create new peers. And monarchs did so. We have already encountered courtier-administrators such as Russell. But Queen Elizabeth was sparing in her creation of peers (James I would create many more). All that meant that 'parliamentary peers' was not a stable category. To compare peers of 1558 with those of 1602 is not to compare like with like. They included noblemen of ancient lineage who owned large tracts of land but also rising courtier-administrators.

Since evidence of noblemen's incomes is patchy, historians have used a range of sources. Rentals, annual surveys, tax assessments, inquisitions post mortem, marriage contracts, materials prepared for legal cases have all been exploited. But while they can be illuminating, they are not firm ground on which to build. And when scholars have counted manors they have quickly run into controversy. Manors were much too diverse to permit the drawing of large conclusions.

And we have to be careful to recognise just what we are counting. At a first glance, that in 1602 parliamentary peers had only 71 per cent of the manors that they had had in 1558 appears to constitute irrefutable evidence for the crisis of the aristocracy: 63 families in 1558 held 3,390 manors or 54 each; 57 families in 1602 held 2,220 manors or 39 each. Yet look more closely and it soon appears that it was not the nobility as a whole but two noble families who were in trouble. In 1569 the earls of Northumberland and Westmorland were caught up in a spectacularly unsuccessful rebellion and lost most of their lands as punishment. Include those lands in the sample for 1558 and the decline of the nobility seems clear. But leave them out of the sample, and the proportion of manors held by parliamentary peers in 1602 would be much the same as that for 1558. So what this exercise measures is not the relentlessly declining fortunes of the nobility as a class but the gross political miscalculation of just two noblemen.[18]

It remains quite unproven that the nobility as a whole suffered a financial crisis in the sixteenth century. The only convincing method of throwing light on that question is to study systematically the wealth and income of individual families over a long period. That has been attempted for the Radcliffes earls of Sussex, and that evidence suggests that noble families could readily hold their own, given due care and attention to their estates. That reinforced the conclusions of earlier studies of the Stanleys earls of Derby and of the ninth earl of Northumberland. It has also become evident that debt was by itself not compelling evidence of economic troubles but rather a common feature of aristocratic life. Spectacular collapses such as that of Richard Grey (d. 1524), third earl of Kent, who it seems gambled away his inheritance, were quite possible, but they were rare and the result of an individual's inadequacy, not the failings of a whole social class. Whatever difficulties some families may have experienced—and this is not to minimise the anguish that individual noblemen, their families and their descendants consequently suffered—their experiences were not typical.

In broad terms, economic and social trends in this period favoured the larger landowners. The population increased. Demand for food and for clothing increased. That in turn increased demand for land. In the second half of the sixteenth century, there were also improvements in farming techniques. Larger landowners stood to gain from that. True, this was an age of inflation. The key was raising rents, and that was a challenge. Typically lands were let out on long leases without built-in rent reviews or according to 'custom', in other words unalterable fixed rents. Attentive management could, however, help. Eric Kerridge's thorough and thoughtful study of the estates of the earls of Pembroke showed that rents and revenues from lands did rise.[19] Noblemen were better placed than the crown to manage their estates—the crown lands were vast and monarchs were always involved in governing the country.

If, then, there is little to suggest that noblemen were in financial crisis, that is not to deny that broad social trends are worth considering. The significant increase in agrarian productivity meant that lands that in 1540 allowed one man to live like a gentleman could by 1640 allow several to do so. Undoubtedly, there were more gentry in 1640 than a century earlier. But it is wrong to write of 'the rise of the gentry' if that is taken to have happened at the expense of the nobility and greater landowners. If any social group did badly in that century it was the church. Monasteries and chantries had been dissolved and their lands sold. They were mostly bought at market prices, that is to say by men who were already wealthy and could meet the costs of consolidating their landholdings by acquiring ex-monastic lands. And the debate over the rise of the gentry and crisis of the aristocracy would have benefitted from at least a brief glance at the fortunes of noblemen and large landowners over a longer period than the reign of Queen Elizabeth. Julian Cornwall, studying the social structure of early Tudor England, remarked that 'individually most of the nobility were men of great wealth'; move forward to the later seventeenth and eighteenth centuries and the great wealth of great families is palpable—as many grand country houses vividly show.

If the power of noblemen rested on their wealth, and on their ownership of large estates, there was another much less tangible dimension, which was nonetheless real and, I should want to argue, vital. That is that the cultural values of Tudor England were aristocratic in a broad sense. We have seen that what ambitious and successful non-nobles aspired to was the ownership of a landed estate. Quickly they proclaimed their standing in heraldry. That shows the enduring appeal of the noble way of life. Humanist thought has sometimes been seen as challenging the nobility, but it did so much less than might be supposed, offering as it did an emphasis on virtue that might easily be combined with a belief in a hierarchical society. When they criticised noblemen for behaving badly, writers such as Thomas Elyot and Lawrence Humfrey were implying that noblemen ought to behave better than other men, and consequently that when noblemen were indeed virtuous, virtues glittered more brightly in them than in others. Hierarchy was thus inherently good. In the Tudor century there were no alternative models: not the enlightenment rhetoric of all men being born equal, nor the new liberalism or socialism of the late nineteenth and twentieth centuries, with their emphasis on redistribution of wealth to produce a more just society. And that ideological pre-eminence of noble values in sixteenth-century England both reflected and immeasurably reinforced the social and political standing of the nobility. The nobility drew enormous strength from the common acceptance of the belief that its inherited position conferred a special and privileged place upon it.

Who ruled Tudor England? Noblemen played a vital role, not least as overseers of regions. The Tudor nobility was a service nobility. Noblemen expected to serve the monarch and almost all the time did so. If there was not a constant *identity* of interest, there was a considerable *community* of interest. The government of Tudor England is best described as a partnership between the crown and the landed classes.

That was the conclusion that emerged from the research I undertook as a graduate student working towards my doctorate and that I have refined since. What I wish to attempt next is to offer an account of how I came to such views and how they began to affect my attitude towards Elton's model of *The Tudor Revolution in Government*.

Set by my tutor Jennifer Loach, whose special interests lay in mid-Tudor parliaments, to write an essay on whether Philip II's power depended primarily on his wealth, I can remember, in a week in which I devoted a long day to reading and skimming Braudel's *Mediterranean* in French, walking in the gardens of my college, St Catherine's, along the river Cherwell, and working out that power is 'the ability to reach a decision independently and to enforce it effectively'. And if one of the obstacles that Philip faced was the tyranny of distance, another obstacle was the objections to his policies by noblemen in the Netherlands in the mid-1560s and beyond.

Reading about the French wars of religion as an undergraduate also forcefully brought home the power of noblemen: not just the obvious rivalries provoked by the Guises but most pointedly, the extent to which, in the late 1580s and early 1590s, France seemed to be disintegrating into a congeries of semi-independent noble principalities under the very nominal rule of a king—not so unlike the condition of sixteenth-century Germany.

I suspect I thought all that my own discovery, but in retrospect I think I was being subtly guided by Jennifer Loach. Meeting her at a seminar the following term, I asked her about her own thesis-in-progress on opposition in parliament in Mary's reign—since I was then writing essays on the Tudors and Stuarts, including one on the mid-Tudor crisis—and in particular asking where did she differ from Sir John Neale's account of Elizabethan parliaments. Neale, said Jennifer, had neglected the role of the House of Lords and noblemen within it.

A few months later, in October 1970, regretting that there was then no Special Subject in Tudor history, I can remember escaping from the sources for the Commonwealth and Protectorate by borrowing from the History Faculty Library and reading with great enthusiasm Ralph Smith, *Land and Politics*, the newly published book of his earlier thesis on the West Riding of Yorkshire, and especially his very vivid chapter on the Pilgrimage of Grace, which in the end he presented as a noble-and-gentry-led conspiracy, an argument that was reinforced by Mervyn James's paper on the Lincolnshire rising that appeared at the same time in *Past & Present*. I had earlier read James's studies of the Percies that evoked a culturally rich world of magnate households.[20]

At the end of that month, seeing that Conrad Russell was giving a paper at the Stubbs Society, I asked Cliff Davies, whose Special Subject classes I was attending, whether it would be worth going to—Conrad had by this time published only a handful of specialist papers. It was a wonderful talk, given in Merton, one of the wittiest I have ever heard. Mercilessly Conrad showed how John Pym—apparently the leader of the parliamentary opposition to Charles I—enjoyed only very limited success in his ventures in the 1620s and 1630s, and that his apparent prominence was an illusion. Stressing Pym's dependence on the earl of Bedford in 1641, Conrad presented Pym as 'the errand boy for the last baronial revolt but one in English history'.

All that, reinforced by a set of lectures that Cliff Davies gave a term later, made me very receptive when the following summer Cliff suggested that I embark on a study of the Talbots earls of Shrewsbury for my DPhil (I had wanted since I was fifteen to write on John Dudley, duke of Northumberland, but I was deterred—as Jennifer Loach had been four years earlier—by being warned that news of a graduate student starting on that topic would be just the stimulus that Andrew Malkiewicz at Edinburgh—the editor of the less important half of the eye witness account of the coup of 1549—would need to bring a decade and a half's researches to completion). Gordon Batho had just published a calendar of the Talbot Papers then in the College of Arms. My expectations were that I should be uncovering a previously unemphasised aspect of English society and politics, the considerable power of the nobility in Tudor England.

But as I very committedly pursued all that I could find about Francis, the fifth earl (1500-1560), and then George, the fourth (1468-1538) earl of Shrewsbury, what I found did not altogether fit my expectations. The earls' leading part in military campaigns convinced me of the importance of war in early Tudor England and hence the general importance of the nobility in a society in which massive resources were devoted to war. But try as hard as I could, the earls could not plausibly be made into leaders of opposition to the crown, instigators of rebellion, political plotters: at most at times they warned, they raised eyebrows. Yet for all that, they were undoubtedly powerful: they could raise substantial armed forces, as in 1513, 1544-5, 1548, 1557 or more tellingly in 1536 against the Pilgrimage of Grace, they were large landowners, but they did not behave as if they were always spoiling for a fight.

Two writers helped me here. As a graduate student freed from the demands of the weekly essay, I read a great deal of fiction, including Trollope's Palliser novels. And the Duke of Omnium taught me a good deal about the role of the nobility. I had often referred, in the then minimal paperwork for the equivalent of upgrades, to my thesis as pursuing 'the career' of the fifth earl of Shrewsbury. But in many respects, the function of the earl of Shrewsbury, like that of the Duke of Omnium, was simply to *be* the earl of Shrewsbury: he was not pursuing any sort of career advancement in the modern sense. That also reinforced my sense that attitudes and perceptions counted for a good deal. Noblemen were powerful not least because it was generally accepted that there should be noblemen, that an hierarchical society was just.

Secondly, K.B. McFarlane's Ford Lectures, *The Nobility of Later Medieval England*, were posthumously published in February 1973. I devoured the book, and at once I recognised in his depiction much that made sense of the materials that I had been uncovering about the earls of Shrewsbury: the nobility was a service nobility, part of the structure and the web of government; conflict between noblemen and the crown was exceptional and a reflection of unusually bad royal government; noblemen were predominantly concerned with the perpetuation of their families through marriages and alliances, and with the management of their patrimonies, and, on the whole, a few remarkable exceptions apart, pretty good at that. McFarlane's book did not exactly give me those ideas (though since I had been taught by his pupil Gerald Harriss, I may well have absorbed them earlier without altogether realising it); rather it helped me understand what I was finding and gave me greater confidence to develop them and related perspectives for the early and mid-Tudor period. And so I tried to work out a balanced position, seeing Tudor noblemen as powerful, but also as men who deployed that power as willing and constructive partners in royal government. I argued that the continuing importance of noblemen in Tudor England can readily be seen in their wealth, in the extent of their ownership of land, in their indispensable role in raising and leading armies, in their general supervision of the localities and repression of rebellion, in their role as royal counsellors and, not least, in the continuing ideological pre-eminence of aristocratic values.

The early 1970s were a remarkable and exciting moment in the study of history. Many scholars in many different fields were consciously seeing themselves as 'revisionists' as they challenged long-established interpretations which had become solidified as fact. For my part, I came to question the views of a declining nobility in England. Several scholars—my fellow student and friend Kevin Sharpe, Conrad Russell, John Morrill and Mark Kishlansky—were questioning the traditional belief that parliaments were rising in power and bent on a struggle to win sovereignty from the crown that would culminate in the Civil Wars of the 1640s and the execution of Charles I. Others, notably William Doyle and Colin Lucas, were repudiating the dominant social interpretation of the French Revolution, denying that the revolution was ever intended as, or achieved, the triumph of the bourgeoisie over the feudalo-absolutist monarchy. And in those years a group of scholars was revising the history of the late medieval church, calling into question the protestant grand narrative of the speedy, inexorable and successful progress of the English reformation. For my part I came to assert with revisionist zeal—against the orthodoxy that saw noblemen in inexorable decline—the continuing political importance of the nobility.

I had begun my researches into the nobility of Tudor England against the background of Elton's claims for a Tudor Revolution in Government. That revolution struck me as plausible enough when I encountered it in Elton's *England under the Tudors* at school and then as an undergraduate. But what I was finding out about the nobility as a graduate student increasingly gave me pause. Noblemen and noble power barely feature in Elton's history. And it was my increasing realisation that the nobility remained powerful as a group and that individual noblemen—such as the fourth earl of Shrewsbury—played crucial part at key moments that led me to question the great emphasis that Elton placed on financial administration. However important changes in the departments that dealt with revenues and expenditure may have been, any proper assessment of government, and especially any claims for a revolution in government, needed to take due account of the nobility—which Elton failed to do. And consequently I came to see Elton's grand claims as more and more inadequate. Administration is not the same as government.

To that I shall return in later chapters. In this chapter, my focus has been on the nobility, on the parliamentary peerage. It is now time to broaden the inquiry and look at the political nation in the round, which is best done by looking at parliaments.

3

Parliament

The political nation

Noblemen undoubtedly ruled Tudor England in partnership with the crown. But crown and noblemen did not, indeed could not, rule alone. Those substantial landowners who held no title of nobility were also involved in the running of the localities. Land was fundamental. But trade and manufacturing, centred on cities and towns, generated wealth too, and the merchants, especially of the larger towns, were also much involved in matters of government. Landowners and merchants together made up the political nation, those actively concerned with the running of the state nationally and locally. In England representatives of that political nation had long come together at meetings of Parliament. Noblemen sat in the House of Lords. Gentry and merchants made up, as we shall see, the bulk of the members of the House of Commons, the lower house of Parliament. Who ruled Tudor England? The shortest answer is the political nation represented in Parliament.

And that raises large questions about the role of Parliament—of the political nation—in the sixteenth century. Was the relationship between the Crown and Parliament, especially the House of Commons—between the crown and the political nation—a struggle for power, for sovereignty? Should the history of Parliament—of the political nation—be seen as a grand narrative in which the seventeenth-century Civil War was decisive? Should we use biological metaphors—the gestation, the growth, the rise, the flowering, maturity of parliaments—of the political nation? But few professional historians of Tudor England would now feel altogether comfortable writing, as S.B. Chrimes did in his study of *Henry VII* (1972), that 'If it be true that England showed a greatness and a marked flowering of her spirit and genius in the course of the sixteenth century' then Henry VII's 'steady purposefulness saved England from mediocrity'.[1]

Did the Tudor century see a great enhancement of the role of Parliament—of the political nation—because the so-called Reformation Parliament (1529–36) agreed to laws dealing with religion and laws about succession to the throne? Did the procedures of parliaments become more formal and more systematised, and did that indicate a greater maturity? Was there a special significance to the efforts, albeit always unsuccessful, of a group of MPs to impose on Queen Elizabeth religious change, a more interventionist foreign policy and a named successor to the throne? Is it justifiable to focus on criticism expressed in Parliament, on what is presented as 'opposition'?

And should that be linked to constitutional liberties and to the rise of social classes—especially the supposed rise of the gentry or the 'middle classes'?

There is something in all that in the broadest sense. Over more than a millennium, the nature of the representative institution that would come to be called Parliament changed profoundly. Assemblies called by the king to discuss matters of state date back to the reign of Athelstan in the tenth century but membership was largely confined to the greatest landowners. In the mid-thirteenth century Henry III's repeated demands for taxation led to the summons of knights—county gentry who were not magnates but who were locally important. From the later thirteenth century it was customary for monarchs to invite as representatives not just knights from the counties but also leading men, known as burgesses, from the towns. Long before the sixteenth century, the period with which this book is primarily concerned, parliaments had become a vital feature, and by the sixteenth century the English monarchy had thus evolved into a constitutional monarchy in which conventions and explicit laws constrained the expression of sovereign power by monarchs. It was royal demands for taxation that stimulated such developments, especially when, as in the 1290s, 1370s, 1380s and 1450s, lack of success in war was seen as the fault of incompetent councillors, even of monarchs. Unpopular ministers could be impeached—tried and punished—in Parliament. But such conflicts, however dramatic, were not the norm, and parliaments in the sixteenth century were, as we shall see, much calmer, summoned because monarchs found them useful. Greater changes lay ahead. Unsuccessful wars lay behind the very different experience of parliaments under Charles I. Ultimately Charles faced what he saw as a rebellion in the name of Parliament, though in 1642 the political nation split down the middle into royalists and parliamentarians, a split that made civil war possible. The parliamentary and army leaders who emerged victorious in the late 1640s were a minority of the king's parliamentary critics in 1641, let alone of the MPs returned in 1640, and the execution of the king in 1649 was the work of a small group of men. What they did divided the political nation irremediably. Military, rather than parliamentary, rule followed. And when the monarchy was restored in 1660, in important ways it was the ancien regime that came back. It was James II's provocative incompetence and the seizure of the throne by William of Orange in 1688-9, followed by William's willingness to surrender royal powers in return for financial support from the political nation to fight Louis XIV, that led to fundamental constitutional changes that enshrined the position of the political nation in Parliament. From that time onwards monarchs were compelled to choose as their leading ministers only those who could command a majority in Parliament. That led in turn to the formation of informal groupings, reinforced by the proliferation of newspapers and periodicals after the effective abolition of licensing in 1695 and the burgeoning of coffee houses and clubs, and in due course to political parties which from the nineteenth century dominated parliaments. From the late nineteenth century the monarch turned into the ceremonial and charitable figurehead he or she is today.

The relevance of all that—and no more than a thumbnail sketch can be offered—is that it is hard for us to look back at sixteenth-century parliaments without latching on to developments that seem to anticipate, or to contribute to, the far-reading changes of the last three hundred years. But we must be careful not to assume that Tudor parliaments were more like their modern counterparts than they really were, and we must above all be alert to, and suspicious of, any suggestion that the modern transformation of the relationship between Crown and Parliament was in any way an inevitable, or even a highly likely, development. In many other European monarchies in the sixteenth and seventeenth centuries representative institutions declined in importance and even disappeared. It is worth recalling that Conrad Russell entitled his textbook of English history covering the period 1509–1660 'the *Crisis* of Parliaments', using the word 'crisis' in its technical sense as a turning point in a fever. It was in those years that Parliament would atrophy or would develop substantially: there was nothing pre-ordained about the latter outcome.

Parliaments in the sixteenth century, it should be emphasised, met infrequently and irregularly. They met only when monarchs summoned them. They could not assemble by themselves, nor were there any conventions that they had to meet every so many years. Henry VII summoned just one Parliament between 1497 and 1509, and that remained in session for only nine weeks. Under Henry VIII, nine parliaments met for a total of just 190 weeks between 1509 and 1547. Parliaments met for 46 weeks in Edward VI's reign, for 28 weeks in Mary's reign and for 140 weeks in Elizabeth's reign. In forty-three years out of ninety-four between 1509 and 1603 there was no Parliament. There was no meeting in 1505, 1506, 1507, 1508 and 1509; in 1516, 1517, 1518, 1519, 1520, 1521 and 1522; in 1524, 1525, 1526, 1527, 1528; in 1568, 1569 or 1570. If frequency of meeting is an index of the standing of Parliament, it is salutary to contrast that record with the reign of Edward III when Parliament met in forty-eight of the fifty years of his reign running from 1327 to 1377. Conrad Russell went so far as to deny that Parliament was an institution, insisting that it was rather an event, an occasion, and that accordingly we should speak not of 'Parliament' but of 'a Parliament'. Sir Geoffrey Elton disagreed: Parliament was 'an institution frequently in suspension' and 'it took but the pressing of a button—the issuing of a writ of summons—to bring it fully fledged into action'. There is little sign that MPs or anyone else wanted more frequent parliaments. 'What can a commonwealth desire more than peace, liberty, quietness, little taking of base money, few parliaments', asked Sir Thomas Smith, the Elizabethan lawyer.[2] 'Everyone is tired of parliament and every day someone asks for leave of absence', noted Eustache Chapuys, the imperial ambassador, in March 1531.[3] On 7 May 1536 a circular letter from Henry VIII to sheriffs insisted on the necessity of calling a Parliament, but assured the sheriffs 'that the charge and time . . . shall be very little and short, the matters being such as shall not long detain them'.[4]

Sixteenth-century MPs were not seeking to wrest sovereignty from the crown. What characterised their mentality was an instinctive sense of justice based on a deep-rooted commitment to the defence of property, the maintenance of order and stability, and the protection of trade and shipping. MPs were neither political philosophers nor students of politics seeing parliaments in constitutional terms. 'It is hard to see most county squires, after a hard day in the hunting field, settling down with a copy of [Machiavelli's] *Discorsi*'.[5] It was accepted that kings were God's lieutenants who ruled by divine right. It was accepted that kings enjoyed prerogatives, as we have already seen, to make war and peace, to marry whom they pleased, to appoint their ministers, officials and judges, to issue coin, to make policy. Tudor parliaments never contested such royal prerogatives in principle. MPs believed that national government was properly the responsibility of the monarch. Tudor MPs did not want to take over that national government. The Tudor century was very different from the eighteenth and especially the nineteenth and twentieth centuries. MPs respected monarchs and deferred to monarchy—criticism made them uncomfortable, even if it was sometimes necessary. The expression of opposition, especially protracted opposition or criticism of royal policy in Parliament, was seen as a failure, as a sign that things were going wrong. The ideal was harmony, consensus, unanimity. As Jennifer Loach wisely observed,[6]

> instead of approaching sixteenth-century parliaments as if they were battle fields we should perhaps see them as meetings of share-holders, in which all those present accept that their interest is the same, and so are their aims, but in which criticism of the way in which those aims are being achieved is permitted, and may lead to a change of strategy.

That image made MPs more like shareholders of a joint-stock company meeting to discuss matters of mutual interest than men seeking to oppose the crown. It can usefully be compared to Conrad Russell's image of parliaments as being like a modern party conference.[7] Another telling image is that of MPs as members of a single political party in a one-party state rather than like the party politicians of modern democratic parliaments. Religious belief—religious divisions—would come to complicate that picture, but for much of the century there was no public argument over politics and policies.

Let us look more closely at MPs and at how they came to become MPs. In the thirty-seven English shires seventy-four MPs 'emerged' from the leading families in the counties and were then chosen—elected—unopposed. Ninety-seven per cent of county 'elections' in Tudor England did not come to a poll. There were consequently no general elections in the modern sense and consequently little electioneering or public debate over political issues. On the rare occasions when there were more candidates than there were seats, a poll—what we would call an election—was called. Since 1430, all men who received an annual income from lands held by freehold of at least £2 were eligible to take part. That was quite a broad franchise, including men well below the gentry. But its significance was limited by the extreme infrequency of county elections. To be returned as an MP was a recognition and reinforcement of one's local standing. It was better to be returned unopposed than to win in a contest. Most shire MPs were men from the county for which they sat, that is to say they were leading gentry who owned land, and who, increasingly, had acquired legal training at the Inns of Court in London. Such men served as MPs above all as a tour of duty.

In the boroughs, leading local merchants involved in the running of the town formed the largest category of MPs. But increasingly in the smaller towns fewer and fewer MPs were true townsmen: 23 per cent in 1559, 14 per cent in 1601.[8] The author of a set of proposals considered by the leaders of the Pilgrimage of Grace at Pontefract in November 1536 urged that every burgess should live in the borough for which he had been elected: 'a great many' did not.⁹ Many borough MPs were not townsmen but rather local gentry and lawyers. Clearly, being returned for a county conferred greater prestige. But gentry were increasingly ready to sit for towns. Between 1510 and 1558 no fewer than eighty-three knights sat for boroughs.

There was another significant category of borough MPs, namely lawyers. They were often in the service of landed magnates or the crown. Some of them were especially ambitious for a career in royal service. They would not have easily secured election in a county or a large town. But in small boroughs the franchise was often restricted and the crown or a nobleman might have decisive influence. In 1539 Thomas Howard, third duke of Norfolk, listed the towns in Sussex where 'in times past I could have made burgesses of parliament': Horsham, Lewes, New Shoreham and Steyning.¹⁰ And so quite a few MPs owed their seats in Parliament to crown or noble patronage, a practice that was well known and accepted.¹¹

Many MPs were royal servants. They were members of the royal household in which they held posts to which they had been appointed by the monarch and to whom they swore individual oaths of loyalty on appointment. In the fifteenth century roughly 25 per cent of MPs can be so identified. In the so-called Reformation Parliament (1529-36) some 125 (40 per cent) were broadly connected to the crown: including not just men holding posts in the royal household but also those holding posts such as constables of castles or membership of regional councils. In Edward VI's reign the ratio was around 45 per cent. So the chronicler Edward Hall exaggerated, but nevertheless noted a vital feature, when he wrote that 'the most part of the commons were the king's servants'. And the increase in the number of borough seats (to which we shall return) accommodated more and more of them. What all that meant in practical terms was that monarchs could rely on a core of perhaps a quarter or a third of MPs to support government legislation. They were not a majority but they were the largest recognisable group.¹²

And they were vigorous in support of the king's wishes. In 1523, as we shall see, and in 1529, they stood firm by the king's financial demands, in the former year over the details of a large grant of taxation, in the latter securing the writing off of loans made to the crown in 1522–3. We shall return to this when we consider the statutes enacting Henry VIII's break with Rome in the 1530s. And it is worth noting the grounds on which Sir Thomas Tempest objected to the act suppressing the smaller monasteries. Where it was claimed that the king had authority granted him by Parliament to suppress these abbeys, Tempest declared that

> I think that these parliaments was of none authority nor virtue, for if they should be truly named, they should be called councils of the king's appointment, and not parliaments, for parliaments ought to have the knights of [the] shire and burgesses for the towns at their own election that could reason for the wealth of the shire or town . . . not such men as the king will appoint for his private lucre.

What did Sir Francis Bigod, landowner and scholar, know of the town for which he was burgess?¹³ Tempest, who was preparing a paper for the meeting of the leaders of the Pilgrims of Grace at Pontefract in November 1536, declared roundly that 'The old law or custom was that none of the king's servants should be of the Commons House and it is not unknown that the most part of the same House were the king's servants'. Perception matters more than strict accuracy here.[14]

Noting the presence of crown servants in parliaments, Alasdair Hawkyard insisted:

> What this amounted to was that the crown's insistence on absolute fidelity by its dependants, combined with a degree of bullying and manipulation of the pliable members not in its service, more or less guaranteed the eventual outcome in the regime's favour of any part of its legislative programme. Under the Tudors, members lacked any real freedom of choice or action. If any man were to forget this, the existence of the lower row made up predominantly of councillors and household officers was a constant reminder.

There is much in that. It is hard to show that, for example, Parliament significantly affected the passage of the Reformation Statutes in these years. Yet as Hawkyard at once qualified his bleak perspective by insisting that 'even so, no Tudor regime could rely automatically on getting its way in the Commons'.[15] We shall return to this when we consider the evidence of dissent and opposition in Parliament. But it is worth noting here that none of this fits well with the teleological narrative of the rise of Parliament. Far from seeking parliamentary sovereignty, a great many MPs were primarily concerned with essentially local interests. Far from wishing to reduce the prerogatives of the crown, there was a goodly number of MPs who held some crown position and who were correspondingly loyal and supportive. Far from being obstructive, there were quite a few MPs who were careerists looking to rise in crown service and seeing service as a member of Parliament as a helpful stepping stone to appointment to the monarch's council, especially from the 1530s when churchmen were more or less excluded.

If we look back to the earliest years of representative assemblies, we find two brilliantly imaginative scholars offering a shared vision. In the late Anglo-Saxon state James Campbell sees a remarkable depth of political involvement, indeed a constitutional monarchy. He noted attitudes and mechanisms that make sense only if there was a substantial political nation meeting at shire courts and hundred courts. Here we see a vertebra: thus we may infer a backbone.[16] Campbell's sometime pupil John Maddicott carefully delineated assemblies of knights and thegns that gave consent to taxation from the tenth to the thirteenth centuries, extending and reinforcing Campbell's vision. The evidence is substantial and the reasoning rigorous.[17] But sometimes, nonetheless, and also when pondering the writings on communities by Susan Reynolds, I do worry that such claims offer too rosy a view of late Anglo-Saxon and Anglo-Norman society. When men attended assemblies, were they autonomous participants, or would it make better sense to think of them as simply being involved in, indeed associated with, royal policies in the making of which they had no great say. Was attendance at meetings more a test of loyalty, as Paul Hyams has wondered, than an opportunity to wield influence? Did these assemblies have the character of consensual Oxford college governing bodies, or were they more like those modern universities in which a management team is less interested in the views of staff than it is to get them to absorb and acquiesce in its policies? Campbell's and Maddicott's visions are thrilling constructs, but they need to be read against the grain. I should like to think them persuasive. But maybe what mattered much more was the masterfulness of monarchs and the goodwill of the greater nobility.[18] And in assessing the significance of voting, the jibe of Shakespeare's Third Citizen in *Coriolanus* after Coriolanus's election[19]

> When we granted [him our voices]
> Here was 'I thank you for your voices,
> I have no further with you

must be borne in mind. But perhaps we should take a more nuanced view. Any representative assembly needs a ballast of supporters of the monarch or the government if it is to function. And we need to test more subtly whether in some circumstances parliaments could and did refuse to acquiesce.

But first, let us ask how far governments attempted to influence the composition of the House of Commons more directly. Letters dated 1 December 1514 addressed to the boroughs and sent from Henry VIII and Archbishop Warham in his role as Lord Chancellor asked the boroughs to return the same members as in 1512. The letter sent to Wells survives. What was clearly a similar letter sent to York was summarised in the civic records: the king expected the electors 'to elect and name to the said parliament these knights and burgesses that was present and expert in those businesses and matters treated upon at the said last parliament'.[20] We know from the returns that by no means all boroughs returned the same men as they had in 1512, but of course a variety of reasons, including death or illness, could explain that. In February 1523 the king and Wolsey (by then Lord Chancellor) sent a similar circular letter to boroughs. Those for Wallingford and Dover survive. They ask for the election of 'the most expert, wise and discreet persons' and issue an order: 'ye by common consent, will and agreement name and appoint and choose two [of] the most discreet, expert and sufficient persons continually resident and inhabited there'.[21] On 7 May 1536 Henry VIII issued what was obviously a circular letter to all sheriffs. He justified his decision to call a new Parliament and exhorted sheriffs to ensure that 'such personages may be elected as shall serve and for their worship and qualities be most meet for the purpose'. But sheriffs were not given more explicit or detailed instructions. Nor were they asked to return the same MPs as in 1529.[22] In early 1553 a circular letter was sent out with no variation. It directed that 'there shall be good regard had that the choice be made of men of gravity and knowledge in their own countries and towns, for their understanding and qualities, to be in such a great council'.[23] Mary issued a similar letter in 1554 asking that her loving subjects choose men 'of the wise, grave and catholic sort'.[24] All these letters and instructions were general. Even those asking for the return of MPs chosen at the previous election did so without exception. Monarch and ministers were not explicitly urging the return of this man or the exclusion of that man.

Monarch and ministers did, however, intervene more directly and personally. Henry VIII appears to have nominated Sir Christopher Dacre and John Pennington for Cumberland and Sir William Bulmer for Yorkshire in 1523. Thomas, Lord Dacre, Christopher's brother, wrote to Wolsey informing him that Christopher could not be spared from the west marches and pointing out that Pennington was sheriff. It would be better if Wolsey named John Hennage or another of his servants.[25] Bulmer wrote to Wolsey to find out whether he should come up to Parliament or stay on the borders.[26] That obvious problems had been overlooked suggests that this was not a carefully planned effort to recruit loyal MPs.

But in autumn 1536 the writer of proposals for the council held by the leaders of the Pilgrimage of Grace at Pontefract in November complained that 'such persons as were elected to the said parliament were named in the king's letters' (unfortunately the manuscript is torn and the precise sense is not easy to elucidate).[27] And there is some supporting evidence. George Giffard informed Cromwell in May 1536 that he and Thomas Pope had been nominated as burgesses by the inhabitants of the town of Buckingham according to Cromwell's letters and the request of the Lord Chancellor.[28] Cromwell also successfully recommended William Ashby as a knight of the shire for Leicestershire.[29] In the same month William Fleurs, mayor of Oxford, had received letters from the Lord Chancellor and Cromwell urging the return of the outgoing MPs William Fleming and John Latton; he pointed out that Fleming was aged and could neither see well nor walk, and asking if he should be replaced.[30] Most notoriously, Thomas Cromwell ordered the election of John Bridges for Canterbury in the face of opposition in the borough.[31] When the sheriff, John Hobbys, held the election, John Starkey, an alderman, and Christopher Levyns, common clerk, were returned. Later that day—so John Alcock, the mayor, claimed—arrived a letter to the mayor from Thomas Audley, Lord Chancellor, and Thomas Cromwell, informing the mayor that the king's 'pleasure and commandment' was that the outgoing MPs, John Bridges and Robert Darknall, should be re-elected. The mayor responded that, had he known the king's pleasure beforehand, he would have done his best to accomplish it. In no uncertain terms Cromwell threatened him with 'his highness's displeasure'. The king 'doth not a little marvel', he wrote ominously, that the mayor had disregarded the king's command. Consequently Cromwell required him on the king's behalf to proceed to a new election and to elect those whom the king wanted. The mayor yielded 'to the king's command'. The difficulty facing us is to know how typical, and how effective, such interventions were.[32] And we can note how Cromwell throughout presented himself as executing the king's command.[33]

There are comparable scraps of evidence for 1539. In that year the mayor and aldermen of Norwich chose their members before the arrival of Cromwell's letter requesting they return John Godsalve, clerk of the signet. They complied as the mayor of Canterbury had complied three years earlier. The duke of Norfolk wrote about the counties of Norfolk and Suffolk (and other unnamed shires within his commission) that 'I have put such order that such shall be chosen as I doubt not shall serve his highness according to his pleasure'.[34] In the same year Thomas Wriothesley, earl of Southampton, was much involved in the business of selecting MPs. He called on Sir

Richard Weston at Sutton Place to see if he would stand as knight of the shire, but Weston was too sick and promised to do his best for Southampton's half-brother Sir Anthony Browne and Sir Matthew Browne. At Guildford, Southampton called the mayors and others together and informed them that the king had summoned his Parliament. If they followed Southampton's advice they would be spared the great charge that would fall on them if they sent their burgesses. What Southampton was offering was MPs who would not claim any expenses. The borough wanted to return Daniel Modge, a resident townsman, but would defer to Southampton's pleasure as for the other member. Southampton was also working for the return of Sir William Goring and Sir John Gage in Sussex.[35] Southampton reported further that he had deferred the election till the next county day. He enclosed a 'schedule of the best men' of the county of Hampshire for Cromwell to choose from and he urged the freeholders of the county to return his brother and Sir Matthew Browne 'according to the king's pleasure'. But he was unable to do much in Farnham where Stephen Gardiner, bishop of Winchester, had already moved men after his own desires.[36]

Clearly Henry VIII and Cromwell were involved in the selection of MPs, but the overall impression is that they were opportunistic, exploiting possibilities and recognising obstacles. No one can be shown to have had overall control.[37] In March 1539 Cromwell wrote to Henry that 'I and other your dedicated councillors [the earl of Southampton surely prominent among them] be abouts to bring all things so to pass that your majesty had never more tractable parliament', but it is far from clear that they could deliver that.[38]

In August 1547, the first year of Edward VI's reign, the council instructed Sir Thomas Cheyne, Lord Warden of the Cinque Ports, so to recommend Sir John Baker to those who had the naming of the knights of the shire that he might be knight of the shire in Kent. The sheriff was also approached but when the council heard that he had treated their request as a commandment, they wrote that they had not and did not mean 'to deprive the shire of their liberty of election', but if they would in satisfaction of the council's request grant their voice to Mr Baker, the council would take it thankfully.[39] The paradoxes of power are plain here. The council was both giving, and denying having given, a commandment. Councillors wanted the gentry of Kent freely to choose as a knight of the shire the man that Councillors wanted.

We are better informed for 1552. In that year the council pressed the claims of fifteen men in eight counties, in four of them successfully nominating both knights of the shire, in two counties securing one but not both.[40] In 1553 the earl of Pembroke received a letter praying your good lordship 'to cause such good order to be taken in the election' of knights and burgesses 'within your circuit' as 'are grave, wise, discreet and conformable'. The sheriff of Suffolk was told by the Privy Council that 'men of gravity and knowledge in their own countries and towns fit for their understanding and qualities to be in such a great council' should be elected, but 'where our Privy Counsil or any of them within their jurisdictions, in our behalf shall recommend men of learning and wisdom, in such cases their directions' were to be obeyed.

What do these scraps of evidence of governmental efforts to influence the composition of the House of Commons reveal? Perhaps the years 1552–3 saw a more determined effort, by Northumberland's government, to secure appropriate members—certainly several letters from councillors survive—but again it is not clear that such an effort (if that is what it was) was particularly successful.[41] In the counties all freeholders worth £2 could vote in the event of a contested election, and that meant that control from above would be difficult if it came to a contest. In the boroughs matters were more mixed. In some there was a large franchise. Some sixteen cities and towns were regarded as counties. In London the court of aldermen, numbering twenty-five men, nominated men who then had to be confirmed by the common council, numbering a hundred. In York the city council of thirty-six chose the MPs. In Norwich the aldermen and common council, some ninety strong, made the choice. In Lincoln it was some forty members of the common council. In Hull some twenty to thirty-two could vote. In Gloucester there was acrimony in 1555 when some 400 to 500 assembled at the county court, but only around twenty were recognised as voters. Beyond the urban counties, there was no statutory regulation of the franchise and, not surprisingly, there was a great diversity of practice. In some the franchise was broad. In Preston the mayor, bailiffs, burgesses and all the commons were entitled to vote. At Malden the freemen and commonalty voted. But often the franchise was restricted. In Shrewsbury, just the aldermen and common council voted, as was the case at Bath, Colchester and Wallingford. In some boroughs ownership of specified properties conferred voting rights, in Knaresborough on nearly ninety men. But in others, only a handful of men were entitled to vote—only one in Gatton, Surrey—and here governments could do much more to manipulate, including securing the return of non-resident outsiders. Ministers often sat for such boroughs. Governments were keen, as we have seen, that 'useful' men sat in the Commons and helped manage its business. And governments might well also benefit, as we have seen, if MPs were returned who were royal servants in a broader sense. But the exercise of electoral patronage was never automatic.[42]

Interestingly the crown could and did increase the number of boroughs which returned burgesses to the Commons. The number of seats in the Commons rose from 296 in 1509 (74 knights of the shire, 26 from urban counties and 196 burgesses) to 398 in 1558 (86 knights, 33 from urban counties and 279 burgesses)[43] and 462 over the century, overwhelmingly an increase in the number of borough, especially small borough, seats. It is not always possible to know exactly when enfranchisement occurred. Henry VIII added some forty constituencies. The thirty-one from Wales and Cheshire reflected changes in their position. They had long borne the brunt of supporting military campaigns and had been exempted from standard taxation. Now that exemption would end but in return they were given representation in Parliament. Under Edward VI thirty-four boroughs were created; Mary added twenty-five; Elizabeth sixty-two. Why did such an expansion take place? Local concerns may well explain why some new boroughs were created. One of the consequences of the dissolution of the monasteries was that abbots no longer sat in the House of Lords. It is likely that it was the loss of their abbots that led to the enfranchisement of Abingdon, Peterborough, St Albans and Westminster in 1545. But the undoubted increase in the population in the sixteenth century does not offer a persuasive explanation. There was no clear rhyme or reason behind the choice of new boroughs. Was it monarchs and governments who were keen on increasing the number of MPs and in the hope of securing more supporters? Some new boroughs—such as Abingdon, Higham Ferrers and Banbury—were given just one member of Parliament: if crude 'packing' of the house was intended, that was an opportunity missed. With the exception of the Welsh seats, the new seats created were overwhelmingly in boroughs, usually small towns with low populations. A good number of these new boroughs were on crown estates, notably the duchy of Cornwall and the duchy of Lancaster. Often the franchise was restricted here too. Maybe this was a way for the crown to influence Parliament without directly interfering in the choice of counties and larger boroughs, subtly increasing its influence without being overtly provocative. Thus, as we have seen, every Parliament had its share of royal nominees: a small number, it is true, but often a large proportion of the most active MPs. To say that Tudor parliaments were 'packed' by the crown is excessive, but undoubtedly the crown did exercise a measure of influence over who did, and perhaps who did not, sit, which again reinforces criticisms of any view of parliaments as bent on power. We shall return to this when considering opposition.

The principal function of MPs was to legislate. MPs themselves presented bills—draft laws—on an enormous range of issues, from the preservation of woods to weights and measures, from fraudulent conveyances to street paving, from prohibitions on the import of foreign hats to the lease of a marsh outside Calais. Often MPs took the initiative in such matters. At other times the government had business—law-making—for parliaments to undertake. Laws, however, were, and are, only part of government. Parliamentary statutes were no substitute for decision-making executive government or the resolution of conflicts of interest. Laws are a mechanism, not in themselves answers to problems. Moreover, laws did not enforce themselves; yet the enforcement of laws duly made was crucial. Laws were interpreted by judges and lawyers in the law courts, and their interpretations were sometimes far removed from the intentions of the governments which had first made them. For governments, laws were useful, but there were other ways of getting things done: instructions from the council, circular letters to JPs, proclamations, martial law, the vice-gerency in ecclesiastical matters, ad hoc commissions of noblemen and gentry. For individuals, or groups such as the London livery companies (the great mercantile gilds that monopolised London's trade), pressing for new laws in Parliament was one means of pursuing grievances—perhaps as much a way of drawing public attention to them as of resolving them—but it could be more effective to bring an action in the law courts under existing law, or to lobby the monarch and councillors for a licence to do something or a conciliar letter ordering someone else not to do something. Parliamentary lawmaking was an inescapable feature of Tudor England, yet its importance compared with other ways of pressing interests was surprisingly limited.

Governments often simply wanted to use parliaments as a means of disseminating information about their policies, especially when these were controversial. In March 1531 Thomas More, the Lord Chancellor, and Brian Tuke read the opinions of carefully selected European university theologians and canon lawyers justifying Henry VIII's divorce to MPs so that they 'may report in your countries what you have seen and heard and then all men shall openly perceive that the King hath not attempted this matter [the divorce] of will or pleasure, as some strangers report, but only for the discharge of his conscience and surety of the succession of his realm'.[44]

The account of Parliament presented thus far is incomplete because so much attention has been paid to the House of Commons. That is a common failing. It is vital, however, to note that the House of Lords was in many ways more important than the Commons. After all, its roughly fifty lay members, those men holding titles—duke, viscount, marquess, earl, baron—of nobility were, as we have seen in an earlier chapter, among the most powerful men in the realm. Most of them had inherited their titles along with substantial holdings of land. A few peers had been freshly created, for it was one of the prerogatives of the monarch to ennoble commoners. The Tudors did that fairly sparingly but often on the eve of a Parliament (for instance Henry VIII created five new peers in 1529). Bishops, and, before the break with Rome, several abbots, also sat in the House of Lords. Monarchs appointed bishops and often had a say in the election of abbots of the wealthiest religious houses. In moments of controversy, individual bishops could be excluded from the Lords, as Mary excluded the bishops of Hereford and Lincoln in 1555 or Elizabeth excluded the bishops of Winchester and London in 1559. Its powers of patronage gave the crown a degree of control of the House of Lords. And it was very likely that noblemen would be personally known to the monarch, through attendance at court and, possibly, service on the council or in war, so, up to a point, they would be open to influence by the crown and its ministers. Thus the upper house of Parliament was always likely to show particular devotion to the monarchy and only in unusual circumstances would the House of Lords be willing to criticise the crown. But if it did, its criticisms could be especially telling.

So was there opposition in Tudor parliaments? Yes, but it was limited and focussed, not to be seen as part of some teleology in which Parliament was inevitably and successfully wrestling with the crown over sovereignty. We have already seen how a significant proportion of MPs were in various ways royal servants and thus not the most likely of dissenters. And that also raises the extent to which MPs felt cowed, the extent to which dissent, and especially organised opposition, would be difficult to plot and, to sustain.

Taxation was overwhelmingly the main reason why monarchs summoned Parliament. And, given the obvious impact of demands for taxation, it is over taxation that opposition and resistance to the monarch might have been thought most likely to be found. Yet what is remarkable is how little objection to taxation there was over the Tudor century. It was a long-standing convention (and we shall return to this in the chapter on taxation) that taxation required consent and that consent to taxation had to come from parliaments and in particular from the House of Commons. That principle had been reasserted in 1496 when Henry VII had asked a great council—a meeting exclusively of noblemen and bishops, rather like the House of Lords—for taxation. It agreed to make a grant but said it did not have sufficient authority for the levying of the tax proposed: accordingly, a Parliament was summoned, and it confirmed the grant. It was of course possible for the government, pleading necessity and emergency, to seek forced loans and other grants without parliamentary approval. Sometimes these did succeed, spectacularly in 1522–3, but, as we shall see, the failure of the Amicable Grant in 1525 showed the limits to such an approach. Usually the crown went to Parliament when it needed taxation.

The generally accepted theory of necessity held that in an emergency, especially war, the king could demand assistance from his subjects and that they could not refuse in principle. They could, however, make pleas of poverty and bargain over the amount, the rates and the timing of taxation. But that amounted to negotiation, not principled opposition, and it is vital to examine such negotiations in the round. In 1523 it was reported that[45]

> since the beginning of the Parliament there hath been the greatest and sorest hold in the lower House for payment of ii*s*. of the li. [2*s*. in the £—or 10%] that ever was seen I think in any parliament. This matter hath been debated and beaten xv or xvi [14 or 16] days together: the highest necessity alleged on the king's behalf . . . and of the contrary, the highest poverty confessed . . . by knights, squires, and gentlemen . . . as by the commoners, citizens & burgesses.

Often this report has been interpreted as evidence of Wolsey's mismanagement of Parliament and as fundamental resistance to taxation. But it was nothing of the sort. Ultimately Parliament granted taxes payable in two instalments, one in 1524 and one in 1525, each of which produced a far higher yield, as we shall see, than either the standard tax or earlier attempts at reform, as well as two further instalments payable by the wealthiest. True, the yield was indeed far lower than the £800,000 which Wolsey asked for at the beginning of the Parliament, but that was so impossibly high that it can never have been more than a negotiating position. Warham, Lord Chancellor in 1512, had similarly asked for £600,000, before settling for much less, but still considerable sums. From Henry VIII and Wolsey's perspective the Parliament of 1523 had been a success: they had secured an enhanced grant to be assessed on new principles (to which we shall return). If Parliament ultimately gave Henry and Wolsey what they sought, had there nonetheless been unprecedented opposition along the way? Maybe. As we have just seen, the anonymous correspondent wrote how there had been 'the greatest and sorest hold in the lower House for payment of ii*s*. of the li. [2*s*. in the £—or 10%] that ever was seen I think in any parliament' and that the matter had been debated for fifteen or sixteen days. Would that we knew more. In his *Chronicle* Edward Hall, on a hasty reading, appears to suggest that it was the king's servants and the knights of the shire who pushed through the grant of taxation. After further reasoning, Hall claimed, MPs were asked to say Aye or No. It was not clear which of the Ayes or the Noes had it. So the House was divided, with the knights of the shire and the king's servants agreeing to taxation while the commons 'severed themselves from the knights of the shires', calling those who urged on the demand 'enemies to the realm'.[46]

Stirring stuff, implying that MPs for boroughs were hostile to taxation to the point of calling those who were in favour 'enemies to the realm'. But is Hall to be believed here? The anonymous correspondent noted 'the highest necessity alleged on the king's behalf' but on the contrary, 'the highest poverty confessed . . . by knights, squires, and gentlemen ... as by the commoners, citizens & burgesses'. Here knights and townsmen were seen as responding as one. And closer attention to Hall's report reveals that the dispute he relates that led to the knights of the realm being called enemies to the realm was not over the main demand but over the third and fourth instalments. The knights of the shire agreed that men with lands worth £50 or more should pay 12d in the £ in the third year but insisted that men with goods worth £50 or more should pay 12d in the £ in the fourth year. The particular argument here did not affect the bulk of taxpayers but only the wealthiest. And Hall tells us that the Speaker—Sir Thomas More—finally persuaded the townsmen to agree.[47] In the end this once again sounds more like vigorous bargaining than fundamental opposition. And generally in Henry VIII's reign taxation was granted without—as far as we know—any great fuss. There was one exception. In February 1532 the Primer Seisin Bill—allowing the crown to claim what we would call death duties on the lands of some landowners—met with sustained opposition in the House of Commons and, despite concessions, was defeated. We know very little about the details and circumstances of an obscure episode but on the face of it, Parliament—the political nation—was able to resist what might have proved a significant fiscal innovation.[48] Perhaps this is best compared to what happened in Henry VII's reign. In 1504 the king asked for two feudal aids—payments by the king's subjects at key moments in the lives of the royal family, in this case the knighting of Henry's son Arthur and the marriage of his daughter Margaret—but the Commons, defending an important point of legal principle against the king, refused to agree to that but granted instead a subsidy worth £30,000, justified on the traditional grounds of the defence of the realm.[49]

Under Elizabeth, there were few immediate problems over taxation. Her government asked for taxation twelve times (in every Parliament except that of 1572) and received twelve grants (including double subsidies from 1589 and a quadruple subsidy in 1601), that is, significantly more in number than under Henry VII or Henry VIII. The obvious necessity—the needs of defence, the threat of invasion, war itself—made the sustained denial of financial assistance unlikely, not least since it would in itself damage national defence. There were qualms about the ways taxes were raised. Yields of taxes fell—from £136,500 in 1559–60 to £73,500 in 1602–3—but the sums granted were in total considerable, even if in real terms less in the 1590s than in the 1540s.

If one looks at the broad sweep of English history, war taxation was often—as in the 1380s or 1620s—a source of parliamentary difficulties for governments and ministers, with criticisms of the government's financial mismanagement, attacks against corrupt ministers and incompetent military commanders, followed by efforts to place controls over the conduct of war by appointing ministers or setting up separate treasuries. It is worth noting in passing that even in such circumstances, criticism was inspired by immediate political circumstances, not by constitutional theories. But what is notable here is how rare such criticism was under the Tudors. Even the Parliament which met in 1558 after the loss of Calais was noticeably smooth. There were some rumbles of discontent, especially over some of the other ways in which the government was raising money, in the 1590s and in 1601, but, compared with the parliaments of the 1370s, 1400s, 1620s or 1640–1, there was relative calm. Monarchs in the sixteenth century by and large managed and financed their wars without running into serious parliamentary opposition.

Moreover, there was little sign that the Commons were making much attempt to use their undoubted right to consent to taxation as a bargaining counter to increase their powers on other matters or to insist on redress of grievances before granting supply. There are just a handful of examples from the Tudor period, and they reflect immediate concern over policies—Henry VIII's divorce, Elizabeth's succession, the use of grants of monopolies—rather than over fundamental constitutional principles. In 1532 two MPs, one called Temse, were reported by the imperial ambassador as having said, in response to a request for taxation to strengthen border defences against the Scots, that if Henry took back Catherine of Aragon and maintained an alliance with Charles V, Holy Roman Emperor, and Catherine's nephew, then such taxation would not be necessary. There is little evidence for this obscure episode and nothing to show any sustained bargaining. It seems as if the Commons did eventually agree to grant taxation, after Henry had summoned a majority of MPs to hear him make a long speech in defence of his actions over the divorce. But Parliament was prorogued, ostensibly owing to an outbreak of plague, before any bill could be passed and so no taxation was granted that year.[50]

More telling links between taxation and redress of grievances are found in Elizabeth's reign. In 1566 concerns over the succession and the queen's demands for a subsidy were linked by John Molyneux: 'if her Majesty will grant us the one we will the more willingly grant her the other'. Elizabeth gave up one of the three subsidies which she had been granted rather than yield over the succession. In 1601 the Commons granted an unprecedented four subsidies but delayed the implementation of the subsidies until the issue of monopolies had been dealt with. Already a contentious matter in 1597, monopolies were royal grants to favoured courtiers—such as the monopoly of the right to import sweet wines—which could easily be abused. They were granted by monarchs under their prerogative. At one level monopolies could be seen as another version of charters given by monarchs to corporations to oversee their trades and, sometimes, to enforce what was in effect royal policy. It was a way of regulating old industries and stimulating new ones. The Stationers' Company was charged with enforcing the licensing of books: in return, members were given a monopoly of printing. In the later years of Elizabeth's reign private agencies were entrusted with more of what might be thought to be the work of government. Military supplies were often entrusted to contractors. In 1581 Edward Stafford was granted a patent giving him a monopoly over searching for lands properly the crown's but concealed by their tenants who paid no rents. Informers were paid for drawing attention to infringements of economic regulations. Customs duties in London and some other ports were farmed out to a single lessee, Smythe, from 1570 to 1589, those due from the outports were farmed out to Sir Francis Walsingham between 1585 and 1590. All this was in various ways potentially dangerous territory. The crown could be presented as abusing its prerogative powers to raise substantial sums of money, 'meeting part of the cost of government by what was in effect a tax on consumption'.[51] Those granted patents of monopoly would pay the crown large sums—and then seek to recoup their expenditure by charging higher prices for inferior products. Critics who urged that statute limit or control monopolies could be seen as calling into question the royal prerogative by which they had been granted.[52] But it is worth noting that the queen's critics concentrated on abuses, rather than on the principle of the powers monarchs enjoyed by virtue of the royal prerogative—that is to say on criticising a bad policy rather than making a bid for parliamentary supremacy. And Elizabeth, showing political good sense, met the considerable concern over abuses by quickly conceding a proclamation and by delivering the famous 'golden speech' in which she recognised the justice of much of the criticism and promised reform. While the actions of James I and Charles I can be defended much more reasonably than their critics (whether peers and MPs at the time, or modern historians) would allow, nonetheless it is interesting to note how Elizabeth never got herself into the awkward controversies of her successors or some of her predecessors.

In the light of what we have been considering, it is misleading to see Tudor parliaments as generally and constantly exploiting royal financial needs in order to strengthen their powers: that was not how they worked. There were no Tudor parliamentary protests over customs duties, regularly granted to kings for life at the beginning of their reigns and substantially enhanced without controversy at the end of Mary's reign. But, in a very broad sense, the convention that taxation required parliamentary consent simply because it was the convention, because it was the normal way of doing things, imposed limits in practice on royal ambition. Governments did not seek unlimited taxation because they knew that that would be unacceptable. In this respect England was a constitutional monarchy very different from that of France, where, against the background of repeated invasions in the fourteenth and fifteenth centuries, kings had achieved the right to tax at will to pay for their armed forces,[53] and in that sense the English Parliament was undoubtedly a restraint on royal power. That is not to deny that so-called absolute rulers were less absolute in practice than they might at first appear and that even so-called absolute monarchs did best when they succeeded in harnessing the collaboration of their leading subjects and social elites.[54] But that, constitutionally, they could act without that collaboration sent them off with a flying start.

So, to return to the question posed earlier, 'Was there opposition in Tudor parliaments?', the response must, be that there was but in the sense that opposition was opposition to specific measures and thus routine. Over taxation there was clearly vigorous bargaining at times, and MPs who agreed to taxation could, at least on one occasion, be labelled enemies of the realm by MPs who did not. But to claim, as Alasdair Hawkyard has done, that 'throughout the early sixteenth century, turbulence was the predominant trait of the house of commons' is to go too far.[55]

Much has been made of the Reformation Parliament (1529–36) as leading to significant changes in the relationship between monarch and Parliament, but that is unpersuasive. Henry VIII's search for an annulment of his marriage to Catherine of Aragon and his break with Rome did at times lead to criticisms in Parliament. In the early 1530s Henry VIII asked Parliament to endorse his break with Rome. From time to time reservations were expressed in Parliament. But there was no sustained campaign.

And our knowledge is patchy and often rests on a single source, especially Eustache Chapuys, the imperial ambassador, who was very unsympathetic to what Henry VIII was doing. In December 1530 he reported that three or four members had seen him to ask whether he could offer them some papal provision on which they could ground their opposition.[56] In early 1531 the Commons wanted to be granted an exemption from *praemunire*, the offence allegedly committed by churchmen. After great murmuring in the Commons, Henry yielded.[57] When in March 1531 Thomas More, Lord Chancellor, read out university opinions favourable to the king on the divorce, the Commons, according to Chapuys, showed its displeasure.[58] In 1532 a bill in restraint of annates (fees amounting to one or two years' income paid by newly appointed bishops to Rome when presented to their sees) which Henry was using in order to put pressure on the pope to grant him his annulment, ran into trouble. There was opposition in the House of Lords where all the bishops and William Fitzalan, eleventh earl of Arundel, opposed it so vigorously that the king had to come in person to the Lords to secure the passage of the bill. Then in the Commons the king agreed to defer implementing the measures against the pope for a year and also agreed to allow the pope 5 per cent of what was previously paid instead of totally abolishing it (a significant concession since it retained the principle of papal involvement in the appointment of new bishops). Even that compromise proved controversial. It was finally agreed to when the king came to the House of Commons in person and forced a division of the house—those who agreed with him stayed on his side, those who did not went to the other side, one of the earliest recorded divisions in the Commons (we have noted that there was a division over taxation in 1523). Chapuys believed that some MPs had remained with the king for fear of his indignation. But the king's efforts proved sufficient: the bill passed with a small majority.[59] It is likely that the revisions to the bill of annates—delaying its implementation for a year, allowing a token payment to the pope—were forced on the king by the Commons, but there is no definite evidence. A little later—as we have seen—two MPs, one called Temse, were reported by the imperial ambassador as having said, in response to a request for taxation to strengthen border defences against the Scots, that if Henry took back Catherine of Aragon and maintained an alliance with Charles V, Holy Roman Emperor, and Catherine's nephew, then taxation would not be necessary.[60] In 1533 there was some dissent over the Act of Appeals: merchants' anxieties over trade were voiced in opposition. In 1534, Robert Fisher, MP for Rochester and brother of John Fisher, bishop of Rochester, reported that there was 'never such a sticking at the passing of any act in the Lower House as was at the passing of the same'; the majority of MPs insisted on the insertion of the word 'maliciously'.[61]

But in these years Henry VIII essentially got his way. What helped was that his measures were presented piecemeal over a number of years, not as a complete package on a single occasion. It is hard not to conclude that Henry was using Parliament as a rubber stamp, securing the public endorsement of the break with Rome and its consequences. There may have been some compromises on detail, but essentially Parliament endorsed the king's will. 'In theory, the king took counsel on important matters in parliament; in practice major policies were announced, rather than decided, there.'[62] It is tempting to write that 'Parliament enacted' such-and-such a statute, but it is quite plain that the initiative for the famous Reformation statutes did not come from Parliament.

Intriguingly, in these years the Commons did not defend the liberties and privileges of the church. Were they reluctant to get involved in religious controversies? In these years possibly a few MPs—scarcely a group let alone a faction—who all knew Sir Thomas More, Lord Chancellor, till he was dismissed by Henry in 1532—may have got together to oppose various bills connected with the break with Rome, but the evidence is slight.[63] Several bills did meet with some opposition, as we have noted, but all were passed. Were MPs intimidated? When the Pilgrims of Grace called for a Parliament to be held in York, were they implying that MPs sitting in London had felt intimidated? Here the case of Sir George Throckmorton is instructive. A Warwickshire MP, Sir George recalled in 1537 that four years earlier he had spoken out on the bill of Appeals 'whereupon the king's grace did send for me and spoke with me in diverse matters'. That the king should have sent for an MP who criticised royal policy is intriguing. Sir George emphasised 'how good and gracious lord you were to me . . . to pardon and forgive all things past concerning the parliament'. That an outspoken MP should need royal pardon and forgiveness for speaking out in Parliament is another illustration of the limits of freedom of speech. Throckmorton confessed that he met four other MPs over dinner and supper to discuss Parliament matters. He boasted to his friends that when summoned, he had spoken defiantly to the king—not least saying to Henry that it was thought that Henry had 'meddled' both with Anne Boleyn's sister and her mother— but he admitted in 1537 that he had pretended to have said this. Throckmorton had wanted to show his friends that he had not been intimidated by Henry—but he had.[64] And it is worth noting that when rebellion broke out in 1536, Sir George had raised 300 men to serve in the king's army against the rebels. Thomas Tempest, writing during the rebellions of autumn 1536, remarked bitterly that 'a parliament they have devised that men may not speak of the King's vices which . . . men may say truly had most need to be spoken on, and reformed of [all] thing, [for if] the head ache, how can the body be whole'.[65] It is revealing that the Pilgrims of Grace should call for a Parliament. What they envisaged was surely that a Parliament meeting in York would repeal the statutes that enacted the break with Rome and the act dissolving the smaller monasteries. That cast doubt on the legitimacy of the Reformation Parliament.

That is reinforced by the terms in which the deal between the leaders of the Pilgrimage of Grace and the duke of Norfolk and earl of Shrewsbury on behalf of the king was presented. Oswald Wolsthrop wrote how Henry VIII 'has by mouth declared unto me Sir Oswald Wolsthrop that we shall have our Parliament at York frankly and freely for the ordering and reformation of all causes for the common wealth of this realm'. They would also have 'his frank and free convocation for the good stay and ordering of our faith and of all spiritual causes'.[66] On 8 January 1537 Robert Aske, noting that the king intended to hold Parliament in York, added that he 'has granted his free election of knights and burgesses and like liberty to the spirituality to declare their learning without his displeasure'. That rather pointedly implied that knights and burgesses had not been freely elected. And the liberty the king promised to churchmen to speak without risking his displeasure hints at how Parliament had recently felt intimidated.⁶⁷ Thomas, Lord Darcy, sent out a circular letter on 21 January saying that the duke of Norfolk would soon arrive and declare 'a free parliament to be kept and also free liberty to the spirituality and temporality to utter their learning truly as they may justify'.⁶⁸ Again that all but said that recent parliaments had not been free.

All that makes it hard to see that the so-called Reformation Parliament (1529-36) marked a qualitative shift in the role of Parliament (as is so often asserted) just because Parliament legislated over religion. That was in any case not altogether new, as the heresy laws of the early fifteenth century show. What was truly new was the emergence of religious diversity and religious division across Europe. That arguably weakened more than it, strengthened parliaments. It would, however, have been easier to make a case for the Reformation Parliament as marking a transformation if, from then on, MPs had consistently pressed the crown to agree to the *same* religious measures. But they did not. Parliament undoubtedly legislated on religious matters in the reigns of Edward VI, Mary and Elizabeth, but the legislation that MPs supported or put forward was not the same. That shows that parliaments largely responded to what monarchs wanted. It is hard to sustain an argument that the Reformation Parliament increased the power of parliaments.

What of the impact of religious change later in the century? After Henry VIII's reign, as religious divisions hardened, men were bolder and more willing to speak out in Parliament on matters of faith. In Edward VI's reign conservative lay peers and bishops fought every religious change, especially in 1547 over the bill introducing communion in both kinds, and in 1552 over the bill allowing clerical marriage. In 1547 there was some opposition in the Commons to the dissolution of the chantries, led by the representatives of Coventry and Lynn. They were bought off by the promise that their corporations would be granted all the gild lands and properties free, but the bargain was then largely dishonoured.⁶⁹ In Mary's reign there was opposition to the exiles bill in 1555—which proposed the confiscation of lands owned by protestants who had gone into exile—but that was much less for doctrinal reasons than from fear of undermining security of tenure. At the beginning of Elizabeth's reign there was a good deal of parliamentary opposition to the new government's religious policy. What lay behind it is highly controversial, but most likely the united opposition in the Lords of the catholic bishops Elizabeth inherited from Mary's reign, together with some pressure from religious radicals in the Commons, drove her into dependence on more committedly Protestant churchmen than she would ideally have wished, and so led to a more radical religious settlement, even if that radicalism was limited, than she had initially sought. Throughout her reign religious radicals—puritans—pushed bills in Parliament intended for further reformation of the church. But this was not a campaign by a united House of Commons against the government: we should not write about it in terms of '*parliament* becoming more assertive' since it was a campaign by a persistent and well organised (but nonetheless small) minority, sometimes receiving tacit support and encouragement from some of the queen's councillors. In 1566, 1571, 1576, 1581, 1584--7, 1589 and 1601 radicals introduced bills reforming the clergy in various ways; in 1571 William Strickland (d. 1598) attempted to reform the Prayer Book and was sequestered (excluded) by the queen; in 1586-7 Sir Anthony Cope

(1548x1550–1614) attempted to push a Presbyterian system of church organisation. Elizabeth tried to silence parliamentary debate over religion, usually successfully, as in 1572, 1576, 1584, 1587, insisting that this concerned her prerogative alone. But if puritan parliamentary campaigns to reform the church achieved very little, nonetheless they do vividly show how some men saw Parliament as a useful arena in which to agitate for their views. And it may be that all this had indirect effects. The presence of a bloc of MPs complicated relations between the queen and Parliament—between the queen and the political nation—and this may well have been a factor inhibiting Elizabeth from allowing any significant revision of the religious settlement made in the first year of her reign. But that did not mean that Parliament had become stronger.

Historians who reject the constitutional interpretation of the House of Commons seeking sovereignty tend to reinterpret opposition as the work of factions, that is to say groups of noblemen, courtiers and politicians using parliaments for their own ends, rather than reflecting in any sense the will of the nation. Kevin Sharpe entitled an influential and provocative collection of essays on the early Stuart period, *Faction and Parliament*. What appeared at first glance like the constitutional demands of the commons were, Sharpe and several of his contributors claimed, in reality court factions using Parliament for their own ends. Since I am far from convinced of the existence of court factions battling away (a subject to which we shall return), I am not persuaded by this reinterpretation, but I do believe that sometimes individual noblemen, courtiers and politicians did try to make use of parliaments to further their own ends. That happened especially in periods of weaker government—the minority of Edward VI, the first year of Mary's reign—but it reflected the ambitions and grievances of individuals, not organised factions. Nevertheless, it shows how parliaments could be used for political purposes that had nothing much to do with constitutional issues relating to the rights of parliaments. In the reign of Edward VI, Protector Somerset's brother Thomas, ennobled as Lord Seymour of Sudeley, stirred up trouble in Parliament in 1547 and 1548 directed against his brother. He tried to recruit his fellow noblemen and assembled a group of servants and associates in the Commons, threatening 'to make the blackest parliament that ever was in England'. In 1554 William Paget who hated Stephen Gardiner, bishop of Winchester and Lord Chancellor, opposed Gardiner's legislation to make heresy a crime and succeeded in defeating it in the Lords by exploiting fears that the government would confiscate monastic lands: Mary and Gardiner were compelled to offer a compromise on that issue before they could secure the passage of their heresy bill. Paget and Gardiner were rivals for favour, but there was an underlying issue of principle and interest too. But it did not turn into a constitutional issue involving the role of Parliament.

In Elizabeth's reign concerns were raised in Parliament over a range of issues, but it was the issues themselves, not the constitutional role of parliaments, that prompted concern. That was especially true over the queen's succession. This was a subject which obsessed ruling circles during her reign. Elizabeth for her part deeply believed in doing nothing. Ministers and courtiers feared that the stability of their government depended on the queen's life. That anxiety spilled over into Parliament. In 1566 John Molyneux called upon the queen to name her successor and linked that with the granting of the subsidy, as we have seen. In 1571 efforts were made to exclude Mary Queen of Scots from the succession. Elizabeth tried to stop such debate. In 1563 she instructed Cecil to tell the commons to end their discussion; in 1571 and 1572 she made her hostility to discussion of the future of Mary Queen of Scots quite plain. Once again parliaments were involved in 'political' matters, however much the queen disliked this. Moreover, conflict in Parliament could arise from just such royal efforts to stop debate. Peter Wentworth (1524–1596), MP, was provoked in 1576 and 1587 not so much into defending abstract principles of freedom of speech or denying the queen's right to let her views be known and so influence MPs, but more simply to claim the freedom to speak and to discuss, without harassment and interruption, those matters of great importance, such as the succession, the future of Mary Queen of Scots, further reformation of the church, which, as he saw it, the queen herself had placed on the agenda. Wentworth was unusually angry and outspoken, and he won little support. The issues he raised did not, however, go away—a point that Cliff Davies forcefully made to me just before he died.

That unease over the queen's efforts to stop debate was part of wider semi-constitutional concerns. Once again, these did not amount to a constitutional conflict in the sense of Parliament seeking to wrest sovereignty from the crown. They were more subtle than that. What sometimes troubled MPs was the enlargement of the scope of royal discretion, for example in the definition of an offence punishable at law; the risk of punishing the innocent if laws were not clearly worded and the scope of the law vague; examples of when authority was given to those unfit to exercise it; and infringements of their own dignity as MPs. None of those concerns was new, and such concerns were not obviously increasing; but they all had the potential, in some circumstances, to flare up into significant disputes.

As he studied Elizabeth's parliaments, Geoffrey Elton came to formulate an apolitical model in which the only legitimate purpose of parliaments was to enact the legislation that governments sought. In the preface to his *The Parliament of England 1559-1581* Elton mused that

> the customary concentration on [parliament] as the centre of public affairs, however traditional it may be, is entirely misleading. This is a message, it seems to me, that needs to be absorbed into the general history of England. We have been misled by the Victorians and their obedient successors who read the modern parliament back into history. . . . I now wonder whether the institution—one of the crown's instruments of government—ever really mattered all that much in the politics of the nation, except perhaps as a stage sometimes used by the real contenders over government policy.

Elton's counter-model was somewhat extreme, contradicted not least by Elton's earlier claims that parliaments served as a point of contact between the monarch and the political nation, and his claims (to which we shall return) for Cromwell's reform of Parliament. Moreover, his claims for apolitical parliaments would have been harder to sustain had his book covered the whole reign rather than leaving out the parliaments of 1597 and 1601. By contrast I have here drawn attention to potential political conflict, though not presenting that as pointing the way to constitutional conflict. Perhaps I have given too much time to these disputes given that I do not see them as of fundamental significance, but if I had simply given an account of a typical day in an Elizabethan Parliament, you would soon have been bored rigid. That of course does make the point that most of what happened in parliaments was routine, useful and uncontroversial. And it is important to emphasise more broadly that Tudor government was a partnership between crown and governing classes, and that there was a fundamental community of interest between king/queen, ministers, courtiers, lords, bishops and commons, all anxious to avoid the sort of disputes and struggles that could degenerate into a civil war. There was nonetheless always the potential for political conflict, usually over the means rather than the ends, as in the example of the succession to Queen Elizabeth, but usually in the Tudor period such potential conflicts remained within conventional limits and did not threaten the essential stability of the regime. Once again there are paradoxes of power here. It is intriguing how different the political climate became soon after James I's accession and how matters, seemingly smoothed over in Elizabeth's reign, flared up again. Elizabeth could do what James could not.[70]

Did Tudor parliaments, then, help or hinder the task of governments? Highly important and controversial issues could provoke difficulties: war (especially if mismanaged), foreign policy (especially if religious differences made diplomacy ideological), taxation (though not much in the sixteenth century), religion (as a result of the emergence of religious diversity in the sixteenth century). Ambitious politicians in search of office could stir up MPs. Parliament offered an arena for voicing concern and, occasionally, for expressing dissent. More commonly, Parliament could serve as Elton's point of contact, or as a safety valve, a forum in which concerns could be brought to the monarch's attention and neutralised before any great damage was done. In many ways that built on the medieval practice of petitioning. From the 1270s 'private petitions delivered in parliament constituted a significant point of contact between the subject's needs and the king's authority'. Nearly 18,000 are preserved in The National Archives and there are more on the Parliament rolls. Technically, petitions were allowed only when it could plausibly be claimed that the common-law courts could not provide an appropriate remedy. And from the later fourteenth century the Court of Chancery expanded the scope of its jurisdiction to deal with the kinds of grievance that had been voiced in petitions. From c. 1420 most petitions were not just delivered in Parliament but addressed to the commons and the adoption of a petition by the commons was crucial—numbers smaller by then and petitions were more concerned with matters of state. Some petitions turned into bills that were debated and amended in Parliament and ultimately became laws.[71]

All in all, the crown derived considerable strength from the fact that the political nation as represented in Parliament had acquiesced, or had been persuaded and cajoled into acquiescing, in taxation or in the break with Rome. As Sir Thomas Smith put it, 'the consent of parliament is taken to be every man's consent'. Moreover, the consent of Parliament was seen as more than the consent of just the political nation.

Of course no MPs came from the poor commons. 'All the members were drawn from the ruling elite.'[72] But it was accepted that the House of Commons represented the whole community. 'Every Englishman is intended to be there present, either in person or by procuration and attorney', as Thomas Smith put it. In effect the political nation had long before appropriated the rhetoric of the 'commons' to defend its own interests against the crown and the crown's officials in the name of the commons (though the Commons was none too keen on any consultation and indeed prevented the public from entering the Commons chamber and restricted the reporting of parliamentary debates).[73] But the crown benefitted too. Securing a law from Parliament meant that those who disobeyed it could in future be punished in the courts: that was why it was so helpful to the crown to secure parliamentary statutes. And the crown could plausibly claim that the consent of Parliament meant that the legislating was not a reflection of the whim of the monarch but the wish of the political nation and indeed the realm as a whole. The sense of solidarity achieved by a show of unity and consensus from a Parliament well managed by a strong ruler and seen as representing both the political nation and the wider community of the realm greatly increased the strength and effectiveness of the monarch's government.

4

Finance

The power of the crown was obviously dependent on its wealth and income. By and large Tudor monarchs secured the revenues they needed without too much pain, though in many ways they tailored their ambitions, especially in foreign affairs, to match their resources, which were much less than those available to the king of France, with its greater population, or the Habsburg emperors and kings of Spain, with the wealth of the New World silver mines at their disposal. But an important question is whether the Tudor governments faced a fundamental problem in raising sufficient revenue.

What did the Tudor monarchs spend money on? They had to maintain themselves and their families in a style appropriate to their station, which meant spending on palaces, on ceremonial, on servants. Henry VIII in particular spent lavishly on his buildings, notably at Hampton Court, Whitehall and Nonsuch. They had to meet the costs of government, that is to say the fees paid to the bureaucrats in the central administration and the lawyers who served as judges and legal officials. They were expected to reward their chief ministers generously. They were expected to make charitable donations. Most costly of all, they spent on war, broadly defined: on resisting rebellion, on defending the realm from foreign invasion and on fighting wars overseas. That meant paying for the wages of soldiers on campaigns, for ordnance and artillery, for coastal fortifications, for permanent or near-permanent garrisons. War was by far the greatest drain on the monarchy's resources.

Sometimes wars overtook them unwanted: the Spanish Armadas from 1588 and the troubles in Ireland in the 1590s can be seen in such a light. More often, in the sixteenth century, the wars on which Tudor monarchs embarked, or joined in assistance to others, were more a matter of choice: Henry VIII's wars against France, for example, were not campaigns which Henry needed imperatively and unquestionably to undertake. The French may have encouraged the Scots to invade England in 1513 and 1523 but that was in response to Henry VIII's aggression in France. In 1542 it was Henry who chose to invade Scotland.

Once war was engaged, then the costs imposed themselves; and they were enormous. In a broad sense, the resources that Tudor monarchs could raise constrained and limited their military ambitions. If Henry VIII had been able to mobilise vastly greater resources, he might well have waged war against France more intensively and more continuously: his plans of campaign would have been different. That conceded, it is not, however, obvious that in what Henry actually did, lack of money, rather than other factors, affected the outcomes. In autumn 1523, Charles Brandon (c. 1485–1545), duke of Suffolk, led an invasion of France that reached within 70 miles of Paris, but the campaign then collapsed ignominiously, with soldiers straggling back to Calais. Very bad weather, especially heavy rain, and inadequate supplies from Henry's Low Countries allies were the key factors: the invasion had begun far too late in the year to avoid bad weather, and hoped-for noble-led rebellions in other parts of France did not materialise. Correspondence suggests that money to buy supplies was often tight, but not that it was lack of money that caused the invasion to peter out.[1]

War apart, governments could watch over their expenditures and avoid extravagance. Elizabeth I was notorious for her personal parsimony, in contrast to the extravagance of her successor James I. But again circumstances played a part here. Elizabeth, the Virgin Queen, had neither husband nor children. Monarchs with families inescapably found themselves spending far more on their courts—though compared to expenditure on war the costs of even the most opulent and luxurious royal court were relatively insignificant. And James as a Scottish king who had become king of England felt that he needed to distribute patronage more widely in order to win and hold political support.

From what did the crown draw its revenues? First, the crown was the greatest landowner in the country. Its estates were mostly let out and the crown's tenants paid rents and other miscellaneous dues. Tudor governments do not seem regularly to have made overall assessments of these revenues: what survives are accounts from individual manors (we should say estates), together with a range of related documentation that is not straightforward to interpret. But the best estimates are that the crown's tenants paid some £40,000 in 1509, £78,000 in 1559 and £100,000 in 1603. These revenues reflected the weather and economic and agrarian trends over which the crown, like other landlords, had little control, the efficiency or otherwise of its estate management, which was in the hands of an army of minor local officials, and the extent to which crown lands were used for reasons of patronage, to purchase or to reward political loyalty.

There was one dramatic change in the Tudor period. The dissolution of the monasteries between 1536 and 1540 added lands worth some £135,000 a year to the crown estates. But much was quickly alienated, initially given out to satisfy a backlog of claims from those longest in crown service, then in the 1540s sold at market prices to finance the wars against France and the Scots, and finally distributed rather cheaply to win political support during the minority of Edward VI. As a result, by the mid-1550s most of the ex-monastic lands had been sold or given away. The dissolution of the monasteries had far less effect on crown finances in the long run than one might have expected. Obviously if the monastic land had been retained by the crown, it would also have retained additional annual revenues for the long term and that might have made a crucial difference to political developments in the seventeenth century. What would Charles I have done if he had not been short of money in 1640?

Since the second half of the sixteenth century was an age of modest inflation, the increase in yields from crown lands was more apparent than real. The sums received at the end of Elizabeth's reign would need to be adjusted to take account of inflation;

and that would eliminate much, if not all, of that increase. Moreover, even in nominal terms, the yields from crown lands seem to have been declining. Lands were sometimes used, especially in periods of political instability (such as the minority of Edward VI), to reward councillors and courtiers, in the form of grants of long leases of lands below market-rents. The immediate cost of any individual grant was small, but cumulatively and over time many such grants did affect the crown's overall landed income. Under Elizabeth, the crown's vast estates were, it seems, largely left alone. The crown seems to have done little by way of investment on its estates for agrarian improvement: this was an age of significant innovation (new fodder crops, techniques such as floating of water meadows) but the crown estates do not seem to have been much involved.

The problem, as we have already noted, is that landholdings had to be actively managed. Lands needed to be surveyed regularly. It is necessary to bargain with tenants over terms. Many of the crown's tenants held land according to 'custom' (in other words, they paid fixed rents that, according to custom, could not be increased). There were all sorts of technical mechanisms that could be used to overcome this. When a tenant died, his heir would be asked to make a one-off payment, an 'entry fine', and so make up for a rent that could not be increased. But this required local knowledge and vigilant management. The crown relied on an army of local officials—bailiffs and stewards—who might overlook a transfer of a lease in favour of a relative or neighbour. The failure to increase rents in line with inflation was something that got worse and worse. An intriguing measure of the problem is the ratio between the cost of buying land and the rents it yielded. In the 1540s the normal ratio was 20:1: that is, a buyer paid twenty times the yield from rent. That is very like a modern home. Multiply the annual rent by twenty and you get something like the price of the house. But, by the later sixteenth century, the price: rent ratio on crown lands had gone from 20:1 to 60:1. In other words, those who were eager to buy land reckoned that the rents on crown lands were ludicrously low and that with skilful management they could be increased considerably: even paying sixty times the current annual rent seemed a good investment. But that just shows by how much rent on crown lands had failed to rise in line with inflation. Why had this happened? Partly because inflation was a relatively new phenomenon; partly because the underlying rate of inflation was not so high, maybe 2 per cent a year; the compounding effect of gradual but persistent inflation would be felt over time, not at once. Moreover, the crown was immensely richer than anyone else, and a gradual decline in its income from lands in real terms (i.e. allowing for inflation) still left it with a very considerable income. And even inasmuch as the crown grasped that there was a problem, it was tempting to put off trying to deal with it, since raising rents would raise all sorts of political difficulties. Whatever the reasons, the consequences were plain: by the end of the sixteenth century, the English crown was like an elderly widow subsisting in an age of inflation on a fixed income. And what the crown increasingly did was to sell its lands—on a quite considerable scale in the 1590s. That met the financial demands on the crown in those years: but meant that in future yields from crown lands would be diminished.

Another important and constant source of crown revenue was the customs dues paid when goods were imported or exported. These produced some £40,000 a year in the later years of Henry VII's reign, a little less on average under Henry VIII, though with some very marked fluctuations from year to year, much less in the mid-sixteenth century, but substantially more—around £90,000 a year—after important and surprisingly uncontroversial changes in the book of rates in the last years of Mary's reign. A comparison of the customs accounts with private records of Bristol merchants suggests that the merchants declared most of their trades (including iron, wine, soap, oil, lead and cloth) but not a large part of their exports of grain and leather: in other words, smuggling (or tax avoidance) was a carefully organised, widespread and highly profitable business.[2] One wonders how effectively the crown tapped into mercantile wealth. Against that, when in the early seventeenth century James I's minister Robert Cecil, earl of Salisbury, attempted to revise the book of rates, left unrevised in Elizabeth's reign, that provoked a storm of protest and protracted legal actions against what were seen as 'impositions'. In the very long run, much greater taxation on buying and selling, at home as well as on imports and exports, would raise huge additional sums of money. In the eighteenth century, following some experimentation during the Interregnum, the excise tax (very roughly equivalent to modern value added tax) dramatically increased the crown's income.[3] Should the English monarchy have followed the example of the French monarchs and introduced a *gabelle*, a tax on salt? Nothing like that was attempted in the Tudor period.

A third source of revenue was what some historians have called 'fiscal feudalism'. When the crown's leading landed subjects—or 'tenants-in-chief'—died leaving heirs who had not reached the age of majority, their lands were temporarily held by the crown or sold by the crown to someone who would hold them temporarily in wardship until the heir was of age. The temporary holder of these lands was entitled to all the revenues. The crown's revenues from such wardships fluctuated but averaged some £10,000 p.a. in Elizabethan England.

Such revenues from lands, from customs, from wardships—described at the time as the 'ordinary' revenues of the crown—were substantial but they were not sufficient to meet all the costs incurred by governments, above all the costs of war and defence, so monarchs from time to time turned to their subjects for assistance, asking them to pay taxation.

It was generally held that kings should themselves meet the costs of government from what were seen as 'their own', as, in a sense, their private resources: the crown lands, customs revenues and feudal dues. But since the thirteenth century, as we have seen, it had also been accepted by the political nation that, in necessity in an emergency, monarchs could ask their subjects for assistance and that their subjects were obliged to give freely to assist their rulers in their necessity. Refusal and opposition were morally indefensible. But what the king's subjects could do was to plead poverty, to say they would dearly wish to assist the king but their powers to do so were more limited than the king realised: in effect to bargain over the timing and the rates at which taxes were levied. Moreover, since the late thirteenth century it had been held that consent to taxation had to come from parliaments and in particular from the House of Commons. In 1496 Henry VII had asked a great council—a meeting of noblemen and bishops—for taxation. It agreed, but, as we have seen, said it did not have sufficient authority for the levying of the tax proposed: accordingly, a Parliament was summoned, and it confirmed the grant.

It was of course thinkable for the monarch, pleading necessity and emergency, to seek forced loans and other grants without parliamentary approval, and sometimes these did succeed, as spectacularly in 1522–3, but the failure of the Amicable Grant in 1525 showed the limits to such an approach. In 1522 commissioners were sent out to make fresh valuations of men's wealth and income. This was a massive inquiry known as the General Proscription. Men were asked to swear an oath that the valuations they gave were true. And these valuations were then used as the basis of a great loan. The king's subjects were instructed to lend 10 per cent of their valuation (higher percentages were demanded from the best off). This produced the quite fantastic sum of £204,000 from the laity in 1522–3. Compared with the yield of fifteenths and tenths (to which we shall return), it was astonishing. Indeed it was perhaps the greatest yield that any government had obtained from a single demand since the danegeld of the tenth and eleventh centuries.

According to the justification offered by the government, these loans were to be repaid from future taxes granted by Parliament. But their size made that unrealistic, and the Parliament of 1529 retrospectively cancelled the crown's obligation to repay them. But by then it had become obvious that just making financial demands was not a viable way of proceeding. In 1525 Henry and Wolsey attempted to raise what they called an 'Amicable Grant', a gift by the king's subjects of up to one-sixth (16 per cent) of their wealth and income, based on the valuations of 1522. Commissioners were appointed, two for each county, usually the leading nobleman or a bishop, and everyone was asked to agree to make a specified payment. In East Anglia Thomas Howard, duke of Norfolk, worked hard to persuade the gentry to agree to pay. But the demand met with so many refusals elsewhere, so many complaints of poverty, and even a short-lived insurrection in south Suffolk/Essex centred on Lavenham, that Henry and Wolsey abandoned the demand without receiving a single penny. The problem was surely in part that this was an unconventional demand. But it failed also because the king had taken the bucket to the well too often. Something of a law of diminishing returns operated in the sphere of revenue raising. Monarchs could ask for and receive high sums, as Henry had done from the great loan of 1522–3. But they could not go on doing so indefinitely. In 1523, Parliament was asked to grant another huge sum, as we have seen; the subsidy granted then yielded £72,000 in 1524 and £64,000 in 1525. The Amicable Grant was one demand too many. The sums demanded stretched merchants' cash flow and disrupted local economies. Suffolk clothiers claimed that if they paid up they would have to lay off textile workers. Not for two decades was anything comparable attempted, and the means used in 1545, a 'benevolence'—richer subjects were invited to contribute a sum of their own choosing—was much more successful, because, unlike the Amicable Grant, it concerned only the better-off, and the effective rate in the £ was much lower, but, as a consequence, it yielded far less than the loans of 1522–3. All the same, it provoked an isolated case of resistance. Alderman Reed of London 'upon a disobedient stomach' refused to pay. He was promptly drafted into the army marching to Scotland 'whereby he might somewhat be instructed of the difference between sitting quietly in his house, and the travail and danger which others daily do sustain'. Placed in the front rack, he was captured and had to pay a ransom. Did the willingness of others to pay reflect fear that if they refused it would cost them dear? But was Henry VIII taking a political risk in raising money in this way?[4]

Under Elizabeth there were few immediate difficulties over securing grants of taxation. There were, as we have seen, just two occasions on which there were difficulties, over the succession in 1566 and over monopolies in 1601. Overwhelmingly, Elizabeth's government successfully obtained taxation from parliaments. In the emergency following the Armada of 1588, the Council called for a forced loan. The deputy lieutenants of Northamptonshire appealed and secured a reduction from £3,500 to £3,000.[5]

Once taxation was granted by Parliament, it was paid without much fuss. An exception to that generalisation was the rebellion of the Cornish in 1497. What provoked them was that they were being asked to pay taxation to support war on the northern borders with Scotland. That infringed an informal division of fiscal labour, whereby the north of England defended the borders and the south and the Midlands paid for war against the French. A similar sense that the taxation demanded was misdirected may account for the remarkable, but as far as we know unique, resistance to the taxation of the 1510s in the Craven district of the West Riding of Yorkshire: Did the men of Craven feel that they had done their bit by serving on the Scottish borders? Such protests are intriguing, but they were most unusual. Taxes, by and large, once granted, were duly paid: people recognised that the crown was morally entitled to ask for and to receive support. It is worth emphasising that the taxes granted were indeed collected and paid, itself a significant administrative achievement, not to be overlooked.[6]

Some historians, notably Sir Geoffrey Elton, drawing on the researches of his pupil Roger Schofield, have argued that there was a fundamentally new departure in 1534 when Thomas Cromwell, Henry VIII's leading minister, introduced a new principle, that taxation was being raised to meet the running costs of government in peacetime and that that marked the emergence of the state.[7] That claim has provoked a long-running historical debate, beginning with Gerald Harriss's challenge.[8] My judgement is that taxation was still being requested by the crown essentially to meet the costs of war and defence, including retrospective grants of taxation to pay for expenditure already incurred. For example, the preamble to the Subsidy Act of 1534 justified taxation on grounds of the great sums of money the king had spent in his last wars against Scotland, on fortifications at Calais, the wars in Ireland, the strengthening of the Scottish borders, the new haven at Dover.[9] Richard Hoyle has pointed out that taxation was not being used to finance the royal household or the central administration or royal extravagance. In years of war far more was spent by monarchs on war and defence than was ever raised by parliamentary taxation.[10] Taxation was never sufficient to pay for war. That was a European-wide phenomenon as the reign of Louis XIV illustrates: taxation served as a foundation for heavy borrowing.[11] The wars between 1511 and 1514 cost £892,000, much more than was raised by taxation: between 1512 and 1517 c. £300,000 was raised in taxes. Between 1542 and 1547 some £2.1 million was spent on war but lay taxation in those years produced only £530,849. Even in years of relative peace—1559-85—parliamentary lay taxation and government military expenditure were much the same: £1.1 million for the former and £1 million for the latter between 1559 and 1585. So when governments justified their demands for taxation by citing the needs of war, including defence, they were telling the truth; they were not using war as a pretext for raising taxes which they spent on something else, they really were spending the proceeds of taxation on war and defence.

The oldest tax paid by the laity was the fifteenth and tenth. Once it had meant those fractions of wealth and income, but in 1334 it had been fixed as a set sum of money paid by each locality, levied by collectors appointed by the Commons in Parliament who apportioned the quota within their own area, most likely by set sums on property. We know very little about how this was done in detail. But it worked. Every time the Commons granted a fifteenth and tenth, the crown could be sure that it would raise around £29,000. The drawbacks with the fifteenth and tenth were that £29,000 was not a great deal of money measured against the costs of war and that neither between different regions of the country nor between individuals in each locality was the tax related to actual wealth and income. Indeed it may have fallen disproportionately on the poor.

So governments had been experimenting in the fifteenth century with ways of increasing the amount paid in taxes by their subjects while levying taxes more fairly according to their subjects' wealth and income. Under Henry VIII and Wolsey there was a significant development. The wealth and income of individuals were assessed, and then they paid, as individuals, taxes—or subsidies as they were known—calculated as so much in the £. In 1513 such a tax, including a payment of 4*d* by everyone, and a sliding scale for the richer, produced £32,500. In 1514 a tax of 6*d* in the £ (2.5 per cent) produced £49,000; in 1515 two such taxes each produced £40,000. Those were higher sums than the £29,000 produced by each of the fifteenths and tenths that were levied in 1512, 1513, 1514 and 1517. Wolsey took the subsidy further in the early 1520s. In 1523, Parliament granted a subsidy of 2*s* in the £ (10 per cent) for those with goods and lands worth over £20, half that rate for those worth between £2 and £20 and a flat charge of 4*d* each year for those worth £2 in goods or £1 in wages, to be levied in two instalments, one in 1524, one in 1525. This tax produced £72,061 in 1524, £65,000 in 1525. These were remarkable sums compared with the standard £29,000 from a fifteenth and tenth. Earlier attempts to raise taxation based on direct assessment of individuals' wealth had been unsuccessful: here Henry VIII and Wolsey made it work. And the clergy were also taxed more heavily in the early 1520s, contributing £24,000 p.a. from 1524.

But Henry VIII and Wolsey pushed their luck too hard in these years. The lessons of the early 1520s point both ways. The crown did raise unprecedented sums of money. The loans of 1522-3 were astonishing and the subsidies granted by Parliament in 1523 much greater than the fifteenth and tenth. And these demands were based on valuations of their wealth and income that men and women made on oath. All that showed a strong, resourceful and creative government. But the limits were quickly reached. When Henry and Wolsey tried once more to raise unprecedented sums, they failed. The Amicable Grant of 1525 was quickly met by refusals. Does the failure of the Amicable Grant show that Tudor government was essentially weak, that it could not raise enough money to sustain war against the French? Or was it more that the war against France which it was being demanded to support was an optional war, not a matter of survival? Henry VIII could choose, as he was to later in 1525, to make peace with France rather than to continue the aggressive pursuit of his dynastic claim to the kingdom. Was that policy of peace caused by his inability to raise more money from his subjects? Was that a measure of his relative weakness? Or could he have successfully pressed on with the Amicable Grant, crushing resistance and raising the money? Was it more that he was reluctant to run the political risks of continuing when there was so much reluctance to pay and that it simply was not worth the political risks of renewed taxation?

For a decade and a half Henry remained at peace with France. Then the revived conflict of 1540s was broader and more costly, but here the windfall gains of the dissolution of the monasteries made fiscal reform unnecessary: the sums the nobility and gentry paid for monastic lands served to finance the wars. Of course that could not be repeated on such a scale. But it was open to an English government to make peace, as Northumberland did in 1550: once again these were not wars of national survival. Neither the military campaigns of 1557-8 nor the various ventures in the early part of Elizabeth's reign lasted long enough to force fundamental questions of financing on to governments. Elizabeth had managed to accumulate a surplus amounting to £300,000 by 1585. She achieved that by avoiding protracted wars, by raising parliamentary taxation towards the costs of such military and naval ventures as had been pursued, and by economy in the running of her household (plenty of dresses but no new palaces). Then came the war years from the Armada of 1588. Large sums were again raised in taxation: £76,000 between 1589 and 1593, £94,000 between 1594 and 1598 and £146,624 between 1598 and 1603. When national emergency demanded greatly increased expenditure, heavy taxation was required—and was secured by the crown. Such taxation was not welcome, but it was borne without either popular revolt or significant parliamentary protest. In 1601 there was much criticism voiced over monopolies, but Elizabeth's conciliatory response was sufficient to secure the grant of large sums of taxation.

So was there nonetheless a fundamental problem? Although the sums granted in the last years of Elizabeth's reign were large, they were, if adjusted to take account of inflation, lower than the sums granted in the 1540s. Moreover the yields of each individual subsidy fell. Each time a subsidy was granted the total receipts were lower. Under-assessment of wealth and income was scandalously common. From 1563, assessments were no longer made on oath. Commissioners accepted low valuations. The central government made little attempt to monitor and to raise yields. Instead, the government compensated by asking for two, or three, or four, or six, subsidies at once. From the government's point of view, what mattered above all was to raise funds to pay for national defence against the Spanish, and this they managed to do in years of economic hardship without provoking rebellion. That was more important to them than whether the fiscal system was in itself fair and efficient. And since large sums were indeed raised, that no doubt explains why the government accepted the situation and why there was no attempt at reform in the 1590s. Some historians would say that this gives too rosy a picture of English public finance in the 1590s, and that the evasions and failures to reform would cause serious problems later. Are such modern historians right to conclude that 'the key failure of the later sixteenth-century monarchy was its inability to tackle the problem of under-assessment of the rich'?[12] One might well argue that they were not, and that a government fighting a war might reasonably have different priorities. If its needs could just about be secured by the existing system, however much it was ramshackle or unfair or by modern historians' standards in need of reform, then it should not be surprising that no radical reforms were undertaken.

But let us look at this a little longer and in broader terms. Did Tudor governments raise enough money from their subjects? Did they raise it fairly and efficiently? Some historians would argue that the Tudors failed adequately to tap the wealth of the country and so had to make do with inadequate resources which increasingly deterred them from intervening in continental conflicts. Many historians would claim that the fiscal system of the Tudors became less and less effective and that the Tudors did not dare remedy matters for fear of upsetting the political consensus on which their authority rested. They relied on expedients that by their very nature could only be temporary. In the early 1520s Henry VIII and Wolsey raised large sums as loans that were never repaid: their efforts to continue raising money on demand, in the Amicable Grant in 1525, provoked such dissatisfaction and resistance that the crown gave up. In the 1540s Henry was able to sell vast amounts of ex-monastic land. He also embarked in 1542 on a policy of debasement of the silver coinage (by as much as 5/6 by 1551), which produced large immediate profits—between 1544 and 1551 £1.27 million—followed by monetary disorder, vigorous efforts to restore the coinage in the early years of Elizabeth's reign and, ironically, the steady inflation of the later century that so gnawed away at the crown's income from its landed estates.[13] In the 1590s Elizabeth's government again sold crown lands on a large scale and had recourse to the sale of monopolies. That in years of war, Tudor governments spent far more than their normal incomes, far more than what taxation parliaments granted, and had to borrow, or sell lands, or debase the coinage, or rely on devices such as monopolies, does offer some support to those who think the Tudor financial system somewhat precarious.

But perhaps that is somewhat unfair. The natural resources of France and Spain were much greater than those of the English monarchy. Eighteenth-century British governments were able to raise vastly greater sums than their Tudor predecessors, but the comparison misleads. The Tudors did not try at all hard or for long to raise very large sums of money in taxation. They did not need to. They were not faced by such protracted and urgent demands that would compel them to reform. When, by contrast, William III and then Anne were locked in conflict with Louis XIV's France with little respite for over two decades from 1689, the imperative of securing greater revenues stimulated fiscal innovation. Nothing so pressing occurred in the Tudor century. The wars of the early 1510s, early 1520s and 1540s were in a sense wars of choice. The first two were conducted on a fairly limited scale. The wars of the late 1580s and 1590s were more wars of national survival, but while there were fearful moments, there was never a single disaster that might have prompted a revolutionary change. Ireland apart, English monarchs did not need to fight wars of national unification. The expedients that the Tudors relied upon proved just about sufficient, and the difficulties and political costs of doing more deterred governments from pursuing reform. They recognised that there was a limit to the willingness of their subjects to pay taxes and that fiscal untidiness and expediency was the price to be paid for political community.

Maybe they were right! It is revealing to consider the introduction of ship money on the ports, intended to raise money to pay for ships to protect trade. In Suffolk in the 1590s it was Ipswich that bore the brunt, but the deputy lieutenants were ordered to levy a rate on the county to reduce the burdens imposed on the town. Sir Robert Jermyn and Sir Nicholas Bacon, in the west of the county, objected: 'they would not be overreached with a crooked measure.' They informed the high constables that they had at first argued against the demand before ultimately agreeing. But far from ordering the high constables to secure the money, they urged them 'to use your best endeavour to persuade' the better-off to contribute. The Council was angry that that would more encourage the people 'to discontentment than to concur in her Majesty's service'. The deputy lieutenants were summoned to attend the Council but, in the event, while they were admonished, they secured a reduction in the county levy from £740 to £500.[14] There was more argument in 1599. In effect some sort of bargaining was taking place. But the crown could not easily dismiss local commissioners. And all this may well have weighed heavily on the queen and her councillors and encouraged them to muddle through rather than embark on fundamental reforms that would have been sure to provoke many in the counties. Some £260,000 a year was spent on war between 1590 and 1603; in the 1690s it would be £4.9 million annually, in Queen Anne's reign it was £7 million a year. Such increases would have been politically impossible in Elizabeth's reign.

5

Military organisation

The strength of any government depends ultimately on its ability to levy and to deploy armed force. This was no less true of Tudor England. In the final resort, when facing an invasion or a rebellion, the power of a Tudor monarch depended on how many men could be raised. When did Tudor monarchs require armies? Henry VII did in 1485, 1486 and 1487 in order first to win and then to secure his throne; in 1492 against France; in 1497 against rebellion. Henry VIII did against France in 1512 and 1513 (30,000 men), against Scotland in 1513 (26,000 men: against France and Scotland in 1522 and 1523);[1] against Scotland in 1532; against the Pilgrims of Grace in 1536–7; against France and Scotland from 1542 to 1550 (32,000 men in France, 15,000 men in Scotland in 1544). In Edward VI's reign, Protector Somerset drove forward the wars, especially that against Scotland, in 1547 (21,500 men) and 1548 (15,000 men). Mary fought against France and Scotland in 1557 (7,000 men in France) and in 1558.[2] Elizabeth intervened in Scotland in 1560 (7,000 men); in France in 1562 (6,000 men); in the Netherlands especially from 1585; prepared to resist Philip II of Spain from 1588; and sent armies to prevent Ireland from becoming a bridgehead for invasion in the 1590s.

The Tudors had no standing army, that is to say soldiers who had undergone intensive training and served full-time. At no point was the formation of one seriously considered, though a proposal from the mid-1530s survives. Briefly under John Dudley, duke of Northumberland, companies of men-at-arms—heavy cavalry men—a thousand strong, were set up in 1550, no doubt in response to the serious rebellions of 1549, but they proved far too expensive to maintain and were disbanded in 1552. Yet the lack of any lasting standing army, whether of infantry or of horsemen, was not necessarily a reflection of weakness; it was sensible allocation of resources, as we shall see. No European state had sufficient resources to train and maintain huge numbers of soldiers.

Monarchs had bodyguards to protect them at court: the Yeoman Archers of Henry VII's reign; the King's Spears of the 1510s but disbanded in 1515; the Gentlemen Pensioners, established as a force fifty strong in 1539. They were surely not 'a minor version of the military establishments developing at continental courts';[3] they were quite simply bodyguards. Monarchs maintained a few permanent garrisons of soldiers: notably in Calais, the last surviving English possession on the French mainland, where there were some 551 men in 1502,[4] on the northern borders (especially Berwick and Carlisle, where there were around 100 men). There were endemic quarrels between garrison soldiers and townsmen. In Ireland there were small armies of between 200 and 700 men in 1534, 1,000 or somewhat more thereafter.[5] What the Tudors did not have is anything like modern special forces, small but well-trained hit-squads capable of effective action behind enemy lines, for example seizing castles, destroying bridges or reporting on enemy activity.[6]

From time to time, as we have already noted, monarchs and rulers hired foreign mercenary troops: for the 1512 campaign in Guyenne; some 5,000 men in 1513; 6,000 men for the 1544 campaign in France; Spanish troops under Peter de Gamboa; for the 1545 campaign against the Scots and, increasingly, intermittently in the reign of Edward VI, when Italians and Germans were used to put down the Western Rebellion and Ket's rebellion in 1549. But the money for mercenaries ran out by 1552.

Thus when they needed soldiers, the Tudor monarchs were largely dependent on their own subjects rallying to their service. There were two ways in which armed force was raised.[7] The first was that individual noblemen and greater gentlemen, and also bishops and mayors of towns, would be sent a letter under the king's privy seal or privy signet authorising them to raise a specified number of soldiers from the ranks of their tenants, servants and friends, selecting officers for every 100 men and requiring that they came with defensive armour, handweapons and horse. A memorandum of 1522 laid down that the king's letters were to be sent to noblemen and gentlemen of England, to put themselves and their servants in readiness, and send in the details of the numbers they could make. Serving Henry VII against the Cornish rebels at Blackheath in 1497 were several lords and gentlemen who had come to the king's aid with 'as many men of war as they could put in a readiness'. In 1492 it was by such methods that Henry raised 12,000 men. The great bulk of the army of 30,000 which Henry VIII took over to France in 1513 was raised under contract by individual noblemen and gentlemen. Henry Percy (d. 1537), fifth earl of Northumberland, brought 100 demi-lances, 300 archers and 100 billmen, all wearing black and red hats in the Percy livery, white Percy crescents on their coats of green and white Tudor cloth, and a red raised cross of St George.[8] The same methods predominated in the 1540s. In 1544, 48,000 men including 4,000 horse and 35,000 foot were raised in England. Noblemen and gentry raised forces to serve in the Netherlands from 1570, especially in 1585 when the earl of Leicester wrote 200 letters to his servants and friends asking them to be ready to serve in the Low Countries. And in the emergencies of 1569, 1588 and 1599, individual noblemen were called upon to provide soldiers.[9]

Within this method, noblemen were in effect contractors, raising men whose wages and travelling expenses were met by the crown, according to terms specified in contracts, that is to say formal and written agreements, or 'indentures' in contemporary language. And noblemen led the armies that were raised in person. It does seem to have worked in the sense that the numbers required were indeed mobilised without any great fuss or protest. Service in war was seen as a fundamental duty of noblemen. Noblemen turned to those who held offices on their estates or in their households to serve as captains. Tenants provided a good deal of the soldiers raised in this way. 'Friends' and neighbours were also numerous. On the whole, tenants were willing to serve. It is worth emphasising that the soldiers raised in this way were not permanent bands: their leaders were substantial men with peacetime duties in a noble household or on noble estates; the soldiers were labourers or artisans. They were brought together because of the needs of war. Towns were also asked to supply men in similar ways: for example Canterbury supplied 183 men in 1557–8; York supplied 250 men in 1548–9, more typically 60–100, out of a population of 6,000; Exeter 30 in 1514 and Norwich 40 in 1542.[10] But 'the numbers of soldiers provided by towns to royal armies in this period remained small in comparison with those raised by rural landlords'.[11]

There was a second way in which armed forces could be raised. Groups of commissioners appointed by the crown on the authority of the king's great seal or of commissions of array would levy the numbers of soldiers required from among the ablest men in the shire. That procedure rested on the Statute of Winchester of 1285, which laid down that all able-bodied men aged between sixteen and sixty were to be prepared to serve in war if necessary, not least by keeping arms and armour appropriate to their rank in readiness, and by being ready to assemble when commissions of array were issued. 'So it is the bounden duty of all subjects, of what degree so ever they be, to serve their country in such sort as their prince and head shall appoint them', wrote the scholar Richard Morrison (best known as Henry VIII's leading publicist).[12] Such methods were used briefly in 1511 when the Statute was reissued, rather more in the mid-1540s, and significantly more under Mary in 1557–8, when an act laid down a scale of weapons, horses and armour required from individuals according to their wealth. How could monarchs be sure that these county militias were fit for purpose? Annual or twice-yearly 'marching watches', with armed parades, were quite common.[13] From time to time, especially in moments of feared invasion such as 1539, general musters were held across the country: inhabitants of towns and villages had to assemble and show that they had the weaponry appropriate to their social rank ready for use. In London 20,000 men were reported to have gathered. Certificates were compiled, listing places and the numbers of men. These were drawn upon in 1542 and 1543, even though the armies were raised by individual noblemen and gentlemen: the government now had a better idea of how many men to expect. In 1544 militiamen were raised and sent to France. By the late 1550s this 'national' system predominated. In 1558 levies of militias were to include the tenants of lords and gentlemen (Thomas, fourth duke of Norfolk, appealed for an exemption for his tenants in Surrey).

Why the shift? Steven Gunn points to the changes in landholdings arising from the dissolution of the monasteries, to an apparent decline in tenants' willingness to serve lords, possibly because landlords were raising rents, though it is not clear that this was a Tudor novelty,[14] to the emergence of 'a new breed of assertive large-scale farmers' ready to refuse to serve in war and prepared to go to law or to defend themselves against law suits brought by their lord'.[15] That last observation seems rather speculative. More persuasive is Gunn's point that the sheer demands of constant warfare on two or three fronts in 1540s drove the Tudors to use supplementary methods.[16]

This county militia system developed appreciably under Elizabeth, partly as commissioners were instructed to include the tenants of lords and gentlemen within the county militias, partly in response to the threats from rebellion within and from Spain. Shire levies were used against the rebels in 1569. This was quite an expensive system. Local rates (taxes) were imposed to finance musters and training. Typically one day was allowed for the muster, one day before and after was allowed for travel. Travelling expenses were reimbursed. These arrangements were not set out fully in statute, giving rise to disputes in times of difficulty such as the 1590s. It was difficult to manage so decentralised a system. There were many local variations. Elizabeth's ministers and military commanders sought the best troops and equipment available, while county officials who had obligations to local communities preferred to minimise costs and disruption.[17] Whether the county militias would have proved effective in the event of invasion was of course never tested. But a good deal of government energy was expended on monitoring these county-trained bands. It is worth noting that this method was largely about raising infantry: cavalry were more readily raised by noblemen and gentlemen from their tenants.

Historians have tended to see the second of these methods, the county militia, as preferable and as more 'modern', since it was based on the king's subjects' national obligation to serve, rather than on private contracts between kings and leading noblemen, a system which Steven Gunn has seen as 'in terminal decline' by the end of the fifteenth century. Yet that seems a mistaken judgement, since militia-based armies might be poorly trained, ill-equipped, uncertainly led, whereas noble-raised contingents might be more effective (a nobleman's honour was at stake). When monarchs needed armed forces in an emergency to resist rebellions, they relied heavily on men raised according to the traditional method of contracts with individual noblemen and greater gentry.

But in practice the difference between the two methods was obscured, since the commissioners who raised the militia forces (especially after the practice of appointing lords lieutenant was developed in the second part of Edward VI's reign) tended to be the same noblemen who otherwise raised troops under a different authority. It is not always easy to see the distinction between, on the one hand, the mobilisation of a citizen militia and, on the other, the recruitment on behalf of noblemen of anyone available. In the mid-1540s indeed both methods could be used at the same time. The third duke of Norfolk raised men from Norfolk by calling on gentlemen who served in his household or as officers on his estates, but he was also issued a commission by the king allowing him to raise men from the whole county of Norfolk and the city of Norwich.[18] In 1558–9 the fourth duke of Norfolk raised men from Norfolk and Suffolk as lords lieutenant but his steward at his principal residence at Kenninghall oversaw the musters.[19] Most counties were dominated by one or two noblemen—or, though rarely, by a group of upper gentry, who took charge. Gunn claims that now 'it was no longer the personal authority of a nobleman which was paramount in raising men and commanding armies but the office he held from the queen',[20] and sees a shift 'from the intimacy of the retinue to the formality of the commission'.[21] I am not so sure the difference was as clear as that. Noblemen—both before and after the introduction of the lord lieutenancy—were responsible for military oversight: to supervise the militia forces, to make sure they were trained, to choose men for active service, to raise contributions locally for arms and armour. A note in one of Thomas Cromwell's remembrances may anticipate the lord lieutenancy: 'to appoint in every shire a person whom the king can best trust, to whom as much of the shire as the king shall appoint, may resort.' Deputy lords lieutenant were also appointed, as many, in late Elizabethan England, as six in a county. From mid-century the system was formalised, but it is important to note that what happened was not a transformation but a formalisation. It recognised the existing influence of noblemen. And noblemen continued to exercise military authority beyond their landed patrimonies: not least in towns and cities.

Under Elizabeth, lords lieutenant were appointed in dangerous years and then pretty much continuously from 1585. Paradoxically, the institutionalisation of responsibilities in the office of lords lieutenant may have increased the military role of noblemen: musters and preparations were a more permanent and regular engagement than raising their servants, tenants and friends when the monarch was at war. Moreover in one sense the soldiers raised by individual magnates under the so-called quasi-feudal system were 'national' forces since, like those raised as a militia, they were paid daily wages by the crown. And it was often the crown that made good any deficiencies in the weaponry that these men brought with them: the crown supplied handguns and pikes. Heavy artillery was always a matter for the government, not least because it required complex and expensive transport.

Raising musters was not something done automatically and precisely. Fearing invasion in 1587, the Council ordered men to muster and then to come together as an army attending the queen. In Northamptonshire there were protests against the quota, 1,200 men, and the deputy lieutenants succeeded in reducing the number to 600 foot and 100 horse.

And the belief that a militia-based system was better for the crown and the state rests on the assumption lurking beneath many accounts that noble-raised armies were somehow dangerous, because they might be used against the crown. That in turn rests on a view of the relationship between crown and nobility as one of conflict, an interpretation already questioned. War should be seen rather as an experience that could bind kings and nobility together, not least when things went well and ransoms and booty added to the winning of glory on the battlefield. And arguably standing armies (unless well managed) could themselves turn into a source of serious disorder.

But there was a potential, if small, risk for monarchs in a system in which their greater subjects could in effect raise private armies and use them for private purposes, for example pursuing local vendettas or, potentially much more dangerously (if rarely), when plotting to overthrow the monarch. What monarchs sought to do to meet that potential threat was to control the mechanisms by which noblemen and gentry provided men. In order to 'make men' in time of war, noblemen and greater gentlemen recruited men they swore to serve them. Noblemen were seemingly prohibited by acts of parliament in 1468, 1495, 1497 and 1504 from such retaining, that is to say maintaining by explicit contracts large numbers of men to fight for them. The act of 1504 introduced a system of licensing (though the act itself lapsed on Henry VII's death in 1509). In practice, noblemen and leading gentry were allowed to retain large numbers of household servants and those engaged in their 'lawful service', but not large numbers of gentlemen. When a nobleman too publicly drew attention to his large retinue, then he was disciplined—as was the case with George, Lord Bergavenny, in 1507. Bergavenny was fined £100,000 reduced to £50,000 (was it ever paid?) for retaining 25 gentlemen, 4 clerks and 440 yeomen in 1507; but in 1513 he led a retinue of 521 men to war. For illegal retaining the fifth earl of Northumberland was imprisoned in the Fleet for ten days in 1516. From the mid-century, licences to retain are recorded among the central government's records. What monarchs sought was a measure of control. They depended on the nobility and greater gentry for their armed forces and consequently they did not attempt to replace the system. But they did not want noblemen to misuse it.

In practice, noblemen continued to have the ability to raise large numbers of men quickly. For example, in October 1536 on hearing of the rising in Lincolnshire, George Talbot, fourth earl of Shrewsbury, as we have seen, raised 3,654 men on horseback within a week to resist the rebels. That was a great achievement, not least since Shrewsbury's men may well have sympathised with the rebels. In the mid-century, Francis Talbot, fifth earl of Shrewsbury, would come to court with several score men wearing his livery: 120 horsemen and 30 gentlemen in 1554. And as late as the 1590s, Gilbert Talbot, seventh earl of Shrewsbury, was able to raise men to cause local mayhem in a quarrel over river weirs with a substantial neighbouring gentleman, Sir Michael Stanhope. But broadly speaking, as I have argued, noblemen did not abuse their military might in their own interests (they generally did not need to: they were powerful enough not to need to use force) nor did they use their military might against the crown (except for very few exceptions, exceptions that prove the rule). The famous examples of great magnate retinues, those of John of Gaunt and William, Lord Hastings, in earlier periods were very exceptional even then. Only a handful of noblemen were powerful enough to be able to raise really substantial forces of their own. The earls of Shrewsbury could. But John, Lord Hussey, and Thomas, Lord Darcy, both first-generation peers, men from minor gentry backgrounds who had risen in royal service, were nothing like as powerful, and they could raise only much smaller forces. Many of the men whom such lesser peers could raise were not their tenants directly but connected to them because they held offices on crown lands. If you were steward of the royal manor of X or bailiff of the royal manor of Y or constable of the royal castle of Z, then you would in times of military emergency be expected to raise your subordinates and the tenants on the estates, but you would not be doing it in your own right. In 1513 Darcy promised to raise 500 from his own lands, 1,114 from offices in which he was steward on crown lands.

Of course one of the difficulties of this discussion is that (after the first years of Henry VII's reign) the Tudors were generally fortunate in not needing armed forces to resist foreign invasion. Henry VIII was worried enough to fortify the south coast in 1539–40. In 1545 the French threatened the Isle of Wight. Three great armies were prepared, though never fully mobilised. Some 110,000 adult men stood ready to fight out of perhaps 600,000 living in southern England, the south Midlands and Wales. That is a rate of one in six adult males, or one in three able-bodied men: a contrast to the one in twelve raised in 1513.[22] If brief Scottish incursions occurred in 1513, 1522-3, or threatened as in 1557-8, if the Spanish were certainly threatening in 1588 and through the 1590s, nevertheless no full-blooded foreign invasion occurred. And while

Henry VIII was frequently at war with the French (between 1511 and 1513, in 1522–3, from 1542 to the end of the reign), nevertheless such campaigns were at his choosing, following what Steven Gunn has seen as 'the dangerous chivalric models' of Edward III and Henry V, and not imposed upon him.[23]

From time to time Tudor monarchs faced rebellions—in 1497, in 1525, in 1536, in 1549 (most seriously perhaps), in 1554, in 1569—but on each occasion the rebellions, while real military emergencies, were dealt with without *protracted* fighting, a matter of weeks rather than months or years. The one disputed succession of the century, in 1553, did not lead to a civil war. And in rebellions the leading noblemen usually rallied to the crown and offered loyal and effective support. In short, neither in dealing with rebellions nor in meeting external threats did the Tudors urgently *need* to improve their ways of raising armed forces: they were good enough to do the jobs required of them. There was no Tudor Revolution in military matters, but perhaps none was required. Only Cardinal Wolsey in 1522 made a serious effort to transform the system, as we have seen. He launched the 'general proscription', a great survey of the military power of the realm. It was intended among other things to list the names of all able-bodied men of military age, their wealth, the weaponry, their lords. For the first time the English government would know just how many men it could command. But there was a good deal of resistance to the survey, not least since one of its other purposes was financial, and nothing very significant happened in military matters as a result of it (perhaps all the government wanted was more accurate information). Steven Gunn rather belittles it as no more than an attempt to 'refurbish' the system, but nonetheless only slowing its decay.[24] It was undoubtedly a substantial administrative achievement.[25] Maybe more would have come of it had Henry VIII's interests not been diverted by the divorce.

Fears of invasion in 1538–9 stimulated a remarkably comprehensive scheme of coastal defence. Cromwell made a note of 'letters to be written to said and expert men in every shire near the sea to view the coasts and advise about fortification of places where there is danger of invasion'; 'expert persons', it was proposed, were 'to be sent to view the coasts of Norfolk, Suffolk and Essex, and the dangerous places to be fortified; the like for Kent, Hampshire, Dorsetshire and Devonshire'. These instructions were matched by action. Building works took place in the Thames Estuary, Sandown, Deal, Walmer, Sandgate, Camber, Calshot, Dover, Hurst, Portland, St Mawes and Pendennis. Henry VIII went in person to Dover in September 1538 and March 1539. A sketch for East Cowes was described as a 'platte devised by the king'. All that activity testifies to Henry's fears. But before long Charles V, Holy Roman Emperor, and Francis I, king of France, were quarrelling again and no joint Franco-imperial invasion tested Henry's new defences. A few years later the Crown paid £21,000 for the re-fortification of Hull in 1542–3.[26] In the 1550s Berwick, a border town, in English hands since 1483 but previously captured and lost by the Scots numerous times, was re-fortified with bastions, maybe not quite the latest fashion when constructed but nonetheless a vast improvement on earlier defences. There was a measure of technological innovation in fortifications. Straightforward stone walls were increasingly vulnerable to artillery and ordnance. The response was the expensive elaboration, most vividly at

Berwick, of complex defensive systems: massive walls, deep ditches, polygonal plans, bastions. It is plain that Tudor governments were able to take decisions to strengthen defences and to impose them. Such measures were very much determined by specific challenges, rather than reflecting any overall scheme of fundamental reform. But that was understandable. Most inland towns continued to neglect their surviving walls as they were not needed as defence. Nor did noblemen and greater gentry spend much money or effort on building or rebuilding castles. They did not need to: England was not a society continually facing enemy attack. Most new building by noblemen or courtiers in the sixteenth century was of brick and timber-framed manor houses that were not fortified: they would have withstood a riot by tenants but not a full-blown artillery assault. Only the shielings and bastles of the Scottish borders were obviously defensive in purpose, and that reflected the troubled condition of border society, quite unlike anywhere else in the realm.[27]

In many ways so far the discussion has emphasised continuities and adaptations. But scholars studying early modern Europe have much debated whether there was what Michael Roberts called a 'military revolution'. Essentially what that comes down to is the impact on warfare in this period of technological change. Cavalry, it is said, gave way to massed and well-drilled phalanxes of infantry. Swords (and by implication bows and arrows in England) yielded to gunpowder. Did monarchs, in addition to the challenges we have already considered, also face the even greater challenge of dealing with a technological revolution? While what has been claimed about infantry and gunpowder was surely true in the long run, that qualification is crucial. England in the sixteenth century does not fit that model well. Armies were dependent on supply lines for food, drink and clothing. They needed shelter from heat, cold and rain. That was as important as ordnance. Moreover guns were awkward to transport, especially in bad weather. Gunpowder itself was not easy to make, very much dependent on the quality of materials from which it was composed: charcoal (from alder, willow, hazel or beech trees), sulphur (mostly imported from volcanic regions of Italy) and saltpetre (extracted from soil rich in dung and urine as it was a product of bacterial action on decaying organic matter) were scarce and costly. The consequence was that gunpowder was not always as decisive in practice as proponents of a military revolution have claimed. And English monarchs were well aware of the challenges posed by changing military technology and responded quite vigorously. A significant concern was dependence on imports of many of the materials needed for making gunpowder. There were significant improvements in English gunfounding, including the creation of foundries for bronze cannon, especially in the Weald of Kent and Sussex. Worth, Sussex, was the first double furnace used for ordnance production. Efforts were made from the 1560s to the 1640s to find more efficient ways to make saltpetre.

By 1547 there was something like a staff managing the royal ordnance in the Tower of London—by the 1560s amounting to around fifty—which made it a bureaucratic institution, though perhaps it should more accurately be seen as a maintenance department (ordnance needs looking after). Aware that guns were so expensive that only the crown could fund them, monarchs sent potentially vulnerable coastal towns such as Hull and Rye royal guns: the towns in turn were expected to finance the cost of gunpowder. Similar developments took place in the royal armoury. In the 1540s the increasing sophistication of weaponry and the sustained military campaigns of those years led to the centralisation of arms and armour. Noblemen continued to hold stocks, but not in the quantity and at up-to-date technological sophistication needed, though doubtless the absence of war in England itself contributed to that. From the 1570s county armouries funded by the crown were established but a good deal of what needed was purchased abroad. As well as involvement in the materials of war, governments were concerned by the quality of soldiers. In late Elizabethan England experienced soldiers were hired as muster-masters within counties to provide new technical expertise and train selected bands of men. All that raised legal concerns, and it was not clear how far men were obliged to bear firearms rather than bows. There was no fundamental revision of the laws and obligations relating to military service. Once again, that was largely because the later Elizabethan state muddled through. It might seem obvious that men should have swiftly given up bows and arrows and mastered guns instead. But early firearms were costly and by no means reliable: moreover training was needed if groups of men were to use them effectively in battle; consequently governments proceeded more by encouragement than instruction. And if the English seemed to prefer bills to pikes and bows to shot, even in what, in continental terms, was the great age of pike and shot, that was neither unreasonable nor hidebound conservatism, given the wars the English fought. We should not deny the amateurishness and relatively limited absorption of continental practice that characterised Henry VIII's armies. And there is no denying that the Calais garrison was too small—some 879 men in later days—to have provided the larger disciplined infantry formations characteristic of early-sixteenth-century Italian wars. We might nonetheless allow that, especially in the wars of the 1540s, commander and gunners did learn from their experiences and recognisably 'professional' soldiers can then be found. But the general point being made here remains: the wars of the 1510s, 1520s and 1540s, as experienced by the English, did not demand urgent wholesale adoption of continental practice.

Tudor monarchs did respond rather more actively to developments in arrangements for war at sea. Henry VII inherited some six ships. Henry VIII greatly expanded the navy: forty-seven ships were built (£8,000 was spent on *Henry Grace à dieu*) and thirty-five bought or acquired. There was a shift from ships that were essentially vessels that transported soldiers who would fight when back on dry land into ships that were platforms for guns, in effect purpose-built warships capable of fighting at sea. In 1545 Henry could mobilise a fleet of over 90 ships carrying 12,000 men to counter the threat of French invasion in 1545 (including some 53 royal ships). Something like a Navy Board—a bureaucratic institution—was set up in 1545-6 to run this navy. Henry VII had founded a permanent royal dockyard at Portsmouth in 1496, and Henry VIII developed dockyards at Woolwich, Deptford and Erith. But these had more of the character of storehouses than of permanently staffed shipyards. And all this was costly (£20,000 p.a. in 1551-3). Shipbuilding was a complex business, requiring timber (there were concerns over shortages), canvas (for sail and rope), pitch-tar and metals (copper, iron) had to be imported.

Private shipbuilding was carried out on a small scale in almost every east/south coast town; those vessels could be mobilised in war. Rye could provide several ships, mostly to transport troops. Generally towns were not called upon; rather, private shipowners were encouraged to lend their ships. Many noblemen owned ships. Privateering offered the potential of lucrative prizes: it developed in the 1540s and especially in the later years of Elizabeth's reign: there were as many as 236 vessels in the years 1585–91. But there were no regular naval crews. Merchant sailors, who normally sailed trading vessels, joined royal ships in periods of warfare. Commanders were usually noblemen or experienced privateer captains.

A case could be made that here there was a standing navy in the making, that more professional standards were being applied to that navy than to infantrymen, that there was a significant increase in regulation and training. But to deduce from this that Tudor governments had made a strategic choice in favour of naval defence against foreign invasion rather than a standing army with obvious risks to political liberties is too speculative and would work better as a later seventeenth-century response to the perceived tyranny of army rule in the mid-century.

Nor would it convince to speak of a Tudor Revolution in the provision of supplies for armies and navies. Victualling was largely done by private contractors from whom governments purchased supplies (especially for the navy) or whom they encouraged to trade with armies in the field. Warfare in Tudor England occurred too spasmodically for there to be much incentive to develop any regular bureaucratic structures. The royal household together with local worthies did the work. Wolsey was the dominant figure at the centre in 1510s and 1520s, Stephen Gardiner in the 1540s. Purveyors were appointed locally to do the local buying. In theory the crown had the right to purchase food at the price it set, but in fact the crown paid market prices and used its prerogative to prevent profiteering, rather than to seize supplies cheaply. Still, purveyance was unpopular; it disrupted normal patterns of trade, created local scarcities, payments were slow in coming and petty corruption was unavoidable. Victualling was crucial: the navy was almost crippled in 1513 by deficiencies in victualling. On the Scottish borders in 1513, the English army lacked food at the moment when a decisive battle was about to take place. In 1523 supply services could not possibly victual an army of 10,000 throughout winter: the military strategy adopted could not work. The correspondence of military commanders routinely deals with deficiencies of supply, inescapable, but sometimes damagingly serious.

Distinctive difficulties occurred over efforts to secure saltpetre for gunpowder. They generated many local conflicts and raised questions over the balance between the royal prerogative and the common law. Charges of vexation and oppression held against roving saltpetre men became one of the constitutional issues raised in 1641. Late Elizabethan governments regretfully acknowledged the damage that saltpetremen made but presented it as unavoidable, and no great disputes occurred, perhaps because the Spanish threat was seen as so great.[28]

Why Elizabeth faced the Spanish Armadas is plain. Why Henry VIII waged war is more complex, as Gunn has observed. 'Henry VIII grew up knowing that great kings won battles and made conquests'[29] and in particular knew from chronicles the history of Anglo-French warfare. Edward III's victory at Crecy and Henry V's at Agincourt offered, as we have already noted, a dangerous model. Henry VIII would doubtless have been aware of the battles at Towton and Bosworth Field that determined the outcomes of the Wars of the Roses. The European context was important too: Ferdinand of Aragon defeating the Moors, Maximilian defeating Charles the Reckless, duke of Burgundy, in 1477. In the late fifteenth and early sixteenth centuries, kings of France fought continuously in Italy. No wonder that Henry invaded France in 1513. David, the Old Testament monarch on whom Henry VIII would model himself, was a great warrior who had slain his tens of thousands.[30]

And for the social elite, war remained in the Tudor century a source of fame and social advance. From childhood, noblemen and gentlemen expected that they would serve in war. Thomas Howard, third duke of Norfolk, served Henry VIII regularly as a military commander, in war, in the early 1520s and 1540s, against rebellion in 1536. George Talbot, fourth earl of Shrewsbury, served in the invasion of France in 1513, on the Scottish borders in 1523, against rebellion in 1536. His son, Francis Talbot, fifth earl of Shrewsbury, served on the Scottish borders in 1544, 1545, 1548 and 1557. Only one of thirty-four adult and fit noblemen did not serve in the wars of 1513. Service in war remained 'the *raison d'être* of nobility both as a social cadre and as a pillar of the body politic in the monarchical state'.[31] Noble commanders were given royal permission to confer titles of knighthood on successful warriors. Edward Seymour first came to prominence in the invasion of 1523, serving under Charles Brandon, duke of Suffolk, who knighted him during the campaign. In the 1540s, Seymour, now the uncle to the young prince Edward, son of his late sister Jane, was very heavily involved in the wars against France and Scotland. 'Command of men in foreign wars or against rebels was an essential function of the Tudor nobility, whether new or old.' Gunn has claimed that depictions of noblemen in martial dress increased from the mid-sixteenth century.[32]

Of course, it did not always go well. Sometimes kings and their officials were not quick to reimburse noblemen for their costly expenses; and when noblemen gave fees to men whom they expected to serve them in war, unrecovered costs grew rapidly, as the fourth earl of Northumberland found. Very occasionally Tudor noblemen were captured in war: Lord Grey of Wilton, taken by the French in 1558, was ransomed for £6,000, compelling the sale of the family seat at Wilton.[33] Some noblemen and gentlemen were killed: Sir Edward Howard at sea in 1513, Lord Sheffield against Ket's rebels in 1549; disease took off Thomas Lord Poynings in 1545 at Boulogne. The third duke of Norfolk on the Scottish borders in 1523 lamented that 'I shall consume and waste away . . . the little flesh that I had is clean gone; and yet I am not sick, but in manner I eat very little, and these five weeks day, I never slept one whole hour without waking, my mind is so troubled for fear that any thing should frame amiss.'[34] And if the second duke of Norfolk won glory on the battlefield at Flodden in 1513, his grandson Henry Howard earl of Surrey's defeat by the French near Boulogne in January 1546, blamed on his over-confidence, was 'a devastating blow' that wrecked his ambitions.[35] Noble military commanders sometimes quarrelled with each other, especially when campaigns went wrong, but that was the common change of war.

A sense of duty, a sense of honour, a sense of adventure: these explain why monarchs, nobles and gentlemen fought. Looking at Henry VIII's wars, we are sceptical about the ostensible justifications offered at the time. But at that social level there is little sign that monarchs found it hard to lead the political nation into war. How far did monarchs find it difficult to mobilise the commons? As we have seen, large numbers were indeed raised. Why the commons joined remains puzzling. A sense of adventure may be important. So was pay that was by no means ungenerous. Yet those who served were not necessarily the poorest or outsiders. Scrutiny of tax records shows that men from York serving in 1542 were assuredly not wealthy but nor were they 'sweepings of the streets' (of sixty-eight serving for York in 1542 forty were in the 1545 subsidy, and twenty-nine of thirty-nine in 1545 were taxed on £10+). Of course the more affluent might have found substitutes to serve for them, which undermines the analysis. Urban pride was manifested in civic send-offs with beer, ale and civic breakfasts, as well as livery and badges. At that stage there was occasional reluctance to serve. The standard-bearer of York's company in 1542 was deprived of the freedom of the city when he declined.[36] Reluctance to serve was more likely to manifest itself during the campaigns themselves. Much more common was desertion during campaigns. But desertion was significant in some campaigns and had more to do with the specific campaigns than with any more general reluctance to serve. In autumn 1523 the army invading France under Charles Brandon, duke of Suffolk, got to within seventy miles of Paris. But extremely wet weather crippled supply lines and the army of 10,000 melted away, despite Henry's orders that it should overwinter in France. Paradoxes of power once more. An English army was within striking distance of Paris. But bad weather and insufficient supplies meant that there was no way of exploiting the opportunity. At times, especially in the mid-century, contemporary commentators were anxious that there were not enough able-bodied men to serve in armies, though it was often their lack of training rather than their low numbers that they regretted. In the 1590s mutinies were feared. But all in all Tudors did not have to worry overmuch: pull the levers and armies assembled and, largely, remained together, no doubt 'the sense of camaraderie vital to all armed forces' held units together.[37] The large armies sent to France in 1513 and the mid-1540s were efficiently and firmly brought to ports of embarkation: there were no reports of any difficulties, only occasional instances of soldiers being fined for affrays, for example two in Southampton in 1513–14. There were greater problems in the mid/late 1540s, when there were sizeable bands of foreign mercenaries, but even so the extent of trouble was limited.[38] Of course, if wars had gone badly wrong that would have provoked widespread opposition, under the Tudors they scarcely ever did.

The aftermath of military campaigns could pose challenges to governments. Here the Tudor monarchs were fortunate. There were contemporary fears that service in war brutalised men and turned them into ruffians and vagabonds, but evidence is lacking for any serious misorders sparked off by disbanded soldiers.[39] The lack of sustained warfare on English soil meant that there was less war-spread disease, no ravaged countryside, no ruined cities (unlike say the Low Countries); only on the Scottish borders and in Ireland was there devastation.

The costs of war were considerable and they were felt locally in the towns and villages of England. Money was supposed to be spent on equipment but compliance was patchy, not least since demands were irregular, depending on the incidence of war and rebellion, and since there was no permanent administrative structure through which demands could be enforced. Gunn claimed that more parishes complied from 1539, sometimes financing military spending by selling church goods. But it has to be said that the statistics are more suggestive than compelling. If in the 1540s the proportion of parishes from a sample of 153 churchwardens' accounts (out of some 9,000 parishes) recording military payments rose from one in thirteen to just over a quarter (i.e. from twelve parishes to thirty-eight) that still leaves three in every four (115 out of 155) not recording any such payments.[40] There are plenty of examples of military expenditure and administration but beyond the unexceptionable claim that years of war or feared war saw more military activity and expenditure it is hard to go. As Gunn notes, 'in successive wars different towns faced different demands'.[41]

In some early modern European kingdoms, the demands of war on manpower and financial resources were so great, so pressing, that war led to significant changes in the structure of government, as states demanded, and obtained, much more from their populations, and, when they did so without provoking revolt, creating new institutions, new procedures, that would further strengthen state power when the immediate wars were over. Of course, that qualification, when they did so without provoking revolt, is crucial: wars, even wars that were successful in outcome, could leave countries exhausted and royal authority questioned and undermined. But as far as Tudor England goes, the most significant difference is that England was not the theatre of warfare: its Tudor experience was quite different from, say, the eastern side of France. The fourteenth and fifteenth centuries had also been very different: then wars that went wrong stimulated noble revolt, criticism in parliament and even popular risings.

In the Tudor period there were some attempts to reform the procedures of taxation (as discussed earlier), with taxation reflecting assessments of wealth and income more accurately in the 1520s, though rather less so as the century went on, but no fundamentally new tax was introduced until the 1640s. Without permanent taxation there could be no permanent army. There was no lasting emergency, no prolonged period of intensive warfare, no partial invasion, not even in the 1590s, that demanded substantial or revolutionary change. There was no lasting full military threat, emergencies were brief, there was no substantial defeat; combined with the long years of (largely) civil peace and at most very small-scale foreign campaigns meant that there was little incentive to embark on any fundamental reform. There was no revolution in Tudor military affairs. Of Elizabeth it has been stated that 'essentially, the regime sought to run its military operations on a shoestring' in the belief that war was temporary and that peace would soon return. Maybe that slightly underplays the heavy financial burdens of the 1590. Perhaps it was more that Elizabeth and her councillors did not see the need for aggressive fiscal innovation. There was no attempt to reshape government and taxation to support prolonged warfare. And while financial burdens were heavy, they were not unprecedented in form and scope. Crucially, they did not provoke widespread resistance or rebellion. The Tudors more or less managed with the military resources on which they could make call. The most serious threat was that posed by the Spanish Armadas. If the Armada had landed in 1588 there would undoubtedly have been some military response but just how effective lords lieutenant and county militias would have been is open to debate. How well trained and equipped were the county militias? Maybe Elizabeth was lucky. But what Philip II and his naval and military commanders were attempting was highly ambitious and risky. Some of Elizabeth's military commanders, notably the second earl of Essex, urged a more vigorous war against Philip, with the aim of bringing Spain to its knees, but that was unrealistic when the queen and most of her councillors were reluctant to increase taxes any further. In many European states there were in this period changes in the organisation and prosecution of war that, as we have seen, Michael Roberts was the first to label a 'military revolution'. But there was little on those lines in Tudor England, not least because it was not necessary. It would be the Civil Wars of the 1640s that provoked fundamental change: a standing army, a state navy, trained officers and trained soldiers.

6

A 'Tudor Revolution in Government'?

That any book dealing with government in Tudor England must involve the study of the monarchy, the nobility, parliaments, finance and military organisation does not seem a contentious proposition. But what should we make of bold claims made, as we have seen, by Sir Geoffrey Elton, grounded on a study of administrative and especially financial institutions, that what he called a 'Tudor Revolution in Government' masterminded by Thomas Cromwell, 'the most remarkable revolutionary in English history', took place in the 1530s? Elton never pulled a punch, never held back from making grand assertions. His interpretation not only sought to transform our understanding of Tudor government but was also, as we have already seen, a remarkable example of how historians construct explanations of the past they study. So Elton's ideas need to be considered both in terms of the detailed propositions they make about Tudor government and also as an intellectual construct, a bold and imaginative framework claiming to reorder the past. As we have seen, Ian Harris showed how Elton drew on adapted ideas then current.

For Elton, Thomas Cromwell was 'one of the most remarkable English statesmen of the sixteenth century and one of the most remarkable in the country's history', who 'instigated and in part accomplished a major and enduring transformation in virtually every aspect of the nation's public life'. At the heart of Elton's claims was the assertion that personal government by a ruling monarch and his servants—what Elton saw as 'household' or 'medieval' government—was replaced by Cromwell in the 1530s with government by administrative departments free from the direct detailed personal control of monarch and ministers and free from the accidents of politics, in other words by 'modern', 'bureaucratic' and 'national' government.[1]

Elton claimed that Henry VII (who reigned from 1485 to 1509) and Cardinal Wolsey (who was Henry VIII's leading minister from around 1513 to 1529) personally and closely superintended the internal administration of the country. They used informal and ad hoc methods, improvising as they felt best, with little attempt at systematic reform. While there were officials whose task it was to check the monies coming in and going out, there was no proper bureaucratic organisation; records were not kept in ways that allowed officials to refer back to them; officials had no judicial powers—they could not summon and punish anyone not paying what was due. That, claimed Elton, was not very efficient. Traditionally, crown revenues from rents, customs dues, parliamentary taxation and profits from the courts were paid into the

Exchequer, the central financial institution. But, according to Elton, the Exchequer was unsuitable for making rapid payments of money—for example to finance a military campaign—so kings had money, especially the revenues from some of the crown lands, transferred to their Chamber or their wardrobe, that is to say to a group of officials working in the king's palaces, or household, where money would be held in a room (a Chamber) and a chest (or wardrobe), bypassing the Exchequer. In 1510 the Chamber was formally established by act of Parliament as an office receiving money with legal powers comparable to those of the Exchequer. Similarly a new court, or department, the Court of General Surveyors, was formally established in 1512 to deal with the crown's landed income. Yet such a way of proceeding was, Elton claimed, much too haphazardly informal. Wolsey, Elton asserted, used a variety of men to collect revenues and to render account for them, often men close to him such as Thomas Magnus, archdeacon of the East Riding of Yorkshire, who served Wolsey as receiver-general in his archdiocese of York and was employed in such tasks as acting as receiver-general for the lands formerly held by Edward Stafford, third duke of Buckingham, after Buckingham's execution for treason in 1521. Such informal ad hoc arrangements disappeared, Elton claims, with Cromwell's ascendancy in the 1530s. From then on the royal household was concerned simply with the administration of the king's court and was no longer involved in the government of the country. Central to Elton's argument is that in the 1530s Cromwell created new administrative departments—the Court of Augmentations, the court of first fruits—or transformed old ones—the Court of General Surveyors, the duchy of Lancaster, the Exchequer—so that they were as new. And what Cromwell wrought in these administrative department amounted, Elton asserted, to a revolution in government.

Elton argues that, from the start, Thomas Cromwell set about a transformation following a clear plan. In April 1532 he was appointed master of the king's jewels. He used this position and also his favour with the king to exercise effective control over the officials of the Exchequer, in effect establishing himself as minister of finance. Cromwell, according to Elton, used his position to divert revenues away from the Chamber and general surveyors. Consequently royal revenues worth £40,000 p.a. passed through his hands. Through an act of Parliament in 1536 Cromwell turned the Chamber into a bureaucratic department. In 1536, following the decision to dissolve the smaller monasteries, Cromwell set up a new department, the Court of Augmentations, to receive revenues—mostly rents—previously paid to the monasteries: for Elton, the Court of Augmentations was a bureaucratic department capable of administering the revenues without outside help, standing on its own feet, with extensive jurisdiction over ex-monastic lands. Elton also saw Cromwell as behind the setting up of a new court, or financial department, to receive the new taxes on the clergy, the first fruits and tenths, but as that happened late in 1540, after Cromwell's fall, Cromwell's influence was not direct. Elton also saw Cromwell remodelling the court of wards, which had dealt with wardships, but that too took place in late 1540. It is not obvious that these changes were Cromwell's work rather than a reaction against what Wolsey had been doing.

For Elton, the key feature of these courts was that they were staffed by effective treasurers handling cash on instruction by warrant, with a straightforward audit. Elton did not altogether and unreservedly praise these arrangements: there were, he believed, too many courts. But he saw the amalgamations that came after Cromwell's fall as consolidating Cromwell's new arrangements: in 1547 the Court of Augmentations was merged with the Court of General Surveyors; in 1554 augmentations and first fruits were amalgamated with the Exchequer. Elton saw those amalgamations as the posthumous climax of Cromwell's revolution. All that, he claimed, emphatically separated the king's household from the financial administration. That was at the heart of Elton's claim that Cromwell masterminded a revolution in government. Essentially it turned on how and by whom royal revenues were administered. And at once it prompts the question, can developments in the financial administration, however substantial, really amount to a revolution in government?

For Elton, Cromwell did not simply revolutionise the way in which crown revenues were administered. Elton went on to make further claims. He asserted Cromwell introduced a new principle of taxation in 1534: from then on, taxation was justified in preambles to statutes as a contribution to the general costs of government and not only for war. Cromwell greatly enhanced, Elton claimed, the post of the king's secretary which he held from 1534. Elton claimed that not only did Cromwell make himself the acme of an all-powerful minister, with his hand over and in every event and detail, but that he also turned the post of secretary into the centre and driving force of administration—almost a premiership. This was reflected, Elton said, in the ways in which orders and legal documents were issued.

Wolsey, the Lord Chancellor, whom Elton always disapprovingly saw as a mere amateur in government—'the most disappointing man who ever held great power in England'—took the great seal needed for authenticating documents, which he held by virtue of his office as Lord Chancellor, with him when he was involved in diplomatic negotiations in Calais between August and November 1521: that, Elton says, had a damaging effect on government business at home, since very little could be done in Wolsey's absence as the great seal was needed to authorise the most important administrative actions. Elton sees Cromwell as much more professional because he had his letters, instructions and warrants sealed by the signet, that is to say the king's private seal, held by Cromwell as the king's secretary, or by the privy seal, held by Cromwell when he was appointed Lord Privy Seal. The privy seal had been developed in the fifteenth century as a way by which a king could act without using the great seal: presumably when a king wanted to send instructions quickly or without wanting to leave a formal record, no doubt a reflection of the civil wars we know as the Wars of the Roses. 'The last medieval chancellor was followed by the first modern secretary of state' is how Elton describes these developments. Yet the significance of the difference between great seal, privy seal and signet is somewhat elusive. It was essential for kings and ministers to have their letters and legal documents sealed so that no one could interfere with them and so that their recipients could be sure that they came from the king or his leading ministers; grants in particular required a seal in order to be legally valid. But why using one form of seal rather than another should be of momentous significance is not plain. There would always be a tension between time-consuming formal restrictions and easy-going practice. From time to time procedures would seem either too tight or too permissive, and adjustments would be made, none of them revolutionary.

Elton also claimed that the king's Council was formalised into a governing body for the first time. For Elton the Council before Cromwell enjoyed only an attenuated existence. Vital matters, Elton claimed, were decided by Wolsey or the king alone, perhaps with the assistance of what Elton saw as a shadowy grouping attending upon the king, a fluctuating and random assemblage of individuals. In addition, the Council sat in Star Chamber to deal with judicial business, which distracted councillors from proper business. Under Cromwell, between 1534 and 1536 the Council was deliberately and consciously re-organised. A councillor once appointed would remain a councillor till formally dismissed, meetings were frequent, regular attendance by councillors was required and the Council was allocated its own clerk. 'Government by the king gave way to government under the king', Elton summed up.

In the 1530s Henry VIII broke from Rome, repudiating papal authority. Elton saw Thomas Cromwell as responsible for that: when the king was floundering in his search for a divorce, Cromwell offered him the revolutionary solution which he adopted. As part of the Tudor Revolution in Government, Elton saw the state as now supreme over the church where before there was a duality. And clearly the break with Rome and the explicit repudiation of papal authority had, and has had, lasting consequences.

For Elton the 1530s transformed the status of Parliament. The break with Rome was effected, said Elton, by a series of parliamentary statutes: the Act of Appeals, the Act of Supremacy, the Act of Succession. Parliamentary statute triumphed over the abstract law of Christendom. The Reformation Parliament marked a qualitative change in the role of Parliament, now able to make laws on the church and religion. The use of Parliament intensified: Parliament, capable of legislating on religious matters, had become a truly omnicompetent legislative instrument. Parliament was used in the 1530s when not strictly necessary according to law. Two hundred statutes were passed between 1532 and 1540 compared to one hundred and fifty between 1509 and 1531. Wolsey had dissolved some smaller monasteries by obtaining papal bulls; Cromwell secured the dissolution of the rest of the smaller monasteries by obtaining a parliamentary statute. Instead of putting pressure on judges to convict those who opposed the break with Rome, Cromwell instead secured a new Treason Act 1534 so that those who refused to accept the break with Rome could be prosecuted in the courts. Where Wolsey had been masterful and arbitrary, Cromwell, Elton claimed, consulted and compromised. And for Elton all this established a true constitutional monarchy: king-in-parliament.

That was not all. England now became a self-contained national unit. Henry VIII broke with Rome, declared himself supreme head of the church and, strikingly, his realm an empire—an idea Elton attributed to Cromwell. That was, Elton said, the first time 'empire' had been used to describe a geographical area rather than attribute of kingship. And that way of looking led Cromwell to attack various 'franchises', that is parts of the realm with 'privileges' (private laws), exempting them in some ways from the normal operation of the law and taxation, notably Cheshire, Durham and Wales. And Cromwell invoked, and transformed, notions of the commonweal, self-sufficient, free from papal interference, committed to remedying the ills of the world.

When Elton first developed his views, Cromwell was an essentially secular figure, inspired by humanist sentiments; later Elton came to see Cromwell as influenced by early Protestantism.

So was all this a 'revolution in government', 'a major transformation ... in the relations between rulers and ruled', a decisive shift from 'medieval' to 'modern' government, thus a pivotal moment in the evolution and development of the modern English state? As an intellectual construct—a series of connected arguments bringing together and treating as part of the same phenomenon matters as diverse as the prevention of fraud by Exchequer officials and oversight of the church in England—it is on its own terms magnificent. And from the early 1950s to his death in 1994 Elton boldly and tirelessly drove his interpretation home.

Before considering Elton's claims in detail, it is worth noting that historians and sociologists who have been writing about what they call 'state formation' have been making a very similar general claim about the transformation of government. They have not much bothered with administrative departments and the management of royal revenues and expenditure, and their exact chronology is somewhat different, often making claims for processes of change that operated over a much longer time span than just Elton's decade. But their basic assertion is that it was in what is fashionable to call the 'early modern' period—the sixteenth and seventeenth centuries—not yet 'modernity', not yet how things are now, not yet 'the world we recognise as our own', but nonetheless moving towards 'modernity'—that a centralised government structure, what can reasonably be called a 'state', developed for the first time, uncannily echoing Elton's overarching claim. For that reason to assess Elton's Tudor Revolution in Government is not to tackle some quaint notion of a forgotten and uninfluential scholar from the distant past but rather to assess what can be seen as in many respects an early version of current claims for 'state formation'.[2]

Elton's claims have, it must be emphasised straight away, attracted a good deal of criticism, as we have already glimpsed in the lives of historians with which this book begins. There was a biting review by R.B. Wernham in the *English Historical Review* (1956). In 1963 Penry Williams and Gerald Harriss published a lengthy critique of Elton's Tudor Revolution in *Past & Present*, to which Elton replied. In 1979 Penry Williams's *The Tudor Regime* appeared, much more than a refutation but certainly that as well. In 1986 David Starkey and Christopher Coleman, two of Elton's pupils, edited a collection of essays, the thrust of which was highly critical of Elton's perspectives. On Elton's death in 1994, Rees Davies, the president of the Royal Historical Society, asked Felicity Heal and me, both Tudor historians then serving on the Council of the Society, to organise a conference in Elton's memory: the papers given then were published in the *Transactions of the Royal Historical Society* in 1997. Once again criticism was the dominant theme, prompting one wit, noting that Elton's base was the University of Cambridge, to call the conference 'Oxford's revenge'. I've had my own say: my emphasis on the power of the nobility in my DPhil thesis and subsequent book was an implicit critique of Elton's grand claims; in a review article in the *Historical Journal* published in 1988 I articulated my scepticism; and ten years later in a paper in *History*, reprinted in my collection of essays *Power and Politics in Tudor England*, entitled 'Elton's Cromwell',

I questioned Elton's belief that Cromwell, not Henry VIII, was the real ruler of England in the 1530s. That is a fundamental criticism to which I shall return.

What other objections can be made to Elton's construct? Critics said that he had misunderstood medieval government. It was wrong to see medieval government as exclusively personal and informal government by the king from his household. That flatly overlooks the characteristics of the Exchequer, the administrative department which supervised the collection and spending of royal revenues. It was thoroughly bureaucratic in its forms and operations, keeping careful records of moneys in and moneys out. It was based in Westminster and did not move when the king moved. Its documented origins lie in the twelfth century, but the scale of earlier taxes—in particular the Danegeld—implies the existence of a sophisticated and complex system of financial administration long before. A recent study of accountability in the twelfth and thirteenth centuries shows vividly that monarchs and officials had anticipated Elton's concerns centuries before the period in which Elton saw revolutionary change.[3] Of course accountability was not just about ensuring that officials remained honest and did not steal or misuse (for example, for lending money received before the required date and pocketing the interest). It was also about monarchs and their councillors disregarding established procedures, on grounds of necessity, not least in time of civil war, and transferring large sums from the Exchequer to more informal arrangements, including trusted officials and chests of money in royal palaces. A truly national and modern financial administration would be one in which financial officials would feel able to protest against and resist such measures. That seems too optimistic a reading of early modern finance.

Moreover in the administrative arrangements of the duchy of Lancaster significant precedents for the administrative structures of the 1530s may be found. The duchy of Lancaster—certain estates that had come into crown hands through the complexities of inheritance when Henry IV seized the throne in 1399—were treated separately from the rest of the crown lands. They were carefully and aggressively managed: and they served as a model in the 1530s. So if Cromwell followed the procedures of the duchy of Lancaster, he was not introducing any modern principles of government but simply following late medieval best practice. Elton's view of medieval government as always informal and inefficient is a grotesque distortion, as anyone who has looked at the records of the medieval Exchequer will quickly realise. Elton here made specific aspersions. More recent proponents of 'state formation' tend to be less specific but implicit in their approach is the assumption, rarely articulated, never demonstrated in detail, that medieval government was somehow backward and ineffective: the word 'medieval' is often used pejoratively.

On the other hand Elton's claim that a 'revolution' producing 'modern' government occurred in the 1530s made excessive claims for what happened then and took too little account of the important administrative reforms of the 1690s, the 1780s and, especially, the mid-nineteenth century, when something like the modern civil service, based on recruitment by competitive examinations, took shape. In the Tudor period as before, 'every civil servant who obtained a post . . . did so as a result of the successful operation of patronage by an official or social superior'.[4] There was no career structure, remuneration was by very low salaries and (one supposes) fees charged to those who were assisted, vacancies were known through gossip, and there are some hints that offices may have been bought and sold (though sale of office may well have been intended to provide a pension for the retiring official). The central bureaucracy was tiny, barely a few hundred officials, just ninety of them in the Exchequer: by 'modern' standards, government was very small scale and undeveloped.

Of course things were not static and from time to time there were changes. But the question remains what did such developments reflect? Were they the deliberate, planned, principled work of a reforming minister with a vision? Or were they much more ad hoc, the consequence of decisions taken in a hurry in response to immediate problems and demands? Take the new revenue courts or departments of the 1530s. The crown was dissolving the monasteries and taking over the very considerable landed estates which the monasteries had held. Those lands had to be administered: rents collected, leases negotiated, sales arranged. That a new department—the Court of Augmentations—was set up to do this does not seem in itself revolutionary. Its procedures do not seem particularly novel: they reflected the best current practices, such as that of the Duchy of Lancaster. In many ways a more important development took place in 1554, following a fundamental review of financial administration in 1552, when William Paulet, marquess of Winchester, absorbed the various financial departments—the Court of General Surveyors and the Court of Augmentations—into the Exchequer so that their revenues could be brought together.

Elton presents that as the culmination of Cromwell's work. But on another reading it might be seen rather as a rejection of the much more informal methods of financial administration practised over the previous eighty years. Edward IV, after recovering the throne in 1471, Henry VII, who won the crown on the battlefield, and Henry VIII all wanted to have large sums of money, presumably held in chests to which they had direct access, to spend as they saw fit, quickly, and without any bureaucratic monitoring that might at crucial moments leave them without resources. Hence the importance in this period of the Chamber as a significant financial institution, as a treasury under the monarch's direct control, not just as a department running the king's palaces. Hence the emergence of what became the Court of General Surveyors, which acted as a board of audit for the Chamber. On Elton's definition that would all be very backward. But arguably the period from Edward IV's seizure of the throne in 1460 to the later years of Henry VIII was, in administrative terms, not so much backward as unusual, reflecting the conflicts of the Wars of the Roses, and kings' concern to have money readily available and under their immediate control exercised by a small number of trusted counsellors. Much more normal, before 1460, and again from the end of Henry VIII's reign, were bureaucratic structures in which money was administered by larger numbers of office-holders outside the king's court. Elton mistakenly saw the loose ad hoc arrangements that the political instabilities of the later fifteenth century had prompted as standard rather than exceptional.

And Elton then misleadingly presented attempts, by Cromwell and others, to formalise and systematise those arrangements as a revolution leading to modern government when what they were doing was going back to the arrangements that obtained before the Wars of the Roses and making the Exchequer once more the primary institution dealing with financial administration. Cromwell was by no means the only minister to be involved in that. And his own contribution was somewhat mixed, since, as Elton admits, once appointed master of the king's jewels, he informally handled large sums of money. Under Cromwell it was the king's jewel house, more than the Chamber, that became the key location of more informal ways of financial management. Elton's suggestion that under Cromwell personal interventions by the minister 'were then no longer the true mainspring of financial action but merely the frills and extravagances on the edges of a bureaucratic organisation' strains credulity. And it was under Edward VI and Mary, not least thanks to William Paulet, marquess of Winchester, that the Exchequer again became the supreme institution responsible for the bulk of the crown's revenue, keeping full records, and following a careful procedure.

On questions of finance, Elton focussed almost exclusively on financial *administration*; there is very little on the raising of revenue, whether the management of crown lands or alternative forms of taxation. There is next to nothing on the sums raised and spent. Elton once admitted to me that 'I don't understand money (I still don't; throughout my life I have never known what my salary actually was)', yet figures are vital to any understanding of finance. And a true financial revolution would have involved a fundamental transformation of the resources of government: taxation based on much more accurate assessment of wealth and income, and taxation of goods and services within the realm. Nothing like that was substantially attempted: Wolsey's Great Proscription in 1522 and his subsidy in 1523 came nearer than anything Cromwell did. The one relevant matter on which Elton made larger claims was that Cromwell in 1534 introduced a new principle of taxation, namely that taxation was now granted as a contribution to the normal costs of government and not just for war. But this is unconvincing, as we have seen. The preamble to the subsidy of 1534 claimed that it had been made necessary by the costs of preventing a feared Scottish invasion in 1532. And what was spent on war was so much greater than what was granted in taxation in this period.

What of the king's Council? Here what misleads is the emphasis on a particular moment when its membership and duties were formalised (and there has been much debate whether this happened in 1534, 1536 or 1540). Yet in a broader perspective, no monarch could rule entirely alone, all monarchs needed a group of advisers meeting regularly to discuss policy, to take decisions, to supervise their enforcement and (what took up a great deal of their time and energy) to respond to the multitude of requests and petitions addressed to the king from people seeking redress of grievances. Something like a Council can be seen in existence much earlier than the 1530s, not least in the immediately preceding decade. It is only from the early 1540s that Council registers survive: arranged chronologically by dates of meetings, these list the names of councillors present and give brief summaries of matters discussed. But similar registers were clearly kept in Wolsey's ascendancy from the mid-1520s to 1529. We know that only because in the early seventeenth century Thomas Egerton, Lord Chancellor Ellesmere, lawyer and judge, evidently read through them, took notes and arranged his material not chronologically but by theme. But it is plain that regular meetings of the

Council took place in much the same way in the 1520s and in the 1540s. There may well have been some changes in the 1530s in the way the Council operated and membership may have become more formalised, but it is not altogether clear what such changes amounted to. No doubt all committees benefit from periodic reinvigoration, but such reorganisation should not be treated as revolutionary change. It is not clear that the changes of the 1530s were as unique or as dramatic or as long-lasting as Elton asserts.

It is reasonable to claim that the most effective Council is a small one composed of professional councillors meeting frequently and regularly, and Cromwell's Council as presented by Elton fits that description, as do the privy councils over Elizabeth's long reign. But what we know of Wolsey's Council suggests that the arrangements of the mid-1530s were not especially novel. True, the formal membership of the Privy Council was small. But analysis of the Council in the 1520s would suggest that in practice that was the case then too. There were undoubtedly councillors—including noblemen—who in practice hardly ever attended. So the difference between the Council in the 1520s and 1530s was not as great as Elton claims. In Mary's reign, however, many men were given the title of privy councillor, but they were not expected to attend several times a week, nor did they. They had been appointed privy councillors in the aftermath of the disputed succession of 1553 and their appointment was an expression of Mary's gratitude for their loyalty. None of that got in the way of the work carried out by what was in effect a small working Council that dealt with business. During the minority of Edward VI the Council had included several noblemen—who did attend. That most likely was a response to the political instability and popular rebellions of the minority. Politics drove the Council rather than concepts of rational administration.

In Elton's grand scheme there is surprisingly little place for the courts of law. These were long established, with recent enhancements under Wolsey. The Court of King's Bench exercised criminal jurisdiction: that was where those accused of the most serious offences would be tried. The Court of Common Pleas dealt with civil cases. In practice there was overlap and encroachment, not least as lawyers sought business. The Exchequer of Pleas heard cases involving crown revenues. The Court of Chancery was a newer development, more willing than the Court of King's Bench and the Court of Common Pleas to hear arguments based on equity, not just precedent. The king's Council had long heard petitions and complaints and it came to act formally and judicially as the Court of Star Chamber. Wolsey, as Lord Chancellor, significantly increased its activity, especially dealing with disputes over land. A Court of Requests developed especially on the face of it to hear cases brought by the poor, and as such can readily be seen as a successor to the petitions to Parliament characteristic of the fourteenth century, though plaintiffs' laments about their actual or feared poverty may have been more an attempt to gain a moral advantage than strictly true.[5]

Perhaps more revealing than such adjustments in institutional or judicial organisation are attitudes to information. Here there were some interesting sixteenth-century developments, but nonetheless they fell far short of anything that could be described as 'modern' government. On a number of occasions, early Tudor governments attempted to gain information on a national scale about certain issues. In 1516–17 Wolsey co-ordinated the work of commissioners who were investigating the extent of enclosures. In 1522 he masterminded the 'general proscription', that great survey of military power, wealth and income. In 1535 commissioners supervised by Cromwell compiled the *Valor Ecclesiasticus*, a minutely detailed statement of the wealth of the monasteries. Similar enquiries were conducted into the chantries and the possessions of parish churches in the reign of Edward VI. These were all substantial achievements. But it is worth noting that such surveys were the exception, not the rule. There was little by way of regular, systematic, collection of information. Not much was done to keep the information acquired up to date. What tended to happen was periodic detailed investigation of particular problems—for example the condition of royal revenues, the staffing and organisation of revenue courts or the costs of a military campaign—and some attempt to resolve them, but not on a regular or systematic basis. For example, in Henry VII's accounts, items of military expenditure are mixed up with the king's gambling debts.

When Sir William Compton, Henry VIII's great favourite, died in 1528, officials had to draw up lists of the posts he had held by going through the bulky rolls on which such appointments were recorded as they were made: there were, however, no standing lists to show the king just which, or how many, posts anyone had, no filing system, no easy way of gathering or retrieving information. The recent invention of printing was not yet much exploited in the procedures of government. New laws, proclamations and propaganda were printed, but governments do not seem to have used printed forms as a way of collecting and ordering information.[6] Where new procedures were introduced, such as the compulsory recording of baptisms, marriages and burials in parish registers from 1538, the information was simply kept locally, where it might well be used to resolve local disputes, for example over inheritances, but it was not transmitted centrally, for example to allow reliable estimates of national population to be made. It was only in the later sixteenth century that Tudor administrators started keeping maps showing, for example, where noblemen and gentlemen lived. Most government decisions, then, were made on the basis not of detailed information or considered analysis but on hunch or prejudice, in response to lobbying, on knowledge acquired personally from experience, on the personal initiatives of monarchs and ministers, rather than from reflection on systematically collected hard information. A great deal still depended on the commitment, energy and ideas of a king or queen or a chief minister. In these senses government was not what we should understand by modern.

Perhaps, though, one should be wary of idealising the efficiency and rationality of modern administration as the study by Anthony King and Ivor Crewe of *The Blunders of Our Governments* all too vividly shows. We now see utter incompetence as normal. In our own dealings with bureaucracy we seem to be in a Kafkaesque world in which (to give a personal example), in response to my claim that a property is my main residence, a succession of officials inform me that it cannot be my main residence because it is not my only residence, a chain of reasoning that defies logic. And again and again examples of incompetence abound. In September 2018 I read of the government's plan to reduce the cost of a pay increase to the armed forces of 2.9 per cent by paying 2 per cent straightway but deferring the 0.95 per cent for six months and paying it as a bonus rather than as consolidating it into salaries, thus saving money in future years as the salaries to which future increases will be applied will be lower. But this ingenious plan has foundered on the apparent inability of the software used by the Ministry of Defence to make such unconsolidated bonus payments.

And maybe that points to a weakness in Elton's approach, in that he stressed too much the place of reason and order in Tudor administration. His arguments were refined when he was a graduate student in the late 1940s. I once put it to him that he was influenced by the then Attlee government's sweeping reorganisation of British government, including the nationalisation of the utilities (coal, electricity, gas, water) and the extension of central planning (notably the Town and Country Planning Act) and the role of civil servants in national life, in a mood of high-minded post-war optimism hard to recover nowadays, when it was felt the man from Whitehall really did know what was best. Elton thought my supposition absurd and angrily replied that it showed how little I understood his approach. But I still wonder whether he was not subtly influenced by the spirit of the age in which he lived into exaggerating the purposefulness and effectiveness of Thomas Cromwell's administration.

While I am sceptical about the emphasis on factional politics and manipulation which Eric Ives and Elton's pupil David Starkey have elaborated, as we shall consider later, in one limited sense their interpretation is relevant here, for Cromwell was not so much the high-minded public servant that Elton would present, but rather both a loyal and ferociously hard-working servant of the king and an ambitious man eager to advance himself and his family. He was building up a landed estate, converting the possibly temporary favour of the crown into something that might be more permanent. His acquisitions were concentrated in Kent, Sussex (where with estates centred on Lewes he became one of the leading county landowners) and, latterly, Essex. Landholding was not the basis of his power, which was rather the king's favour, but those acquisitions show him as a magnate-in-the-making in much the same way as those of Sir William Compton. There was then a significant personal side to the career of the man whom Elton saw as introducing impersonal national government.

Elton saw Cromwell as responsible for the transformation of Parliament: 'Cromwell was fascinated by the work and potentialities of parliament'; 'he well deserves the name of England's first parliamentary statesman'. But was Elton mistaken in supposing that medieval parliaments did not make law but only declared it? Parliaments had legislated on matters concerning the church and heresy in the fourteenth and fifteenth centuries. Conversely, parliaments in the 1530s were largely used by Henry as a rubber stamp, as we have seen, to associate the political nation with by no means popular policies, to secure the means of punishing those who disobeyed, to allow the king to claim to an international public opinion that his divorce was supported by the political nation. Elton wanted to present Cromwell as rescuing the common law from threats, Cromwell as ensuring the survival of Parliament at a time when representative institutions elsewhere in Europe were in jeopardy. But this is all implausible. Henry VIII and Cromwell did not always use parliaments. Elton pinpointed the use of Parliament to dissolve the smaller monasteries; what he did not go on to say was that the larger monasteries were persuaded to surrender in the years between 1538 and

1540 by pressures put upon them by groups of commissioners, not by parliamentary means. It is thus hard to see the Reformation Parliament (1529–36) as marking a qualitative shift in the power of Parliament just because it legislated over religion. That was not new, as we can see from the heresy laws of the early fifteenth century. What was new in the early sixteenth century was the emergence across Christendom of lasting religious diversity and religious division. Religious divisions would very likely be reflected in parliaments. Monarchs and governments could, for example, seek to set down true religion in legislation. MPs unhappy with the state of the church could try to use Parliament to achieve a more palatable settlement. But none of that conferred additional powers on parliaments. Arguably, religious divisions would weaken more than they strengthened or empowered parliaments.

What of Elton's claims for Cromwell's role in the break with Rome and particularly for developing the theories of royal supremacy and empire? The difficulty here is that these ideas were not quite as novel as Elton supposes. Long before the 1530s men thought of England in terms of a unitary state focussed on the monarchy. In the fourteenth century monarchs had secured parliamentary statutes prohibiting obedience to foreign powers, intending the pope: they were known as statutes of praemunire after the writ (the legal instrument) by which those suspected of breaking the law could be accused. Popes had long ago ceased to have any real influence in England. The English church was already a 'monarchical church'. Henry VIII always held a high view of his powers. By invoking the Bible as his authority for seeking an annulment of his marriage to Catherine of Aragon, Henry was from 1527 implicitly questioning papal power; from 1528 to 1529 he and his ministers and agents were making quite explicit threats against the papacy. Elton was mistaken in supposing that the break with Rome and the theories justifying it were Cromwell's. Moreover Elton mistakes the role that Parliament played in all this. What was enacted in the 1530s was not a parliamentary supremacy over the church but Henry VIII's royal supremacy, less a constitutional monarchy than something more troublingly tyrannical. And this is the context of the legislation removing the franchises of Cheshire and Durham and reordering the local administration of Wales into counties on the English model. But that was done not out of some idealistic and rational reforming zeal or from imperial aggrandisement but because the break with Rome led Henry VIII to fear that those parts of his realm over which he had less than full legal control might become havens from which those who opposed the break with Rome might stir up trouble. England—unlike the territories ruled by kings of what they called France—had been a unified and integrated state for centuries before the reign of Henry VIII, with far fewer and much less wide-ranging liberties, immunities and privileges than France. This was not just a matter of constitutional principle. From the 1440s, if not earlier, in what could be seen as 'a revolution in transport', carters provided regular services across England facilitating trade and in broader senses unifying the country.[7]

Moreover there is one aspect of government that Elton initially neglected, and that is the matter of enforcement (to which we shall return). When, later, in his study of the implementation of the break with Rome in the 1530s, *Policy and Police* (1972), Elton came to study enforcement, what he showed was that Henry VIII and Cromwell relied heavily on the traditional rulers of the localities, noblemen and gentlemen, to impose their policies: there was no attempt at any Tudor Revolution in local government, there were and there remained very few full-time salaried officials at local level. Such success as was achieved was due 'not to the creation of new machinery or the introduction of new principles, but to . . . energy . . . , to the vigorous encouragement, by exhortation as much as by threats, of the loyal cooperation of all sorts of Englishmen on which Tudor government depended at all times'.[8] That is also the pervading theme of Penry Williams's study of *The Tudor Regime*, in which he emphasises how much the effectiveness of Tudor governments in dealing with disorder, religious division, dearth or inflation depended not on formal administrative procedures but on the maintenance of effective collaboration between the central government and the leading noblemen, gentlemen and merchants in the localities whose wealth, local influence and more or less willing service made up for much of the administrative inadequacy of central government. Gerald Harriss, who joined with Penry Williams to attack Elton's claims in *Past & Present* in 1963, noted thirty years later that[9]

> The development of the English state is now read as the interpenetration and coalescing of centre and locality, rather than as the spread of government from the centre through the increasing executive authority of the crown and its agents. This depended on the formation of a governing elite and a governing mentality, at both central and local level. . . . The crown could only govern the realm through this local political elite.

There is, then, not much of the Eltonian edifice left standing. And it is unlikely, I think, that any future historian will make quite the claims for Thomas Cromwell and the 1530s that Elton did. Certainly governments in that decade were ambitious in what they aspired to do and they did interfere in myriad ways in the lives of their subjects, as C.S.L. Davies pointed out. Justifications in preambles of statutes and in circular letters to JPs and in proclamations made lofty claims. The break with Rome and consequent religious changes were large matters with important consequences. Was there more activity than before? Yet Wolsey in the late 1510s and 1520s was a great activist, as Peter Gwyn has insisted, and it would thus be misleading to single out Cromwell's decade. It may be that the survival of Cromwell's papers gives a misleading impression that much more than usual was going on then. By contrast maybe government was less aggressive, more careful to avoid confrontation and conflict, and consequently less reforming under Elizabeth, but Council minutes nonetheless suggest much activity. Looking back from our perspective, a good deal of what Tudor governments did or aspired to do may strike us as naïve or unlikely to prove effective. Yet we ought to give them credit for trying. Elton's *Reform and Renewal* counts as his most successful book, discounting his tendency to see Cromwell as behind everything and his reluctance to allow continuities. What does emerge very clearly is an activist government aware of social and economic challenges and doing what it could in response.

To deny that there was a Tudor Revolution centred on the financial administration is not to say that Tudor government was weak or that it failed. What I wish to emphasise is its relative strength but to note its vulnerability in some circumstances. In the chapter on monarchy I noted that Tudor monarchs defeated challenges to their titles and remained on the throne till they died: pretenders and rebels did not overthrow them. But that, I argued, was not inevitable: it required personal courage and political skill. Royal authority was reinforced by political theory which stressed monarchy as the only plausible system of government and by the church which presented monarchs as God's lieutenants on earth. At times what Elton saw as no more than the assertion of royal authority was seen by some as tyrannical, even despotic. Government remained personal, much more so than Elton allowed, as we shall see in the next chapter. The military and financial resources of Tudor monarchs were, as I have argued earlier, considerable but not limitless: the Tudors succeeded in getting by without needing fundamental reforms. In some respects their administration was remarkably effective, for example in compiling the survey of monastic wealth, but also, by modern standards, surprisingly rudimentary. On the whole Tudor government worked, but because it did not attempt too much too quickly and because it sought and largely obtained the compliance of its leading subjects. Much depended on circumstances. The monarchy was at its weakest on the death of a king, on the accession of a minor or of a usurper with rivals to defeat and debts to pay off. But once established, a monarch was hard to oppose, since he or she could lay claim to traditional loyalties and to ties of patronage; and obedience and loyalty to the monarch was very much in the interests of the landed classes, as I have already argued. The importance of circumstances highlights a further weakness of Elton's approach. Government could never be a fixed, or a permanent, achievement: royal authority had constantly to be remade by monarchs and ministers.

But if Elton was wrong in his principal claims, nonetheless he was raising important questions. Government matters, however fashionable it is to elevate the personal and the private. And administration matters a good deal too, even if looking in great detail at how a state is administered is not always rivetingly interesting. A ubiquitous characteristic of the modern world in which we live is the large part played in all our lives by the state. How we came to get here is a legitimate line of inquiry and Elton was consciously making an attempt to explain that. Manifestly the break with Rome in the 1530s and what proved to be the lasting repudiation of the papacy (Mary's short reign apart) has been very important in England's subsequent religious and political development: maybe contemporary Euroscepticism reflects in some measure the centuries of English detachment from Catholic Europe. Whether Elton quite got the significance of the break with Rome right is another matter. I think he failed to see just how far the church in England was already a monarchical church and how far the crown was already for all practical purposes supreme. I think parliamentary statute was already seen as dominant: English common law had already long developed independently from the Roman law practised on the continent. I think England was already 'a self-contained national unit': indeed when between 1529 and 1532 Henry argued forcefully that legal cases should be settled in England, not in Rome, he was playing on that already existing sense of England as an independent nation-state. The long-term consequences of the break with Rome undoubtedly consolidated and reinforced that sense, but the break with Rome was possible only because it was already there. Elton was also undoubtedly right to think that how England became a constitutional monarchy in which the powers of the crown were defined and restricted by law is a highly important matter: but he gave the 1530s far too much importance, grossly neglecting the political and constitutional struggles of earlier periods (to cite just taxation and Magna Carta), as well as fundamental changes in later periods, especially in the late seventeenth and the nineteenth centuries when monarchs lost their control over government first to politicians who could command a following in the House of Commons and then to organised political parties. And Elton was also undoubtedly right to see administration—bureaucracy—as a key feature of government, though his association of bureaucracy and modernity is unconvincing. Was administration, let alone government, as impersonal as Elton wanted to claim?

7

The personal

Elton made great claims for the revolutionary nature of the administrative reforms he saw in the 1530s. He presented them as introducing modern impersonal government, immune to the influence and interference of individuals. But do his claims fall because administration and government can never be simply a matter of structures but inescapably involve personalities and hence differences of opinion, ambitions, jealousies and disputes? Was Elton's model flawed because it offers only a very partial description of government, focussing on the institutional arrangements but overlooking the larger context—especially the human context—in which all institutions must operate? Was Elton in this respect making the same mistake as sociologists and anthropologists who see politics and government in terms of groups, whether classes or peoples, similarly overlooking or underestimating the significance of human personalities and relationships?

There is an immediate tension in Elton's approach between his emphasis on the new administrative arrangements that he sees in the 1530s and his emphasis on Thomas Cromwell as their author and as the man who worked tirelessly to implement them. If so much depended on one man, then can what he created (if we allow Elton's claims for the sake of argument) be seen as impersonal? Elton presents Cromwell as acting vigorously in various ways, exploiting the offices he held to introduce changes. Such a system is as much personal as it is bureaucratic. And there is little reason for supposing that one man's actions are more likely to prove lasting than another's.

Moreover Cromwell was not a disinterested ascetic reformer. He was building up his own wealth in these years. Interestingly, Elton's last published paper was a communication 'How Corrupt Was Thomas Cromwell?'[1] And Cromwell undoubtedly received all manner of gifts—food, birds, horses, luxurious clothing. He also expected a range of fees for issuing writs and sealing documents. Elton accepted that Cromwell 'probably did on occasion take what to modern eyes look like straightforward bribes'. But what Cromwell did was standard, not corrupt.

My sometime student Michael Everett went deeper. As he has convincingly shown, Cromwell's wealth increased as he rose in royal favour. In his will in 1529 he bestowed £900 in cash; in his will in 1532 £1,830. Cromwell also came to receive many annuities, that is to say regular payments from institutions and individuals. Between March 1525 and June 1534, some ninety-four are recorded. Between 1525 and 1529 Cromwell was granted thirteen, ranging from £1 to £13 6s 8d, in 1531 alone nine, in 1532 twenty-one, in 1533 thirty-three. The annual totals rose from £54 in 1529 to £94 in 1531, £129 in 1532 and £437 in 1533. In the single month in October 1537, Cromwell received

£500. Annuities were general gifts, perhaps rewarding some past favour and certainly offering an inducement for future favour. Does all that make Cromwell an unscrupulous and corrupt minister? Everett would claim that it certainly does: 'ultimately, yes; he took bribes and probably made considerable sums when doing so.'[2]

But what Cromwell was doing was conventional; all courtiers and officials behaved in this way, if on a smaller scale. One of the difficulties is that it is exceptionally difficult to provide detailed evidence that would clearly convict him of wrongdoing. It is impossible to prove that Cromwell did something that he would not otherwise have done (or that he did not do something he would otherwise have done). He was certainly charged with bribery in the act of attainder that cost him his life in 1540. But no evidence was given for just the sort of charge that could easily be thrown into the pot in such circumstances. In 1536 the Pilgrims of Grace voiced their hostility to Cromwell but that was because they saw him as author of religious changes they feared, not because he was corrupt. In 1538 one George Poulet accused Cromwell of being 'a great taker of money': 'he will speak, solicit, or do for no man, but all for money'. But again there is no detailed evidence in support.[3]

Yet even if we follow Elton and exonerate Cromwell from charges of corruption, nonetheless all this does show the continuing, very personal nature of government and administration. Crown officers were paid salaries, but they also charged individuals for whom they performed administrative services fees, fees that the officers kept for themselves. Modern administrative departments do often charge fees for services rendered—for example, fees are charged when you ask for a passport or seek probate of a will—but, crucially, those fees do **not** go into the pocket of the individual officer who is doing the administrative work for you. In Tudor government they did. Nor, today, would offering a larger or additional payment—for example to the civil servants who process passport applications—be tolerated or produce more rapid service (though you can get preferential treatment by going to a post office and paying a little more). In fact it is hard to show that it did in the Tudor period—and it may be that the fulsome gifts should be seen more as conventional than as intended to bribe in the sense of securing some special favour or unusual attention. Nonetheless, the overall impression is of an administrative set-up that is significantly more personal and less bureaucratic than what exists now; and there is absolutely nothing to suggest that Thomas Cromwell did anything to change that system. That would have been a revolution.

Moreover Cromwell built up his own wealth in the service of the crown. Perhaps he deserved it because he pushed through great reforms—but even then it could still be said of him, following the proverb, that 'he did well by doing good'. What Cromwell did was to build up estates in Sussex and the south-eastern home counties. It has been claimed that 'he apparently never used them as a platform for landed local influence',[4] but that rather misleads. What he was doing, just as all successful courtier-administrators were doing, was turning the rewards and opportunities of royal service, which were by their very nature likely to be temporary and certainly would not last longer than their own lives, into a permanent landed patrimony that would provide for them and their families in retirement or after political disgrace, and even more importantly serve as a basis of a lasting landed endowment for their descendants. That sort of ambition makes Tudor courtier-administrators very different from modern career civil servants—and underlines again that 'modern' is a misleading word to apply to Tudor government.

That courtier-administrators were interested in their own enrichment does not necessarily mean that they were not good administrators, but it does add another dimension to any study of government. The attitudes, the habits, the mentalities of those individuals who were doing the administering are a significant part of government. Interesting too is that the term 'courtier-administrators' seems the most apt characterisation, rather than simply officials, much less bureaucrats. For these officials were servants of the crown and in a real sense members of the king's or queen's court. And that militates against the very sharp distinction that Elton made between 'household' and 'bureaucratic' government: the two overlapped too intimately. There was no rigid distinction to be made, as one suspects Elton would have wished, between creative and hard-working administrators who got on with things and courtiers who were frivolously wasting everyone's time.

It was such perspectives that led Geoffrey Elton's pupil David Starkey to attack his mentor with great vigour. Starkey's valuable initial insight was that the royal court was an essential feature of government. Elton's approach to government, focussing on units of financial administration, on the formalities of the membership of the king's council, on the differences between different seals and signets that authorised government documents, missed out a vital feature of government—that it was the king's (or queen's) and that it was personal. Starkey urged the political and administrative importance of the royal court. On such a view—shared by other historians—study of ceremonies and artistic patronage were as revealing about the nature and purposes of government as were administrative departments.[5] Moreover Starkey claimed that Elton had got his financial administration badly wrong. Elton had, he claimed, overlooked the importance of the privy chamber. And here Starkey built up an image of the privy chamber—the small group of courtiers, headed by the groom of the stool, who managed the king's private apartments at court, making sure the king had clean bedding and toilets, performing a miscellany of domestic chores—and increasingly becoming involved, so Starkey claimed, in financial administration and in politics, not least because they had regular access to the king, and could allegedly keep those they did not like away from the king. The groom of the stool became responsible for a good deal of the king's expenditure, meeting his gambling debts, making payments when the king travelled, but also rather more substantial payments, not least in times of war. All that, Starkey pointed out, was outside the control of the exchequer and the other various financial departments set up or developed under Cromwell. Arguably for the king's close body servant to hold and to spend large sums of money reflects a rather basic system of government: nothing very bureaucratic or 'modern'. And that led Starkey into a vehement and gleeful denunciation of the Eltonian Tudor Revolution.[6]

In many ways Starkey was convincing. Elton's counter that the privy chamber was transformed under Cromwell into a 'proper institution charged with administering the private finance of the crown' is weak. But in elevating the privy chamber to a place of central importance, Starkey was himself repeating Elton's mistake, that of seeing changes in the structures of financial administration (in this case, the establishment of the privy chamber as a formal department in 1495) as all-important. But much more important than how monies are administered are the questions of how money was raised and how much money was raised. The privy chamber never raised money. Officers of the privy chamber simply received money—from the exchequer, from the other revenue courts—and held or spent it as the king determined. The privy chamber was essentially parasitic and its significance can only be understood within the broader context of national finance as a whole. And here Starkey had little to say: certainly no overall figures. Starkey, like Elton, tended to reify institutions and administrative departments; that is to say, to write about the chamber, the household, the privy chamber, the Ccourt of General Surveyors and so on, as if they were living entities with a collective identity of their own. The key, however, is never to forget that they were staffed by individuals, and that much of what was achieved was the work of individual officers, and when things went wrong, that often reflected the jealousies and quarrels of office-holders. And individual officers often made all sorts of accommodations that ignored or transcended the apparently clear demarcations of their posts: for example, John Heron of the chamber had as his clerks two exchequer officials. Realities were often messier, less clear-cut, than formal administrative boundaries.

Starkey also went too far in minimising the more formal and bureaucratic elements of government, indeed by seemingly playing down the extent to which the realm was subject to government. Increasingly, Starkey focussed on politics seen as rivalries of competing courtiers and factions; government itself fades out of Starkey's presentation. Starkey valuably qualified Elton's claims by pointing to the personal dimension of government. Elton admitted that 'the book about the Tudor Revolution was not about politics: it was about administration, about the instruments used to transform decisions into actions and to run the ordinary, daily active government of England'. Starkey would deny the distinction between politics and administration-government. All government, for Starkey, inescapably involves politics—struggles for power—and therefore administration, Starkey claims, cannot be hived off and treated separately from politics. But he then went much too far. The claim that all government is always 'political' is excessive: in Starkey's world no one is ever doing anything for its own sake or for the general good but merely for personal advantage. More sensible analysis would suggest a mixed model that allowed degrees of interaction between administration and politics but also degrees of separation.

One of the bones of contention between Elton and Starkey was the location of the Privy Council. It is remarkable that we have little certain evidence of where exactly it met. Elton thought it met in the old Westminster palace, Starkey believes that from 1536 it met in the new palace of Whitehall. Why should that be significant? Because, says Starkey, if it was in the new palace of Whitehall, then it was ever more closely part of the king's court, situated directly opposite the king's privy chamber. Because, counters Elton, if it was in the old palace of Westminster while the king and his courtiers lived and slept in the new palace, the council was therefore national, bureaucratic, impersonal, not part of the court. My reading of what little evidence there is suggests that it is Elton, not Starkey, who is correct on the physical location of the council chamber. But it seems to me that where the council met cannot bear the polemical weight that Elton and Starkey would place upon it. After all, the old and new palaces of Westminster and Whitehall were very close, barely 200 yards apart. And more generally, even if councillors met opposite the king's privy chamber, as Starkey claims, they could still have been acting as impersonal bureaucrats; after all that a prime minister sleeps above the Cabinet Office does not make government personal, informal, medieval. It is what governments do, and how they do it, that counts. Where they do it may offer some useful clues but no more.

Starkey went on vastly to exaggerate the place of the privy chamber in politics—the influence that the small group of courtiers who held offices in the privy chamber could wield, treating the groom of the stool as the most important financial officer, treating the privy chamber as more important than the Privy Council. And that led on to a view of politics as a struggle between competing courtiers, a factional view of politics. Here Starkey joins forces with Eric Ives and many other historians. And indeed even Elton can be found espousing a factional view of politics, notably in his account of the fall of Thomas Cromwell in 1540.

How factional then was the Tudor court? Are Starkey and Ives and other historians right to see factions as central? Did high politics come to be dominated by events in the monarch's antechamber (or indeed bedchamber) on the one hand and by cliques and factions on the other, every member of the court gravitating around those with direct access to the king, exchanging personal services along the line of access? Was it courtiers and factions who ruled in Tudor England? If they did, that obviously has implications for any understanding of government, since the more that politics turns on the unpredictable outcomes of struggles between courtiers or groups of courtiers aiming to manipulate the king, the less can government be plausibly seen in terms of the administrative machinery so lovingly described by Elton, and the more important is the royal court in the sense of the place in which struggles over power were played out. If everything turned on who could bend the king's ear, then the fine details of the exchequer or the Court of General Surveyors, the signet or the great seal, seem irrelevant. 'The object of a faction', says Ives, 'was . . . to influence the king as he made his decision and hence to be rewarded with the duty to implement it. Instead of Henry VIII governing according to his own autonomous will, government emerged from the shifting political and individual context around him'. Thus what mattered was the manipulation of the king. Monarchs are seen as vulnerable in a variety of ways to such factions. 'Government policy and initiative did not arise from the monarch's executive will'; they emerged from 'the shifting political and individual context around him'. 'The more contentious the issue, the more the full battery of tactics might be tried: restricting access to the king, the claque, the innuendo, the bribe, the diversion. These brought Wolsey down, Anne Boleyn down, Cromwell down and the Howards and Gardiner'.[7]

If that were correct, then monarchs would be much less important and factional intrigue much more so; though a political world dominated by factional intrigue is a world in which power is enjoyed but momentarily, a world in which political instability is the rule. But historians have been too quick to reify their understanding of the court, to see it as an abstraction with a life of its own. Elton was briefly aware of the problem:

the court at times 'seems to be to no more than a convenient conceptual piece of shorthand, covering certain people, certain behaviour, certain attitudes'.[8] Bafflingly, Elton thought the court could not exist till 'alternative sources of political loyalty' had been destroyed and opted for the beginning of Henry VIII's reign in 1509 since before then magnates offered alternative patronage. That is wrong-headed on many counts. The English nobility, as has already been argued, was a service nobility, serving monarchs rather than conspiring against them. Only the households of brothers or uncles of monarchs had ever come close to matching the households of monarchs and even they were a long way short. Yet as overseers of the regions noblemen continued to play a vital role. Elton was on firmer ground when pointing out that the court comprised a host of grooms, pages, cooks and scullions: not everything was inherently 'political'. Courtiers were on a spectrum. Some performed essential but menial tasks but were known to the monarch and received some favours. Others were what we would see primarily as politicians but spent most of their time at court. Clearly courtiers who enjoyed access to monarchs as in the course of fulfilling their duties might attempt to exploit their position by presenting petitions for the monarch to sign and by charging their clients an appropriate fee. But it is hard to see that such practices greatly affected Tudor government. And the difficulty overall is that interpretations of government emphasising the court work only when monarchs are presented as ineffective in exercising discipline, embarrassed to be told home truths or out-argued by their councillors. If Henry VIII and Elizabeth had been as weak as that, then we would be right to focus on the court.

But Henry VIII was far more dominant than such a model would suggest, more aware of what he wanted and much more skilful in pursuing his ends than such factional interpretations allow. The life of Sir William Compton (d. 1528), groom of the stool 1509–26, is instructive. Far from being the *eminence grise* of early Tudor politics, the real power behind the throne, Compton played no significant political role. There is nothing to suggest that he had views about foreign policy or taxation or the king's divorce. What Compton did was to enrich himself, building up a landed patrimony that would be the foundation of a noble dynasty that endures to this day: the current fifth marquess of Northampton lives in Compton Wynyates, the dream early Tudor house that Sir William Compton built. In the words of Lord Herbert of Cherbury in the mid-seventeenth century, Compton was more attentive to his private profit than to the public weal.[9] Similarly, it is far more persuasive to see Cardinal Wolsey as *The King's Cardinal*, the title of Peter Gwyn's magisterial biography. It was Henry VIII who chose and promoted Wolsey as his leading minister. And their working relationship, which lasted from 1515 to 1529, was a partnership, but one in which Henry determined policy—notably war and peace and the divorce—and Wolsey dealt with daily detail, working tremendously hard. Not the least of Wolsey's functions was to serve as a sort of political lightning conductor for Henry, taking the public blame for mistaken policies such as the Amicable Grant in 1525: despite its name a demand for a huge sum of money, as we have seen. So successful was Henry in using Wolsey in this way that many historians continue to think that Henry was not involved in such important policies.

The Amicable Grant was a massive financial demand of one-sixth of every man's wealth or income, not sanctioned by parliament, and one that produced refusal and, in Lavenham and neighbouring towns in southern Suffolk and north-east Essex, a small-scale insurrection. There were various, by no means compatible, factional interpretations of the Amicable Grant. One historian held that Cardinal Wolsey deliberately sabotaged the Grant by setting it at an impossibly high rate and by provocatively threatening leading London merchants when they would not agree to it: Wolsey, on this view, was pro-peace and attempting to restrain and to undermine the bellicosity of the king. Other historians have claimed that Wolsey's supposed critics, Archbishop Warham, and the dukes of Norfolk and Suffolk, exploited the resistance to the Amicable Grant to damage Wolsey's position. But close examination shows that there were no such divisions and that there was no manipulation at the heart of government: Wolsey, Warham, Norfolk and Suffolk were working together to try to make things work. And Henry VIII, far from being manipulated, was not only very much involved in, but fully responsible for, the Amicable Grant. A chance discovery by Richard Hoyle (and published by us in *Historical Research*, 1994) of a set of instructions to the lay commissioners in Gloucestershire—presumably identical instructions were sent to commissioners in every county—proves that Henry was fully involved. The instructions name the two commissioners in Gloucestershire, 'to whom the king's highness hath *by his own mouth* in the presence of the residue of the council largely and amply spoken and declared the whole weight and importance of this matter', and going on to assure them, as they might do the people,

> that there is no thing mentioned in these instructions which hath not proceeded of the *king's own mouth* and by the deliberate and substantial advise of his whole council and not only from the king's said mouth but also from the most inward parts of his most noble heart and mind as that thing which as highly concerneth the honour of his highness and this his realm as ever did [any]thing in time of man's memory.

The commissioners were further informed both 'what sum of money must necessarily be had for maintenance and performance of the king's said intended voyage' and 'how and after what rate it will amount and be had' were decided 'after long devising and substantial debating in divers and many consultations had by the king's highness and the nobles and other of his most honourable council by great and mature deliberation upon every thing requisite and necessary to be considered in this matter'.[10] That makes it very hard to justify claims that the Amicable Grant was the work of Wolsey alone.

Wolsey fell from office in 1529. Factional historians see this as the result of a coup by his supposed enemies the dukes of Norfolk and Suffolk: it is much more likely that it was Henry VIII who was responsible. By then Henry wished to secure an annulment of his marriage to Catherine of Aragon so that he could marry Anne Boleyn. Perhaps Henry came to suspect, unfairly, that Wolsey was not wholly enthusiastic about this; more significantly still, Henry saw that to humiliate Wolsey, cardinal and papal legate, would be an excellent way of threatening the pope and intimidating churchmen in England. In other words, there is no need to invoke a factional explanation for his downfall.

That is also my view of the fall of Anne Boleyn, married to Henry in 1533, but arrested, convicted and executed for adultery with five men including incest with her brother in 1536. This has produced a full-scale historical controversy. Anne may well have been guilty of at least some of the adulteries of which she was charged, and Henry was sincerely convinced of her guilt. Anne was not, then, brought down by a political faction, whether conservative supporters of Catherine of Aragon or by Thomas Cromwell, anxious to remove an obstacle to his foreign policy or to his desire to dissolve the monasteries, as Eric Ives has successively claimed.

Most historians have assumed that Cromwell, not the king, was determining policy. That is what Elton believed too. But did Elton misunderstand the relationship between king and minister? For Elton, as we have seen, Cromwell was 'one of the most remarkable English statesmen of the sixteenth century and one of the most remarkable in the country's history', who 'instigated and in part accomplished a major and enduring transformation in virtually every aspect of the nation's public life'. Since Henry VIII, in Elton's words, had 'an unoriginal and unproductive mind', one 'unable to penetrate independently to the heart of a problem', 'the details of government, the day-to-day work of the executive, the control and reform of the administrative machine, these were in [Cromwell's] hands'. 'In Cromwell's years of power the king rarely interfered in administrative matters and . . . Cromwell, not Henry, was really the government.' Above all, Cromwell was the architect of the Tudor Revolution in Government. By and large Elton's interpretation commanded the field, owing not least to his indefatigable presentation of it over forty years.

Elton's arguments for Cromwell's role relied heavily on his reading of parliamentary drafts. But here in many ways Elton became a prisoner of his sources, as he himself momentarily recognised. 'It may be', Elton wrote, 'that Cromwell appears to dominate his age because his papers have survived.' Hastily Elton corrected himself. 'The accident of preservation ought not to be ignored, but it must not be overstressed', he insisted. 'The record . . . cannot really be suspected of serious distortion when it sets the stamp of Cromwell on nearly everything done in these ten years [the 1530s].'[11] His early articles on Cromwell's work in preparing the parliamentary statutes that gave legal sanction to the break with Rome rested on a minute scrutiny of surviving drafts of the supplication against the ordinaries, the act of appeals and other statutes. But Elton assumed, rather than proved, that the ideas expressed in these acts were Cromwell's. Just because these drafts—or more often, corrections written on to those drafts—were in Cromwell's handwriting does not prove that the ideas which they expressed were themselves devised by Cromwell.

In 1536 a law was passed by parliament that is routinely taken to be Cromwell's poor law. Yet Henry VIII was much more closely involved in the making of this law than Elton allowed. A letter by one Thomas Dorset to the mayor of Plymouth described how on Saturday [11 March] 'the king's grace came in among the burgesses of the parliament, and delivered them a bill', asking them to examine it and weigh it in conscience, 'to see if it be for a common weal to his subjects'.[12] He would come there again on the Wednesday to hear their minds. 'There shall be a proviso made for poor people', Dorset continued, 'sturdy beggars . . . shall be set at work at the king's charge'.

For Elton all this shows that Cromwell was responsible—'he mobilised Henry VIII to help through a commonwealth measure.' A more compelling reading would be that Henry was clearly taking a leading part in the parliamentary passage of what became the poor law, a crucial moment in the development of poor relief. Alasdair Hawkyard has noted 'the close involvement of, and interest shown by, Henry VIII in every stage of the assembly and proceedings of the house of commons'.[13]

Much of what was done was simply obvious and necessary, such as the administrative arrangements to deal with the monastic lands acquired by the crown. It is best to see Cromwell as the king's hard-working secretary, writing his letters,—'why keep a secretary and write letters yourself?', as Wernham wisely inquired many years ago in his review of *The Tudor Revolution in Government*—sending out his instructions, dealing in a routine executive way with a mass of day-to-day concerns, contributing, no doubt, to the working out of details, but in the end much less influential than he has been presented and probably less independent in action than Wolsey had been.

Among Cromwell's papers are notes that he regularly made of things to do. They often begin with notes in a secretary's hand: additional reminders in Cromwell's hand then follow. Much was just listed. But often Cromwell made a note of the need to know what the king wanted done. So he frequently wrote 'to know whether the king will . . .' or 'to know the king's pleasure' or 'what the king will have done with . . .'. Matters treated were important. They included dealings with foreign powers, both Henry's ambassadors abroad and foreign ambassadors in England: 'For knowledge of the king's pleasure in the points to be treated of with the ambassadors';[14] 'to speak with the king touching the duke of Bavaria's ambassador for his despatch and what shall be the effect of the king's letters that his highness will write, and what gifts he will give him'.[15] When Stephen Vaughan and Christopher Mont were negotiating with the duke of Saxony in autumn 1533 (not especially fruitfully since the duke was reluctant to add to his quarrel with Charles V by taking on Henry's cause as well), Cromwell noted: 'to know the king's pleasure whether Vaughan shall go forward or return'. In the same set of remembrances he noted: 'To declare Cristopher [Mont's] and Stephen Vaughan's letters and to know answer'.[16] That is sufficient to dispose of claims that Cromwell was masterminding a German alliance independently of the king. Henry's attitude would appear to be crucial and Cromwell emerges as the executor of the king's wishes. Strategic decisions were clearly the king's: 'what order the king's highness will take if the Scots do not sue for peace after this truce and abstinence of war and what provisions shall be made in that behalf by cause the truce lacketh but a year.'[17]

Several remembrances refer to Elizabeth Barton, the nun of Kent, who prophesied doom for the king if he married Anne Boleyn. 'To know what the king will have done with the Nun and her accomplices';[18] 'what shall be the king's pleasure for sending the Nun to Canterbury and whether she shall return';[19] 'to know whether the king will have all the rest of the monks and friars [involved with the nun of Kent] sent for',[20] 'to know what way the king will take with all the said malefactors'. In 1535 Cromwell's notes, in a set of 'remembrances at my next going to the courte', included the following: 'to advertise the king of the ordering of Master Fisher [John Fisher, bishop of Rochester]'; 'to know his pleasure touching Master [Thomas] More and to declare the opinion of the judges'; 'whether Master Fisher shall go to execution, with also the other'; 'when shall be done farther touching Master More'.[21] The remembrances included religious matters: 'first touching the anabaptists and what the king will do with them';[22] 'to know the king's pleasure for Tyndale, and whether I shall write or not';[23] 'for the convocation of the clergy and what shall be the kings pleasure therein'.[24] More general policy questions and practical decisions also occur: 'to know the king's pleasure touching a general pardon';[25] 'to know what the king's pleasure shall be for such persons as be outlawed in all shires of this realm and what process shall be made against them';[26] 'to know the king's pleasure when he will have musters of his gunners'; 'general musters to be made through the realm if so shall stand with the king's pleasure'[27]. If Cromwell was making decisions and ruling the country himself, he would not have made such notes. There would have been no point in reminding himself of the need to find out the king's pleasure. These remembrances strongly suggest that the minister did not act before knowing what the king wanted. They show that the king was very much in command and that Cromwell referred constantly to him on any questions that needed judgement. Henry was asked to decide who should go abroad and when, to say at what moment ambassadors should be brought to see him and to determine what answers should be made to letters, messages and requests from abroad. Henry was asked for instructions on how the principal opponents of the king's policies—the Nun of Kent, More, Fisher—should be dealt with. The strong impression is of a minister doing the daily executive work of government, drawing his master's attention to the need to fill vacant posts but asking the king for guidance on how to act in all issues of importance. There is no sense whatsoever here of a minister acting on his own initiative, or manipulating his master, or making substantial suggestions to the king, or trying to temper the king's proposals. Government was thus the king's. England was a monarchy in fact as well as in name. Yet Elton's vision of Cromwell's supposed revolution in government constantly plays down Henry's role. Intriguingly, David Starkey, long a vigorous proponent of a factional reading of the politics of Henry VIII's reign, has in recent years been taking a view much closer to mine. At a conference at Hampton Court Palace in July 2009, Starkey noted my presence in the audience of his lecture and, referring to the break with Rome and what followed, declared that 'yes, it was the *King's Reformation*'—alluding to my book. Most recently when interviewed by *BBC History Magazine*, Starkey remarked, 'I wonder whether we have powerfully underestimated Henry VIII as a political operator.'[28] He went on to add:

> We've been taught to regard the king as tempestuous, babyish, self-indulgent—Donald Trump-like. Well there were aspects of Henry like that but when it came to the pursuit of a strategic goal, I think it would have been difficult to have operated more impressively.

This view is a thousand miles away from that of Sir Geoffrey Elton's characterisation of Henry as 'a bit of a booby, a bit of a baby'. It is also a long way from the view of Henry VIII that Starkey put forward in *Henry VIII: Personalities and Politics* in 1985.

8

Enforcement, dissent and rebellion

Thus far much attention has been paid to government at the centre: the monarchy, the royal court, the Privy Council, the central administration, especially the administration of finance. Taxation and military organisation have been considered very much from the perspective of rulers seeking to raise armies and the revenues to pay for them. And Elton's grand claims for a Tudor Revolution in Government focus on the centre. Yet government is not just about rulers—whether kings or their ministers—making decisions. Government also crucially involves enforcement. In any evaluation of government, looking at how far governments succeeded in enforcing their policies and in imposing their demands is crucial.

Tudor monarchs did not command a standing army. They did not control a police force. Thus what Tudor monarchs could routinely do by using or threatening force was limited. They enjoyed a measure of coercive authority, but they could not rule by force alone. There was no network of full-time salaried local officials appointed by Tudor monarchs. Thus monarchs and their councillors could give orders, but would they be obeyed? Monarchs inherited a complex body of laws and they could attempt to make new laws. There were well-established courts of law and professional judges. But how would offenders be found, how would they be brought before the courts? That at once leads on to consideration of the relationships between kings and counsellors on the one hand and those who implemented policies locally on the other. In this respect noblemen were, as we have already seen, highly important as regional supervisors, their position formalised in the post of lords lieutenant in the later sixteenth century. But what of those below the nobility in the social hierarchy?

Monarchs appointed a sheriff in every county as an unpaid representative responsible for overseeing the collection of royal revenues, the mustering of soldiers, the administration and execution of justice locally, holding courts, executing writs—that is to say instructions from the central courts—and acting as returning officer in parliamentary elections. Sheriffs were often portrayed as villains in popular literature, accused of partiality and corruption in parliaments, and the inability of successive monarchs to prevent this has been seen by some historians as a serious weakness in English government, though others have questioned the objectivity of such evidence. From the mid-fourteenth century sheriffs were joined, and in many ways superseded, by the justices of the peace, but sheriffs continued to fulfil their legal roles, receiving and forwarding as appropriate thousands of writs annually. They tended to be most effective and most successful when the monarch was strong and vigorous in ruling.[1]

By the sixteenth century the crucial position was that of justice of the peace. JPs were appointed from the greater gentry—men with lands worth £20 or more yearly—in every county. They met together regularly at the quarter sessions held in the county town. Formally they were all equals, working collegially. Formally they heard and determined—dealt with—felonies (serious crimes) and trespasses (such as unlawful occupation of land or property) committed against the peace, and they meted out reasonable punishment according to the law. They dealt with straightforward offenders, such as those who robbed, committed less serious assaults or behaved in a disorderly way. They had the power to pursue and arrest and imprison wrongdoers. In this they did not usually act as modern policemen or detectives: rather, they responded to information brought to their attention, by parish constables or by paid informers.

If any man occupied another man's property by force, JPs, 'after they be complained unto', were to go with the power of the shire and commit them to the nearest gaol. If there was a riot or unlawful assembly, JPs, together with the sheriff or under-sheriff, should take such power as would be necessary to arrest the rioters. They were expected to deal with murders, including murder by poisoning, and manslaughter. Rape fell within their purview. They dealt with robbery, theft, arson and burglary. They referred more serious crimes to the monarch's assize judges to deal with on their twice-yearly visits.

JPs were expected to raise money to pay for gaols. They were to deal with broken bridges, organised their repair. They were to see that highways were in good shape. They carried out a range of administrative tasks. They licensed alehouses. They set local wage rates. At the two sessions between Easter and Michaelmas, they were to use their discretion if there was a dearth of victuals and make proclamation how much a mason, a carpenter, a tiler and other craftsmen, workmen and labourers should be paid by the day. Where statutes laid down which days and hours they should work, ensuring that what was prescribed was enforced fell within the responsibilities of the JPs. They investigated vagrants and dealt with them. They dealt with unlicensed beggars (a matter to which we shall return when we consider poverty). They bound men over for good behaviour. JPs were expected to arrest suspected heretics. They were expected to investigate fairs kept in churches. They were to take action over the counterfeiting of coins. Again and again statutes—laws—were passed which JPs were expected to enforce. JPs were expected to inquire into the quality of work done by tanners, blacksmiths and clothmakers. Victuallers—selling food—should have 'but reasonable gain'; if they did not, they should be punished at the discretion of the JPs. JPs were to watch that weights and measures were uniform. Moreover, JPs were the figures of authority to whom anyone with a grievance or a problem could appeal: JPs often dealt informally with a range of such matters. They reported to royal ministers—to Thomas Cromwell, to William Cecil, Lord Burghley—on all sorts of problems, from serious local disputes to issues arising from the implementation of government orders. If special needs arose, such as a grant of taxation, the JPs would very likely find themselves serving as commissioners. But it is interesting here to note that when some matter of special importance or sensitivity arose, such as the General Proscription of 1522, Wolsey's great survey of wealth and income, or the attempt to secure an Amicable

Grant in 1525, monarchs often used temporary commissions that included noblemen rather than relying on JPs alone. Overall, the inescapable impression is of just how many and how varied the tasks of JPs were and how overwhelming the demands on them may have been. One can only guess that while, like modern local councils, they did do a great deal, they could not do everything, and some of what was required of them was left undone.[2]

JPs were technically appointed by the Lord Chancellor, the king's chief legal officer. But, in practice, how much choice did governments have? In any county there were only so many gentlemen with the leisure and means to take on what was an onerous activity. Many JPs must in effect have selected themselves for service: the largest landowners could scarcely be omitted. Indeed, provision was made that men worth less than £20 yearly could be named as JPs if there were not sufficient men worth £20. There does not seem to be much evidence to support the notion that court faction spilled over into the localities: indeed a study of Edward VI's reign offers a rebuttal.[3] JPs were not paid, though their expenses when they attended the assizes were in effect refunded. If the largest landowners were named time and again, among the rest there was quite a turnover. The government would try to find able and competent gentlemen fit to serve. William Cecil kept lists of likely JPs. There are signs in the mid-1530s and in Elizabeth's reign that the central government did not appoint or reappoint those whose religious convictions were seen as out of line with government policy. But even in religion the government would find it hard to insist to total conformity, for example in counties such as Cumberland or Sussex in which Catholic sympathies remained strong throughout Elizabeth's reign. When in the 1570s Richard, bishop of Chichester, summoned thirty-five gentry whom he suspected of being crypto-Catholics, three protested to the Council, and Curteys appears to have apologised. Historians have often tried to interpret changes in the composition of county benches as factional or political, but it is hard to substantiate such explanations. And perhaps the turnover of names reflects less suspicions by governments of disloyalty or local factional strife than the sheer burdens of the office; many gentlemen would accept the burdens for a limited tour of duty but would not wish to serve continuously and permanently.

Among the roles of the JPs was to supervise the parish constables, two for each parish, chosen annually by the parish. Constables dealt with minor offences in their village: they could put offenders in the stocks. They searched out wrongdoers, reporting those accused of more serious crimes to the JPs and presenting them to the quarter sessions for punishment. Literary sources, notably Shakespeare, are less than flattering about the work of constables: historians who have painstakingly studied the administrative records are much more impressed by their constant and detailed attention to their duties. What is intriguing is the involvement of significant numbers below the level of JPs and town magistrates in some aspect of local administration. A significant proportion of the inhabitants of any parish would at some point in their lives serve as constables.[4] Similarly each parish had two lay churchwardens. In the towns especially there was a plethora of minor offices. One in ten of the population of London was at some point an office-holder. Up to the reign of Edward VI in many towns there were gilds and fraternities whose principal purpose was religious but whose members were not only engaged in defending the interests of particular crafts and trades but also involved in what can reasonably be termed local government. All that meant that 'government' was not something alien to those not in the political elite: in important ways, and for significant periods of time, many such people were involved in the daily running of their villages, churches and towns.

It has even been suggested that a village assembly in Swallowfield set up a series of subordinate assemblies. 'We will be esteemed to be men of discretion, good credit, honest minds and Christian like behaviour, one towards another in the name of God', the villagers declared.[5] The role of such village assemblies was not to make policy, and often they simply responded to orders, sometimes orders that they cannot much have liked (such as removing images from churches or levying taxes), but broadly they conformed and did the tasks required of them. In myriad smaller matters, they obviously exercised a measure of power themselves. We simply lack information, but it is plausible that there was what could be called 'a politics of the parish'. Much of that might be exerted over their neighbours, enforcing standards of sexual morality or reproving drunkenness, for example. Alison Wall has observed, perhaps extravagantly: 'there were people on the ground everywhere to monitor what was happening and crucially with the power to take action if anything was amiss: little brother was watching you.' Paul Griffiths emphasises how the poor were scrutinised and controlled by urban institutions. But that emphasis on 'the official surveillance system' is overdone.[6] More plausibly it was the unavoidable need to organise daily and annual activities that imposed scrutiny. The agricultural year created its own demands: the common fields needed to be managed. Manorial courts remained integral to local government.[7] So did the liturgical year. And taxes, when demanded, had to be paid over and managed. This was a complex and sophisticated society: 'free riders' (in modern terminology) who accepted the benefits but avoided the costs were especially unpopular. What gave English society its depth was the larger involvement of men in the administration of the villages and towns in which they lived, an involvement that went back a long way. We know little in detail about how such men were chosen and exactly by whom, but it is not fanciful to see the emergence and development of civil society here and that may well have mattered much more in the sixteenth century than any study of ancient Roman history. The village of Swallowfield was remarkable. Most of it was in Berkshire but three parts were detached portions of Wiltshire and that might explain the setting up of subordinate assemblies. Yet there were active groups to be found in other towns and villages. As we have repeatedly seen, there were large numbers of offices to be held at relatively low levels of society. But we need to strike a balance between seeing such office-holders as exercising power and as simply obeying instructions.

How effective was this system of government? Did kings and ministers find JPs and constables loyal, willing and conscientious executors of their instructions? Or did JPs and constables largely ignore what the central government demanded and simply run things in their own interests? Was this a remarkably effective and (from the central government's point of view) cheap system of government (since JPs and constables served unpaid)? Or did it leave kings and ministers at the mercy of their leading local subjects, who simply ignored any instructions they did not like? Would a system of crown appointees, paid a salary and with no local ties to the areas in which they served, have worked better? Or was the very rootedness of JPs and constables in their own local societies a source of great strength for the king?

JPs and constables were not free to ignore and disregard instructions from the centre. If they were largely left alone, it is because they did what they were expected to do. If they ignored or refused to obey royal and conciliar commands, that would sooner or later come to light. My impression of the 1530s is that most JPs were very ready to do government's bidding and in particular to enforce the break with Rome. I would endorse Simon Walker's conclusion from an earlier period that JPs 'considerably increased the ability of the royal administration to enforce its will in the localities'.[8] For the later sixteenth century, there are far more surviving sources, especially collections of gentry correspondence, and these show JPs working very conscientiously.

What strikes me is that there was a sense of community, of common interest, between the king and his ministers at the centre and the noblemen and greater gentlemen in the localities. The king and his ministers sent out orders—indeed—but they were obeyed because those who received them expected to obey them, seeing that as their role and function. That is not to say that they would have slavishly done something wicked or something absurd, but that their working presumption was that the king's government was for the good of the realm. Much of what they were asked to report on or to do did not after all directly affect their own interests. Noblemen and gentlemen grew up in a monarchical society: they would have seen the monarch's palaces, surpassing the houses of noblemen in number and scale and opulence; in learning the history of the realm, they would have heard about great monarchs of the past; at church they would have heard much that declared the authority of monarchs as God's lieutenants. They would have absorbed a sense of duty: that their social standing was justified by the service that they performed to those it was their role to rule. And what they did, in performance of their duties, often went beyond the call of duty, and what they would have done if simple self-interest accounted for all their actions. Moreover, they would not have seen themselves as distinct from the 'government', the 'centre': they were themselves in a real sense part of that government. This was what A.B. White, writing about the first quarter of the thirteenth century and referring to the extent to which Englishmen in the shires were compelled to take part, called 'self-government at the king's command'.[9]

Moreover governments worked hard to inform and to justify. They did not just send out instructions. Royal proclamations—437 under Henry VIII, 382 under Elizabeth, to be read out at market crosses—explained and defended royal policies: why the king was going to war, why taxation was being raised, why such and such religious measures were being taken. Acts of parliaments included substantial preambles, explaining and justifying the laws they declared. Circular letters to JPs were common. Parliaments were in a sense occasions at which the king and his leading counsellors would inform representatives of the political nation of what they wanted and needed. Sometimes, if the need were pressing, the king summoned ad hoc groups of gentry to court to hear royal justification, as over the Amicable Grant of 1525, when the king presented his policy 'by his own mouth'. The aim was to reassure the gentry that what was being done was necessary and worthwhile. True, governments could also coerce. JPs and town magistrates who did not do what they were asked to do could find themselves reprimanded, even summoned before the king's council. Of course, such coercion could not be deployed on a large scale. The king could punish a handful of JPs, but not most of them: the king needed JPs, and in any county there were only a small number of men who were in a position to serve. Since, however, there was in practice a strong sense of community between king and gentry, what might strike us as a potentially awkward relationship did not in fact cause many problems in practice.

More effective than coercion was monitoring. Governments were regularly asking JPs to report on what they had been doing. Special commissioners could be sent out to check local arrangements. And JPs did not act in isolation: noblemen, clergy, townsmen, parish constables could in different ways report and complain if a JP was in some way failing in his responsibilities. Tudor society was complex and sophisticated: JPs were part of an interlocking system. Governments might also seek to reward, by grants of patronage. Clearly the monarch was at the centre of a network of patronage. Monarchs could make outright gifts. They could offer leases of crown lands at below market rents. They appointed to a vast number of offices, many of them involving routine duties that the recipient of royal patronage might delegate to a deputy while pocketing half the proceeds. Simply naming a local gentleman a JP conferred a measure of status. But that there was sufficient patronage available to the crown to buy the loyalty of the whole political nation is very doubtful. Only a few courtier-administrators could hope to amass grants sufficient to serve as the basis of a landed patrimony. And many of the offices to which the crown appointed were real jobs-of-work: even if recipients found deputies to do them, they were nonetheless formally answerable and would not wish for things to go wrong.

When urban history became a fashionable area of inquiry, historians (not least those with a sociological bent) tended to write about those who ruled towns in terms of oligarchy—that a small group dominated urban government and perpetuated its power over the generations. In a similar vein it was often held that monarchs effectively controlled towns by striking bargains with the leading citizens. Royal charters protected the economies of towns from competition from outside and allegedly reinforced oligarchic rule. Colin Philipps cut through such theorising. In a world of low expectancy of life, even among the affluent, oligarchic rule in the sense of a son succeeding his father was demographically all but impossible. Few leading merchants would be succeeded by a son and almost none by a grandson. Thus urban society was not dominated by— could not be dominated by—a closed elite based on a handful of families. Historians should be wary of lazily using 'oligarchy' as a label and as an explanation. Surely, men did not rise up from the dust in early modern towns, but the ruling elites were much more open and necessarily compelled to recruit from a larger pool of townsmen than the fashionable claims of 'oligarchy' allowed. But clearly there were communities of interest between monarchs and those who ruled the towns. London was exceptional in its population—over 100,000 by the end of the sixteenth century—and in its wealth. Most of the international trade of England went through London.

All this suggests that governments largely got what they sought. But how far were the policies that Tudor kings and their leading counsellors pursued themselves the product of negotiation and consultation between crown and its leading subjects? How far were parliaments in many ways a reflection of just such negotiation and consultation? How were local rulers—JPs, town magistrates, parish constables—engaged in a continuous and continuing process of negotiation? How far is it convincing to say that country gentlemen 'not only responded to, but themselves shaped, the demands of government'?[10] Is it fair to say with John Watts that 'political integration ... arises from below, as well as from above: it cannot be imposed by authorities, however powerful; it is always the product of some kind of negotiation between interests groups, including the various governments'?[11] At a very basic level, there is something in this. Tudor monarchs grasped that there were limits to what they could demand. They broadly accepted the convention that taxation had to be granted by parliament—that is to say agreed to by the political nation represented in parliament—and they did not insist that parliaments consented to hugely high levels of taxation. Tudor governments made little attempt to circumvent the constitutional conventions relating to taxation. A more plausible case could be made that the under-assessments of wealth and income under Elizabeth should be seen as a kind of 'negotiation' with the government. From 1563 assessments of wealth were no longer made on oath; assessments steadily declined, not least in relation to inflation. But perhaps 'negotiation' is too strong and purposeful a term here. Governments were, as we have seen, nonetheless securing large sums in taxation, notably in the 1590s, and that mattered more to them than the fairness of the assessments. Undoubtedly, many of their leading subjects disliked precise assessments being made of their wealth; Elizabeth's governments were ready to go along with this, rather than impose more rigorous monitoring, since, given that parliaments agreed to multiple subsidies, not just one, monarchs did receive large sums. Yet it is not so much that Elizabeth's governments engaged in negotiation or bargaining; it is rather that they took the view that taxation was better raised in much the way it had been rather than embark on systematic reform. Still, it is fair to argue that taxation always involved a measure of negotiation or bargaining over rates and terms.

It is harder, however, to claim that the Tudor monarchs' (very different) religious policies were much open to 'negotiation'. Henry VIII insisted absolutely upon his break with Rome and on his supremacy over the church. On that issue no compromise was possible. Brutally tough measures were taken against those who would not acquiesce. Those who would not conform risked imprisonment and death. Oaths were imposed on every adult male in 1534: refusal was treason. No negotiation was possible. J.M. Gray accepts that this was true for the Carthusian monks but claims that persecuted evangelicals could secure substantial concessions, including the content and terms of the oaths.[12] But that proves, rather than disproves, my point. Henry VIII's primary concern was his royal supremacy and the break with Rome. On that, to repeat, no negotiation was possible. Evangelicals, while in danger of falling into heresy, did at least support Henry over the break with Rome. Moreover evangelicals were asked to swear as part of the legal proceedings against them when they were tried for heresy. Henry VIII's oaths relating to his royal supremacy were imposed on everyone.

Andy Wood has highlighted one of a number of disaffected men in Walsingham, Norfolk. 'There was precious little negotiation going on', Wood rightly notes, 'as Ralph Rogerson's "cankrede" words were choked off in Norwich marketplace in May 1537.' We do not know what, 'according to his cankered stomach', Rogerson said just before his life was halted by the hangman's noose. But earlier, Rogerson, a yeoman farmer, also employed as a lay chorister at Walsingham Priory, had complained against the dissolution of the monasteries and urged that 'when these men [the king's commissioners] shall come to put down the abbeys some must step to and resist them and I will assay to get them company for that purpose' and then 'come up to the king to complain'. Any such complaints against the dissolution of the monasteries were most uncompromisingly received by Henry VIII.[13]

When Edward VI's government required churchwardens to take down images and rood screens, no 'negotiation' was allowed. Those in positions of local responsibility who acquiesced in such religious changes did so from a mixture of motives. Some may genuinely have been persuaded by the government's propaganda or, more likely, have already encountered protestant teaching and found it spoke to them. Some were careerists, won over by hopes of profit and advancement; some felt a deeply ingrained sense of loyalty to the crown; some accepted that policy making was properly the king's; some were surely aware that disobedience risked punishment; and some were fearful. Up to a point, there might be some scope left for local inaction at least, but not much. Elizabeth's government was, it seems to me, much less intrusive in religious matters. Open Catholic worship was proscribed (and many Jesuit missionary priests would be executed for treason); vigorous campaigning for a more fully Protestant Church was also squashed (including Archbishop Grindal whom Elizabeth suspended from his duties when he refused to stop encouraging clerical prophesyings). But that still left a good deal of space for a variety of interpretations of the Elizabethan religious settlement, its various elaborations soaked in ambiguity. Yet that was not exactly 'negotiation'. Michael Braddick claimed that 'the settlement, like most policies, was the product of negotiation between a number of interests in the light of a number of political opinions'[14] but that fails to convince because the religious settlement largely reflected Elizabeth's own preferences, except where, on specific matters, she had to yield to those in parliament, both the Lords and the Commons, who would not accept what the queen sought. That, despite Elizabeth's preferences, unreformed Catholicism survived, and both reformed Catholicism and Puritanism spread, does not 'reflect ... a failure of enforcement'.[15] The term 'failure' is ambiguous. It can mean trying to do something but not succeeding in one's aim. But failure can also mean not trying to do something very hard, or at all, and so consequently not achieving it. Elizabeth did not try at all hard to crush Catholicism and Puritanism. Of course, Elizabeth's reluctance to enforce her preferences directly with the greatest rigour may reflect a realistic assessment of what her chances of success would have been, and a calculation that indirect methods would be preferable to open confrontation. Yet that is hardly to be described as 'negotiation' or bargaining: Elizabeth was simply making her own calculations, given the circumstances in which she operated, of what would work best.

'Negotiation' was more plausible on matters on which the monarch had no obvious personal interest. The wide-ranging measures to relieve poverty enacted and developed in late Tudor England were largely based on local initiatives, as we shall see, showing that those who ruled in the localities enjoyed a measure of autonomy in the ways in which they responded to the problems they encountered, and that the central government could respond favourably and creatively to such local solutions.

Dissent

Yet while generally people did comply; nonetheless, there were dissenters of various kinds. How far did Tudor governments face dissent or public opposition to war? What did people think of war? If there was no public outcry against war, if in a monarchical and hierarchical society the common people were not consulted on the merits of war, there was nonetheless at least some disquiet. The Sarum rite, the most common liturgy, included a prayer for peace in our time in the canon of the mass, and English instructions at the bidding of the beads to pray for 'the unity and peace of all Christian realms and in especially for the good state, peace and tranquillity of this realm of England' and for 'peace both on land and water', sometimes even 'for the peace of these lands England and France, that God make perpetual peace betwixt them'.[16] The implication is that peace is the ideal. Cranmer's first English Prayerbook in 1549 used collects for peace at every matins and evensong and prayed at matins: 'Give peace in our time, O Lord/Because there is none other that fighteth for us, but only thou O God.' A remark reported to Thomas Cromwell in 1539 hinted at hesitations. Men say nothing against the king's acts so long as peace followeth; but when it was said that we should have war, people were uneasy, saying God have mercy upon us all. Edmund Dudley, previously Henry VII's councillor, noted that war was 'a great consumer of treasure and riches' and that there are 'many ways to enter it, and the beginning seems a great pleasure, but the way is very narrow to come honourably out thereof'.[17] Cautiously discussing the case for intervention in Scotland at the end of 1559, Sir Nicholas Bacon, Lord Keeper, noted[18]

> the unwillingness that . . . the greater part of all the estates of this realm have to make war by invasion. And the cause is the ill fruits that they daily see war bringeth forth. It is evident to their eyes that it brings and breeds spoil and slaughter of innocents, overcomes all laws, and fills the realm full of felonies, burglaries and robberies . . . when men remember what famine, penury and misery have ever followed wars in time of plenty, is it any marvel though in this time of scarcity of money, men and friendship, they be unwilling to make war.

In *Utopia* Thomas More bitterly satirised monarchical devotion to winning glory in war.[19] Shakespeare's *Henry V* can be seen as subverting the heroic image of the warrior Henry V as model ruler. Shakespeare casts doubt on the justification of Henry's war against the French: bishops supported it to draw his attention away from their vast landed endowments; his father urged his son to fight abroad to avoid aristocratic disorders at home. And when on the eve of battle Henry wanders incognito among his forces, Williams, the Welsh soldier, bluntly tells him that 'If the cause be not good, the king himself hath heavy reckoning to make, when all those legs and arms and heads chopped off in a battle shall join together cry out all "we died at such a place"', a charge that the king never answers.[20]

But there was no sustained objection to war in our period. Tudor military and naval campaigns were relatively infrequent. By and large they were, if not wholly successful, then at least not disastrous failures to be blamed on incompetent monarchs and corrupt commanders (should the 1512 campaign be seen as coming close?[21]). Tudor parliaments were not arenas of angry protests against war. Of course, when war came, it was the common people who primarily bore the brunt—injuries and death in battle, vulnerability of soldiers to infectious diseases, civilians pillaged, women raped, soldiers readjusting awkwardly to peace. And, as we have seen, it was not the common people who were present in parliaments. This, too, was a society used to force and bloodshed. Husbands beat their wives, fathers beat their children, heads of households beat their servants. Bears were baited, cocks encouraged to fight. Deer were hunted. Men were armed and drunken quarrels readily turned to violence. War appeared banal, commonplace. And for some war was an adventure, as we have seen.

From time to time, parliaments, as we have already noted, were the arena of debate and dissent on other matters. Though our knowledge of the parliaments of Henry VIII's reign is very limited (the sources are meagre), there was clearly (as we have seen) hard bargaining over taxation in 1523 and some bold individuals spoke out against the break with Rome in the 1530s. In Elizabeth's reign—for which the sources are much richer—we know that from the 1570s there was something of a campaign, never successful, but nonetheless recurring, to reform the church in a more protestant direction.

And occasionally—very occasionally—in the Tudor century, there were full-scale rebellions that directly challenged royal policy. In 1525, there was effective refusal of the Amicable Grant, a huge financial demand not sanctioned in parliament and intended to finance an invasion of France. Enforcement was placed in the hands of two commissioners in each county, often noblemen and bishops; refusal was widespread at every social level below that of the political elite. There was something approaching a popular rising in and around Lavenham, Suffolk: weavers, labourers, artisans, fearing the effects on local employment in the cloth industry if the rich clothiers had to make huge payments, angrily demonstrated. The dukes of Norfolk and Suffolk managed to face them down, persuading them to go home. But Henry VIII then abandoned the financial demand. Peter Gwyn has argued that the king had never seriously intended to invade France and that this financial demand was simply intended to impress the Emperor Charles V, but there would have been other ways of impressing him than making a huge and predictably unpopular financial demand. And if Henry really meant it but decided not to press it home, then that reveals Tudor government at its most ambitious (a huge financial demand, and attempted without parliamentary consent, so potentially setting a precedent for royal taxation at will) and its least effective (because it failed). Maybe Henry could have pressed on, and secured the money, at the price of imprisoning refusers and of raising constitutional issues: Henry chose not to, maybe partly because the chances of an invasion of France were receding as the emperor's reluctance became ever more obvious. That qualification highlights complexities of passing judgement on the strength of governments: but overall the Amicable Grant does seem to me to lay bare the limits of royal power.[22]

In 1536 there were a series of rebellions in the north of England. From October to December, and beyond, the king's writ did not run there, as some 30,000 men were up in arms. The rebels did not see themselves as rebels, of course; they saw the king as misled by evil councillors (naming Cromwell and Cranmer among others) and called on him to change his policies. In a sense they were offering the king advice—counsel—and emphasising the strength of their feelings by their armed assemblies. And, by blaming Cromwell and Cranmer, they offered the king a way out should he have wished one. The difficulty of judging what this rebellion shows about the strength or weakness of Henry's government is that exactly what the rebellions were about, and who first started and then led them, have been matters of heated controversy. If, with Geoffrey Elton, you see the rebellions as stirred up by dissident noblemen Lords Hussey and Darcy, angry that they had lost favour at court, then you will see it as one of the last doomed throws of a supposedly declining nobility and consequently see the failure of the rebellion as revealing the growing strengths of the central government. If, with Michael Bush, you see the rebellions as a protest against taxation and in particular the introduction in 1534 of a new principle of peacetime taxation, then you will rather see the rebellions as highlighting the weaknesses of the king's government.

Neither reading persuades me: the risings were not essentially over taxation, which continued to be for the costs of war and defence, and which in 1536 affected only a very small number of the rich; nor were the risings the work of Lords Hussey and Darcy, who were first-generation peers unable to raise large armies, but rather that of people below the political elite; Darcy, like a great many other northern noblemen and gentlemen, was compelled by armed crowds of commons to join in the rebellion; Hussey fled from his house in Sleaford for fear that the commons would seize him. The threat of force was real. Sir William Sandon was one of the Lincolnshire JPs engaged in levying taxation. The commons 'took and swore him whether he would or no . . . one of the rebellious . . . said he should go on foot as they did, and so they carried him forth the space of half a mile by the arms for half an hour towards Horncastle till he was for heat and weariness almost overcome'. Gentlemen did not walk in the sixteenth century, they rode. This could not have been more pointed.[23] That large numbers of northerners demonstrated against royal policy vividly shows the limits to royal power. What in my view they were protesting against were the religious policies Henry had followed since he sought an annulment of his first marriage to Catherine of Aragon: the break with Rome, the royal supremacy, the dissolution of the smaller monasteries, changes in long-established patterns of worship and fears that still more radical change, including the confiscation of processional crosses and the wholesale closure of parish churches, was in the offing. So passionately provoked did people feel that they gathered together in large numbers and overwhelmed local noblemen, JPs and urban magistrates, who were powerless to resist them, impotence exacerbated by the fact that many of the political elite felt as uneasy about royal religious policy as did the commons.

How was the rebellion defeated, and what does that say about the nature of government and royal power? First, some noblemen, notably, as we have seen, George Talbot, fourth earl of Shrewsbury, whose estates were centred on Sheffield, mobilised his forces against the rebels: that prevented the rebellion from spreading further south. Secondly, outside the north, the nobility remained loyal to the king and in particular the duke of Norfolk raised forces at the king's command and joined with Shrewsbury to confront them. Thirdly, Norfolk, on Henry's behalf (but accepted only with great reluctance by the king) made a deal with the rebels. Not only would they be pardoned for any offences but a parliament would be held in York at which they could speak their minds freely: and till parliament met, abbeys would stand. Fourthly, Henry and Norfolk then exploited the dispersal of the commons: no such parliament was ever called, and soon the dissolution of the monasteries resumed. Noblemen and gentlemen, caught unprepared by the outbreak of rebellion in autumn 1536, were now more attentive; and when small-scale risings flared up, they were quickly and bloodily put down. Writing of France, Peter Lewis remarked that 'peasant movements were not, in the later middle ages, serious political things'.[24] It is easy, nonetheless, to imagine alternative scenarios in which Henry's throne would have seemed less secure. Faced with protests against the Amicable Grant in 1525, Charles Brandon, duke of Suffolk, wished to attack and destroy them. But Thomas Howard, third duke of Norfolk, would not agree because 'the serving men and tenants had let drop many words which showed their reluctance to fight against their kindred and companions who, they deemed, were suffering from utter injustice'.[25] Norfolk and George Talbot, fourth earl of Shrewsbury, would twice make deals with rebels in 1536 because they were outnumbered and because they feared that their men would not fight the rebels.[26] What the Pilgrimage of Grace reveals are the complexities of power. Henry was a dominant ruler. The break with Rome and the declaration of the royal supremacy was a bold step. The dissolution of the smaller monasteries and the changes in worship in 1536 were again strikingly radical. Many of the king's subjects did not want them. Henry achieved his ends by his political skills: initial caution gave way to bold assertions; consent was demanded from the political nation in parliament and his subjects in general through the swearing of oaths; ruthless pressures were exerted against those who did not conform. Until the rebellions, Henry prevented any grand outburst of disaffection; he then rode out the rebellions by a mixture of force, deceit and luck. It was not the structures of government and administration—certainly not any Eltonian Tudor Revolution in Government— that saved Henry's throne; but rather the king's political skills and ruthlessness, the active loyalty of a key nobleman, the earl of Shrewsbury; the devious forcefulness of another, the duke of Norfolk. The strength of government is not a given, not something that grows steadily: it is rather something that is related to the dynamics of politics, something that ebbs and flows. Rebellions were both unlikely to succeed, but also, dangerously, because unpredictably, threatening—paradoxes of power indeed.

Rebellions are inherently fascinating and reveal much about the workings of government that is usually hidden. But focussing on rebellions may give a misleading impression. So unequal was Tudor society by modern standards that it is surprising that there were not more popular rebellions and riots. In the mid-century there was a good deal of contemporary awareness of the plight of the commons and commentators urged monarchs and councillors to alleviate the lot of the poor. Edward Seymour, Protector Somerset, appears to have shown a remarkable sympathy. It is likely that the lot of the poor was at its worst in the mid-1590s. Yet there was no popular rising in that decade. Why did the commons not rebel against their lot? Why were there not more risings such as Ket's rebellion in 1549, provoked by a range of social and agrarian grievances and directed against exploitative gentry?

Before answering that question we should note a recent interjection that denies the premiss and asserts that there were in fact more risings than those highlighted and discussed in textbooks: the Cornish rising of 1497, the Amicable Grant in 1525, the Pilgrimage of Grace in 1536, the south-western rising and Ket's rebellion in 1549, Wyatt's rebellion in 1554 and the northern rising in 1569. In York, it is suggested, with the implication that York's experience was typical, there were riots over the election of the mayor in 1489, 1504, 1516–17, enclosure riots in 1484, 1486, 1492, 1494, 1534 and 1536 and two uprisings against the city's rulers in 1504 and 1529. Escalating tensions in the 1480s and 1490s led in particular to a great riot in 1504 when some 3,000 people imprisoned the mayor and town council in the Guildhall and compelled them to do their bidding, releasing them only once they had agreed to the rebels' demands. Yet the argument here is forced. None of these amounted to a rebellion. The near-annual riots over common rights eventually prompted Henry VII to summon the mayor and leading citizens to Greenwich. There the king gave them an ultimatum. 'I may not see the city go in utter ruin and decay in default of you that should rule, for rather of necessity I must and will put in other rulers that will rule and govern the city according to my laws.' And these enclosure riots ceased.[27] The course of a rebellion would have been very different. What we are dealing with here are not rebellions, but rather demonstrations in defence of specific rights. Of course, they might have escalated into rebellion, for example if outrageous force was used against them, but that these demonstrators were very much part of the government of York, often members of craft gilds, and that the riot of 1504 was characterised by carefully directed actions, drawing on conventions of collective assembly and petitioning, again suggests that here we are dealing with bargaining rather than incipient rebellion.[28]

Another recent inquiry has proposed, counter-intuitively, that far from being destructive, rebellions were part of the natural order. P. Lantschner, looking at Florence in 1378 and Tournai in 1420, sees rebellion 'as intensification of existing processes of negotiation that were ordinarily taking place around the multiple nodes and layers of the city's political structure'; 'revolts were an intrinsic part of a political order in which conflict ... was not the subversion but the essence, of politics'. Yet is it not the case that substantial revolts occurred when customary processes of negotiation broke down and when those revolting sought to use force, or the threat of force, to prevent unwelcome impositions and charges?[29] A similar objection can be made to the suggestion that 'conflict arose not from the commons' exclusion from power but from their inclusion within the urban political community'.[30]

So the large question, why there were not more social rebellions, protesting against, and trying to overturn, an indefensibly unequal society, stands. To that large question, there are many answers. First, rebellion was a very serious offence punishable by death, so it was never going to be undertaken lightly. It was regularly denounced from the pulpit in parish churches. Second, among the most important responsibilities of noblemen and gentlemen and town councils was the maintenance of order: usually they acted quickly and effectively to prevent disaffection getting out of hand. Ket's rebellion, in July 1549, occurred in a royal minority, at a moment when Protector Somerset's government was distracted by an earlier rising in Devon and Cornwall against religious change, and in a county, Norfolk, whose leading nobleman and landowner, Thomas Howard, third duke of Norfolk, was in the Tower (following charges of treason against his son the earl of Surrey at the very end of Henry VIII's reign) and, crucially, unable to respond to and deal with the angry concerns of those who rose and then rebelled. Usually, in Tudor England, noblemen and gentlemen were able to nip any incipient risings in the bud. Following the rebellions of 1549, local gentry were much more alert to potential trouble. In 1550 an 'Act for the punishment of unlawful assemblies and rising of the king's subjects' that if twelve people gathered to change the laws made by parliament for religion or *any* other laws, they would be judged guilty of treason if they did not disperse within an hour. Breaking down hedges would be a felony. So would the ringing of bells or firing of beacons.

Third, although risings often began with petitioning and negotiation, ultimately governments were able to stop negotiating and to mobilise overwhelming force, including foreign mercenaries, and shatter popular risings bloodily. The weapons of the weak were limited. Some rebellions ended tragically, notably the Prayer Book rebellion in the south-west and Ket's rebellion in Norfolk, both ending with some thousands of commons left dead on the battlefields after Lord Russell and the earl of Warwick respectively gave them battle. In July 1549 Lord Grey ordered after the execution of rebels in Oxfordshire 'their heads to be set up in the highest places of the towns for the greater terror of evil people'.[31] That must have been a deterrent.

Fourth, and more positively, the substantial involvement in local administration— as village constables, as church wardens, as holders of a variety of urban offices—of men from below the social elite bound them into the society in which they lived. If that society was hierarchical, the hierarchy was complex: not just powerful and powerless but shades of power and inequality. Villages were not uniformly peopled by poor peasants equal in their poverty; there were indeed very poor people, but there were also what French historians call *coqs de village*, men who were quite substantial figures in a village society, well above subsistence levels, if well short of the gentry. There were many prosperous urban merchants. Such men held local office; such men characteristically employed servants themselves; such men were ready to resort to litigation in defence of their property; they were involved in the day-to-day administration of the criminal law; consequently they were not the sort of men to enter lightly into rebellion. If they had specific grievances they knew how they could present them peacefully in petitions to the JPs, to noblemen, even directly to the monarch for redress. They knew how to portray themselves as loyal, honest, hard-working and deserving even when their motivation was more self-serving. And when they did rebel, they were able to control and discipline the commons: the orderliness of Tudor rebellions is remarkable. Popular force was directed not against noblemen and gentlemen as such but against those individual noblemen and gentlemen who would not join in the commons' rebellion.[32] The commons did not, as Mark Stoyle has brilliantly shown, cry out 'kill all the gentlemen' in an apparent outburst of pure class hatred, but rather 'kill the gentlemen', intending those who like Sir Peter Carew were resisting the commons' rising and thus immediate threat to the rebels.[33] The heavy toll of lives occurred when government forces attacked them.

Fifth, the world in which the commons lived was the only world they knew: the reforms they sought in rebellion were very often simply a return to how things had been—there was little sense that the world could be made better. There was much resignation, acceptance of fate and God's will. What will be, will be. That was not the same as saying that 'whatever is, is right'. Resignation was quite compatible with a deep undertow of social resentment and contempt for lords. But it took a lot, and very exceptional circumstances, to provoke a rebellion.

Sixth, there were many shared values and experiences. Religion, of course, could be bitterly divisive as well as unifying: but it is worth here emphasising the unifying aspects of a faith in which all were equal before God. Growing up and living in a locality, in a region, could produce strong ties of identity. Englishmen—certainly in the face of the Spanish Armadas—felt themselves to be Englishmen, with rights and liberties, a way of life that was worth defending, a shared political culture, that is to say a common framework of ideas that bound men together.[34] And the mere fact of threatened invasion reinforced and consolidated that sense of Englishness whose origins and development can be seen over many centuries.

Seventh, a somewhat contrary argument has been advanced, notably by Keith Wrightson, namely that from the second half of the sixteenth century there was increasing social polarisation in villages. It is held that there was a long-run trend in which small farmers lost out, holding land according to custom they could not easily prove or modify, vulnerable to bad harvests, and in danger, in moments of crisis, of losing their relative independence and their involvement in the running of the parish and becoming agricultural labourers or, worse, undeserving poor and vagrants. Those in the upper reaches of village society identified less and less with the commons and more and more with the gentry, with whom they collaborated when serving as constables and minor office-holders, a social trend allegedly intensified by puritan religious convictions including heavy emphasis on sexual morality. And that made these village worthies, these coqs de village, less and less likely to join the commons in rebellion.[35] The difficulty with such an interpretation is that it implicitly takes too rosy a view of social harmony, and it attributes to the village worthies too great a propensity to rebel, in the preceding period. Moreover social polarisation is likely, by its very nature, to emerge over a long time, not suddenly in response to particular events. Village worthies had long been involved in raising taxation or soldiers locally when governments required. Their role in the administration of the poor law intensified but did not transform their role. Moreover the nature of Ket's rebellion in 1549—especially the hostility voiced by quite substantial men against their social superiors—cautions against seeing the integration of yeomen and gentry as a straightforward process. As controversy over the practice of foldcourse shows in large parts of Norfolk, instead of the land being divided geographically, with some fields given over to arable and others to pasture, the division was chronological, that is to say that at certain times of the year fields were cultivated for grain, while at others they were open for grazing by sheep. Such a practice risked quarrels over the dates by which sheep were moved on and off the land. The longer the sheep stayed, the greater the pressures on farmers who wished to use the land to grow grain. It seems that in 1549 there was a strong feeling that the larger sheepowners were taking more than their fair share. Moreover 'custom' was more multi-faceted than it is often presented. It was not just the poor who invoked custom.[36] It is worth emphasising in passing that there were relatively few rebellions even before the mid-sixteenth century and generalising from a small number is inherently risky.

How far did governments adjust their policies and their methods in response to rebellion and to fear of rebellion? Arguably the half-century after the mid-century rebellions was a period of quiet government. Debasement ceased. Inflation did not hit mid-century heights. Taxation did not touch the poor and demands on the rich were less frequent. Queen Elizabeth allowed her subjects a measure of freedom of choice of religious practice. Military and naval ventures did not end in disaster nor were they conducted in the heated political atmosphere of the mid-1620s when Charles was trying to take on the French and the Spanish against the background of acrimonious criticism of his favourite George Villiers, duke of Buckingham. In short, there were fewer obvious causes of rebellion.

There were no revolutionary changes in the mechanisms by which Tudor governments sought to enforce their policies. Tudor governments continued to rely on noblemen, JPs and town magistrates. There was no radical change. No intendants—legally-trained officials, without local connections, appointed by the crown, and supported by armed force at their disposal—on the French model were ever considered, let alone introduced. There was no Tudor Revolution in the enforcement of policy. Interestingly, when Geoffrey Elton came to study enforcement of the break with Rome in the 1530s he showed how fully Henry and Cromwell relied on existing mechanisms of government, above all the local roles of noblemen and JPs.[37] No network of spies, no centrally appointed paid officials, replaced them. In the mid-Tudor period, lords lieutenant were introduced, not least to resist popular rebellion more effectively, and from the middle of Elizabeth's reign their role was spelled out more precisely, but, as we have seen, these posts were less a transformation than a formalisation of the role of noblemen. All that was not a sign of weakness but rather a reflection of governments' beliefs that they were coping, that they were able to secure their aims, in short that no great changes were necessary. And consequently that meant that men of some substance in the localities did not feel angered by unwelcome intrusion by the central state.

There was a marked paternalistic tone to Tudor government. It would be wrong to see paternalism as simply a disingenuous reaction to popular rebellion, whether from weakness or from fear. Its origins were no doubt Christian and humanist. All governments claim to be governing in the interest of the people; that was, and is, not necessarily a hollow claim. Governments were probably wrong to see enclosures as a widespread and increasing social evil—agrarian historians show that it was the mid-fifteenth century rather than the sixteenth century that was the time of extensive enclosing—but Wolsey's great inquiry into enclosures in 1516-17 reflects the deep conviction that government was for the good of the governed. Governments would intervene if noblemen pressed too hard on their tenants as the seventh earl of Shrewsbury found when he attempted to raise rents paid by his Glossopdale tenants. He received no fewer than seven letters from the council and five from individual councillors, as well as one from the queen, urging him to respect the principles of good lordship. In 1592, Thomas (1527-1608), Lord Buckhurst, wrote that[38]

> in the policy of this common wealth, we are not over ready to add increase of power and countenance to such great personages as you are. And when in the country you dwell in you will needs enter in a war with the inferiors therein, we think it both justice, equity and wisdom to take care that the weaker part be not put down by the mightier.

Tudor governments did not tolerate wantonly selfish behaviour by members of the elite. And Tudor governments, often responding to local initiatives, laid down quite sweeping measures aimed at the alleviation of poverty, as we shall see in the next chapter.

Of course, such measures can be seen as social control, as attempts by the government or by political elites to reinforce their authority and to confirm the existing social order, but they were not just, or even mainly, about power, I should claim: they were too detailed, too deliberate for that. Only small numbers of people were assisted in any town or village and they were not the kind of people to come together and to organise to petition and to fight.[39] And while there is plenty of evidence that courtier-administrators were enriching themselves in royal service, there is little to suggest that blatant fraud was taking place on a provocative scale. Certainly, set against modern aspirations, this was a grotesquely unequal society, though those words are written less confidently than they would have been before the transformation of advanced world capitalism from the 1990s. It was also, by modern standards, a much poorer society in aggregate. Consequently even if the wealth of the richest had been confiscated and redistributed, it would have only slightly added to the resources of the poor. It is hard to strike a balance between a bland and cosy picture of the paternalism of Tudor governments on the one hand and a recognition of deep suffering on the other. The lot of the poorest was not happy. Harvest failure was all too common. In a sense it was the weather that ruled Tudor England. There were back-to-back years of high wheat prices in 1556-7 and 1596-7, the latter crisis 'galvanised government into enacting a national poor law which thereafter guaranteed the basic food entitlement of many of those most vulnerable to scarcity'. Before then 'scarcity . . . was commonplace . . . England was poor, under-developed and heavily dependent on the current year's harvest'.[40] There was little security of employment. Poor relief was in practice patchy. There was a trend away from occasional aid to regular payments to a selected subset of the local poor. The undeserving poor were not well treated. The weapons of the weak, as we have already noted, were limited. Thomas More, sounding like a modern criminologist, wrote of men driven into crime by poverty.

And those convicted of crime could be harshly punished. The penalty for grand larceny—the theft of goods worth more than a shilling—was hanging, death by slow strangulation. Steve Hindle has calculated that, astonishingly, some 75,000 felons went to the gallows in the century before 1630: 'it is arguable that more English men and women were hanged in the years 1580–1630 than between 1630 and the virtual abolition of capital punishment in 1967.'[41] Given that the population of England was some 2.5 million in the mid-sixteenth century, that is a remarkably high figure. It averages at about nineteen executions annually in each English county. The survival of records is uneven so we can never be certain. The assizes, or their equivalents such as the Court of Great Sessions in Chester, could execute felons. Very occasionally executions could follow quarter sessions. Boroughs with rights of gaol delivery could execute. So large numbers of executions were theoretically possible. It is likely that in the late sixteenth century and early seventeenth century there were indeed high levels of executions. An examination of Devon in 1598, both assizes and quarter sessions, found seventy-four executions.[42] Extrapolating that figure over England as a whole over the century 1530–1630 would yield an overall figure even higher than Hindle's 75,000. Over a hundred people were executed for property offences on the Home Circuit of the assizes that year. The year 1598 was of course a very difficult year: the harvest was terrible. A study of the Middlesex Sessions between 1547 and 1625 estimated that there were 6,476 executions in London and Middlesex, that is about 62 annually. That adds some further credibility to Hindle's overall figure of 75,000.[43] Since such national figures depend on extrapolation, it would be as well to be cautious. That figure may well be too high. But that a great many were executed for felonies seems incontrovertible. Branding of cheeks and foreheads, ripping and cropping of ears, slitting of nostrils, boring through tongues, whipping and despatch to the galleys were considered lenient sentences. Enforcement varied. Much depended on the discretion of constables and JPs. They could show pity, especially to known residents. They could be harsh, especially towards vagrants and outsiders, with parishes unwilling to take on additional burdens. 'Local reaction to the arrival of strangers and vagrants in a village was not unlike that of too many towns towards asylum seekers today', Penry Williams has written.

These are necessary qualifications to the more positive assessment that follows. By and large, and despite the incidence of rebellions, despite some dissent, despite some reluctance to implement policy, Tudor governments and their subjects, from the nobility and gentry down quite some way along the social scale, felt that they were engaged in a common enterprise. Government was not just a matter of the king and his councillors issuing orders which noblemen and gentry JPs and parish constables and town magistrates unquestioningly implemented. There was too much awareness of a common purpose and shared values for that. Government was not intended by kings and councillors as something done against the localities. Of course, demands for taxation, especially extra-parliamentary finance, and for military support, were burdensome and unwelcome: but, broadly speaking, Tudor governments secured what they sought. And sometimes Tudor governments could be remarkably bold: the General Proscription of 1522, that great military and fiscal survey, the *Valor Ecclesiasticus* of 1535, itemising the wealth of all the monasteries, the dissolution of the monasteries in the late 1530s, the imposition of a range of religious changes such as the dissolution of the chantries in the late 1540s—these are all testimony to the ability and the power of Tudor government.

It was not exactly, however, through a process of bargaining and negotiation that Tudor monarchs operated, fashionable though the term 'negotiation' has become in some recent writing. They would not have recognised noblemen and gentlemen and towns as independent centres of power, something that the concept of 'negotiation' seems to assume. Nor did local noblemen and gentlemen and town councillors and parish constables, through their participation in government, significantly affect the making of policy, except in the relief of poverty, an area in which local initiatives, notably those in Norwich, were taken up by Elizabeth's Privy Council and generalised. More significant in accounting for the relative success of Tudor government is Penry Williams's insight that the key to that success was not just bureaucracy—and certainly not any Eltonian revolution in the central administration—but rather the willingness of kings, queens and councillors to deploy a combination of formal and informal methods of ruling. Many aspects of government were indeed formal—the procedures by which taxation was collected, for example, the administration of royal finances by the exchequer and by the various departments that Elton lovingly described—but Tudor monarchs very much resorted to less formal methods and approaches as well. The regional authority of landed noblemen was crucial in the Tudor period: this was to some extent formalised in the late Tudor office of lord lieutenant, but that position did not confer authority on noblemen, it confirmed it. Gentry JPs played a vital role in the enforcement of royal policies. The very dependence on Tudor monarchical government for the implementation of its policies on noblemen and greater gentlemen whom it could certainly cajole, sometimes discipline and occasionally (but not generally) punish, severely qualifies claims that Tudor government was essentially bureaucratic, impersonal, modern. Tudor government did not work at all badly, I should argue, but it did so because Tudor monarchs and councillors worked energetically and skilfully to maintain harmonious relationships with those who enforced their policies in the localities.

9a

Poverty and policy

One way of considering enforcement is to take a theme and to explore how governments set about enforcing their will on it. We have already considered how successfully governments managed to raise taxation and levy armies. Next we shall consider how Tudor governments responded to the challenge of poverty.

Jesus taught that 'the poor you will always have with you' (John 12:8) and encouraged those who heard him preach to support the poor (echoing Deut. 15:7-11), but Jesus's admonitions were personal, aimed at individuals, not structural. The medieval Christian Church encompassed various activities involving the relief of the poor, from hospitals for the infirm and chronically ill to the distribution of food, drink and money to the needy. But like Jesus's teachings, this was not systematised, and, like Jesus's teachings, rested more on charitable impulses than on investigation and analysis. There are always people who are ill or disabled who cannot earn their living. There are orphaned babies and young children, widows with children, unmarried mothers. There are often victims of economic circumstances and of dearth, fire and flood. Economic historians would claim that the incidence of poverty nonetheless fluctuates. Paradoxically, the very high mortality of the Black Death and subsequent outbreaks of plague led to a century and more in which the common people who survived the plague were relatively more prosperous, and poverty, while not absent, was not an acute social challenge. That may reflect too rosy a view, but however that may be, matters changed towards the end of the fifteenth and the beginning of the sixteenth centuries. Population began to rise, and by the mid-sixteenth century an increased population was putting inflationary pressure on the economy. Contemporaries recognised a growing problem of poverty. But there was also a sense that there were more and more able-bodied men who did not work, relying instead on begging and even on petty crime. That was seen as troubling in itself and also as potentially threatening to social stability.

And there were various responses. It would be wrong, however, to assess sixteenth-century poor relief simply in terms of the introduction and imposition from above, by the government, of a uniform and national policy. Increasing concern and increasing activity in the parishes most likely arose from local concerns, from the reality of the problem of poverty, rather than from new laws.[1] Indeed at times it seems that laws passed by Parliament were more a codification and extension across the realm of measures already taken in some localities. It is interesting that at no point in the sixteenth century was a national scheme of taxation and corresponding distribution of charity considered. All the measures set out in parliamentary statutes were based on parishes. There was no sense of solidarity between parishes. The churchwardens of Ashburton, Devon, were unique in providing regular (weekly) alms for the poor in the mid-1540s, that is before the legislation of 1547 in Edward VI's reign. By 1553 half of the sample of parishes chosen by Marjorie McIntosh were taking some action for the poor.[2] Over the sixteenth century as a whole the key development was the collection of what were in effect local taxes, the yields of which were then distributed in various ways to the local poor. That went hand in hand with vigorous measures against begging. The twin aim of policy was to relieve poverty but also discourage begging unless a beggar's circumstances were so compelling that he or she was individually licensed to beg. A statute in 1531 expressed anxiety that vagabonds and beggars 'daily do increase in great and excessive numbers by the occasion of idleness, mother and root of all vices', notably thefts and murders. Begging was from then on subject to licensing by JPs, the first time that requirement was to be insisted upon nationally. Punishments for those caught begging outside their home territory without licence were severe: they were to be beaten or whipped till they were bloody.

There was a growing awareness that the consequences of the religious changes of the 1530s and 1540s, notably the dissolution of the monasteries and the suppression of the chantries, had had a major impact on the relief of poverty, leading to a substantial reduction in the numbers of hospitals and almshouses. Even Henry VIII quickly recognised these challenges. In 1536, at the same time that Parliament dissolved the smaller monasteries, Henry came in person to the Commons, as we have already noted, to urge MPs to accept a bill dealing with poverty. It was to become the first statute to lay down that parishes should organise poor relief. Collectors of alms were to gather charitable donations on Sundays and holy days in order to relieve the poor, the lame, the impotent, the sick, the feeble and the diseased unable to work. But poor people were not to wander begging. The statute encapsulates the acceptance of the need to raise money in the parishes to relieve the poor but also the vigorous condemnation of idle beggars.

That division of the poor into the deserving and the undeserving poor, although vigorously asserted throughout the sixteenth century and often treated as a distinctive feature of the sixteenth century, is perhaps better seen as timeless. The challenge is that the deep and instinctive charitable urge to alleviate suffering by grants of food, drink, clothing and shelter can be exploited by anyone able to work but unwilling to do so. But it is a myth to suppose that until the early-sixteenth-century charity was undiscriminating and consequently encouraged men to feign poverty. Barbara Harvey's moving researches into the Benedictine monks of Westminster Abbey in the fifteenth century show clearly how discriminating the late medieval monks were.[3] Christopher Dyer has emphasised that many late medieval villages were already doing what has been seen as new in the sixteenth century.[4]

Arguably the policies of Henry VIII's and Somerset's governments intensified poverty, especially the very costly wars between 1542 and 1550. What the right hand did that worsened the problem, the left hand attempted to mitigate. In Edward VI's reign successive governments, parliaments and bishops formulated legislation that went beyond that of 1536: parish officials were now instructed to implement continuous relief. Injunctions in 1547 laid down that parish churches should contain a strong chest with a hole for contributions.⁵ The statute in 1547 required collections to be made every Sunday and holy day to allow distribution to be made to those 'in unfeigned misery'.⁶ The 1552 Act contained detailed instructions for the collection and distribution of alms. Parish ministers and churchwardens in villages and equivalent officers in towns were to compile a register of inhabitants highlighting those who were impotent, aged and needy. Two gatherers and collectors of alms were to be chosen each year for relief of the poor. Collections and distributions were to be made weekly, accounts to be presented quarterly.⁷ It was envisaged that some would need to be persuaded to contribute. The poor could be set to work. How fully such instructions were met is very hard to say. Marjorie McIntosh found 29 per cent of her sample of parishes reported setting up a poor box, half (as we have noted) taking at least some steps to help the poor.⁸ Exceptionally severe measures were announced against able-bodied alms seekers in 1547. The letter V was to be branded on their chest. They were to be enslaved. But the act was not enforced and was repealed in 1550.⁹ McIntosh has argued that the broad principles of the system of poor relief that was to operate into the early nineteenth century were consolidated by the mid-century. Further legislation refined details, for example that of 1563 adding teeth to enforcement by empowering collectors for the poor, or by specifying harsher punishments of the undeserving poor, for example in 1572 by requiring grievous whipping and burning of the right ear. But such statutes could also recognise explicitly what had long been implicit in all these measures, namely that some able-bodied men were unable to find paid employment through no fault of their own.¹⁰ There were no new statutes or injunctions between 1577 and 1598. But there were deep concerns over swarms of beggars by the mid-1590s, not least in the light of disastrous harvests in the late 1580s and 1590s. Seventeen bills were presented in Parliament in 1597, consolidated into a single statute in 1598, and modified slightly in 1601. For McIntosh these dealt with problems that had arisen over many decades rather than introducing a new system of support.¹¹ In many ways she is correct, but the impact of the consolidation of various strands may have been greater than she allows. It became clearer than ever that the state accepted that it had a moral obligation to help all meet basic needs: contributions from the wealthier enabled that obligation to be met. JPs were to assess the charges falling on each parish. Royal briefs would allow charges for specific purposes. Overseers of the poor would replace collectors, emphasising the continuing concern that idle beggars should not exploit the system. Licensed begging was abolished. Those who begged illegally faced gaol, banishment, forced employment in galleys, though such theoretical harsh penalties were often not enforced. Overall there was more supervision and recording.¹² It was indeed a continuation and refinement of initiatives taken over many decades, but the combined effect was significant and appears to us the more so since the pattern set endured until 1834.

In the reign of Henry VII migrants arrived in England, the tail end of a Romany diaspora. They were believed, wrongly, to have come from Egypt. They made their way by palmistry and fortune-telling and before long they were accused of robbing. Statutes of 1531, 1554 and 1563 imposed harsh penalties but it seems as if enforcement was half-hearted and haphazard. Gypsies were not known for begging and dealing with them was not a priority.¹³

9b

The crown and religion in Tudor England

That men and women were prepared to rebel—to risk their lives—over religious policy shows that we cannot look at rebellion simply as a violent kind of negotiation in which the commons urged the monarch to withdraw financial demands or to prevent landlords from encroaching on the common fields. Do rebellions over religion suggest that ideas—religious ideals—must be given weight in any consideration of who—or what—ruled Tudor England? If religion was so central and so important a feature of Tudor life, if some men and women felt so strongly that they were prepared to be martyrs for their faith, then the ways in which governments formulated and enforced their religious policies, and the successes and failures of such attempts, will shed revealing light on the strengths and weaknesses of Tudor government. Were religious ideas and liturgies elaborated by a Martin Luther, a Philip Melanchthon, a Thomas Cranmer or a Reginald Pole more powerful than the armed force and patronage of monarchs? Was not the least paradox of power that while kings and queens could issue declarations of religious doctrine and demand that their bishops and clergy impose them, they could ultimately do no more than secure outward public conformity (and sometimes not even that) while failing, or not even trying, to open windows into men's souls? But was another, and as significant, a paradox of power that if monarchs could not compel compliance from everyone, they could nonetheless exert considerable influence in the long term over what men and women believed and on how they worshipped? All Tudor monarchs and their councillors and churchmen sought to enforce religious uniformity. All believed that there was only one true faith. None accepted the viability of a multi-confessional state. But all, to some extent, faced the problem of religious dissent. And some responded by following ambiguous policies, amounting to a fluctuating degree of tolerance in practice. The challenge for the modern historian in evaluating the effectiveness of attempts to enforce religious policy is that for much of the period no single and unambiguous religious policy was consistently pursued, except in the most general terms. Monarchs and rulers saw religious dissent as a challenge. In this chapter I shall treat religion from the perspective of those in authority. How effectively did they deal with that challenge?

Before the break with Rome, religious dissent was limited. There was general agreement on the basic tenets of the Christian faith and on the styles of worship that were appropriate. That consensus was not incompatible with vigorous theological debates within the universities, nor with the emergence from time to time of fashionable new cults or approaches. When John Wyclif (d. 1384), Oxford don and theologian, attacked what he saw as superstitious popular practices, he was handled with kid gloves, and his teachings influenced some of the knights of Richard II's court in the 1390s. But he never won royal favour, and Henry IV and Archbishop Arundel countered vigorously, not least by securing parliamentary legislation allowing the burning of heretics and by lavish endowments of new religious foundations. Wyclif's ideas were discredited by their association with a small-scale popular rising in 1414 and a plot in 1431, and largely disappeared from the universities.

But what of the survival of Wyclif's ideas? Governments can deal with people and they can invest in new religious foundations, but controlling belief is more challenging. In the early sixteenth century from time to time men and women were prosecuted for heresy. If the prosecutions are taken at face value, then 'groups of fervent readers, listeners and learners',[1] mostly skilled artisans, weavers, wheelwrights, smiths, carpenters, shoemakers, tailors, met together in taverns and in their own homes to read, to listen, and to discuss the scriptures, sharing manuscript books of translated extracts from the Bible and commentaries. Their numbers, however, were not great. In the Chilterns around sixty were accused at Amersham in 1506 and some twenty at Buckingham in 1506–7. Two were burnt, the rest did penance and there were further abjurations in 1508. In 1511 there were two more burnt and twenty-one did penance. In 1521 some 350 were accused before Bishop Longland: four were burnt, around 50 abjured and did penance. In Kent some five people were burnt and nearly fifty abjured in 1511–12, particularly in Tenterden, Halsen, Ashford, Maidstone, Benenden and Cranbrook. In Coventry some seventy-four people were accused and seven burnt in 1511. There were isolated cases in other parts of the country. On the face of it, the church authorities discovered heretics and brought them before the church courts with determination and efficiency. Of course it is possible that the heretics whom the authorities detected were just the tip of the iceberg and that there were thousands more that were never detected nor troubled. 'There can be little doubt that heresy drives uncovered only a very few of the total number of heretics.'[2] There is no certain way of disproving such a claim, but it is worth remarking that the martyrologist John Foxe disagreed.[3]

> Neither were there any assemblies nor readings kept, but both the persons and also the books were known; neither was any word so closely spoken, nor article mentioned, but it was discovered. So subtly and sleightly [cunningly] these catholic prelates did use their inquisitions and examinations, that nothing was done or said among these 'known-men', so covertly, fifteen or twenty years before, but it was brought at length to their intelligence.

If he was right, the authorities, then, successfully contained the problem—successfully from their point of view.

Of course, that assumes that those who were persecuted were indeed heretics. Yet it is possible that they were simply awkward or difficult people who had expressed some mild criticism of the church, perhaps rooted in a simple person's moralising, contrasting of the ideals of the church and the realities of the behaviour of its priests, or some commonsensical 'first principle' questioning the plausibility of doctrines such as that of transubstantiation. They were then turned into more or less coherent heretics by the processes of examination, assisted perhaps by the prejudiced testimony of lay neighbours whom they had annoyed, not necessarily over religion but possibly for what might have appeared as their self-righteousness. Did churchmen too readily assume, sincerely and in good faith, that those who criticised them, or dabbled in unorthodox literature, were fully paid-up members of an organised group, of an antichurch? Did they impose a stereotype, based on their institutional memory of late-fourteenth-century Wycliffitism, which was itself a negative caricature of features of orthodox belief and practice, on what were much more diffuse and variegated notions? If there is anything in such doubts, then, far from dealing effectively with a challenge, the 'dissent' they were tackling was largely their own invention.[4]

If too much is uncertain about the supposed 'lollards', there is little doubt that the ideas of Martin Luther, Huldrych Zwingli and other German and Swiss theologians who challenged the Catholic Church in the 1520s spread quickly in England. It is clear that during the 1520s some academics and students at the two universities, Oxford and Cambridge, met and read and discussed the works of the continental reformers. As early as February 1519 Luther's correspondents informed him that his books were being exported to England. Archbishop Warham reported that Oxford University was infected with Lutheranism in March 1521.[5] Many later reformers were at Cambridge at some point in the 1510s and 1520s, including William Tyndale, George Joye, William Roy, Robert Barnes, Miles Coverdale, Thomas Bilney, Hugh Latimer, Thomas Cranmer, John Frith, Nicholas Ridley, John Taylor and Thomas Arthur, though the evidence that they knew each other and met as a group is later and patchy. In 1527–8 Wolsey's new foundation Cardinal College, Oxford, did, if Foxe is correct, contain a group who were reading Luther, Melanchthon, Zwingli and Bucer. In London some merchants took an interest in Lutheran ideas. From early 1526 Tyndale's translation of the Bible was being printed in Antwerp and imported into England. It was considered heretical because of the way in which some key words were translated and because of the Lutheran theology in the preface. All this amounted to a significant problem for the government. Religious orthodoxy was being challenged. How did the authorities respond?

A first step was to declare certain books prohibited and make the ban public in a grand book-burning. Luther's works were prohibited in England in April 1521; the papal bull declaring Luther a heretic was publicly proclaimed in May 1521. A ceremonial burning of Luther's books then took place at Paul's Cross. Further book-burnings were organised in Oxford and Cambridge. In October 1524 Bishop Tunstall of London warned booksellers that no new works should be printed, and none imported, without episcopal permission. In 1526 the printing of Tyndale's translation of the New Testament was met with another grand public book-burning at Paul's Cross. In May 1530 the bishops issued a full list of prohibited books and organised another spectacular book-burning. That was followed by a royal proclamation the following month against pestiferous English books printed abroad. They were books 'to the intent as well to pervert and withdraw the people from the catholic and true faith of Christ, as also to stir and incense them to sedition and disobedience against their princes, sovereigns and heads, as also to cause them to contemn and neglect all good laws, customs and virtuous manners'.[6] According to Edward Hall 'it was alleged that Tyndale and Roy were not truly translated, and also that in them were prologues and prefaces which sounded to heresy'. Robert Ridley, a priest, wrote to Henry Gold, a chaplain of Archbishop Warham, that there were not three lines without fault.[7] Book dealers were dealt with vigorously. But whether ideas could be disposed of by being burnt is a very different matter. Henry VIII and his bishops could burn suspect works but little would that avail if fresh books were printed.

A more positive measure was to organise polemics and preaching against heresy. Henry VIII himself wrote against Luther, a remarkable step for a king to take. He was at work by April 1521; by June the *Assertio Septem Sacramentorum*, the defence of the seven sacraments, was in print. Just how much the king himself wrote is debated, and the text itself is simply a very competent statement of orthodoxy, but that the king was directly and actively associated with the rejection of Luther's teachings is plain. Henry attended the book-burnings at Paul's Cross in May 1521 and February 1526, at each of which Bishop John Fisher of Rochester preached sermons which were later published. Thomas More also took up his pen, appointed by Cuthbert Tunstall, bishop of London, and in the late 1520s and early 1530s wrote several works attacking Luther and defending the late medieval church.

Individuals suspected of heresy were investigated and prosecuted. At first the authorities were lenient, especially towards young scholars. An interesting example of this was Thomas Bilney (c. 1495–1531), who had studied at Cambridge. Tried for heresy in 1527, he repeatedly refused to recant, but at last he agreed to do so, provided he could abjure in a form in which he declared that all sorts of views were heresy but never admitted to having held such views himself. And while he was being tried, Bishop Tunstall engaged him in theological correspondence. Clearly what the authorities hoped to do was to wean him away from the temptations of heresy. But the government's hopes were disappointed. In 1530 he started preaching again and distributed copies of Tyndale's translation of the New Testament, actions which were to lead to his arrest, trial and burning at Norwich in 1531.[8] His experiences are typical of the evolution of government policy: relative toleration and mild disciplining, in an effort to win back young scholars in the late 1520s; greater rigour and severity, including burnings, in the early 1530s.

How successful were such policies? It was not possible to keep books out of England. Several thousand copies of the New Testament must have been imported from the Low Countries in the late 1520s, judging by the number of editions. On the other hand the number of Protestants in England was no more than a few hundred at the most. The authorities detected and prosecuted vigorously between 1528 and 1532. Those recorded in the pages of Foxe amount to some 230, but only perhaps half a dozen of these were clearly Lutheran. Of course, how far this should be seen as the 'success' of the authorities is debatable. It could be argued rather that the majority of the population was perfectly satisfied with the late medieval church, as the levels of involvement in activities such as church rebuilding and donations to chantries show. Dissent was a tiny problem and on this view readily contained.

With the break with Rome and the assertion of the royal supremacy over the church in the 1530s, matters changed. Now it was Henry VIII who was publicly making grand claims and requiring general agreement to them. Open opposition was vigorously crushed. Between 1529 and 1532, forceful measures were taken against the church in England to compel churchmen to acquiesce in the king's supremacy. On several occasions they were accused under the fourteenth-century statute of praemunire which restricted papal powers in England. But since all they had done as bishops was thoroughly conventional and wholly transparent, it was disingenuous of the king to accuse them of such offences. Some dissent was voiced in parliaments, as we have seen, but pressures and threats were used, for example when Henry VIII came to the Commons in person to secure the passage of the Annates Bill in 1532. The Nun of Kent, a woman called Elizabeth Barton, who, she claimed, had seen visions and then became the centre of a local cult in Kent, prophesied that if Henry and Anne married, they would not live long. That was held to be treason and the Nun and two priests, two monks, two friars and a layman who had assisted her were executed in November 1533.

In spring 1534 the act of succession imposed the taking of an oath which implied not just approval of Henry's new marriage but also the break with Rome itself.[9] As far as we can see, it was generally applied, with all men aged over sixteen being required to swear. Very few refused. Among those who did, Thomas More and Bishop Fisher of Rochester stand out. Many Observant Franciscans refused. Their houses were dissolved, carts full of friars were taken to the Tower of London, where some died; others were allowed to go into exile and some were placed under a sort of house arrest in the households of trusted noblemen. The prior, John Houghton, and the procurator, Humphrey Middlemore, at first refused to swear but then agreed to do so. Nine refused to swear an oath in autumn 1534 that committed them to acknowledging Henry VIII as supreme head of the church. Houghton and the priors of the Charterhouses of Axholme then refused to swear a further oath in spring 1535. They were executed for treason in May 1535: three London Charterhouse monks, including Middlemore, followed in June 1535. The remaining Charterhouse monks were placed under great pressure. In May 1537 twenty swore. Ten who still refused to take the oath were sent to Newdigate, where they were chained and starved: nine died by September, one survived until he was executed in August 1540. Two priests associated with the Brigittine nunnery at Syon, Reynolds and Hale, were executed in May 1535. The details of all this are complex and the sources frustrating. Gray goes as far as to assert that 'there is no evidence of the government demanding or the inhabitants of Syon [including Reynolds], actually taking' an oath to the supremacy. They were, he concedes, subjected to a preaching campaign, but the sisters of Syon were held to have acquiesced in the royal supremacy when, challenged to leave the chapter house if they refused to swear, they sat tight. Yet there seems no doubt that the nuns took the oath to the succession in spring 1534 and that they continued to be placed under considerable pressure to acknowledge the king's supremacy in some form over the following year.[10] And Thomas More and Bishop Fisher were executed in July 1535. They refused to swear an oath that committed them to accepting the break with Rome and the right of the king of England to detach the English church from Christendom. They did not die for freedom of conscience—they had both been involved in persecuting heretics earlier—but for their belief in what was right. Thus, Henry VIII and his leading minister Thomas Cromwell had faced some determined dissent but had crushed it.

How effective, from Henry VIII's perspective, had the policy of imposing oaths been? Forced to choose between offending God by taking the oath and offending the king by refusing it, the king's subjects overwhelmingly swore. Doing so was compromising. It made it harder to argue against what you had just publicly sworn to uphold and harder to protest against future religious changes. Gray would claim that 'the English people were participants in the process of implementation in that they swore oaths' and that 'oaths gave the people a voice'.[11] But participation is empty if you have no choice. It is to empty the term of all meaning to claim that people could exercise 'agency' over the swearing of the oaths the king required. What made the swearing of oaths so nasty a measure was precisely that the procedure was designed to appear as the expression of a free choice. But it was not. Gray's double claim that 'oaths were a central way if not the central way in which Henry *both* coerced his subjects into obedience *and* secured their consent to many of his policies' quickly falls.[12] Any seeming consent given by people who have been coerced into obedience should not be taken as evidence of their real feelings. The claims that 'a decision to take these oaths indicates some kind of acceptance of the content of the oath, or at least a willingness to co-operate with the regime regardless of the juror's own personal opinions' rest on a hollow understanding of acceptance and co-operation.[13]

To be sure, there were those for whom none of this was a problem. When in November 1538 the abbot of Athelney asked the parson of Holforde, sent to him by his master Lord Audley, whether Audley was of the new sect or after the old sort, he replied that he was of the best sort, subject to the king and a good Englishman.[14] Maybe many reasoned as did the Observant Franciscan John Forest, declaring that 'he had denied the bishop of Rome by an oath given by his outward man but not in the inner man'.[15] Others were very likely aware that in taking the oath they would avoid the king's wrath but would offend God and risk divine retribution. All hangs on just how completely and sincerely men and women believed. Some versions of the oaths were general, allowing a measure of equivocation. It is interesting to note that there were significant variations to the wording of oaths. Individuals who had been openly critical were required to swear oaths explicitly condemning Henry's marriage to Catherine of Aragon, accepting Anne Boleyn as queen and any children as legitimate and setting out the royal supremacy. Perhaps some were aware, as they swore, that oaths imposed by force, in this case accompanied by the threat of prosecution for treason, were not binding in the eyes of God for that reason alone. Chapuys observed that 'people swore because they dared not offer opposition, the penalty being forfeiture of life and property, and no one in these times wished to become a martyr; besides which, several reconciled themselves to the idea, by the notion that oaths taken by force, against good customs, were not binding'.[16] But that cut little ice. The oaths allowed the king to claim that his policies had been widely endorsed.

Perhaps it is surprising that there was not more opposition. Only one bishop, John Fisher, refused to go along with the break with Rome. Some of the others, notably

Stephen Gardiner of Winchester and Cuthbert Tunstall of Durham, were probably unhappy, but they conformed. More generally, the government relied on the existing machinery of local government to enforce the break with Rome. Great reliance was here placed on the leading landowners, noblemen and gentlemen, in every county. Noblemen, as we have seen, were regarded as the general supervisors of their regions and were expected to watch out for dissent. The greater gentry, as we have seen, served as justices of the peace, a post to which they were appointed by the crown, but which they then tended to hold for life and were required to hold regular meetings, the quarter sessions, at which a whole range of local offenders would be dealt with by them, or, for more serious offences, referred to the assize judges, or to the king's council. That system of administration of the law was now applied in the 1530s to the enforcement of the religious changes of that decade. JPs were expected to deal with dissent and to report to Thomas Cromwell. Many—but by no means all—did, and Cromwell was able to investigate such reports of people who had criticised the king's marriage to Anne Boleyn or regretted the break with Rome. For example Sir Peter Edgecombe reported from Cornwall in December 1533 that, according to Cromwell's letter, he had 'committed to ward for a time and punished by pillory and stocks in the market place such persons as hath come to my knowledge to have had a seditious and opprobrious speech of the queen's grace'.[17] Some were then tried for treason. The law of treason was extended in 1534 explicitly to cover treasonable speech, but the ways in which men and women who expressed dissent were discovered were thoroughly traditional— there was, it must be emphasised, no Tudor Revolution in local government. No doubt with men such as JPs in mind, the government prepared several works of propaganda in the 1530s and issued several circular letters, explaining the reasons for the king's divorce and justifying the break with Rome. By and large the government succeeded in securing compliance, with the very large exception of the Pilgrimage of Grace in 1536.

In 1536 Henry VIII and Cromwell began the dissolution of the monasteries. It is worth considering their methods. In 1535 commissioners—a dozen or so men, mostly lawyers—carried out a nationwide survey of the monasteries, listing the numbers of monks and nuns, and the income of the houses from lands and donations. That in itself was a remarkable achievement. An act of Parliament in 1536 dissolved the smaller monasteries, those with fewer than twelve monks—although that later became those with an income of less than £200 a year. That measure passed through Parliament without much opposition. But when commissioners were sent out to implement it, there was so much opposition that, as we have seen, it grew into a large-scale rebellion, the Pilgrimage of Grace, which affected most of the north of England—Lincolnshire, Yorkshire, Northumberland, Durham, Cumberland, Westmorland and Lancashire—in the autumn of 1536. The rebellion was the expression of a range of grievances, and some historians play down the role of religion. But I think that the dissolution of the monasteries was crucial.

Several dissolved monasteries were restored by the rebels. When, outnumbered, the duke of Norfolk and the earl Shrewsbury concluded a truce on 6 December, what they were offered was a free pardon for any offences committed, the promise of a Parliament at York and, crucially and revealingly, a pledge that till that Parliament met, abbeys should stand. The rebellion was ultimately ended by good fortune and trickery. When the commons of the north-west besieged Carlisle in February 1537, Sir Christopher Dacre recklessly but successfully charged into them. Martial law was then imposed. And then the leaders of the rebellion, Lord Darcy, Sir Robert Constable and Robert Aske, discovered that they had been tricked and that Henry had never had any intention of calling a Parliament or allowing monasteries to stand. After the ringleaders were executed, the dissolution of the monasteries gathered pace, and soon it involved not just the smaller monasteries dissolved in 1536 but all of them. And instead of relying on parliamentary legislation, the government sent commissioners from monastery to monastery from late 1537 through to early 1540, and they cajoled and persuaded the abbots to surrender their monasteries to the crown, even though the legality of such action was questionable. Three abbots—Reading, Glastonbury and Colchester—who continued to refuse were eventually executed in 1540. And by then all the monasteries had been dissolved. It was in its way a remarkable political and administrative achievement, though hardly just in its methods. And once more the paradoxes of power are glaring. In late 1536 Henry felt he had no option but to invite Robert Aske, leader of the Pilgrimage of Grace, to spend Christmastide at court; the following spring he would be executed at York. In December 1536 the monasteries seemed safe; by early 1538 it was clear that they were not; and by the autumn of 1538 they were doomed.

As we have already seen, in the 1520s Protestant religious ideas were spreading into England. Up to 1532 the authorities vigorously resisted them. But thereafter Henry VIII relaxed the repression of heresy. Some of the early Protestants were instead recruited by the government to help in the break with Rome. The most ardent defenders of the government's policies included those who welcomed them—but as a first step to the introduction of religious reforms on the lines of the newly reformed churches in Germany and Switzerland. Thus by the mid-1530s there was religious division in England. Some were unhappy about the break with Rome and associated changes. Others wanted far-reaching religious reform and campaigned to secure it. Yet all continued to believe that there was only one true faith, that the price of religious diversity would be social subversion and anarchy. And the government responded to the emergence of religious diversity by trying to set out what true religion, both in terms of belief and in terms of practice in church worship, really was. Henry VIII's remade church was a curious hybrid. He broke with Rome and declared his royal supremacy but he would never have any truck with Lutheran teaching on justification by faith nor Zwinglian characterisation of the mass—the eucharist—as a remembrance, not a daily miracle. And yet Henry dissolved the monasteries, effectively ended the practice of pilgrimage and attempted to root out what he saw as superstitious images while retaining those which were useful. Clearly this was not simply Catholicism without the pope but nor was it Protestant.

Imposing and securing compliance with *The King's Reformation* was challenging. Henry knew well enough what he wanted, but he was enough of a politician to know how and when to compromise. He realised that there were practical limits to his powers of compelling belief. He grasped that among churchmen and, increasingly, among the educated laity, religious convictions were polarising. If he were to win acceptance for the break with Rome and the royal supremacy, the pope would have to be denounced, but if radical religious changes were to be enforced, or even if they were simply to be advocated from the pulpits, he risked provoking further religious rebellions such as the Pilgrimage of Grace. The law passed in 1539 that we know as the Act of Six Articles was in fact termed an act abolishing diversity of opinions, but for all such extravagant claims, Henry's policy was the more realistic one of steering a path between the extremes. A proclamation in April 1539 set out this middle way. It criticised some who 'minding craftily by their preaching and teaching to restore into this realm the old devotion to the usurped power of the Bishop of Rome, the hypocrite religion, superstitious pilgrimages, idolatry and other evil and naughty ceremonies and dreams justly and lawfully abolished and taken away by authority of God's word'. But it also rebuked those who

> taking and gathering divers Holy Scriptures to contrary senses and understanding, do wrest and interpret and so untruly allege the same to subvert and overturn as well the sacraments of Holy Church as the power and authority of princes and magistrates, and in effect all laws and common justice, and the good and laudable ordinances and ceremonies necessary and convenient to be used and continued in this realm.

My suspicion is that Henry was also prepared to accept a measure of ambiguity in the codifications of religion that were drawn up in these years: if what he wanted was included, it did not unduly trouble him if elsewhere an almost contradictory passage was also included. At least his opinion was endorsed; and Henry could hope that in due course his wishes might be articulated more exactly. Once more we glimpse the paradoxes of power. Henry had broken with Rome and imposed his royal supremacy, he refused to accept the Lutheran Confession of Augsburg, he insisted on the mass as traditionally understood. But he could not at once impose his convictions on every article of religion.

How effectively was Henry's policy imposed? Without Tudor opinion polls, it is hard to measure the trends in religious belief. From time to time stiff measures were taken, but they were—perhaps deliberately—never pushed for too long. In 1539–40 some 500 Londoners were charged with heresy but very few were punished: were the indictments intended as a warning? It is clear that, especially in towns, for example Rye in Sussex, religious views polarised and there were vigorous quarrels. But in the long run what Henry set out to achieve—a middle way—does seem to me to have characterised the later church of England. The government did secure remarkable levels of compliance in its policies of religious reform. From 1538 the setting up of candles before images of saints in churches was prohibited: an analysis of churchwardens' accounts suggests that the prohibition was effective. Relics were to be dismantled; once again the evidence of churchwardens' accounts suggests that they were, if not always immediately. By the end of the reign virtually all parishes had purchased a copy of the Bible in English, as required by the injunctions of 1538, although again quite a few delayed, and a fresh proclamation was issued in 1541. But how many convinced Henricians were there?[18]

In the mid-Tudor period the governments of Edward VI and then of Mary adopted very definite religious policies, abandoning Henry's hybrid and ambiguous church. Under Edward VI, religious radicalism was enforced from the centre. Injunctions in 1547 set out a radical agenda. In 1547–8 an inquiry into the wealth of parish churches led to the dissolution of the chantries and the prohibition of the doctrine of purgatory. Conciliar orders called for the destruction of images, altars, roods and Catholic service books. In 1549 and 1552 parliaments passed acts of uniformity requiring the use of new prayer books in churches, the second of which was especially radical.

How effectively were such measures enforced? There was outright resistance in Devon and Cornwall, where a large-scale rebellion took place in 1549 clearly directed against religious change, notably the introduction of the Prayer Book in English. That rebellion was ultimately crushed with much loss of life. There was also opposition to religious change in the West Riding of Yorkshire and in Oxfordshire. The rising in Oxfordshire was 'one of the most effectively handled Tudor rebellions on record', blamed on a handful of papists rather than, as would have been more accurate, on several hundred commons, concealment that has proved effective until recently. Most of those who went from Thame to Woodstock were pardoned but some received exemplary punishment. And the troubles were quickly brought to an end.[19] Churchwardens' accounts reveal payments for the pulling down of images and altars, for the whitewashing of medieval wall paintings and for the purchases of the new prayer books, and they record the disposal of parish plate and vestments. Thus, the level of outward compliance in the religious changes in Edward VI's reign was considerable. But just how much inward sympathy there was for them is the question raised by an examination of the religious policies of Mary's reign.

Examples of spontaneous rejoicing at Mary's accession suggest that many had been far from won over. Once established as queen, Mary ordered the restoration of Catholicism. In the parishes there is much evidence of the re-acquisition of vestments, of the setting up of altars, statues and painted windows, of the purchase or recovery of liturgical books and church plate. Clergy who would not conform were deprived. Gentry who stuck to their Protestantism were encouraged to go into exile: some 472 did. Heresy statutes were revived and some 300 men, women and children were burnt for heresy in campaigns in which lay JPs were prominent. The burnings which have so harmed Mary's posthumous reputation do not seen to have provoked the revulsion that we feel today.[20] The martyrologist John Foxe can cite only one example of someone who was converted to Protestantism when he witnessed the horrors of a burning, Julius Palmer, an Oxford don. Attempts were made to prevent the circulation of Protestant pamphlets printed abroad but with little success—though as they were aimed at the influential but barely toyed with notions of resistance, their impact was limited. By contrast, Bishop Bonner of London issued a catechism for teaching children and a short book of homilies (in effect model sermons which parish priests could use). Once again in terms of outward compliance Mary's government was successful: there is no sign of any incipient religious rebellion in England in the later years of Mary's short reign. The religious rebellions of Tudor England—1536, 1549, 1569—were all directed against religious change: there were no popular rebellions in favour of further reformation. But Mary's religious persecution proved to be a damaging legacy. If Mary had lived, if she had borne a son who became an adult king, if the Catholic Church reinvigorated itself, if leading noblemen were won over by patronage, Catholicism might have re-established itself. In such circumstances the Marian persecutions would have been remembered only by the losers. That was not to be. And the memory of the burnings has been a lasting stain on English Catholicism.[21]

Elizabeth's reign saw a return to her father's policy of a hybrid church, a middle way. That is a controversial claim, but I find it the most plausible characterisation of her religion. As Anne Boleyn's daughter, she would have found it hard not to repudiate the papacy. And she clearly welcomed an English liturgy and communion in both kinds. But there is very little sign that she wished to go further. In her own religious practice, in her concern for ceremonies, proper clerical dress, crucifix and images, she was remarkably 'Catholic'. A book of prayers probably in her own hand is wholly conventional, revealing little more than that she was a Christian. She never saw the more radical Scottish or continental reformations as models. She disliked excessive preaching. She was remarkably concerned about the fate of cathedrals and church music, not obvious Protestant priorities. On progress in summer 1561 she was appalled by the condition that many parish churches were in and issued orders that better order be taken. And she saw the religious settlement of the beginning of her reign as final: she never sympathised with demands for further reformation. But she grasped that if many of her subjects were still essentially Catholic, others wanted that further reformation. So she agreed to a profoundly, perhaps deliberately, ambiguous settlement. What she wanted was a comprehensive church, a church that would embrace all her subjects. So religious debate was silenced if it went too far. That was particularly so over the vexed issue of predestination—the belief that God had chosen some men to be saved but that most would be damned. When disputes over this raged in the University of Cambridge in the 1590s, Elizabeth thought it 'a matter tender and dangerous to weak ignorant minds' and attempted to quieten the arguments. For religious division risked turning into civil war, as it had in France and the Low Countries. Elizabeth could rather thank God (in the French prayer in her book of devotions) for 'the good things I have enjoyed until now to thy honour and the relief of thy church, while my nearest neighbours have felt the evils of bloody warfare'. If the avoidance of civil and religious war is a test of the effectiveness of Elizabeth's policy, then it may be seen as a success, with the revolt of the northern earls in 1569 no more, as it turned out, than a brief threat. Of course it might be claimed that Elizabeth merely deferred the clash over religion to the 1640s and that the deliberate ambiguities of Elizabeth's church were doomed attempts to reconcile the irreconcilable. It is undoubtedly true that at the end of Elizabeth's reign there were serious divisions. A minority remained Catholic. Outward Catholic worship had virtually disappeared. Clergy had been deprived in the early years of the reign—though rather more, nearer 1,000 than the 200–300 that has been the standard estimate for over a century.[22] Only in areas where Catholicism was especially strong, such as

Lancashire, did many survive into the 1560s and 1570s. Later Catholic priests were concentrated on gentry households where they could be given a measure of protection. But that meant a gradual erosion of public Catholicism and with it the restriction of Catholicism to a minority of committed adherents, rather than as the religion of all or most, though along a spectrum ranging from strong devotion to lukewarm social conformity. County commissions were remodelled: known Catholics were not named as JPs, though this proved harder to enforce in counties where Catholicism was strong. Laws were passed imposing fines on recusants—people who did not attend church— but enforcement varied greatly, and it was difficult for the central government to compel JPs to punish gentry recusants. Moreover, Elizabeth was concerned not to push Catholics into open opposition.

Meanwhile there were those who wanted further religious reformation, on the lines of the model established in Calvin's Geneva. They mounted vocal campaigns in parliaments, as early as 1559 and 1563, they published theological tracts and they debated in the universities. They failed to realise their most ambitious goals. But, partly assisted by the imposition of forms of worship from above, partly from the increasing availability of the Bible in English and later of John Foxe's Book of Martyrs, partly from the impact of individual preachers, partly from the informal influence of friends, Protestants did succeed in building congregations confident that faith in Christ had redeemed them from their sins and living godly lives marked by attendance at church on Sundays, by prayer, by Bible reading, by psalm-singing and by sermon-gadding. But these were often small minorities in the towns and parishes in which they lived, often bitterly divided among themselves over the true interpretation of the word of God they preached. And their religious zeal, especially when it was directed to the reformation of manners and meant the suppression of alehouses or popular sports and the strict observance of the Sabbath, often antagonised the more lukewarm majority of people, who are best characterised as 'parish anglicans' or 'rustic pelagians', that is a religion based on the Prayer Book but reflecting not so much any theological insights as an untutored and very human belief that the way to salvation lay in an honest life of charity, good works, regular attendance at church, participation in the rituals of the church, especially communion, catechising their children but in the essentials of the faith rather than in the finer points of theology.

Such an approach was powerfully reinforced by the church buildings inherited, and also the pious practices remembered, from the Catholic, medieval past; it also reflected the social and inclusive aspirations of the Elizabethan religious settlement itself. Thus far I have deliberately avoided the term 'toleration'. The queen manifestly did not tolerate missionary priests who might threaten her life nor did she tolerate provocatively puritan clergy. She suspended Edmund Grindal, archbishop of Canterbury, when he refused to suppress prophesyings, gatherings of clergy who expounded the Bible. She did not plead for liberty of conscience. But within broad limits she did allow, or create, a space in which men and women of rather different persuasions could worship and teach. And at the level of parishes as well as division there may also at times have been neighbourly recognition that not everyone will agree, but as an implicit acceptance of peaceful co-existence and a reluctance to bring matters to the courts rather than any positive endorsement of religious diversity for its own sake.[23] In Amsterdam tacit acceptance of faiths other than Calvinism developed in the early seventeenth century into full-blown toleration of public worship for Lutherans and Jews.[24] It would take the experience of civil war before something comparable developed in London in the later seventeenth century.

How successfully then did Tudor governments enforce their religious policies? Very successfully, if the test is avoiding a civil and religious war of the sort that ravaged France and the Low Countries, though perhaps they were lucky that none of the rebellions grew into something more serious and that the disputed succession of 1553 proved short-lived. Quite successfully, if the test is the successful prohibition of the outward expression of a proscribed belief or practice. Reasonably successfully, though often only slowly, if the test is some positive action, requiring expenditure, such as the dismantling of an image or the purchase of a Bible. Not very successfully, if the test is persuading people to hold beliefs, especially new beliefs, or to change their religious practices and to conform not simply in a spirit of resigned compliance but with informed enthusiasm. But perhaps that last is too demanding a test. Governments could use force: they could burn, execute, imprison, exile, fine, frighten. But their means of oppression were relatively limited. Sometimes they dared to act radically, dissolving the monasteries and the chantries. At other times, they largely accepted what they found and attempted to work with the grain of local society. Thus some JPs were removed from the bench but mostly governments endeavoured to secure the compliance of existing members. What could they do? It was difficult not to choose as JPs the leading landowners in a county: outsiders parachuted in, or even minor local men raised up in dignity, would find it hard to exert the same authority, not least against popular unrest. So there were clear limits to the control the central government could wield. Some clergy—more, at the beginning of Elizabeth's reign than has generally been thought, as we have seen—were ejected from their livings when regimes and religious policies changed, but generally clergy remained in post throughout the shifts and turns of policy. That might mean willing acceptance but more likely it reflected the 'relative unwillingness on the part of the authorities to mount anything resembling a thorough, nationwide purge of malcontents'.[25] It would have offended against contemporary notions of property rights to have embarked upon more wholesale policies—and, in any case, it is difficult to see where any government could have found the necessary replacement clergy. No Tudor government could then hope fully to control those who in the last resort implemented its policies in the localities and parishes and reported on dissenters. But JPs and clergy in turn showed a considerable degree of loyalty to the crown and, with obvious exceptions, general compliance with the more forcefully expressed wishes of central governments. In some senses they were placing their own self-interest above religious principle, hoping to gain personal favour (possibly at the expense of less willing local rivals) by serving the government and carrying out its sometimes unpopular policies. More fairly, they can be seen as subordinating religious principle to the maintenance of social order and stable government or convincing themselves that they were the same. The extent of that conviction among those who ruled in the localities was not the least of the successes of Tudor government. But arguably it was not a lasting success. In the 1640s these religious divisions were at the heart of the Civil Wars. Yet contingency played a significant part in the outbreak of Civil War in 1642. Alternative scenarios are readily imaginable. Religious divisions complicated, to say the least, the tasks of governments, but they did not make civil war inevitable.

9c

The exception of Ireland

Historians studying Tudor England, especially those studying early and mid-sixteenth-century England, have usually ignored Ireland, unless Irish matters impinged directly on English concerns. In that they were responding, or not responding, rather like Tudor monarchs. Ireland was in many ways an exception. Neither the Romans nor the Normans had effectively conquered the Irish. But nor did the Irish manage to repulse the English. Instead an extraordinarily complex political society evolved. The Normans and English soldiers and settlers more or less established themselves around Dublin, under a chief governor appointed by the king, but beyond the Pale the writ of Norman and English monarchs barely ran, even allowing for a series of gradations.[1] At upper social levels the English intermarried and assimilated: from Normans to Old English, fundamentally dependent on English monarchical power, not Irish, but yet with political and social interests that did not match those of English monarchs. And similarly the elite Irish did not become English, unlike the Welsh gentry in the fifteenth and sixteenth centuries. Briefly in Henry VII's reign Dublin was a centre of support for Yorkist pretenders. But Ireland was not, rather astonishingly, a factor in Henry VIII's break with Rome and subsequent religious changes. If the predominantly political disaffection of Gerald Fitzgerald, ninth earl of Kildare, and his son Thomas in 1534 had fused with religious opposition, then Henry could well have faced a serious challenge, and the history of the 1530s would have to be written in a British context. But no such fusion occurred. Partly in response Henry VIII heightened his claims to rule Ireland, though to little practical effect. Rhetoric is not the same as reality.

In Elizabeth's reign the position of Ireland began to change, not for the better, neatly sketched by C.S.L. Davies in a model review. 'The ideal was an Ireland anglicised' at least at the level of the political and social elites, rather like Tudor Wales. 'The Gaels were to be won over to English manners and ultimately, no doubt, to the English language.' Ireland as a whole, and not just the territories within the Pale, would be under English, not Irish, law, administered by officials working in counties and answerable to the English monarch rather than being subject to the will of Irish chiefs or Old English magnates. Increasingly Englishmen, and in the last years of the reign, Presbyterian Scotsmen, exploited the uncertainties of Irish land tenure with the aim of expelling native Irish. The policy of 'surrender and regrant' would allow Irish landholding to be 'recognisable in Lincoln's Inn'.[2] 'Tudor attempts to establish English rule in Ireland deteriorated sharply into violence, rebellion and war over the course of the latter half of the sixteenth century.'[3] That was colonial, racist and bloody. When a senior Conservative Party politician today rejoices in the triumphant history of British institutions, not least monarchy and parliament, I fear I am tempted to heckle 'Ireland'. During Elizabeth's reign the always precariously delicate balance of power was unsettled. 'The repeated large-scale rebellions headed by Old English magnates (Kildare, Desmond) or Gaelic chiefs (notably the O'Neills in Ulster and a host of lesser fry)' set up, as Davies has noted, 'a vicious circle of ruthless suppression, confiscation of land, the introduction of planned settlements of Englishmen, and further resentment'. Munster offers an especially unhappy example. That meant that when Philip II of Spain came to be at war with England, there were sufficient discontents within Ireland for there to be a danger of it becoming a base for French or Spanish soldiers. Conflicts internal to Ireland were exacerbated by external interventions.[4] Small wonder that Robert Devereux, second earl of Essex, proved unable, as we have seen, to impose English order. Late Elizabethan Ireland was thus another illustration of the paradoxes of power. English royal authority outside the Pale was very limited, yet ruthless English settlers could, at times, in places, forcefully impose themselves on the native Irish.

It remains puzzling that efforts to establish English rule became so violent. Awareness of how the Spanish used and justified the use of force in their colonies hardly offers a compelling explanation of the treatment of Ireland. Nor does a recent claim that what happened in Ireland was foreshadowed in the Boulonnais, the territory around Boulogne, captured by Henry VIII in 1544. Certainly ruthless measures were taken to impose order. But it is hard to see them as some kind of embryonic 'colonisation'. The awkwardness of claiming that the Treaty of Camp (7 June 1546) 'paved the way for the development of an English colony' is that the Treaty provided for the return of Boulogne and all lands occupied by the English to be returned in good condition once the French had paid 2 million crowns and a further sum to redeem their debt to the English. The rhetoric of 'colonisation' is not the most appropriate way to characterise the ways in which the English temporarily administered the Boulonnais until its return to the French.[5] Within Ireland, more pertinent were mid-century religious divisions which undoubtedly added a new set of deeply felt differences. The compromises and ambiguities characteristic of Henry VIII's and Elizabeth's remade church could not easily temper the passion of Catholics who had never accepted the break with Rome and radical Calvinists determined to build a church of the saved. But it was as much both the weakness and the strength of English royal power that made things worse. In practice, as C.S.L. Davies has insisted, 'neither assimilation nor conquest was practicable in a pure form'.[6] Too many settlers were 'vicious, exploitative and bad'. Maybe the rhetoric of English claims allowed them to believe that in seizing lands for themselves they were also capturing Ireland for the English crown.[7] Once more there are paradoxes of power to be noted. The Irish could at times feel the victims of overwhelming and arbitrary force, and that underlies the history that the Irish learn. Yet English monarchs and their ministers were all too conscious of how little sustained authority they could exert in Ireland. Once more power was everywhere, power was nowhere.

Conclusion

Paradoxes of power

Who ruled Tudor England? Where did power lie in Tudor England? Were there dramatic changes? It is tempting when writing a book on any subject to exaggerate its importance. That is especially the case if that subject is not specific to a period. Power is ubiquitous. All settled societies need to be governed and many features of government perdure over the centuries. That makes it even more tempting, perhaps necessary, to assert that changes and developments in the period you have chosen to study have been of unusual and dramatic significance. That is what Geoffrey Elton did in laying his claims for a Tudor Revolution in Government. It made his chosen period pivotal in the evolution of England. Elton's interpretation was, and remains, a powerful intellectual construct that offers, or appears at first blush to offer, a framework that can explain the long-run development of English government. Power lay with an exceptionally energetic and creative leading minister, Thomas Cromwell, and with the officials in the financial departments at the heart of government that managed the monarch's revenues and expenditures. In the 1530s England took a big leap towards modernity, away from household, personal and improvised government towards impersonal, bureaucratic government. Yet, for the reasons we have seen, Elton's model has always been shaky.

More commonly, and less provocatively, many historians have presented the Tudor century as a recovery from the supposed collapse of the monarchy a century earlier into the civil wars we know as the Wars of the Roses. They may have been unconsciously influenced by works of justification written at the time celebrating the end of civil strife. The question 'Who ruled?' is answered by emphasising bold kings, notably Henry VII, and claiming that they deliberately weakened the nobility, a claim that has been challenged here. For the first half of his reign he was beset by pretenders challenging his right to rule but he won through and then consolidated his power. The conflicts of the mid-century were put aside. Noblemen remained important, but they were not associated with regional sentiments nor did they try to set up states which they alone ruled. England had long been unified.

It has been easy, too, as we have seen, to fall for seductive biological metaphors. It is tempting to see the state as growing in maturity, in authority and in scope, and thus as an example or illustration of 'state formation', the ways in which an embryonic state turned into what, perhaps a touch optimistically, we tend to see as the finished state of our own time. And in such analyses, whether Elton's revolution or the seemingly more modest claims of state formation, the historian's chosen period is often presented as especially significant.

Manifestly, there is an element of truth in all such analyses. However effective the late Anglo-Saxon state may have been, clearly where we are now is a very different place, and it is not the least of the tasks of any historian to contribute to understanding how that came to be so. But the historian should resist any teleology, any sense that what has happened over the centuries was inevitable or even likely. Historians should be ever alert to the possibility that it could have been otherwise.

It is clear that England was a monarchy in fact as well as name. The monarch's role in the sixteenth century was not simply ceremonial or symbolic, however much ceremonies and symbols reflected, and maybe increased, the monarch's power. Sixteenth-century England was not a de facto republic in which the monarch was a powerless figurehead. Leading ministers were appointed by monarchs and entrusted with authority by them. They were not politicians jostling to become prime minister. They were not organised into political factions with groups at court and in the localities. There were no political parties in Tudor England that could give their leaders support and thus power independent of the monarch. And yet monarchs were not all powerful, nor were they unusual in as much as they attempted to increase their power—all rulers do that. But that is not to say that they set out with carefully defined plans to make themselves absolute rulers. Much political action was reactive and instinctive. Monarchs inherited royal prerogatives, the power to make foreign policy, to undertake defence, to raise taxation and to spend it. They appointed judges, chose their leading councillors and married whom they pleased. Unlike modern rulers, they did not have to concern themselves as a matter of routine with education, housing and health, although they were increasingly involved in dealing with poverty and begging. Monarchs and their councillors could not attend to everything. And in many ways monarchs depended on a larger political nation, the noblemen (especially those serving as lords lieutenant), the greater gentry (serving as JPs), the most prominent merchants in towns for the implementation of policy and the punishment of those who disobeyed. Taxation depended on the consent of the Commons in Parliament: the MPs who consented were gentry, merchants and lawyers, not the poor commons, but they felt they represented all those who lived in their constituencies. Increased and reliable taxation consolidated the power of the monarchy but—the paradoxes of power—the consequent involvement of the political nation represented in Parliament also made monarchs more accountable to the political nation, both in terms of principle (since the political nation had agreed to taxation) and in terms of practice (since Parliament offered a specific practical mechanism by which that accountability could be exercised). Accountability did not have to be directly invoked; an awareness that monarchs' officials were in principle accountable affected their behaviour. Administration became more complex, more sophisticated, which potentially both helped and complicated the challenge of ruling.

Thus monarchs, while undoubtedly powerful, were compelled to take note of MPs' sentiments, especially their complaints. Monopolies were a vivid issue in the 1590s. Politically skilful monarchs, as Tudor monarchs were, responded to such concerns; less astute monarchs in other centuries stood fast on their prerogative rights and suffered politically. The Tudor monarchs were adept at knowing when to press on and when to let go. And many rulers shied away from fundamental reform, even though objectively the need for fundamental reform may have seemed compelling, preferring to muddle through and to maintain political stability, rather than to find the perfect form of government or even an imperfect, but better, government. Power in some senses lay with those who articulated such caution.

There was a large political nation, including noblemen, gentry, substantial men in their villages, leading merchants, lawyers, scholars, churchmen. Men from these social ranges were involved in the administration of their localities. If monarchs and leading ministers lost the support of a significant proportion of this political nation, then they were in trouble. In 1525 noblemen and senior churchmen worked hard to try to get those deemed liable for the Amicable Grant to agree to pay, but men who were usually obedient taxpayers protested that the demand was too great and in many counties and towns they refused to agree to pay. But such dissent was unusual. And most monarchs were well aware of the need to secure the acquiescence of the political nation in their policies. That was why Henry VIII and his publicists prepared justifications of his stand over the divorce. By and large the political nation reacted to royal policy rather than taking initiatives in promoting any cause. Religious policies could provoke and increasingly divide the political nation.

It is hard to claim that those outside the political nation ruled Tudor England. The common people did not rule. That is not to say that the poor commons did not have opinions. Edward Hall noted that in 1531 Henry VIII stopped seeing Catherine of Aragon, 'wherfore the common people daily murmured and speake their foolish fantasies'.[1] Some scholars have sought to show that the common people were more continuously and effectively involved in politics than that allows. But the evidence for such 'popularity' is slight. Edward Seymour, duke of Somerset, Protector of the Realm in the first half of Edward VI's minority, undoubtedly showed unusual sympathy for the plight of the poor commons, but the notion that he envisaged reordering the political system to involve the commons as a matter of routine is far-fetched. Somerset's use of conventional metaphors of the body shows his fundamental rejection of any idea that the poor commons were equal partners in government. They had views on political issues; they could very occasionally take matters into their own hands and rebel. But what historians label 'popularity' is probably best seen as a legacy of the Civil Wars of the 1640s that came to be significant in the early eighteenth century after monarchs from William III and Anne onwards came to choose their leading—from George I's reign it would be prime—minister from those politicians who could command a majority in the House of Commons. Eighteenth-century politicians did then look beyond Parliament—'out of doors'—for reinforcing support from the people. But very little of that can be found in the sixteenth century. Still, the interests of the commons, and especially their plight, did influence government attitudes. Poor laws are the most obvious illustration; so are the inquiries into enclosure of common fields. The common people could and did rebel: briefly and very rarely the commons did seem to rule, did threaten the social order. But never, in the sixteenth century, for long.

Could, and did, women rule in sixteenth-century England? Nothing in English law or conventions prohibited a woman from reigning. Henry VIII's daughters Mary (by Catherine of Aragon) and Elizabeth (by Anne Boleyn) did. They were contested and patronised because of their gender (though it is hard to disentangle that from opposition to their political, and especially religious, allegiances) yet (in my view, though I accept that these are controversial judgements) they were eminently capable of ruling. How far have historians who have seen Mary and Elizabeth as weak rulers been misled by the patriarchal and misogynist assumptions in so many of our sources? That opposition to policies was much more important than opposition to gender was vividly shown in 1553 when Mary's rival was another woman, Lady Jane Grey. In Elizabeth's reign some Catholics would wish to see Elizabeth replaced by another woman, Mary Queen of Scots.

But if queens in their own right could rule effectively, there was nonetheless a gap below the level of monarchy. Unlike descent of the title of monarch, descent of noble titles was according to male primogeniture. Women were to that extent seen as inferior to men. The nobles who sat in the House of Lords were all noble*men*. Tudor society was permeated by patriarchal and misogynist assumptions and, indeed, boldly articulated beliefs. Technically, elite women were 'covered' by their husbands, depriving them of their independent legal identity; they were not to act on their own initiative, for example in entering contracts or bringing a case to the courts of law, except with the approval of their husbands. In practice life was more complex than that. On marriage, elite women had typically been granted a dower, that is to say a share of the lands of their husband. Patriarchy was then qualified because husbands did not always outlive their wives. That meant that among the elite, there were heiresses and widows whose dower, inheritances and allowances conferred a measure of financial independence, and, with that, the capacity to live as they, not their late husbands, chose, not least in exercising the freedom to choose another husband or not to remarry. Notable examples are Dorothy Wadham, founder of Wadham College, Oxford, and Frances Radcliffe, countess of Sussex, founder of Sidney Sussex College, Cambridge.

And even within the constraints of obligation to parents and husbands, women could create space to exercise at least some authority. Here literature is revealing. Shakespeare's women can be more 'masculine' than men: Lady Macbeth is the supreme example. More positively, Portia is eloquent, learned in the law and wise. Their circumstances are often tangled and complex, but Shakespeare's women do exercise a measure of 'agency', acting independently in their own interests as they saw them. And there is enough evidence from real life to support that. Here we again see the paradoxes of power: women were expected by the writers of conduct books to be passive and weak, yet are to be found manifestly assertive.

Women were excluded from sitting in parliaments and could not vote when there were contested elections. We do not know whether male members of Parliament were accompanied by their wives when parliaments were in session. But women can be found in the late thirteenth, fourteenth and fifteenth centuries petitioning the crown in Parliament for redress of grievances, especially over their lands. Petitioning was, as we have seen, an important procedure. What we shall consider here are women petitioners. Within the first 7,910 documents in The National Archives series SC8, Mark Ormrod identified a total of 926 petitions in which women appeared as petitioners, alone or jointly. If less than a sixth of his sample petitions involved women, that shows 'how far the petitioning system was skewed in favour of men'.[2] From a different perspective, petitions were legal documents and had to follow conventions if they were to be effective. The clerks and scriveners who prepared these petitions were men, and the documents they produced cannot be treated as revealing the pure and unmediated voices of women. Yet allowing for such complications, petitions when sensitively assessed, can nonetheless offer valuable glimpses of the lot of women and in particular what ways were open to them to pursue their interests. If that were possible in the late thirteenth, fourteenth and early fifteenth centuries, then it is hard to see why that should not be the case in the sixteenth century, with which this book deals.

Sources for the history of women in the sixteenth century are scarce. In the seventeenth century there is much more. Yet that could not have sprung from nowhere. Can we safely infer from the richer seventeenth-century sources that in various ways women were exercising agency in the sixteenth century as well? Were sixteenth-century women engaged in battle and defence, in crime, in writing, in large-scale economic activity, in religious debates, in painting? Seventeenth-century examples are plentiful. Would that sixteenth-century sources were plentiful also.

Matters that had long been pursued by petitions to the king through Parliament were in the sixteenth century increasingly pursued through the central law courts and in particular through new or expanded courts of law that were less bound by the precedents set by the older courts. Star Chamber, transformed by Cardinal Wolsey, grew in popularity measured by the number of plaintiffs bringing cases. And while it is obvious that a great many records have been lost, some 5,000 cases with nearly 1,000 female litigants have been identified by John Guy from the reign of Henry VIII.[3] Deborah Youngs has searched through STAC1, STAC2 and STAC10 and found 735 cases, or roughly 14 per cent of the total, involving at least one female plaintiff.[4] Those women were, like those who petitioned from the thirteenth to the fifteenth centuries, 'both proficient in the legal process and able to make informed, strategic decisions' about what legal procedures to follow. Study of women litigants in Star Chamber readily shows abbesses and noblewomen. It was clearly a court 'for those with some resources'. According to John Guy, among male plaintiffs the gentry were the largest category; yeomen and husbandmen, neither poor nor rich, were almost as large.[5] The social or occupational position of women was recorded much less often. But some did describe themselves as 'working women'. Youngs cites a widow living in Bristol who kept herself by 'manual labour and daily occupation with her hands'.[6] More commonly, however, the women who brought pleas to Star Chamber did so over land and evidently had the resources to do so. All that shows that elite women and some women of lower social status could exercise a measure of agency as litigants in court. But if what they complained about was true, then they should not have needed to go to court. Monarchs and ministers should not have tolerated such high levels of force as the records of Star Chamber reveal. Or maybe, or even more likely, the women's complaints against the use of force were vastly exaggerated in order to persuade Star Chamber courts to hear a complaint. Women who participated in that were once again scarcely exercising 'agency'.

An excellent study of women 'waging law' in the reign of Elizabeth confirms such a nuanced position. More and more women put their names to litigation in the civil courts. 'Significant numbers of Elizabethan women refused to be passive victims of a restrictive legal system and became active plaintiffs or vociferous defendants in a clutch of different law courts.' Of the cases that came before the judges of the Court of Requests in Elizabeth's reign a third were women. We must grasp that that meant that large numbers of women were coming to London, where the Court sat, and spending weeks and months there, 'waging law', the more so since the numbers of cases brought to the law courts typically doubled over the reign. It has been suggested that the judges 'consistently showed sympathy to the poor, the aged, and the intimidated'.[7] But that is not very relevant to the question of women's agency.

It is hard to claim that exercising agency was generally true of 'working women'. In a world with no reliable contraception, women's lives were dominated by pregnancies and the raising of children, against the background of domestic labour poorly paid by the piece or back-breaking agricultural work. The pressures of life were overwhelming; 'agency' seems not so much impossible, for there were certainly assertive women, but rather largely irrelevant in the sense of affecting daily lives. It seems plausible that women might in some circumstances act together in a concerted way as women, though this is not easy to document and, when it is, might be thought to illustrate the weakness rather than the agency of women. After the defeat of the commons outside Carlisle in February 1537, seventy-four men were executed by martial law. All was lost. But their widows, as a last gesture of defiance, during the night took down the dead bodies of their husbands from the various places in which they had been set up as an example and buried them in the churchyards of the parishes in which they lived. That vividly and movingly shows what women could collectively do.[8] And it is worth noting how Thomas Howard, third duke of Norfolk, dealing with concerns arising from the disruption of trade with the Low Counties in 1528, warned that if he had not squashed (true) rumours that English merchants had been detained in Flanders, he would have had 200 or 300 women sueing to him to make the clothiers set their husbands and children on work.[9] But all too often our sources are unhelpful. Some 525 men were indicted for riotous assembly over the Amicable Grant in 1525. No women were indicted. Yet surely women were well aware of the demand.[10]

Belief in witchcraft—and it was overwhelmingly women who were accused of being witches—came to be banal not just generally but among the political nation. That some, mostly women, possessed supernatural powers and were capable of inflicting harm on other people and animals and even crops, perhaps helped by familiar spirits in animal form, was an idea with a long past. But in the second half of the sixteenth century it was held by increasing numbers of educated men and women, including lawyers, and in 1563 it was made a felony, that is to say what we call a criminal offence. In continental Europe it was commonly held that witches made pacts with the devil; not so in England, though that may reflect different legal systems, with the English law demanding specific detailed evidence; or, as we shall see, perhaps England and the continent were not so far apart. Accusations, though, were not made by wealthier villagers against poorer neighbours; rather they reflected relationships, jealousies, fears within villages; what was new in the later sixteenth and early seventeenth centuries was that some clergy, JPs, judges also believed in witchcraft strongly and encouraged prosecutions too. All the same, there were also sceptics, and the total numbers of those prosecuted for witchcraft were small. There were 109 cases in the 1570s, 166 in the 1580s, 128 in the 1590s, 20 in the 1620s, 19 in the 1630s. During the Civil War, however, the disruption of authority gave zealous individuals greater scope to pursue those whom they saw as enemies. And in the circumstances of the Civil War—the many conspiracies and plots, real or imagined—the temptation to demonise your enemies was irresistible. As Mark Stoyle has shown, Prince Rupert's military successes were put down to the workings of his dog Boy, seen by some as a familiar spirit. And in 1645–7 Matthew Hopkins, an obscure Maningtree gentleman, masterminded what can only be called a witch-hunt: in Suffolk, Norfolk and Essex, some 250 were investigated, and maybe 100, probably rather more, were executed. This was by any standard a major witch-panic, with accusations that witches, many of them very young, killed children and cattle. They were accused of consorting with familiar spirits and with making pacts with the devil. Familiar spirits were frequently mentioned in witch trials. But pacts with the devil were more unusual. Did that reflect the use of interrogatories—questions about their beliefs and practices put to suspected witches—that had been influenced by continental ideas? Undoubtedly the process of interrogation could readily induce suspects to confess to all sorts of behaviour. The East Anglian witch-hunt was clearly affected by the Civil War: 'local justices, preoccupied with the problems of keeping the war effort going, had allowed local pressures for witch-hunting to get out of hand.' The collapse of authority allowed individuals unusual influence—and they might use irregular procedures such as deprivation of sleep. But clearly there was popular support too for the investigation and prosecution of witches, though the scale and extent in the sixteenth century never matched what happened in East Anglia in the mid-1640s.

Where then did power in Tudor England lie? Who ruled? If power is the ability to take a decision independently and then to implement it without difficulty, then in many ways the adult Tudor monarchs wielded a great deal of power. Henry VIII's break with Rome and associated religious changes, notably the dissolution of the monasteries, can fairly be described as revolutionary in their consequences. Moreover, apart from the five years of Mary's reign, they have not been reversed. Henry was remarkably successful in achieving his aims. Parliament—the political nation—went along with royal policy with little fuss, passing the famous statutes that implemented the break with Rome. But power is slippery. If imposing an oath of allegiance on every adult male in 1534 marked the acme of Henry's power, in little more than two years circumstances looked very different. For several months in the autumn of 1536, rebellion meant that the king's writ no longer ran in the north of England, the nadir of royal power. On 6 December 1536 Henry's lieutenants, Thomas Howard, third duke of Norfolk, and George Talbot, fourth earl of Shrewsbury, felt compelled to make a deal with the leaders of the rebellion. A Parliament would be held in York, presumably to repeal those famous statutes, and till then the dissolution of the smaller monasteries enacted in the spring would cease. Moreover Henry welcomed Robert Aske, leader of the Pilgrimage of Grace to court, where Aske with impunity gave the king an account of his involvement and an assessment of the grounds of revolt before returning to the north, confident that the king would honour the concessions his lieutenants had made. But Henry's hospitality to Aske was no more than *reculer pour mieux sauter*. And in early 1537, helped by some lucky breaks, the king recovered control and the rebel leaders perished as traitors. It had been a close-run thing. For a while Henry's ability to pursue revolutionary change had been seriously put in check. The paradoxes of power appear very clearly. When, in the autumn, Henry first ordered noblemen and gentry to muster at Ampthill, Bedfordshire, the threat to him was real. Yet when Robert Aske was executed by being hanged from a chain at York on 12 July 1537 no one could doubt Henry's power. Moreover the ultimate defeat of the Pilgrimage of Grace allowed Henry to pursue the remaking of the church on the lines he sought.

Earlier when seeking to wage war against Francis I, king of France, Henry and Wolsey succeeded for a while in raising huge sums of money. But then in 1525 a new demand, the Amicable Grant, was met with refusals so vehemently expressed that Henry yielded, cancelling his demand. That was government at its most ambitious and least effective. What a difference between the monarch who could secure over £200,000 in 1522–3 and the monarch who abandoned the Amicable Grant with not a penny paid. And yet a few years later Henry was able to embark on, and enforce, the break with Rome.

Power depended on circumstances, on personality, on contingencies. And that makes it inappropriate to write about royal power as if it was something tangible that, once attained, could simply be practised. On the contrary. It was as true of power in general as of absolutism that it was always in the making, never made.[11] Monarchs began with many advantages, from the belief that coronations conferred semi-divine status upon them to the revenues from their landed estate. But their estates needed to be managed. Prudent modern historians criticise Queen Elizabeth and her ministers for not doing what was necessary to maintain and increase those revenues. And while that semi-divine status, that standing as God's lieutenant on earth, which coronations conferred on or recognised in monarchs, undoubtedly enhanced the role of monarchs, the potential risk, once God was admitted in such a way, was that the door was open to apply tests as to whether a monarch was, or was not, ruling in accordance with the will of God. When bishops drew up a memorandum in 1572 calling for the execution of Mary Queen of Scots,[12] they implied that there were criteria by which monarchs could and should be judged. Thomas More cast doubt on Henry VIII's claims. Power that seemed absolute, potentially despotic, was hedged with moral and political constraints. Yet at times monarchs were able utterly to crush those whom they saw as their enemies, as Thomas More well knew. But Henry could not compel More to agree to the royal supremacy any more than More could compel Henry to restore papal authority. Queen Elizabeth could suspend Edmund Grindal, her archbishop of Canterbury, but she could not win over her puritan critics. If monarchs, with all the inherited advantages of their calling, faced constraints, how much more so was that true of monarchs' subjects. The political nation was large, and larger numbers served as constables and officials of various sorts. So many ruled, in varying degrees. It was not just monarchs, not just their leading councillors, not just noblemen who wielded power. But if authority was widely, if hierarchically, diffused, that did not mean that in certain circumstances, and when it mattered most, monarchs, or those who ruled in their name, could not bring to bear overwhelming force. Much recent writing, especially that expressed in terms of state formation, tends, perhaps teasingly, to present monarchs as politically weak. If you were uneasy at the break with Rome, if you were a Jesuit missionary priest, if you were a puritan preacher, it would not have felt like that. And yet monarchs could never be altogether certain. Uneasy lay the head that wore a crown. Elizabeth's councillors were fearful of her assassination. It is hard, contemplating the dissolution of the monasteries, a revolutionary measure by any standard, not to see those responsible as truly powerful. Requiring the swearing of oaths of allegiance with explicit or implicit acceptance of the justice of royal policy was a remarkable and effective assertion of royal authority. But if at times monarchs could seem all-powerful, they were not. Power was everywhere, power was nowhere. It was not only monarchs and ministers who ruled. Noblemen who oversaw regions in which they held extensive tracts of land were at times in a position of great power. George Talbot, fourth earl of Shrewsbury, saved the throne of Henry VIII; it is not exaggerating to claim, by his immediate, instinctive and active resistance to the commons who rose in Lincolnshire and in the West Riding of Yorkshire in 1536, raising 3,654 men on horseback in a week. In other circumstances a nobleman could be reprimanded, as Gilbert Talbot (1552–1616), seventh earl of Shrewsbury, was for his oppressive behaviour towards his tenants in Glossopdale. The commons acting together could launch rebellions that if they ultimately, and sometimes very bloodily, came to an end with the power of the monarchy and the social hierarchy reasserted, nonetheless for a time were rightly seen by governments as military and political emergencies. Power was not the exclusive attribute of monarchs. Noblemen and gentry who were called upon to raise armed force in times of war and rebellion clearly could exert a significant measure of power. Lesser men who did the routine duties of constables, churchwardens and of a myriad offices were clearly not powerless but the powers were circumscribed by laws, regulations and monitoring. Ideas and conventions were significant too. Those who were born into the political nation and beyond absorbed an attachment to property, a sense that there were right ways to rule, that taxation required the consent of the political nation represented in Parliament. Religion came newly in the sixteenth century to be the joker in the pack as some men and some women came to be prepared to die for their religious convictions. Martyrs exemplify the paradoxes of power here, utterly weak when set ablaze, yet Hugh Latimer's remark, 'we shall this day light such a candle, by God's grace, in England, as I trust shall never be put out', testifies to a belief in a greater and lasting power. Power implies a relationship between those wielding it and those subjected to it, and ultimately such a relationship could be one way only, but there was scope for relationships that were two-way, and all relationships are potentially affected by personalities and contingencies. Power in Tudor England was widely diffused. But how effectively it was wielded was variable. For all that they achieved, and their achievements were not small, Tudor monarchs could have been forgiven had they concluded, when things went wrong, as, for example, when men refused to agree to make an Amicable Grant in 1525, that power was everywhere, power was nowhere.

Epilogue

The influence and legacy of Sir Geoffrey Elton

This book began with an account of the early life of Sir Geoffrey Elton and his formation as an historian. We followed the development of his ideas, especially his claims for a Tudor Revolution in Government. As we saw, much of what he argued has been rejected by historians. But that in itself poses intriguing questions. Thus far the critics we have noted expressed their reservations in measured academic prose. For an indication of what scholars actually thought, and how deeply they felt, a letter from the medievalist K.B. McFarlane to his sometime pupil Gerald Harriss, then a lecturer at Durham, immediately after the publication of *The Tudor Revolution in Government*, is revealing. McFarlane pulled no punches.

> Elton's book is a great shock. As I began to read it my eyes bulged with incredulous horror. You must read it; it has quite a lot directly and by implication about the fifteenth century exchequer, household, council and government offices. *The Tudor Revolution in Government* he calls it and this consists in making Cromwell responsible for every development in administration between 1397 and 1558 and several outside that period. One would suppose that the historian of a revolution, especially of an invisible revolution like this one, would think it necessary to study carefully the *ancien régime*. Not he; he invents it. The revolution consists in the difference between this invention and the reality of 1558. There's hardly a page without lunacy. Elton is a doctrinaire, a blind Procrustes who stretches and compresses not facts but phantoms of his own creation to fit a wholly ridiculous theory. I cannot remember ever having read a more insane book; it's rendered no more delightful by a crass conceit, a clumsiness of writing. . . . I have sat for hour after hour—it's very long and verbose—in fascinated horror over it. It'll sweep Tudor historians off their feet—all but the strongest planted—and who of them is—though they may carp or hesitate at details. But the slick contrast between medieval, household and informal on the one hand and modern, bureaucratic and organised on the other should catch on.

McFarlane then referred to a paper Elton had previously read in Oxford: Gerald Harriss and others had been impressed, McFarlane had not, and now he claimed vindication: 'the man's an industrious joke'.[1] McFarlane's letter remained a private document until Gerald Harriss included it in an edition of McFarlane's letters in 1999. But McFarlane was not alone in his dismay. I recall meeting M.E. (Mervyn) James by chance on the day in 1983 that Elton's appointment to the Regius Chair in History at Cambridge was announced: 'a black day for Tudor studies' was James's verdict.

How then can we explain how and why Elton rose to the top of his profession and wielded the influence he did? Despite such vigorous critics, Elton's *Tudor Revolution in Government* became a staple in A-level and university syllabuses. Why?

Elton's theory of a Tudor Revolution in Government had a seductive charm. It provided a very neat framework for students studying the continuous development of English society. History students nowadays, as has already been noted, take bits-and-pieces courses: the Tudor Revolution in Government this semester, the French Revolution in that semester, the First World War in year one, politics here, sexuality there. Time was, as hinted earlier, when history students would take long survey courses—England from the Romans to 1330, English History 1330 to 1688, English History 1688 to 1939—in which the emphasis was on political and constitutional developments. In such a syllabus, Elton's theory appeared a godsend, making sense of disparate elements, linking them together in a plausible framework.

Another different but important reason lies in Elton's exuberant personality. Elton did not undersell his claims. He was neither shy nor retiring nor fearful of contradiction. Many Englishmen and women were—and still are—quiet and cautious in social gatherings, prone to understatement. Many English academics are diffident, all too aware of how little they know and how much they do not know, and consequently cautious and slow in putting forward their thoughts. Not Geoffrey Elton. It was said of him that he never sat through a committee meeting without speaking his mind on every item on the agenda, usually speaking first. If he had been a member of a seminar group, then whenever in a seminar the tutor asked for comments or questions after a presentation, he would have jumped in straight away. In Germany such confidence and forcefulness would have been much more common, indeed expected, not least from young scholars seeking deferentially to impress their professor patrons, and consequently the young Elton's interventions would have made less impact because most ambitious young scholars were doing the same. In post-war Britain such behaviour might provoke private concerns—the English have all sorts of put-downs for someone behaving in this way: too clever by half, clever clogs, too big for his boots, needs to be taken down a peg and now, girly swat—but because all that was said privately, Elton was able to take the academic establishment by storm, especially once he had had the exceptional fortune to be appointed to a post at Cambridge so early in his career.

His critics—Wernham, Harriss, Williams, Davies, Loach and Gwyn—whose lives I sketched in Chapter 1, did not behave like Elton did, nor did they make the impact that Elton did and that offers another explanation of how Elton could command the field. I would like them to feature more prominently in this epilogue. But, for varied reasons, they did not seek to respond to Elton in kind.

R.B. Wernham wrote a devastating review of *The Tudor Revolution in Government*. It was lengthy. But even so, in order to make all the points he wanted, Wernham had to compress and allude. You would need to be familiar with the issues in order to grasp just how devastating it was. And having written his review, Wernham did not go round the country denouncing Elton and his claims. His was an academic world in which most scholars set out their criticisms in measured academic prose, making a fundamental point in a brief footnote, in the expectation that, without further ado, it would be noticed and referred to. Wernham's review of Elton had taken him away from his principal interest, Elizabethan foreign policy, and he quickly returned to compiling the *Lists and Analyses* of diplomatic correspondence and preparing a survey of English foreign policy over the sixteenth century. He had said what he wanted to about Elton and had no inclination to hammer away at it. Much later, in 1996, when he was ninety, Wernham gave a talk on 'Sir Geoffrey Elton', who had died two years earlier, to the Senior Historians' conference at Cumberland Lodge. There he indicated his differences with Elton and recalled discussing *The Tudor Revolution* soon after it was published with K.B. McFarlane, whose trenchant letter to Gerald Harriss I have quoted at length. 'We agreed that Geoffrey, mistaking administration for government, had mistaken for *revolution* what was in fact a stage, albeit a crowded and eventful stage, in an *evolution*.' That, Wernham recalled, was 'the central point' in his review. He hesitated, he said, when writing the talk he gave in 1996, about repeating old criticisms of Elton's claims, since Elton and he had become 'old friends', not least at meetings of the Senior Historians, and Elton was no longer there to answer back. Wernham emphasised 'how brief and distracted had been his [Elton's] apprenticeship in Tudor history'. It was hardly surprising 'if in an over-eagerness to make his mark he allowed the depth and excellence of his research to tempt him a bridge too far in the conclusions he drew'. Generously, Wernham saw the debates that Elton provoked as 'one of Geoffrey's greatest contributions to historical studies'. All that reveals a marvellously kindly man, but not someone who could have stopped the pugnacious Elton in his stride. It is hard to imagine Elton writing in quite such a way about those who wrote critically about him.

Gerald Harriss and Penry Williams did launch a full-blooded attack in 1963. But it is significant that they did so not of their own initiative, if my recollections of conversations with Penry are correct, but because Trevor Aston, the editor of *Past & Present*, invited them to do so. While the papers they wrote may have made their reputations as historians (Penry Williams thought that his had secured him his fellowship at New College, Oxford) it is worth noting the limitations of what they did. There is little sign that they had read and absorbed each other's pieces, and Williams did not really endorse Harriss's claims. More important is that, while they replied to Elton's self-defence, both Harriss and Williams rather left it at that. They did not drive home their criticisms, they did not quickly repeat them in print. Harriss concentrated on his interest in crown, parliament and taxation in fourteenth-century England. He did return to confront Elton over whether Thomas Cromwell had wrought a revolutionary change in 1534, namely the introduction of taxation in peacetime, and showed, convincingly to my mind, that he did not. But that was by then just one part of Elton's grand claims, and it turned on how the *preambles* (introductions) to acts of parliament granting taxation were interpreted. Harriss provoked a lively debate but a debate for specialists in the period. Penry Williams did continue studying in Elton's field. I remember lectures he gave to undergraduates in 1970 in which Williams saw administrative institutions as very important and offered respectful reservations about some of Elton's claims. Williams spent well over a decade preparing a study of government, eventually published in 1979 as *The Tudor Regime*. That book is a classic of historical writing. If only Williams had completed it much earlier, if only it had appeared soon after the debates in *Past & Present*, Elton's views might not have secured the dominance they did. Moreover, although Williams offers a very different view of sixteenth-century government to Elton, he never saw it as his purpose to attack Elton. When I asked him, in 1971, whether his book was intended as a refutation of Elton, he responded, somewhat pained, that he hoped it would be more than that. Indeed it was. But by not showing directly and in detail, either in his book or in another shorter and more focussed critique, how Elton had got things wrong, Williams left the field open for Elton to write a dismissive review, unfairly belittling the book in the *TLS*. Much of this on Williams's part was a matter of temperament and distaste for overt polemic. In *The Tudor Regime* Williams came up with a splendid formulation, already quoted, that encapsulates the message of his book: 'the strength of Tudor government lay in a skilful combination of the formal and the informal, the official and the personal'. But the title of his book, *The Tudor Regime*, conveys nothing of that, which is a pity. A younger generation of scholars would write in terms of 'state formation' but Williams did not seek to find a pithy slogan to encapsulate his views.

Cliff Davies was perhaps best placed to mount a devastating challenge. In his doctoral thesis, on the supply services of English armed forces in the first half of the sixteenth century, towards the end he engaged squarely with Elton's revolution, observing, subversively, that bureaucratic forms of administration did not in themselves guarantee effectiveness or efficiency, while pointing out that the most bureaucratic institution by 1550 was the Navy Board, which had not featured in Elton's grand claims. But Davies did not publish his DPhil thesis as a monograph, nor did he go on to write a substantial refutation of Elton. In his textbook *Peace, Print and Protestantism* (1976), Davies offered not a rebuttal of, but a commentary on, Elton's *Revolution*. He did write vigorously against Elton's paper on the Pilgrimage of Grace in 1536, demolishing Elton's attempt to present that commons' religious rising as the work of a disaffected noble faction, but that was tangential to the *Revolution in Government*. A characteristic of Davies's work was his propensity to move on, rather than to consolidate and reinforce. And much of what he researched and wrote was done in reaction to what others had argued. When interpretations he had put forward had become generally accepted, Davies would challenge them and begin afresh. By the mid-1990s few accepted Elton's claims. Characteristically, Davies came to see more in them, though avoiding consideration of the more detailed aspects of administration, but stressing more the sheer scale and scope of what was attempted by Thomas Cromwell in the 1530s. For me, he here underestimated the leading role played by Henry VIII (and we had many arguments over dinner on this) and the activism in government of Thomas Wolsey. It was all very stimulating, but Elton's *Revolution in Government* survived.

Jennifer Loach might have taken on Elton's grand claims but her deep learning was grounded in highly detailed studies of mid-sixteenth-century MPs and of parliamentary procedures, studies which took time to research and write up. The demands of teaching, a young family and, let us be fair, a certain diffidence slowed her down. She viewed Elton's polemical approach with distaste and that increased her natural reluctance to engage in such intellectual jousts herself. She wrote a fine pamphlet on the mid-Tudor crisis, but she did not attempt anything like that on Elton's revolution. A complication was that Elton's position on the place of parliaments changed radically over his career, as we have seen, and anyone writing on Elton's view of parliament was chasing a moving target. When Loach began her researches in the mid-1960s, Elton was presenting Thomas Cromwell as the man who revolutionised the role of parliament, an institution capable from the 1530s of legislating on religion. Loach would express her scepticism in an essay published in 1986. But by then Elton had moved on to a resounding rejection of Sir John Neale's view of Tudor parliaments as seeking sovereignty. On the flaws of Neale, Loach and Elton were well agreed. That, however, would have made writing any critique of Elton's changing views of parliament very awkward for Loach, especially as Elton never explained how and why he had changed his mind. And consequently that would have been unsteady ground on which to elaborate a wider challenge to Elton's notions of a revolution in government.

Peter Gwyn's monumental study of Wolsey was a challenge to Elton. By insisting on Wolsey's enormous energy, his activism, his sense that much was amiss in church and state and needed redress, Gwyn was making Thomas Cromwell much less unique and revolutionary than Elton supposed. In the early 1980s, as he worked away on his book, Gwyn was a daily presence in the Upper Reading Room of the Bodleian Library, and got to know, and influence, not a few academics and graduate students. But the late 1980s were devoted to writing, supported by his sister in Westerham, and he was no longer involved in the cut and thrust of academic debate. His intellectual interests evolved, as we have noted. He was closely involved with Nikolai Tolstoy and 'the tragic events in Austria in the early summer of 1945'. He planned a book on the partition of India. But most importantly, Gwyn migrated to France where he spent the rest of his life, not least pursuing his passion for gardening. He remained interested in Tudor history, as some biting reviews show. And, of course, *The King's Cardinal* made a great impact when published in 1990. It still commands the field today. But Gwyn could no longer be invited to give a keynote lecture at a conference or papers to seminars or talks to branches of the Historical Association. As with his other critics, Elton was fortunate that Gwyn did not mount a direct and explicit and sustained attack on his claims.

Much as I should like to, I cannot here justify giving Wernham, Williams, Harriss, Davies, Loach and Gwyn as much space as I have given Elton. It was not that they had not engaged with Elton. In a variety of channels they had, but what they had not done was to engage in a sustained and systematic campaign.

The generosity of Elton's critics and their distaste for overt polemic allowed Elton to command the field for many years. Moreover, he was surprisingly well regarded by many scholars of other periods: surprisingly, given that his emphasis on the 1530s risked making those who worked on earlier or later periods no more than minor players in Elton's grand theory. Some historians of the mid-nineteenth century latched on to Elton's phrase, 'a revolution in government'. Even though what they meant was completely different from anything Elton had claimed, nonetheless it made looking for revolutions in government appear exciting and important.[2] And that apparent endorsement by scholars working in periods removed from Elton's own reinforced his standing and allowed him to present to them such criticisms as were made of his work by fellow-specialists as no more than petty-minded jealousy.

The most important reason, I suspect, for the extent of Elton's influence was that Elton was a man of demonic energy. In a spate of books and articles, in lectures in Cambridge, in radio talks, in lectures given to Historical Association branches and university history societies, he hammered away at his vision of the Tudor Revolution in Government. He would not let go. In his early fifties he published two further substantial studies of Thomas Cromwell: *Policy and Police* (1972) in which he considered the enforcement of the break with Rome and subsequent religious changes, and *Reform and Renewal* (1973) in which he looked at Cromwell and social policy. In 1977 he published another textbook, *Reform and Reformation*, dealing with the years 1509–58 and reiterating his views. Before then he had also written a textbook on *Reformation Europe* and *The Practice of History*, an introduction to the historian's art. In the late 1970s he moved on to a study of Elizabethan Parliaments, published in 1986, in which he took on his former mentor Sir John Neale.

He read voraciously and reacted instantly. If you published something that disagreed with him, the next day there would be a letter and a thunderous denunciation, followed the following day by another of generous encouragement. He could be bullying and overbearing, he was excessively combative. He was too prone to see himself as a victim of a great Oxford conspiracy. 'I confess', he once wrote to me,

> to being somewhat disquieted by your offhand and unhelpful remarks in the latest *EHR*, till I realized that you were trying to revive the old policy of that journal under which only history produced at Oxford is good and especially anything from Cambridge should be decried. It was a policy consistently applied to me for some 30 years.[3]

But he could also be genuinely kind, especially to younger scholars.

Elton once described his daily round to me. Every day, despite going to bed late, he got up at 5.00 am and wrote 2,000 or 3,000 words before breakfast; then he would get on with the teaching, the committees and the administration that are the lot of academics, and also find time for reading. He smoked untipped Camels; he drank prodigious quantities of beer and malt whisky by the bottle.

Elton attracted many students to study for PhDs with him. Several were already his students as undergraduates, including Jack Scarisbrick, David Loades, John Guy and David Starkey. Many of them were appointed to lectureships: Elton lobbied tirelessly for his pupils. Several of them came to disagree with their mentor over the Tudor Revolution but most of them did so quietly and politely. It was not until the mid-1980s that David Starkey did so loudly and unequivocally. Elton had also attracted many pupils from the United States of America, Canada and Australia. All that reinforced his reputation and made him a global figure.

Elton's energetic exploitation of the opportunities his appointment at Cambridge permitted explains a good deal. Yet in many ways his achievement and his fame remain puzzling. He put forward a doubtful and contested claim about a 'Revolution in Government'. In many ways in his behaviour and in his approach to history he was the acme of the German professor—perhaps he was influenced by his father—even though he saw himself as thoroughly English and came to feel that he should have been born English. Of his Jewish background there was never much sign. And there is another paradox. Elton's politics were not radical. The 1960s were for him 'a welter of trendy leftism' which he deplored, and I wonder how he felt about his brother Lewis's son, Ben, the irreverent comedian. And yet, and yet, in his historical writings, so deeply conservative a man as Geoffrey Elton is to be found praising Thomas Cromwell not for routinely doing the king's business, not just for furthering useful reforms but for launching a *revolution*.

Acclaimed, if controversial, Elton was very much an historian's historian in the sense that he made little effort to pitch his ideas at a lay audience. He did not believe in historical biography as a valid way of proceeding, on the grounds that surviving sources do not offer enough to build up an impression of the characters of those he studied. He would not, I think, have regarded historical novels as an appropriate way of making good the shortcomings of the sources. The study of the past was for Elton the painstaking scrutiny of the surviving evidence. He would surely have given pretty short shrift to the plethora of recent 'popular' biographies of the Tudor royal family and to representations of the Tudors in historical fiction, plays, films and television series.

But if Elton would, I think, have been disapproving and dismissive of historical novels and plays, paradoxically, in a way Elton's greatest and certainly most widespread legacy has been Hilary Mantel's historical novels, *Wolf Hall*, *Bring Up the Bodies* and *The Mirror and the Light*, which present Thomas Cromwell very much in Elton's image. Cromwell is powerful, scheming, controlled, progressive, but also vulnerable, reflecting the title of one of the chapters of Elton's *Policy and Police*, 'Victim and Victor'. There is little space in the novels or their adaptation as television drama or stage play for any kind of revolution in government but there is a strong sense of Cromwell as in control. Pragmatic, a master of detail, Cromwell comes across as just the sort of man who would be able to drive home a bureaucratic revolution, even if we do not see that happening centre stage in the novels.[4] In a way, Mantel has supplied the biography of Thomas Cromwell that Elton did not feel could be written; that the imagination of an historical novelist has been needed for that does rather vindicate Elton's reservations.[5]

Mantel explains at the end of *Bring Up the Bodies* that 'in this book I try to show how a few crucial weeks might have looked from Thomas Cromwell's point of view'. In many places what the characters say comes from the sources—from ambassadors' despatches, from Cromwell's letters, from depositions and indictments, from chroniclers. Such quotations are fairly presented. But obviously there is little opportunity to subject them to any kind of critical analysis. What Mantel then does is to fill the gaps—the chasms— between matters for which there are sources and matters for which there are not.

Interestingly, Hilary Mantel sees historians and novelists as 'engaged in a common struggle with evidence', though she recognises that 'historians are trained in how to handle evidence, novelists have to learn it'. Historical novelists, she declares, 'should not pass on error'. What she wants to do, she says, is 'work with the historical record and with gaps in it'.[6] Mantel insists that historical novelists should hold closely to the evidence. But there is no gainsaying that she does more than that. She goes beyond that historical record and offers inventions of her own devising. So do screenplay writers. Here I was struck during conversation on BBC Radio 3 Nightwaves with Michael Hirst, the television screenwriter who produced *The Tudors* for the BBC, that he sees himself not as making up falsehoods but as imagining what was true but has not left anything in the surviving records and presenting that truth.

All this raises large questions with implications beyond this study of Tudor government. Does it matter if those who write plays, films, television series and historical novels present false, misleading or contentious views of the past? If they said anything false, misleading or contentious about someone alive they would run the risk of being pursued under the laws of libel and slander. Beyond the niceties of the law, we should think badly of anyone who knowingly said unpleasant things about someone else that were not true. If, however, we are dealing with the past, especially the more distant past, can we say anything we please? Are novelists, dramatists and screenwriters free if they choose to show kings as murderers, councillors as corrupt plotters, judges as persecutors, the common people as a mob? Here there is a huge difference between what historical novelists, dramatists and screenplay writers can present and what historians can say. As an historian I am not free to invent my sources; if nothing shows me that X ever met Y, I must not assert that they did meet and then go on to give a report of what they said to each other. The distinction is not entirely clear-cut. So long as I am quite open about what I am doing, I am free as an historian to speculate, to say, for example, that it is quite likely that X and Y did meet, and that if they did, they would have said such and such—but at once duty requires me to add, quite firmly, that this is speculation. And historians are very careful not to use any such speculation as evidence for further speculation. Historians are always well aware of how much they do not know, how much cannot be known.

On the whole, Mantel's interventions—inventions—are limited to those matters for which no sources survive. But in one respect she goes further, indeed a step too far. I have made much of Cromwell's memoranda of things to be discussed with the king, arguing that they show that Cromwell was cautious about making decisions himself and that Cromwell was very much the king's servant. Mantel—in the television adaptation—dismisses them. Instead she imagines Cromwell arriving at mass. 'The king groans. "No escape from your big lists?"' It is, of course, possible that that was indeed how lightly Henry treated the business of government, but the sheer number of surviving memoranda would suggest not. After all, if Cromwell was the ruler in fact of the country, and if Henry did not want to be bothered by Cromwell's lists, it is difficult to see why Cromwell would have gone on making them and bringing them to the king. However that might be, there is no doubt that Mantel's Cromwell, just like Elton's Cromwell, is the dominant figure in the government and politics of Henry VIII's reign. Mantel's Cromwell has given Elton's grand claims for Cromwell's central role a fresh lease of life. And responding to that is not the least of the justifications for this book.

Notes

Introduction

1 E.H. Carr, *What is History?* (1961), p. 22.

Part I

1 I. Harris, 'Some Origins of a Tudor Revolution', *English Historical Review*, cxxxvi (2011), pp. 1355–85.
2 This biography draws on P. Collinson, 'Geoffrey Rudolf Elton 1921-94', *Proceedings of the British Academy: Memoirs of Fellows of the British Academy*, xc (1997), pp. 429–58, to which I contributed.
3 Collinson, 'Elton', pp. 430–1.
4 Collinson, 'Elton', p. 432.
5 Collinson, 'Elton', p. 432.
6 Collinson, 'Elton', p. 433.
7 Collinson, 'Elton', p. 433.
8 Collinson, 'Elton', p. 433.
9 Harris, 'Some Origins of a Tudor Revolution', p. 1359.
10 Collinson, 'Elton', pp. 433–4; Harris, 'Some Origins of a Tudor Revolution', p. 1360, n. 26.
11 Harris, 'Some Origins of a Tudor Revolution', p. 1360, n. 26.
12 G.R. Elton, 'The Terminal Date of Caesar's Gallic Proconsulate', *Journal of Roman Studies*, xxxvi (1946), pp. 18–42, reprinted in G.R. Elton, *Studies in Tudor and Stuart Government*, 4 vols (Cambridge, 1974–91), i. 1–36.
13 Collinson, 'Elton', p. 434.
14 Collinson, 'Elton', p. 435; R.B. Wernham, paper read to the Senior Historians, Cumberland Lodge.
15 Collinson, 'Elton', p. 435; Harris, 'Some Origins of a Tudor Revolution', pp. 1361–2; G.R. Elton, pers. comm.
16 *Oxford Dictionary of National Biography*.
17 G.R. Elton, pers. comm.
18 Collinson, 'Elton', p. 435.
19 G.R. Elton, *The Practice of History* (1967), p. 163, n. 1.
20 Collinson, 'Elton', p. 437.
21 Harris, 'Some Origins of a Tudor Revolution', p. 1373, n. 115.
22 Collinson, 'Elton', p. 437; Harris, 'Some Origins of a Tudor Revolution', p. 1174, n. 118.
23 Harris, 'Some Origins of a Tudor Revolution', p. 1358.
24 Collinson, 'Elton', p. 439; R.B. Wernham to G.W. Bernard, 10 Jan. 1997, cited by G.W. Bernard, 'Elton's Cromwell', *History*, lxxxiii (1998), p. 590, n. 18.
25 A point I emphasised in my 'Elton's Cromwell', p. 590, n. 18.
26 Pers. comm.

27 Elton, *Practice of History*, p. 163, n. 1; Harris, 'Some Origins of a Tudor Revolution', p. 1357–8.
28 Harris, 'Some Origins of a Tudor Revolution', p. 1358.
29 Harris, 'Some Origins of a Tudor Revolution', p. 1358.
30 Harris, 'Some Origins of a Tudor Revolution', p. 1358, and from an earlier draft of Dr Harris's paper.
31 Harris, 'Some Origins of a Tudor Revolution', pp. 1374–5.
32 Harris, 'Some Origins of a Tudor Revolution', p. 1376, n. 26.
33 M. Everett, *The Rise of Thomas Cromwell* (2015).
34 Harris, 'Some Origins of a Tudor Revolution', p. 1376, n. 126.
35 Harris, 'Some Origins of a Tudor Revolution', pp. 1375–7.
36 Harris, 'Some Origins of a Tudor Revolution', pp. 1364–74.
37 Harris, 'Some Origins of a Tudor Revolution', pp. 1378–82.
38 Harris, 'Some Origins of a Tudor Revolution', p. 1381.
39 Harris, 'Some Origins of a Tudor Revolution', pp. 1369–70.
40 Harris, 'Some Origins of a Tudor Revolution', pp. 1369–71.
41 Harris, 'Some Origins of a Tudor Revolution', pp. 1364–8.
42 Harris, 'Some Origins of a Tudor Revolution', pp. 1368–9; M. Greir Evans, *The Principal Secretary of State: A Survey of the Office from 1558 to 1680* (Manchester, 1923).
43 G.R. Elton, *The Tudor Revolution in Government: Administrative Changes in the Reign of Henry VIII* (Cambridge, 1953), p. 2, n 1.
44 This section draws on G.W. Bernard, 'Richard Bruce Wernham 1906-1999', *Proceedings of the British Academy*, cxxiv (2004), pp. 375–96. Much is taken from Wernham's unpublished papers, notes and diaries. I wish to thank Wernham's daughter, Joan Jerrett, for allowing me access and giving me permission to quote from them.
45 R.B. Wernham, *Before the Armada: The Growth of English Foreign Policy 1485-1588* (1966), p. 10.
46 R.B. Wernham, 'The Disgrace of William Davison', *English Historical Review*, xlvi (1931), pp. 632–6.
47 R.B. Wernham, 'Queen Elizabeth and the Siege of Rouen, 1591', *Transactions of the Royal Historical Society*, xv (1932), pp. 163–79.
48 R.B. Wernham, 'Strategic Bombing', *Oxford Magazine*, 17 May 1962, pp. 308–9.
49 Hugh Trevor-Roper, pers. comm. to author, Feb. 2002.
50 P. Williams, 'A Revolution in Tudor History? Dr Elton's Interpretation of the Age', *Past & Present*, xxv (1963), pp. 3–8; G.L. Harriss, 'Medieval Government and Statecraft', *Past & Present*, xxv (1963), pp. 8–38; P. Williams, 'A Revolution in Tudor History?: The Tudor State', *Past & Present*, xxv (1963), pp. 39–58; G.R. Elton, 'The Tudor Revolution: A Reply', *Past & Present*, xxix (1964), pp. 26–49; G.L. Harriss, 'A Revolution in Tudor History?', *Past & Present*, xxxi (1965), pp. 87–94; P. Williams, 'A Revolution in Tudor History?', *Past & Present*, xxxi (1965), pp. 94–6; G.R. Elton, 'A Revolution in Tudor History', *Past & Present*, xxxii (1965), pp. 103–9.
51 P. Williams, *The Tudor Regime* (Oxford, 1979), p. 463.
52 A. Macintyre, 'Gerald Harriss', in R.E. Archer and S. Walker, eds., *Rulers and Ruled in Late Medieval England* (1995), p. x.
53 C.S.L. Davies, 'Tudor: What's in a Name?', *History*, xcvii (2012), pp. 24–42, expands 'A Rose by Another Name', *TLS*, 13 June 2008, pp. 14–15, and 'Representation, Repute, Reality', *English Historical Review*, cxxiv (2009), pp. 1432–47.
54 Davies, 'Tudor', p. 32.
55 C.S.L. Davies, 'Information, Disinformation and Political Knowledge under Henry VII and Henry VIII', *Historical Research*, lxxxvi (2012), pp. 1–26.

56 C.S.L. Davies, *Peace, Print and Protestantism 1450-1558* (1976), p. 12.
57 This paragraph draws on the account that he wrote on 22 March 2015, stimulated by Keith Thomas's reminiscence in the *London Review of Books*.
58 C.S.L. Davies, 'Provisions for Armies 1509-1550: A Study in the Effectiveness of Early Tudor Government', *Economic History Review*, 2nd series, xvii (1964), pp. 234-48; C.S.L. Davies, 'The Administration of the Royal Navy under Henry VIII: The Origins of the Navy Board', *English Historical Review*, lxxx (1965), pp. 268-88.
59 C.S.L. Davies, 'England and the French War 1557-59', in J. Loach and R. Tittler, eds., *The Mid-Tudor Polity c.1540-1560* (1980), pp. 167-8.
60 C.S.L. Davies, 'The English People and War in the early Sixteenth Century', *Britain and the Netherlands*, vol. vi *War and Society* (The Hague, 1978), pp. 1-18.
61 C.S.L. Davies, *English Historical Review*, cxxix (2014), p. 1023.
62 C.S.L. Davies, 'The Pilgrimage of Grace Reconsidered', *Past & Present*, xl (1968), pp. 54-76.
63 C.S.L. Davies, 'Les révoltes populaires en Angleterre (1500-1700)', *Annales, ESC*, xxiv (i) 1969, pp. 24-59.
64 C.S.L. Davies, 'Popular Religion and the Pilgrimage of Grace', in A.J. Fletcher and J. Stevenson, eds., *Order and Disorder in Early Modern England 1500-1750* (1985), pp. 58-91.
65 *English Historical Review*, cxxix (2014), p. 1024.
66 C.S.L. Davies, 'Protector Somerset and Slavery: The Vagrancy Act 1547', *Economic History Review*, new series, xix (1966), pp. 533-49.
67 P.J. Gwyn, 'Wolsey's Foreign Policy: The Conferences of Calais and Bruges Reconsidered', *Historical Journal*, xxiii (1981), pp. 755-72.
68 Polydore Vergil, *Anglica Historia*, ed. D. Hay, Camden Society, lxxiv (1950), pp. 126-30, 132-4.
69 G. Walker, *John Skelton and the Politics of the 1520s* (Cambridge, 1988).
70 *The Comedy of Acolastus*, translated by John Palsgrave, ed. P. Carver, The Early English Text Society, ccii (1937), pp. xxvii, n. 1; *LP*, III ii 29, G.W. Bernard, 'The Fall of Thomas Wolsey Reconsidered', in *Power and Politics in Tudor England* (2000), p. 56.
71 LP, IV iii 5749; Bernard, 'Fall of Wolsey', pp. 55-6.
72 For more, see Blair Worden, *London Review of Books*, xii (Nov. 1990).
73 P. Gwyn, *The King's Cardinal: The Rise and Fall of Thomas Wolsey* (1990), pp. xxii.
74 P. Gwyn, *The King's Cardinal: The Rise and Fall of Thomas Wolsey* (1990), pp. xxi-xxii.
75 I. Mitchell, *The Cost of a Reputation* (1997).
76 P.J. Gwyn, review of T. Betteridge, *Writing Faith and Telling Tales* (2013), *THE* (29 Nov. 2013); review of D. Starkey, *Virtuous Prince* (2008), *THE* (15 Jan. 2009); review of D.R. Starkey, *Six Wives* (2004), *English Historical Review*, cix (2004), pp. 783-5; review of E.W. Ives, *Life and Death of Anne Boleyn: The Most Happy* (2004), *English Historical Review*, cxx (2005), pp. 1081-3.

Chapter 1a

1 Thomas Smith, *De Republica Anglorum*, ed. M. Dewar (Cambridge, 1982), p. 88.
2 The best guides are S.B. Chrimes, *Henry VII* (1972, rev. ed. with my Foreword 1999); S.J. Gunn, 'Henry VII (1457-1509), King of England and Lord of Ireland', *Oxford*

Dictionary of National Biography (2004) and P.R. Cavill, *The English Parliaments of Henry VII 1485-1504* (Oxford, 2009).
3 S. Cunningham, 'Pole, Edmund de la, eighth earl of Suffolk (1472?-1513)', *Oxford Dictionary of National Biography* (2004).
4 The best study is Gwyn, *The King's Cardinal*, pp. 159–72. *LP*, III i 1284; 1336; 1283a.
5 TNA, PRO, SP1/112 fos. 114-16 (*LP*, XI 1244).
6 G.W. Bernard, 'The Fall of Sir Thomas Seymour', in *The Tudor Nobility* (Manchester, 1992), pp. 212–40.
7 The best guide is J. Loach, *Edward VI* (1999), ch. 1.
8 C.S.L. Davies, *English Historical Review*, cxxiii (2008), p. 1537.
9 R.W. Southern, 'The Historical Sense', *TLS*, 24 June 1977, reprinted in R.W. Southern, *History and Historians: Selected Papers of R.W. Southern*, ed. R.J. Bartlett (Oxford, 2004), p. 106.
10 For a scintillating assessment of *1066 and All That*, see J. Rosebank, 'G.N. Clark and the Oxford School of Modern History: Hidden Origins of *1066 and All That*', *English Historical Review*, cxxxv (2020), pp. 127–56.
11 TNA, PRO, SP1/117 fo. 185 (*LP*, XII i 784).
12 S.M. Jack, 'Henry VIII's Attitude towards Royal Finance: Penny Wise and Pound Foolish?', in C. Giry-Deloison, ed., *Francois 1er et Henry VIII. Deux princes de la Renaissance* (1515-47) (Lille, 1996), pp. 145–63. Cf. M. Horowitz, *Historical Research*, lxxii (2009), p. 375.
13 BL, Harleian MS 296 fo. 37 (*LP*, V 363). Richard Hoyle informs me that there is a copy in Northants Record Office F (M) C 13.
14 PRO E36/118 fos. 174–174v (*LP*, XII i 98 (3)).
15 William Shakespeare, *Much ado about nothing*, Act V, sc. ii.
16 J. Loach, *Edward VI* (1999) is the best guide.
17 E. Russell, 'Mary Tudor and Mr Jorkins', *Historical Research*, lxiii (1991), pp. 263–76, esp. pp. 272, 275.
18 The classic exposition is S. Adams, 'Eliza Enthroned? The Court and Its Politics', in C. Haigh, ed., *The Reign of Elizabeth I* (Basingstoke, 1984), pp. 55–78.
19 M.J. Rodriguez Salgado, and S.L. Adams, eds., 'The Count of Feria's Dispatch to Philip II of 14 November 1558', *Camden Society: Camden Miscellany*, xxxiii (1984), pp. 302–33 at pp. 329, 331.
20 P. Collinson, 'The Monarchical Republic of Queen Elizabeth I', *Bulletin of the John Rylands Library of Manchester*, lxix (1987), pp. 394–424.
21 John Fortescue, *The Governance of England*, ed. C. Plummer (Oxford 1885), p. 109.
22 For a splendid recent rebuttal of Collinson's notions, see J. McGovern, 'Was Elizabethan England Really a Monarchical Republic?', *Historical Research*, xcii (2019), pp. 515–29.
23 J. Harington, *Nugae Antiquae*, ed. T. Park, 2 vols. (1804), i. 68–9.

Chapter 1b

1 Richard Hoyle has emphasised the force of such homilies but has not recognised that the public condemnation of rebellion was nothing new. Manifestly, the Homily of 1547 was not a response to the rebellions of 1549: R.W. Hoyle, '"Wrightsonian Incorporation" and the Public Rhetoric of Mid-Tudor England', *History*, ci (2016), pp. 20–41, esp. pp. 32–40.

2 Harington, *Nugae Antiquae*, i. 385.
3 G.W. Bernard, 'Architecture and Politics', in G.W. Bernard, ed., *Power and Politics in Tudor England* (Aldershot, 2000), pp. 175–90.
4 S. Foister, *Holbein and England* (2004), p. 261.
5 Quoted by T. Osborne, *English Historical Review*, cxxiv (2009), p. 156.
6 Cf. C.S.L. Davies, *English Historical Review*, cxxviii (2013).
7 Elton, *Studies in Tudor Politics and Government*, iii. 53.
8 See G. Dodd, 'Kingship, Parliament and the Court: The Emergence of "High Style" in Petitions to the English Crown, c. 1350-1405', *English Historical Review*, cxxix (2014), pp. 515–48 at p. 546.
9 M.H. Cole, *The Portable Queen: Elizabeth I and the Politics of Ceremony* (Amherst, 1999); M.H. Cole, 'Monarchy in Motion: An Overview of Elizabethan Progresses', in J.E. Archer, E. Goldring and S. Knight, eds., *The Progresses, Pageants, and Entertainments of Queen Elizabeth* (2007), pp. 27–45.
10 R. Strong, *Holbein and Henry VIII* (1967), pp. 6–20, 233–4, 247.
11 Payments of 7s 6d per person healed are listed in Henry VIII's privy purse expenses, which survive for the period November 1529 and December 1532: *LP*, V, pp. 747–62.
12 Cf. R. Asch, *Sacral Kingship between Disenchantment and Re-enactment: The French and English Monarchies, 1587-1688* (Oxford, 2014), pp. 1–3.
13 Cf. S. Cunningham, *Henry VII* (2007), cit. C.S.L. Davies, *English Historical Review*, cxxviii (2008), p. 1537.
14 J. Ross, '"Contrary to the Right and to the Order of the Lawe": New Evidence of Edward Dudley's Activities on behalf of Henry VII in 1504', *English Historical Review*, cxxvii (2012), pp. 24–45, esp. 39–43.
15 TNA, PRO, SP1/111 fo. 144 (*LP*, XI 1110).
16 *LP*, XIV i 144.
17 *Times*, 16 March 1972, p. 11.
18 G.R. Elton, *Policy and Police: The Enforcement of the Reformation in the Age of Thomas Cromwell* (Cambridge, 1972), p. 374.
19 TNA, PRO, SP3/12 no. 117 (*LP*, XIII i 462).
20 TNA, PRO, SP1/155 fo. 153 (*LP*, XIV ii 750).
21 *TLS*, 2 Jan. 1964.
22 TNA, PRO, SP1/143 fos. 197–206 at 205v (*LP*, XIV i 402).
23 Cf. P. Williams, *English Historical Review*, lxxxviii (1973), p. 596; (TNA, PRO, E36/118 fo. 4 [*LP*, XI 975 fo. 3]).
24 TNA, PRO, SP1/106 fo. 213 (*LP*, XI, 495).
25 TNA, PRO, SP1/138 fo. 14v (*LP*, XIII ii 695); fo. 35v (*LP*, XIII ii 703); fos. 145-145v (*LP*, XIII ii 722); fos. 185–185v (*LP*, XIII ii 804) (II); SP1/139 fo. 40 (*LP*, XIII ii 830) (1 iv); R. Morison, *An Invective against the great and detestable vice, treason* (1539), (RSTC 18111), sig. E iii–viiv.
26 TNA, PRO, SP1/130 fo. 63 (*LP*, XIII i 519); cf. P. Williams, *English Historical Review*, lxxxviii (1973), p. 596.
27 BL, Cotton MS, Cleopatra, E vi fos. 218-9 (*LP*, VIII 921); Elton, *Policy and Police*, 241.
28 BL, Cotton MS Titus B i 433 (*LP*, XIV ii 399).
29 John Leland, *Collectanea*, ed. T. Hearne (Oxford, 1715), VI. 70: cited J.H. Bettey, *The Suppression of the Monasteries in the West Country* (Gloucester, 1989), p. 101. W.R. Stacy, 'Richard Roose and the Use of Parliamentary Attainder in the Reign of Henry VIII', *Historical Journal*, xxix (1986), pp. 13, 15.
30 Ibid., pp. 13, 15.

31 J. Kaulek, ed., *Correspondance politique de MM de Castillon et Marillac, ambassadeurs de France en Angleterre, 1537-42* (Paris, 1885), no. 241, p. 209 (*LP*, XV 953).
32 Kaulek, *Correspondance politique*, no. 242, p. 211 (*LP*, XV 954).
33 TNA, PRO, SP1/116 fo. 83 (*LP*, XII i 468).

Chapter 2

1 *LP*, III i 1284 (1), 1284 (2-7).
2 *LP*, III i 1284 (3) (8) (2-8), pp. cxxxix-cxxxi.
3 *Pace* J. Watts, 'King, Lords and Men in Renaissance England: The Poetry of John Skelton', in S. Boardman and J. Goodare, eds., *Kings, Lords and Men in Scotland and Britain, 1300-1625* (Edinburgh, 2014), pp.121-35, esp. pp. 125-7.
4 N. Younger, 'The Practice and Politics of Troop-raising: Robert Devereux, Second Earl of Essex, and the Elizabethan Regime', *English Historical Review*, cxxvii (2012), pp. 566-91; N. Younger, *English Historical Review*, cxxviii (2013), pp. 1564-6; S. Alford, *English Historical Review*, cxxviii (2013), pp. 1566-8; J. Dickinson, *Court Politics and the Earl of Essex 1589-1601* (2012), For a different view see A. Gajda, *The Earl of Essex and late Elizabethan political culture* (Oxford, 2012).
5 James Ross offered a fine illustration of this in his paper at the Institute of Historical Research, University of London, in January 2019, which whets the appetite for his forthcoming book.
6 M.E. James, *Society, Politics and Culture: Studies in early Modern England* (Cambridge, 1986), is the classic modern exposition; for a succinct sketch, see S.J. Gunn, 'Off with Their Heads: The Tudor Nobility 1485-1603', in J.S. Moore, ed., *The House of Lords: A Thousand Years of British Tradition* (1994), pp. 52-65.
7 M. Weiss, 'A Power in the North? The Percies in the Fifteenth Century', *Historical Journal*, xix (1976), pp. 501-9.
8 K.B. McFarlane, *The Nobility of Later Medieval England* (Oxford, 1973), p. 120.
9 G. Walker, 'Continuity and Change in the Royal Court in Late Medieval and Renaissance England', in C.D. Baschiera and J. Everson, eds., *Scenes of Change: Studies in Cultural Tradition* (Pisa, 1996), pp. 193-210 at p. 199.
10 BL, Hatfield Microfilms, M485/39 vol. 150 fo. 84 (S. Haynes, ed., *A Collection of State Papers Relating to the Reigns of Henry VIII, Elizabeth and Mary* (1740), pp. 97, 99).
11 G.W. Bernard, 'The Rise of Sir William Compton, Early Tudor Courtier', *English Historical Review*, xcvi (1971), pp. 754-77.
12 J.A. Youings, ed., *Devon Monastic Lands, Devon and Cornwall Record Society*, new series I (1955), pp. 4-7; *LP*, XIV, i 1534 (12, 13); D. Willen, *John Russell First Earl of Bedford; One of the King's Men* (1981), pp. 30-1, 62-6.
13 Bernard, *King's Reformation*, pp. 407-32.
14 TNA, PRO, SP1/110 fos. 73-6 (*LP*, XI 930).
15 R. Holinshed, *Chronicle*, iii. 800.
16 J. Loach, *Edward VI* (1999), pp. 170-9.
17 K.J. Kesselring, *The Northern Rebellion of 1569: Faith, Politics, and Protest in Elizabethan England* (Basingstoke, 2007); P. Marshall, *English Historical Review*, cxxiv (2009), pp. 414-16.
18 C. Thompson, *The Framework of the Crisis of the Aristocracy, 1558-1641* (Wivenhoe, 1986) and *The Counting of Manors: Professor Stone's Reply Confuted* (Wivenhoe, 1990); cf. reviews of Stone, *Crisis*, by D.C. Coleman, 'The "Gentry" Controversy and the

Aristocracy in Crisis', 1558-1641, *History*, li (1966), pp. 165-78, and J.P. Cooper, *TLS*, 7 April 1966, pp. 285-8. I am grateful to Christopher Thompson for advice.
19 E. Kerridge, 'The Movement of Rent 1540-1640', *Economic History Review*, 2nd series, vi (1953-4), pp. 17, 24-5, 28.
20 R.B. Smith, *Land and Politics in the England of Henry VIII: The West Riding of Yorkshire, 1530-46* (Oxford, 1970), esp. ch. v; M.E. James, *Politics and Culture: Studies in Early Modern England* (Cambridge, 1986), esp. 'A Tudor Magnate and the Tudor State: Henry Fifth earl of Northumberland', pp. 48-90, and 'Two Tudor Funerals', pp. 176-87.

Chapter 3

1 S.B. Chrimes, *Henry VII* (1972), pp. 321-2.
2 J. Strype, *The Life of the Learned Sir Thomas Smith* (1820), p. 192.
3 *LP,* V 120.
4 BL, Harleian MS. 283, fo. 256 (*LP*, X 815); Hawkyard, *House of Commons, 1509-1558*, p. 13.
5 I. Roy, *English Historical Review*, cxxiii (2008), p. 1003.
6 J. Loach, 'Opposition to the Crown in Parliament, 1553-1558', Univ. of Oxford D.Phil. thesis (1974), p. 1.
7 C. Russell, *The Crisis of Parliaments: English History 1509-1660* (Oxford, 1971), p. 39.
8 J. Loach, *Parliament under the Tudors* (Oxford, 1991), p. 37.
9 TNA, PRO SP1/112 fo. 28 (*LP*, XI 1128).
10 BL, Cotton MS, Caligula B vi, fo. 319 (*LP*, X 816 [misdated as 1536: *recte* 1539]; Hawkyard, *House of Commons 1509-1558*, p. 18.
11 Hawkyard, *House of Commons 1509-1558*, p. 19.
12 Hawkyard, *House of Commons 1509-1558*, p. 302.
13 TNA, PRO, SP1/112 fos. 114-16 (ms is badly damaged), (*LP* XI 1244); Hawkyard, *House of Commons 1509-1558*, p. 303.
14 TNA, PRO, SP1/112 fo. 28 (*LP*, XI 1182).
15 Hawkyard, *House of Commons 1509-1558*, p. 302.
16 J. Campbell, 'The Anglo-Saxon Origins of English Constitutionalism', in R.W. Kaeuper, ed., *Law, Governance and Justice: New Views on Medieval Constitutionalism* (Brill, 2013), pp. 15-26.
17 J. Maddicott, *The Origins of the English Parliament, 924-1327* (Oxford, 2010).
18 Cf. J. Dunbabin, *English Historical Review*, cxxx (2015), p. 409.
19 A. McLaren reviewing O. Arnold, *The Third Citizen: Shakespeare's Theater and the Early Modern House of Commons* (Baltimore, 2007), *English Historical Review*, cxxiii (2008), pp. 1028-9.
20 Hawkyard, *House of Commons 1509-1558*, p. 12, citing A. Raine, *York Civic Records*, iii, *Yorkshire Archaeological Society Record Series*, cvi (1942), p. 46.
21 Hawkyard, *House of Commons 1509-1558*, pp. 12-13, citing Berkshire Record Office, W/AEp 1 and BL, Egerton MS 2093, fos. 48v-49, v = verso.
22 BL, Harleian MS. 283, fo. 256 (*LP*, X 815); Hawkyard *House of Commons 1509-1558*, pp. 13-14.
23 Hawkyard, *House of Commons 1509-1558*, p. 14, citing J. Strype, *Ecclesiastical Memorials* (6 vols in 3, Oxford, 1832), II ii, pp. 64-5).
24 Strype, *Ecclesiastical Memorials*, III, i. pp. 245-6; *Calendar State Papers, Spanish 1554-8*, p. 67; Hawkyard, *House of Commons 1509-1558,* p. 14.

25　TNA, PRO, SP1/27 fo. 145 (*LP*, III ii 2931). Hawkyard, *House of Commons 1509-1558*, p 15.
26　TNA, PRO, SP1/233 fo. 275 (*LP*, Add. I i 374).
27　TNA, PRO, SP1/112 fo. 28 (*LP*, XI 1182).
28　TNA, PRO, SP1/104 fo. 30 (*LP*, X 916).
29　Lehmberg, *Later Parliaments of Henry VIII*, pp. 4-5.
30　TNA, PRO, SP1/103 fo. 311 (*LP*, X 903).
31　S.E. Lehmberg, *The Later Parliaments of Henry VIII 1536-1547* (Cambridge, 1977), p. 5.
32　TNA, PRO, SP1/104 fos. 38v-39 (*LP*, X 929); TNA, PRO, SP1/103 fo. 274 (*LP*, X 852); BL, Add. MS, 32638 fo. 83 (R.B. Merriman, *Life and Letters of Thomas Cromwell*, 2 vols. (Oxford, 1902), ii. 13-14; Hawkyard, *House of Commons 1509-1558*, pp. 88-9, v = verso.
33　Hawkyard, *House of Commons 1509-1558*, p. 89 (no reference given).
34　BL, Cotton Caligula B vi fo. 319 (*LP*, X 816): but 1539 not 1536, Hawkyard, *House of Commons 1509-1558*, p. 18.
35　BL, Cotton MS, Cleopatra E iv fo. 209 (*LP*, XIV i 520).
36　BL, Cotton MS, Otho, E ix fo. 69 (*LP*, XIV i 573); BL, Cotton MS, Vespasian, F xiii fo. 230 (*LP*, XIV i 564).
37　Hawkyard, *House of Commons 1509-1558*, p. 20.
38　BL, Cotton MS, Titus B i fo. 266 (*LP*, XIV i 538), Hawkyard, *House of Commons 1509-1558*, p. 11.
39　*Acts of the Privy Council*, ii. pp. 516, 518.
40　Hawkyard, *House of Commons 1509-1558*, p. 16, citing BL Lansdown, MS 3 no. 19 fo. 39.
41　Loach, *Parliament under the Tudors* (Oxford, 1991), pp. 92-3.
42　Hawkyard, *House of Commons 1509-1558*, p. 64.
43　Hawkyard, *House of Commons 1509-1558*, p. 108.
44　Vienna, Haus-, Hof- und Staatsarchiv, England, Karton 5, Berichte, 1531, fo. 35 (*LP*, V 171); E. Hall, *Chronicle* (1809 ed.), p. 775.
45　BL, Cotton MS, Titus B i fo. 112 (Ellis, *Original Letters*, 1st series, i. 220; *LP*, III ii 3024).
46　Hall, *Chronicle*, p. 657 (Hawkyard, *House of Commons 1509-1558*, pp. 331-3).
47　Hall, *Chronicle*, p. 657.
48　Hawkyard, *House of Commons 1509-1558*, pp. 300-1.
49　P.R. Cavill, *The English Parliaments of Henry VII 1485-1504* (Oxford, 2007), pp. 210-12; cf. S.J. Payling, *English Historical Review*, cxxvi (2011), pp. 424-5.
50　Vienna, Haus-, Hof- und Staatsarchiv, England, Karton 5, Berichte, 1532, fos. 41-41v (*Cal. S.P., Spanish*, IV ii no. 948, pp. 440-1; *LP*, V 989); Herbert of Cherbury, *Life of Henry VIII*, p. 335; Hall, *Chronicle*, p. 788.
51　N. Tyacke, 'Introduction: Locating the "English Revolution"', in N. Tyacke, ed., *The English Revolution c.1590-1720* (Manchester, 2007), p. 14.
52　Loach, *Parliament under the Tudors*, p. 137.
53　G.L. Harriss, *English Historical Review*, cxxii (2007), p. 532; cf. P. Freedman, *English Historical Review*, cxxiv (2009), p. 138.
54　Cf. G. Hanlon, *English Historical Review*, cxxiv (2009), p. 980.
55　Hawkyard, *House of Commons 1509-1558*, pp. 4, 7-8.
56　Vienna, Haus-, Hof- und Staatsarchiv, England, Karton 4, Berichte, 1530, fo. 679v (*Cal. S.P., Spanish*, IV i no. 547, p. 853).
57　Vienna, Haus-, Hof- und Staatsarchiv, England, Karton 5, Berichte, 1531, fo. 34 (*LP*, V 171).

58 Vienna, Haus-, Hof- und Staatsarchiv, England, Karton 5, Berichte, 1531, fo. 35 (*LP*, V 171).
59 Vienna, Haus-, Hof- und Staatsarchiv, England, Karton 5, Berichte, 1532, fo. 17 (*Cal. S.P., Spanish*, IV ii no. 907, pp. 390–1; *LP*, V 832); fo. 21 (*Cal. S.P., Spanish*, IV ii no. 922, pp. 41–12); *LP*, V 879); fo. 23 (*Cal. S.P., Spanish*, IV ii, no. 926, pp. 416–18); *LP*, V 898.
60 Vienna, Haus-, Hof- und Staatsarchiv, England, Karton 5, Berichte, 1532, fos. 41–41v (*Cal. S.P., Spanish*, IV ii, no. 948, pp. 440–1; *LP*, V 989); Herbert of Cherbury, *Life of Henry VIII*, p. 335.
61 *LP*, VIII 858; TNA, PRO, SP1/93 fo. 40v (*LP*, VIII 856 [2]), v = verso; Hawkyard, *House of Commons 1509–1558*, p. 301.
62 *The Story of Parliament* (2015), p. 34.
63 Bernard, *King's Reformation*, pp. 210–12.
64 TNA, PRO, SP1/125 fos. 202–6 is the original confession (*LP*, XII ii 952 [1]); TNA, PRO, SP1/125 fos. 207–9v is a fair copy (*LP*, XII ii 952 [2]). Peter Marshall thinks that my reading 'does not quite ring true': Sir George could not have 'invented an audacious personal admonition of Henry Tudor'. Yet Sir George did not invent the whole matter. Friar William Peto, warden of the Observant Franscicans, had a short time earlier told Sir George how he, Peto, had berated the king for meddling with Anne Boleyn's sister and mother. Sir George did indeed speak out in parliament over the act of appeals. The king summoned him to explain himself and pardoned Sir George for his opposition after Sir George made a grovelling apology. It was then, I suggest, that the humiliated Sir George first boasted to his friends that he had berated the king for meddling with Anne's sister and mother. But he had not done so. Word of Sir George's boasting to his friends evidently came out somewhat later, in autumn 1537. Hence the interrogation to which he was subjected. What concerned the king at that time was how serious a threat Sir George was, how actively was he in touch with his brother Michael and through him with Reginald Pole in exile. Marshall's remark that 'the interrogatories were not predicated on the contention that no such words had passed between Sir George and the king, and neither did Sir George in his confession explicitly deny that they had' is baffling. The key point is that there is nothing in the interrogatories to support the much-repeated contention that Sir George – by contrast with Friar Peto – had ever berated the king to his face (P. Marshall, 'Crisis of Allegiance: George Throckmorton and Henry Tudor', in P. Marshall and G. Scott, eds., *Catholic Gentry in English Society: The Throckmortons of Coughton from Reformation to Emancipation* (Aldershot, 2009), pp. 40–2.
65 TNA, PRO, SP1/112 fos. 114–16 (*LP*, XI, 1244); Hawkyard, *House of Commons 1509–1558*, p. 107.
66 TNA, PRO, SP1/114 fo. 52 (*LP*, XII i 4).
67 TNA, PRO, SP1/114 fo. 49 (*LP*, XII i 43).
68 TNA, PRO, E36/118 fo. 110 (*LP*, XII i 848 I (2)).
69 J.J. Scarisbrick, *The Reformation and the English People* (Oxford, 1984), pp. 66–8.
70 For a critical view of James I and Charles I, see A. Thrush, 'Survey', in A. Thrush and J.P. Ferris, eds., *The House of Commons 1624–1629* 6 vols. (2010).
71 Cf. J.R. Maddicott, *English Historical Review* (2009), pp. 195–6; G. Dodd, *Justice and Grace: Private Petitioning and the English Parliament in the Late Middle Ages* (Oxford, 2007); W.M. Ormrod, G. Dodd and A. Musson, *Medieval Petitions* (2009).
72 Hawkyard, *House of Commons 1509–1558*, p. 108.
73 Cf. N. Vincent, *TLS*, 4 July 2008.

Chapter 4

1. S.J. Gunn, 'The Duke of Suffolk's March on Paris, 1523', *English Historical Review*, ci (1986), pp. 596–634.
2. E.T. Jones, 'Illicit Business: Accounting for Smuggling in Mid-Sixteenth-Century Bristol', *Economic History Review*, liv (2001), pp. 17–38.
3. D'Maris Coffman, 'Towards a New Jerusalem: The Committee for Regulating the Excise, 1649–1653', *English Historical Review*, cxxviii (2013), pp. 1418–50; M. Braddick, *The Nerves of State: Taxation and the Financing of the English State, 1558–1714* (Manchester, 1996), pp. 99–101.
4. I am grateful to Penry Williams for discussion of this case.
5. I owe this to Penry Williams.
6. See M.A. Faraday, ed., *Shropshire Taxes in the Reign of Henry VIII* (2015), for an excellent case study.
7. G.R. Elton, 'Taxation for War and Peace in Early Tudor England', in J.M. Winter, ed., *War and Economic Development* (Cambridge, 1975), pp. 33–48.
8. G.L. Harriss, 'Thomas Cromwell's "New Principle" of Taxation', *English Historical Review* (1978), pp. 721–38; id., 'Medieval Doctrines in the Debates on Supply, 1610–29', in K.M. Sharpe, ed., *Faction and Parliament: Essays on Early Stuart History* (Oxford, 1978), pp. 73–103.
9. *Statutes of the Realm*, iii. 516–7.
10. R.W. Hoyle, 'Crown, Taxation and Parliament in Sixteenth-Century England', *English Historical Review*, cix (1994), pp. 1174–96.
11. G. Rowlands, *The Financial Decline of a Great Power: War, Influence and Money in Louis XIV's France* (Oxford, 2012).
12. I.W. Archer, 'The burden of taxation on sixteenth-century London', *Historical Journal*, xliv (2001), pp. 627. Cf. P.K. O'Brien, 'The Triumph and Denouement of the British Fiscal State: Taxation for the Wars against Revolutionary and Napoleonic France, 1793-1815', in C. Storrs., ed., *The Fiscal-Military State in Eighteenth-Century Europe* (2009), pp. 267–300; P.K. O'Brien, 'The Nature and Historical Evolution of an Exceptional Fiscal State and Its Possible Significance for the Precocious Commercialization and Industrialization of the British Economy from Cromwell to Nelson', *Economic History Review*, lxiv (2011), pp. 408–46.
13. J. Bishop, 'Currency, Conversation, and Control: Political Discourse and the Coinage in Mid-Tudor England', *English Historical Review*, cxxxi (2016), pp. 763–92 at p. 765.
14. I owe this example to Penry Williams.

Chapter 5

1. Gunn, *English People at War*, p. 17.
2. Gunn, *English People at War*, p. 17.
3. Gunn et al., *War, State and Society*, p. 21.
4. Gunn et al., *War, State and Society*, p. 22.
5. Gunn et al., *War, State and Society*, p. 22.
6. Cf. M. Prestwich, *English Historical Review*, cxxiii (2008), pp. 1006–7.

7 J.J. Goring, 'The Military Obligations of the English People 1511–1558', Univ. of London Ph.D. thesis, 1955, is an outstanding study.
8 Gunn et al., *War, State and Society*, p. 167.
9 Gunn, *English People at War*, p. 55, sees this not as one but as four schemes: (i) raising armies under contracts with captains of individual companies, (ii) lords recruiting retinues of men sworn to their service; (iii) lords calling on a wider following of servants, tenants and friends and (iv) trusted peers, councillors, household men and towns recruiting large retinues sworn to the king's service under licence. But (ii) and (iii) are simply how (i) operated in practice, not a different system. And (iv) is a detailed elaboration of (i).
10 Gunn et al., *War, State and Society*, pp. 51–2.
11 Gunn et al., *War, State and Society*, p. 53.
12 Gunn et al., *War, State and Society*, p. 241, citing Richard Morison.
13 Gunn et al., *War, State and Society*, pp. 97–8.
14 Gunn et al., *War, State and Society*, pp. 20, 139–40.
15 Gunn, *English People at War*, pp. 57–8.
16 Gunn et al., *War, State and Society*, pp. 20, 141.
17 Younger, 'Practice and Politics of Troop-raising', p. 567.
18 Gunn et al., *War, State and Society*, p. 142.
19 Gunn et al., *War, State and Society*, p. 142.
20 Gunn et al., *War, State and Society*, p. 142.
21 Gunn et al., *War, State and Society*, p. 145.
22 Gunn, *English People at War*, p. 18.
23 Gunn et al., *War, State and Society*, p. 6.
24 Gunn et al., *War, State and Society*, p. 20.
25 J.J. Goring, 'The General Proscription', *English Historical Review*, lxxxviii (1971), pp. 681–705.
26 Gunn et al., *War, State and Society*, p. 69.
27 H.G. Ramm, R.W. McDowell and E. Mercer, eds., *Shielings and Bastles* (1970).
28 D. Cressy, 'Saltpetre, State Security and Vexation in Early Modern England', *Past & Present*, ccxii (2011), pp. 73–111.
29 Gunn, *English People at War*, p. 1.
30 Gunn, *English People at War*, p. 1.
31 A.R. Bell, A. Curry, A. King and D. Simpkin, *The Soldier in Later Medieval England* (Oxford, 2013), p. 261.
32 Gunn et al., *War, State and Society*, p. 227.
33 Gunn et al., *War, State and Society*, p. 178.
34 Gunn et al., *War, State and Society*, p. 179.
35 Gunn et al., *War, State and Society*, pp. 191–2.
36 Gunn et al., *War, State and Society*, pp. 53–5.
37 Gunn et al., *War, State and Society*, p. 253.
38 Gunn et al., *War, State and Society*, pp. 276–7.
39 Gunn et al., *War, State and Society*, p. 279.
40 Gunn, *English People at War*, p. 32.
41 Gunn, *English People at War*, p. 34.

Chapter 6

1. The following paragraphs draw out Elton's principal claims in *The Tudor Revolution in Government* and in *England under the Tudors*.
2. See M.J. Braddick, *State Formation in Early Modern England c. 1550-1700* (Cambridge, 2000); M.J. Braddick, 'State Formation and the Historiography of early Modern England', *History Compass*, ii (2004), pp. 1–17; S. Hindle, *The State and Social Change in Early Modern England* (2000).
3. J. Sabapathy, *Officers & Accountability in Medieval England 1170–1300* (Oxford, 2014).
4. P.W. Lock, 'Officeholders and Officeholding in Early Tudor England c.1520–1540', Univ. of Exeter PhD thesis, 1976, pp. 49, 95, 98, 212, 260.
5. Laura Flannigan is completing an important study of the Court of Requests: see L. Flannigan, 'Litigants in the English "Court of Poor Men's Causes", or Court of Requests, 1515-25', *Law and History Review*, xxxviii (2020), pp. 303–37.
6. T. Betteridge and L. Wooding in V. Gillespie and S. Powell, eds., *A Companion to the Early Modern Printed Book in Britain 1476–1558* (Woodbridge, 2014).
7. R. Sharpe, 'Common Carriers in Medieval England: Evidence from Oxford Archives', *Oxoniensia*, lxxxi (2016), pp. 27–62; J. Langdon, 'Horse Hauling: A Revolution in Vehicle Transport in Twelfth and Thirteenth-Century England', *Past & Present*, ciii (1984), pp. 37–66.
8. Elton, *Policy & Police*, p. 375.
9. G.L. Harriss, 'The Medieval Parliament', *Parliamentary History*, xiii (1994), pp. 206–26 at p. 208.

Chapter 7

1. *Historical Journal*, xxxvi (1993), pp. 905–8.
2. M. Everett, *The Rise of Thomas Cromwell: Power and Politics in the Reign of Henry VIII* (2015), pp. 41, 89.
3. TNA, PRO, SP60/6 fo. 48 (*LP*, XIII I 471 (7)).
4. M. Robertson, '"The Art of the Possible": Thomas Cromwell's Management of West Country Government', *Historical Journal*, xxxii (1989), pp. 793–816, p. 795.
5. D.R. Starkey, 'Representation through Intimacy: A Study in the Symbolism of Monarchy and Court Office in Early Modern England', in I.M. Lewis., ed., *Symbols and Sentiments* (1977), pp. 187–224.
6. D.R. Starkey, 'The King's Privy Chamber 1485–1547', University of Cambridge Ph.D. thesis 1973.
7. E.W. Ives, 'Henry VIII: The Political Perspective', in D. MacCulloch, ed., *The Reign of Henry VIII. Politics, Policy and Piety* (Basingstoke, 1995), pp. 32–3.
8. Elton, *Studies in Government and Politics*, iii. 39.
9. G.W. Bernard, 'The Rise of Sir William Compton, Early Tudor Courtier', *English Historical Review*, xcvi (1981).
10. G.W. Bernard and R.W. Hoyle, 'The Instructions for the Levying of the Amicable Grant, March 1525', *Historical Research*, lxvii (1994), pp. 190–202 at pp. 193, 198.
11. Elton, *Tudor Revolution in Government*, p. 5.
12. In passing it might be noted that Henry VIII was using the phrase 'a common weal' to mean the common good, the well-being of his subjects, rather than to 'the

commonwealth, the political community itself'. That rather undermines the premiss of John Watts's analysis, that the meaning of the term changed between the 1450s and the 1530s (J. Watts, '"Common Weal" and "Commonwealth": England's Monarchical Republic in the Making, c.1450–c.1530', in A. Gamberin, J.-P. Genet and A. Zorzi, eds., *The Languages of Political Society: Western Europe, 14th-17th Centuries* (2011), pp. 147–63, esp. p. 149).
13 Hawkyard, *House of Commons 1509–1558*, p. 4.
14 TNA, PRO, SP1/122 fo. 185 (*LP*, XII ii 192).
15 BL, Cotton MS, Titus B i, fo. 448v (*LP*, VIII 475).
16 BL, Cotton MS, Titus B i, fo. 449 (*LP*, VI 1370).
17 BL, Cotton MS, Titus B i fos. 446v and 478v (*LP*, VI 1370).
18 BL, Cotton MS, Titus B i, fo. 422 (*LP*, VII 52).
19 BL, Cotton MS, Titus B i, fo. 462 (*LP*, VI 1382).
20 BL, Cotton MS, Titus B i, fo. 448v (*LP*, VI 1370).
21 BL, Cotton MS, Titus B i, fos. 474–5 (*LP*, VIII 892).
22 BL, Cotton MS, Titus B i, fo. 415 (*LP*, VIII 475).
23 TNA, PRO, E36/143 fo. 69 (*LP*, IX 498).
24 BL, Cotton MS, Titus B i, fo.429.
25 BL, Cotton MS, Titus B i, fo. 450 (*LP*, XII i 1315).
26 BL, Cotton MS, Titus B i, fos. 446v and 478v (*LP*, VI 1370).
27 BL, Cotton MS, Titus B i, fo. 476 (*LP*, XV 438).
28 BBC *History Magazine*, January 2018, p. 47.

Chapter 8

1 P. Nightingale, 'The Intervention of the Crown and the Effectiveness of the Sheriff in the Execution of Judicial Writs, c. 1355–1530', *EHR*, cxxiii (2008), pp. 1–34. Dr Jon McGovern is preparing a substantial monograph on the sheriff in Tudor England.
2 The description of the work of JPs is based on *The boke for a justyce of peace neuer so well and dylygently set forthe* (1544), RSTC 14878.3.
3 A. Bryson, 'Edward VI's "Special Men": Crown and Locality in Mid Tudor England', *Historical Research*, lxxxii (2009), pp. 229–51.
4 J.R. Kent, *The English Village Constable, 1580–1642: A Social and Administrative Study*, (Oxford, 1986). For a study of a parish constable with a high sense of duty, see J. Healey, 'The Fray on the Meadow: Violence and a Moment of Government in Early Tudor England', *History Workshop Journal*, lxxxv (2018), pp. 5–25.
5 S. Hindle, 'Hierarchy and Community in the Elizabethan Parish: The Swallowfield Articles of 1596', *Historical Journal*, xlii (1999), pp. 835–51 at 848–51. Ralph Houlbrooke is completing an important study of Swallowfield.
6 A. Wall, *Power and Protest in England 1525–1640* (2000), pp. 114, 120; P. Griffiths, *Lost Londons: Change, Crime and Control in the Capital City, 1550–1660* (Cambridge, 2008).
7 B. Waddell, 'Governing England through the Manor Courts, c. 1550–1850', *Historical Journal*, lv (2012), pp. 279–315.
8 Cited by S.J. Payling, *English Historical Review*, cxxiii (2008), p. 713 from S. Walker, *Political Culture in Late Medieval England* (Manchester, 2006).

9   A.B. White, *Self-Government at the King's Command: A Study in the Beginnings of English Democracy* (Minneapolis, 1933). See review by M. Powicke, *History*, December 1934. I am very grateful to Ralph Houlbrooke for details of Swallowfield.
10 Hindle, *State and Social Change*, p. 10.
11 J. Watts, *The Making of Polities: Europe, 1300–1500* (Cambridge, 2009), pp. 424–5.
12 J.M. Gray, *Oaths and the English Reformation* (Cambridge, 2013), pp. 14–15.
13 C.E. Moreton, 'The Walsingham Conspiracy of 1537', *Historical Research*, lxiii (1990), p. 29; TNA, PRO, SP1/119 fo. 37 (*LP*, XII i 1056 [2]); A. Wood, 'The Deep Roots of Albion's Fatal Tree: The Tudor State and the Monopoly of Violence', *History*, xcix (2014), pp. 416–17. Wood sees what was going on in Walsingham as a plot to murder the gentry, unfortunately omitting the protests against religious change, especially the dissolution of the monasteries. The gentry were to be murdered for their part in enforcing religious change, *not* for being gentry. There is an instructive parallel in M.J. Stoyle, '"Kill All the Gentlemen"? Misrepresenting the Western Rebels of 1549', *Historical Research*, xcii (2019), pp. 50–72.
14 M. Braddick, *State Formation in Early Modern England c.1550–1700* (Cambridge, 2000), p. 293.
15 Ibid., p. 293.
16 Gunn, *English People at War*, p. 21.
17 Gunn, *English People at War*, pp. 11, 50.
18 I.W. Archer and F.D. Price, eds., *English Historical Documents* vol. V (a) *1558-1603* (2011), p. 95, citing BL, Harleian MS 398 fos. 12v-21.
19 G.R. Elton, 'War and the English under Henry VIII', in L. Freedman, P. Hayes and R. O. Neill, eds., *War, Strategy and International Politics: Essays in Honour of Sir Michael Howard* (Oxford, 1992), pp. 1–17.
20 Shakespeare, *Henry V*, ed. T.W. Craik, 1.i esp. 88–80, 83–9, 1 i.2 esp. 32–94; 4.1.86–183. Cf. C.S.L. Davies, *English Historical Review*, cxxxvii (2012), pp. 967–8.
21 N. Murphy, 'Henry VIII's First Invasion of France: The Gascon Expedition of 1512', *English Historical Review*, cxxx (2015), pp. 25–56. But the blunders and miscalculations were the king's.
22 G.W. Bernard, *War, Taxation and Rebellion in Early Tudor England: Henry VIII, Wolsey and the Amicable Grant of 1525* (Brighton, 1986); P. Gwyn, *The King's Cardinal* (1990), pp. 397–407.
23 TNA, PRO, SP1/110 fo. 126 (*LP*, XI 967 [v]); cf. TNA, PRO SP1/119 fos. 2-3 (*LP*, XI 828[1] [2]); SP1/110 fos. 124-24v (*LP*, XI 967 [i]); SP1/110 fo. 125 (*LP*, XI 967 [ii]).
24 P.S. Lewis, *Late Medieval France. The Polity* (1968), p. 283.
25 *Historical Manuscripts Commission, Manuscripts in the Welsh Language*, 48th appendix, part i. pp. ii–v.
26 TNA, PRO, SP1/110 fos. 6 7 (*LP*, XI 904); SP1/112 fo. 131 (*LP*, XI 1241).
27 D.M. Palliser, *Medieval York 600–1540* (Oxford, 2014), pp. 251–2.
28 C. Liddy and J. Haemers, 'Popular Politics in the Late Medieval City: York and Bruges', *English Historical Review*, cxxxviii (2013), pp. 771–805, esp. 772.
29 P. Lantschner, 'Revolts and the Political Order of Cities in the Late Middle Ages', *Past & Present*, ccxxxv (2014), pp. 3–46.
30 Liddy and Haemers, 'Popular Politics in the Late Medieval City', pp. 771–805 at p. 805.
31 TNA, PRO, SP10/8 no. 32.
32 M.J. Stoyle, '"Kill all the gentlemen"? (Mis)representing the Western Rebels of 1549', *Historical Research*, xcii (2019), pp. 50–72.
33 Stoyle, '"Kill all the gentlemen"?'

34 Cf. S.J. Payling, *English Historical Review*, cxxiii (2008), p. 713. My graduate student Connor Huddlestone is exploring the political culture – the common framework of ideas – of Tudor councillors.
35 K. Wrightson, *English Society 1580–1680* (1972), pp. 140–1, 181, closing pages; Hindle, *State and Social Change*, pp. 51, 28–9; M.L. Bush, *English Historical Review*, cxxxviii (2013), pp. 730–1 ('it was in the reign of Edward VI that the late medieval tradition of risings of the commons came to an end'). For a powerful critique see Hoyle, 'Wrightsonian Incorporation', pp. 20–41.
36 A. Wood, *The Memory of the People: Custom and Popular Senses of the Past in Early Modern England* (Cambridge, 2013), reviewed by H. French, *English Historical Review*, cxxx (2015), pp. 735–6.
37 A point made forcefully by Jeremy Catto, review of *Policy and Police*, *Sunday Times*, May 1972.
38 For Buckhurst's letter see S.E. Kershaw, 'Power and Duty in the Elizabethan aristocracy: George, earl of Shrewsbury, the Glossopdale dispute and the Council', in G.W. Bernard, ed., *The Tudor Nobility* (Manchester, 1992), pp. 259, 15 and 21.
39 Hoyle, 'Wrightsonian Incorporation', p. 31.
40 B.M.S. Campbell, 'Global Climates, the 1257 Mega-eruption of Samalas Volcano, Indonesia, and the English Food Crisis of 1258', *Transactions of the Royal Historical Society*, xxvii (2017), pp. 88–91.
41 S. Hindle, *The State and Social Change in Early Modern England* (Basingstoke, 2000), p. 119.
42 A.H.A. Hamilton, ed., *[Devon] Quarter Sessions from Queen Elizabeth to Queen Anne* (1878), p. 131. I owe this reference to Jim Sharpe.
43 J.C. Jeaffreson, ed., *Middlesex County Records*, ii (1878). I owe this reference to Jim Sharpe.

Chapter 9a

1 M.K. McIntosh, *Poor Relief in England, 1350–1600* (Cambridge, 2012), pp. 224–5; rev. P. Slack, *English Historical Review*, cxxx (2015), pp. 437–8.
2 McIntosh, *Poor Relief in England*.
3 B. Harvey, *Living and Dying in England 1100–1540* (Oxford, 1993).
4 Dyer, 'Poverty and Its Relief in Late Medieval England', *Past & Present*, ccxvi (2012), pp. 141–78.
5 McIntosh, *Poor Relief in England*, p. 128.
6 McIntosh, *Poor Relief in England*, p. 129.
7 McIntosh, *Poor Relief in England*, pp. 130–1.
8 McIntosh, *Poor Relief in England*, pp. 132–3.
9 C.S.L. Davies, 'Protector Somerset and Slavery: The Vagrancy Act 1547', *Economic History Review*, new series, xix (1966), pp. 533–49.
10 McIntosh, *Poor Relief in England*, p. 141.
11 McIntosh, *Poor Relief in England*, p. 293.
12 McIntosh, *Poor Relief in England*, p. 276.
13 D. Cressy, 'Trouble with Gypsies in Early Modern England', *Historical Journal*, lix (2016), pp. 45–70.

Chapter 9b

1. M. Aston, 'Lollardy and Literacy', *History*, lxii (1977), pp. 347–71, at p. 353.
2. S. Thompson, 'The Pastoral Work of the English and Welsh Bishops, 1500–1558', Univ. of Oxford DPhil thesis. 1984, p. 121.
3. John Foxe, *Acts and Monuments* (1570 edn.), pp. 945–6 (John Foxe, *Acts and Monuments*, ed. S.R. Cattley and G. Townsend, 8 vols.) (1837–41), iv. 228.
4. I offer a substantial treatment of this theme in my *The Late Medieval English Church: Vitality and Vulnerability before the Break with Rome* (2012), ch. ix.
5. BL, Cotton MS, Caligula B vi fo. 171 (*LP*, III I i 193); Ellis, *Original* Letters, 3rd series i. p. 239.
6. P.L. Hughes and J.F. Larkin, eds., *Tudor Royal Proclamations*, 3 vols. (1964–9), i. 129 (*LP*, IV ii 6487).
7. BL, Cotton MS, Cleopatra E v. 393 (*LP*, IV ii 3960).
8. G. Walker, 'The 1527 Heresy Trial of Thomas Bilney Reconsidered', in *'Persuasive Fictions': Faction, Faith and Political Culture in the Reign of Henry VIII* (Aldershot, 1996), pp. 143–65.
9. For a fine study of the administration of the oaths, see T. Steel, ed., *Loyalty and Levy: South-West Lancashire in the Reign of Henry VIII. The 1534 Succession Act Oath Roll and 1545 Lay Subsidy Returns for West Derby Hundred*, Record Society of Lancashire and Cheshire, clviii (2021).
10. J.M. Gray, *Oaths and the English Reformation* (Cambridge, 2013), p. 76. (As Gray points out, I mis-dated *LP*, VII 622, as 1535, instead of 1534). *LP*, IX 986. Cf. J. Walter, *English Historical Review*, cxxix (2014), pp. 1193–4.
11. Gray, *Oaths and the English Reformation*, p. 15.
12. Gray, *Oaths and the English Reformation*, p. 7.
13. Gray, *Oaths and the English Reformation*, p. 9.
14. *LP*, XIII ii 744.
15. TNA, PRO, SP1/132 fo. 124v (*LP*, XIII 1043).
16. *Cal. S.P., Spanish*, V (i) no. 58 p. 157.
17. *LP*, VI 1503.
18. The question was posed by C.S.L. Davies, in his review of R. Rex, *Henry VIII and the English Reformation, English Historical Review*, cxi (1996), p. 168. For my latest views see G.W. Bernard, 'Henry VIII: "Catholicism without the Pope?"', *History*, ci (2016), pp. 201–22.
19. K. Halliday, 'New Light on "the Commotion Time" of 1549: The Oxfordshire Rising', *Historical Research*, lxxxi (2009), pp. 655–76.
20. It was Peter Clark who first suggested this to me.
21. See my review of E. Duffy, *Fires of Faith: Catholic England under Mary Tudor, English Historical Review*, cxxvi (2011), pp. 928–30.
22. P. Marshall and J. Morgan, 'Clerical Conformity and the Elizabethan Settlement Revisited', *Historical Journal*, x (2016), pp. 1–22.
23. Cf. A. Walsham, *Charitable Hatred: Tolerance and Intolerance in England, 1500–1700* (2006); *English Historical Review*, cxxiv (2014), pp. 701–3; B. Kaplan, *Divided by Faith: Religious Conflict and the Practice of Toleration in Early Modern Europe* (Cambridge, 2007). For an eirenic Queen Elizabeth and a more sympathetic view of the queen than in his earlier biography, see C. Haigh, 'The English Reformations and the Making of the Anglican Church', St George's Cathedral, Perth Lectures, xiv (2006).

24 S. Middleton, *English Historical Review*, cxxx (2015), pp. 192–4.
25 Marshall and Morgan, 'Elizabethan Settlement Revisited', p. 16.

Chapter 9c

1 S.J. Connolly, *Contested Island: Ireland 1460–1630* (Oxford, 2007), p. 42.
2 C.S.L. Davies, *English Historical Review*, cxxviii (2013), pp. 1224–5.
3 C. Brady, review of R. Rapple, *Martial Power and Elizabethan Political Culture: Military Men in England and Ireland: 1558–1594* (Cambridge, 2009), *English Historical Review*, cxxv (2010), pp. 1247–9, esp. p. 1248.
4 C.S.L. Davies, *English Historical Review*, cxxviii (2013), p. 1225.
5 N. Murphy, 'Violence, Colonisation and Henry VIII's Conquest of France, 1544–1546', *Past & Present*, ccxxxiii (2016), pp. 13–51.
6 Davies, *English Historical Review*, p. 1225.
7 Brady, *Martial Power and Elizabethan Political Culture*, p. 1248.

Conclusion

1 Hall, *Chronicle*, pp. 781–2.
2 W.M. Ormrod, *Women and Parliament in Later Medieval England* (Cham, Switzerland, 2020), esp. pp. 1, 9–10.
3 J.A. Guy, *The Cardinal's Court: The Impact of Thomas Wolsey's Star Chamber* (Hassocks, 1977).
4 D. Youngs, '"A Besy Woman . . . and Full of Lawe": Female Litigants in Early Tudor Star Chamber', *Journal of British Studies*, lviii (2019), pp. 735–50, esp. p. 735.
5 Guy, *Cardinal's Court*, p. 109, n. 19.
6 Youngs, 'Besy Woman', p. 739.
7 T. Stretton, *Women Waging War in Elizabethan England* (Cambridge, 1998), pp. 7–8, 41–2, 174.
8 Bernard, *King's Reformation*, p. 396; *LP*, XII i 1156, 1214 (1, 2).
9 TNA, PRO, SP1/47 fo. 83v (*LP*, IV ii 4044), v = verso.
10 For a fine overall survey of the status of women, see R.A. Houlbrooke, 'Women's Social Life and Common Action in England from the Fifteenth Century to the Eve of Civil War', *Continuity and Change*, i (1986), pp. 171–89.
11 The phrasing is David Parker's.
12 R. Oates, 'Puritans and the "Monarchical Republic": Conformity and Conflict in the Elizabethan Church', *English Historical Review*, cxxvii (2012), pp. 819–43.

Epilogue

1 K.B. McFarlane, *Letters to Friends 1940–1966*, ed. G.L. Harriss (Oxford, 1997), pp. 97–8.
2 O. MacDonagh, 'The Nineteenth-Century Revolution in Government: A Reappraisal', *Historical Journal*, i (1958), pp. 52–67.
3 pers. comm. 25 April 1987.

4 I am grateful to Greg Walker for some especially helpful comments here.
5 D. MacCulloch, *Thomas Cromwell: A Life* (2018), is less a biography than a book-length assertion of MacCulloch's notion that Thomas Cromwell was a religious radical who tried to impose a Protestant reformation in England. In my *King's Reformation* (2005), pp. 512–79, I had earlier shown how such a reading rests on misunderstanding of the evidence of the surviving sources. Unfortunately, an occasional dismissive sentence aside, MacCulloch fails to engage. I stand with Hugh Kearney: 'conflicting interpretations are a commonplace of historical writing, but once their existence is recognised, the historian is no longer free to adopt the simplicity of one point of view alone' (*Strafford in Ireland 1633–41: A Study in Absolutism* (1959), preface, p. xii.
6 H. Mantel, BBC Reith Lectures, 2017, second lecture, pp. 5, 8.

Bibliography

Primary Sources: Manuscript

British Library, London
Cotton MS
   Caligula B
   Cleopatra E vi
   Otho E
   Titus B I
   Vespasian F xiii
Harleian MS
Lansdowne MS
Additional MS
Hatfield Microfilms, M485/39

The National Archives, Public Record Office, Kew
TNA, PRO
SP1
SP3
E36
PRO31/18

Haus-Hof und Staatsarchiv, Vienna
England, Karton 5, Berichte

Primary Sources: Printed

Acts of the Privy Council

Calendars of State Papers, Spanish

The boke for a justyce of peace neuer so well and dylygently set forthe (1544), RSTC 14878.3

Brewer, J.S., Gairdner, J., and Brodie, R.H., *Letters and Papers, Foreign and Domestic, of the reign of Henry VIII* (21 vols. in 36), 1862–1932.
Merriman, R.B., ed., *Life and Letters of Thomas Cromwell* (Oxford, 2 vols., 1902).
Faraday, M.A., ed., *Shropshire Taxes in the reign of Henry VIII* (2015).
Rodriguez Salgado, M.J., and Adams, S.L., eds., 'The count of Feria's dispatch to Philip II of 14 November 1558', *Camden Society: Camden Miscellany*, xxxiii (1984), pp. 302–33.
John Fortescue, *The Governance of England*, ed. C. Plummer (Oxford 1885).

John Foxe, *Acts and Monuments*, ed. S.R. Cattley and G. Townsend (8 vols., 1837–41).
Edward Hall, *Chronicle* (1809 ed.),
John Harington, *Nugae Antiquae*, ed. T. Park (2 vols., 1804).
Haynes, S., ed., *A Collection of State Papers relating to the reigns of Henry, VIII, Elizabeth and Mary* (1740).
Herbert of Cherbury, *Life of Henry VIII* (1649).
Historical Manuscripts Commission, Manuscripts in the Welsh Language, 48th appendix, part i. pp. ii–v.
Holinshed, R., *Chronicles* (6 vols, 1807–08).
Hughes, P.L, and J.F.. Larkin, eds., *Tudor Royal Proclamations* (3 vols., 1964–9).
Kaulek, J., ed., *Correspondance politique de MM de Castillon et Marillac, ambassadeurs de France en Angleterre, 1537–42* (Paris, 1885).
Richard Morison, *An Invective against the greate and detestable vice, treason* (1539), (RSTC 18111).
The Comedy of Acolastus, translated by John Palsgrave, ed P. Carver, *The Early English Text Society*, ccii (1937).
William Shakespeare, *Henry V*; *Much ado about nothing*.
Thomas Smith, *De Republica Anglorum*, ed. M. Dewar (Cambridge, 1982).
Steel, T., ed., *Loyalty and Levy: South-West Lancashire in the Reign of Henry VIII. The 1534 Succession Act Oath Roll and 1545 Lay Subsidy Returns for West Derby Hundred*, Record Society of Lancashire and Cheshire, clviii (2021).
J. Strype, *Ecclesiastical Memorials* (6 vols in 3 parts, Oxford, 1832).
Polydore Vergil, *Anglica Historia*, ed. D. Hay, *Camden Society*, lxxiv (1950).

Secondary Sources

Adams, S., 'Eliza Enthroned? The Court and its politics', in C. Haigh, ed., *The Reign of Elizabeth I* (Basingstoke, 1984), pp. 55–78.
Alford, S., review of J. Dickinson, *Court Politics and the Earl of Essex 1589-1601* (2012), *English Historical Review*, cxxviii (2013), pp. 1566–8.
Archer, I.W., 'The burden of taxation on sixteenth-century London', *Historical Journal*, xliv (2001), pp. 599–627.
Archer I.W., and Price, F.D. eds., *English Historical Documents*, vol. V (a) *1558–1603* (London, 2011).
Archer J.E., Goldring, E., and Knight, S., eds., *The Progresses, Pageants, and Entertainments of Queen Elizabeth* (Oxford, 2014).
Asch, R., *Sacral Kingship between Disenchantment and Re-enactment: The French and English Monarchies, 1587–1688* (Oxford, 2014).
Aston, M., 'Lollardy and literacy', *History*, lxii (1977), pp. 347–71.
Bell, A.R., Curry A., King, A., and Simpkin, D., *The Soldier in Later Medieval England* (Oxford, 2013).
Bernard, G.W., 'The rise of Sir William Compton, early Tudor courtier', *English Historical Review*, xcvi (1971), pp. 754–77.
Bernard, G.W., *War, Taxation and Rebellion in early Tudor England: Henry VIII, Wolsey and the Amicable Grant of 1525* (Brighton, 1986).
Bernard, G.W.,'The fall of Sir Thomas Seymour', in G.W. Bernard, ed., *The Tudor Nobility* (Manchester, 1992), pp. 212–40, reprinted in G.W. Bernard, *Power and Politics in Tudor England* (Aldershot, 2000), pp. 134–60.

Bernard, G.W., and Hoyle, R.W., 'The instructions for the levying of the Amicable Grant, March 1525', *Historical Research*, lxvii (1994), pp. 190-202.

Bernard, G.W., 'The fall of Thomas Wolsey reconsidered', xxxv (1996), pp. 277-310, reprinted in G.W. Bernard, *Power and Politics in Tudor England* (Aldershot, 2000), pp. 51-79.

Bernard, G.W., *Power and Politics in Tudor England* (Aldershot, 2000).

Bernard, G.W., 'Elton's Cromwell', *History*, lxxxiii (1998), pp. 587-607, reprinted in G.W. Bernard, *Power and Politics in Tudor England* (Aldershot, 2000), pp. 108-28.

Bernard, G.W. 'Architecture and politics', in G.W. Bernard, ed., *Power and Politics in Tudor England* (Aldershot, 2000), pp. 175-90.

Bernard, G.W., 'Richard Bruce Wernham 1906-1999', *Proceedings of the British Academy*, cxxiv (2004), pp. 375-96.

Bernard, G.W., *The King's Reformation: Henry VIII and the remaking of the English Church* (2005).

Bernard, G.W., review of E. Duffy, *Fires of Faith: Catholic England under Mary Tudor*, *English Historical Review*, cxxvi (2011), pp. 928-30.

Bernard, G.W., *The Late Medieval English Church: Vitality and Vulnerability Before the Break with Rome* (2012).

Bettey, J.H., *The Suppression of the Monasteries in the West Country* (Gloucester, 1989).

Bishop, J., 'Currency, conversation, and control: political 'discourse and the coinage in mid-Tudor England', *English Historical Review*, cxxxi (2016), pp. 763-92.

Braddick, M.J., *The Nerves of State: Taxation and the Financing of the English State, 1558-1714* (Manchester, 1996).

Braddick, M.J., *State Formation in Early Modern England c.1550-1700* (Cambridge, 2000).

Braddick. M.J., 'State formation and the historiography of early modern England', *History Compass*, ii (2004), pp. 1-17.

Brady, C., review of R. Rapple, *Martial Power and Elizabethan Political Culture: Military Men in England and Ireland: 1558-1594* (Cambridge, 2009), *English Historical Review*, cxxv (2010), pp. 1247-9.

Bryson, A.,'Edward VI's "special men": crown and locality in mid Tudor England', *Historical Research*, lxxxii (2009), pp. 229-51.

Campbell, B.M.S.,'Global climates, the 1257 mega-eruption of Samalas volcano, Indonesia, and the English Food Crisis of 1258', *Transactions of the Royal Historical Society*, xxvii (2017), pp. 88-91.

Campbell, J., 'The Anglo-Saxon origins of English constitutionalism', in R.W. Kaeuper, ed., *Law, Governance and Justice: New Views on Medieval Constitutionalism* (Brill, 2013), pp. 15-26.

Carr, E.H., *What Is History?* (1961).

Cavill, P.R., *The English Parliaments of Henry VII 1485-1504* (Oxford, 2009).

Chrimes, S.B., *Henry VII* (1972), rev. ed. with Foreword by G.W. Bernard (1999).

Coffman, D'Maris, 'Towards a New Jerusalem: the Committee for Regulating the excise, 1649-1653', *English Historical Review*, cxxviii (2013), pp. 1418-50.

Cole, M.H., *The Portable Queen: Elizabeth I and the Politics of Ceremony* (Amherst, MA, 1999).

Cole, M.H., 'Monarchy in motion: an overview of Elizabethan progresses', in J.E. Archer, E. Goldring and S. Knight, eds., *The Progresses, Pageants, and Entertainments of Queen Elizabeth* (2014), pp. 27-45.

Coleman, D.C.,'The "Gentry" controversy and the aristocracy in crisis, 1558-1641', *History*, li (1966), pp. 165-78.

Collinson, P., 'Geoffrey Rudolf Elton 1921-94', *Proceedings of the British Academy: Memoirs of Fellows of the British Academy*, xc (1997), pp. 429-58.

Collinson, P., 'The Monarchical Republic of Queen Elizabeth I', *Bulletin of the John Rylands Library of the University of Manchester*, lxix (1987), pp. 394-424.

Connolly, S.J., *Contested Island: Ireland 1460-1630* (Oxford, 2009).

Cooper, J.P., review of L. Stone, *Crisis of the Aristocracy*, TLS, 7 April 1966, pp. 285-8.

Cressy, D., 'Saltpetre, state security and vexation in early modern England', *Past and Present*, ccxii (2011), pp. 73-111.

Cressy, D., 'Trouble with Gypsies in early modern England', *Historical Journal*, lix (2016), pp. 45-70.

Cunningham, S. 'Pole, Edmund de la, eighth earl of Suffolk (1472?-1513)', *Oxford Dictionary of National Biography* (2004).

Cunningham, S., *Henry VII* (2007).

Davies, C.S.L.,'Provisions for armies 1509-1550: a study in the effectiveness of early Tudor government', *Economic History Review*, 2nd series, xvii (1964), pp. 234-48.

Davies, C.S.L., 'The administration of the Royal Navy under Henry VIII: the origins of the Navy Board', *English Historical Review*, lxxx (1965), pp. 268-88.

Davies, C.S.L., 'Protector Somerset and Slavery: the Vagrancy Act 1547', *Economic History Review*, new series, xix (1966), pp. 533-49.

Davies, C.S.L., 'The Pilgrimage of Grace reconsidered', *Past & Present*, xl (1968), pp. 54-76.

Davies, C.S.L., 'Les révoltes populaires en Angleterre (1500-1700)', *Annales, ESC*, xxiv (i) (1969), pp. 24-59.

Davies, C.S.L., *Peace, Print and Protestantism 1450-1558* (1976).

Davies, C.S.L., 'The English people and war in the early sixteenth century', *Britain and the Netherlands*, vol. vi, *War and Society* (The Hague, 1978), pp. 1-18.

Davies, C.S.L.. 'England and the French War 1557-59', in J. Loach and R. Tittler, eds., *The Mid-Tudor Polity c.15 40-1560* (1980), pp. 159-85.

Davies, C.S.L., 'Popular religion and the Pilgrimage of Grace', in A.J. Fletcher and J. Stevenson, eds., *Order and Disorder in Early Modern England 1500-1750* (Cambridge, 1985), pp. 58-91.

Davies, C.S.L., 'A rose by another name', *TLS*, 13 June 2008, pp. 14-15.

Davies, C.S.L., review of S. Cunningham, *Henry VII, English Historical Review*, cxxiii (2008), p. 1537.

Davies, C.S.L., 'Representation, repute, reality', *English Historical Review*, cxxiv (2009), pp. 1432-47.

Davies, C.S.L.,'Tudor: what's in a name?', *History*, xcvii (2012), pp. 24-42.

Davies, C.S.L., 'Information, disinformation and political knowledge under Henry VII and Henry VIII', *Historical Research*, lxxxvi (2012), pp. 1-26.

Davies C.S.L., review of P. Pugliatti, *Shakespeare and the Just War Tradition* (2010), *English Historical Review*, cxxvii (2012), pp. 976-8.

Davies, C.S.L., review of C. Maginn, *William Cecil, Ireland and the Tudor State* (2012), *English Historical Review*, cxxviii (2013), pp. 1224-5.

Davies, C.S.L., review of C. Richmond, *Doing History*, in *English Historical Review*, cxxix (2014), pp. 1022-24.

Dickinson, J., *Court Politics and the Earl of Essex 1589-1601* (2012).

Dodd, G., *Justice and Grace: Private Petitioning and the English Parliament in the Late Middle Ages* (Oxford, 2007).

Dodd, G., 'Kingship, Parliament and the Court: the emergence of "High Style" in petitions to the English crown, c. 1350-1405', *English Historical Review*, cxxix (2014), pp. 515-48.
Dunbabin, J., review of H. Oudart, J.-M. Picard and J. Quaghebeur, eds., *Le Prince, son Peuple, et le bien commun de l'Antiquite tardive a la fin du moyen age* (2013), *English Historical Review*, cxxx (2015), p. 409.
Dyer, C., 'Poverty and its relief in late medieval England', *Past and Present*, ccxvi (2012), pp. 141-78.
Elton, G.R., 'The terminal date of Caesar's Gallic Proconsulate', *Journal of Roman Studies*, xxxvi (1946), pp. 18-42, reprinted in G.R. Elton, *Studies in Tudor and Stuart Politics and Government* 4 vols (1974-91), i. 1-36.
Elton, G.R., *Tudor Revolution in Government: Administrative Changes in the Reign of Henry VIII* (Cambridge, 1953).
Elton, G.R., *England under the Tudors* (1955).
Elton, G.R., 'The tudor revolution: a reply', *Past & Present*, xxix (1964), pp. 26-49.
Elton, G.R., 'A revolution in tudor history', *Past & Present*, xxxii (1965), pp. 103-9.
Elton, G.R., *The Practice of History* (1967).
Elton, G.R., *Policy and police: the enforcement of the reformation in the age of Thomas Cromwell* (Cambridge, 1972).
Elton, G.R., 'Taxation for war and peace in early Tudor England', in J.M. Winter, ed., *War and Economic Development* (Cambridge, 1975), pp. 33-48.
Elton, G.R., *Studies in Tudor and Stuart Politics and Government*, 4 vols. (1974-1981).
Elton, G.R., 'War and the English under Henry VIII', in L. Freedman, P. Hayes and R. O. Neill, eds., *War, Strategy and International Politics: essays in honour of Sir Michael Howard* (Oxford, 1992), pp. 1-17.
Elton, G.R., 'How corrupt was Thomas Cromwell?', *Historical Journal*, xxxvi (1993), pp. 905-8.
Everett, M., *The Rise of Thomas Cromwell: Power and Politics in the Reign of Henry VIII* (2015).
Foister, S., *Holbein and England* (2004).
Freedman, P., review of T.F. Ruiz, *Spain's Centuries of Crisis, 1300-1474* (2007), *English Historical Review*, cxxiv (2009), p. 138.
French, H., review of A. Wood, *The Memory of the People: Custom and Popular Senses of the Past in Early Modern England* (Cambridge, 2013), *English Historical Review*, cxxx (2015), pp. 735-6.
Gajda, A., *The Earl of Essex and Late Elizabethan Political Culture* (Oxford, 2012).
Goring, J.J., 'The military obligations of the English people 1511-1558', Univ. of London Ph.D. thesis, 1955.
Goring, J.J., 'The general proscription', *English Historical Review*, lxxxviii (1971), pp. 681-705.
Gray, J.M., *Oaths and the English Reformation* (Cambridge, 2013).
Griffiths, P., *Lost Londons: Change, Crime and Control in the Capital City, 1550-1660* (Cambridge, 2008).
Gunn, S.J., 'Henry VII (1457-1509), king of England and lord of Ireland', *Oxford Dictionary of National Biography* (2004).
Gunn S.J., 'The Duke of Suffolk's march on Paris, 1523', *English Historical Review*, ci (1986), pp. 596-634.
Gunn, S.J., 'Off with their heads: the Tudor nobility 1485-1603', in J.S. Moore, ed., *The House of Lords: A Thousand Years of British Tradition* (1994), pp. 52-65.

Gunn, S.J., *Early Tudor Government 1485-1558* (Basingstoke, 1995).

Gunn, S.J., Grummitt, D., and Cools, H., *War, State and Society in England and the Netherlands, 1477-1559* (Oxford, 2007).

Gunn, S.J., *Henry VII's New Men and the Making of Tudor England* (Oxford, 2016).

Gunn, S,J., *The English People at War in the Age of Henry VIII* (Oxford, 2018).

Guy. J.A., *The Cardinal's Court: The Impact of Thomas Wolsey's Star Chamber* (Hassocks, 1977).

Gwyn, P.J.,'Wolsey's foreign policy: the conferences of Calais and Bruges reconsidered', *Historical Journal*, xxiii (1981), pp. 755-72.

Gwyn, P., *The King's Cardinal* (1990).

Gwyn, P., review of T. Betteridge, *Writing Faith and Telling Tales* (Notre Dame, 2013), *THE* (29 Nov. 2013).

Gwyn, P., review of D. Starkey, *Virtuous Prince* (2008), *THE* (15 Jan. 2009).

Gwyn, P., review of D. Starkey, *Six Wives* (2004), *English Historical Review*, cix (2004), pp. 783-5.

Gwyn, P., review of E.W. Ives, *Life and Death of Anne Boleyn: The Most Happy* (2004), *English Historical Review*, cxx (2005), pp. 1081-3.

Haigh, C., 'The English reformations and the making of the Anglican church', *St George's Cathedral, Perth Lectures*, xiv (2006).

Halliday, K.,'New light on "the commotion time" of 1549: the Oxfordshire rising', *Historical Research*, lxxxi (2009), pp. 655-76.

G. Hanlon, review of T. Blanning, *The Pursuit of Glory: Europe 1648-1815* (2007), in *English Historical Review*, cxxiv (2009), pp. 979-81.

Harris, I.C., 'Some origins of a Tudor Revolution', *English Historical Review*, cxxvi (2011), pp. 1355-85.

Harriss, G.L.,'A Revolution in Tudor History? Medieval Government and Statecraft', *Past & Present*, xxv (1963), pp. 8-38.

Harriss, G.L.,'A Revolution in Tudor History?', *Past & Present*, xxxi (1965), pp. 87-94.

Harriss, G.L., 'Thomas Cromwell's "new principle" of taxation', *English Historical Review*, xciii (1978), pp. 721-38.

Harriss, G.L., 'Medieval Doctrines in the debates on supply, 1610-29', in K.M. Sharpe, ed., *Faction and Parliament: Essays on Early Stuart History* (Oxford, 1978), pp. 73-103.

Harriss, G.L., 'The Medieval Parliament', *Parliamentary History*, xiii (1994), pp. 206-26 at p. 208.

Harriss, G.L., review of L. Scordia, *'Le roi doit vivre du sien': la théorie de l'impot en France (XIIIe-XV siecles*, in *English Historical Review*), cxxii (2007), pp. 531-2.

Hawkyard, A., *The House of Commons, 1509-1558, Personnel, Procedure, Precedent and Change* (2019).

Healey, J., 'The Fray on the meadow: violence and a moment of government in early Tudor England', *History Workshop Journal*, lxxxv (2018), pp. 5-25.

Hindle, S., 'Hierarchy and community in the Elizabethan parish: the Swallowfield Articles of 1596', *Historical Journal*, xlii (1999), pp. 835-51.

Hindle, S., *The State and Social Change in Early Modern England* (Basingstoke, 2000).

Horowitz, M., 'Policy and prosecution in the reign of Henry VII', *Historical Research*, lxxii (2009), pp. 412-50.

Houlbrooke, R.A., 'Women's social life and common action in England from the fifteenth century to the eve of civil war', *Continuity and Change*, i (1986), pp. 171-89.

Hoyle, R.W., 'Crown, taxation and parliament in sixteenth-century England', *English Historical Review*, cix (1994), pp. 1174-96.

Hoyle, R.W., '"Wrightsonian Incorporation" and the public rhetoric of mid-Tudor England', *History*, ci (2016), pp. 20–41.
Ives, E.W., *Faction in Tudor England* (1979, 2nd ed. 1986).
Ives, E.W., 'Henry VIII: the political perspective', in D. MacCulloch, ed., *The Reign of Henry VIII. Politics, Policy and Piety* (Basingstoke, 1995), pp. 32–3.
Jack, S.M., 'Henry VIII's attitude towards royal finance: penny wise and pound foolish?', in C. Giry-Deloison, ed., *Francois 1er et Henry VIII. Deux princes de la Renaissance (1515-1547)* (Lille, 1996), pp. 145–63.
James, M.E., *Society, Politics and Culture: Studies in Early Modern England* (Cambridge, 1986).
James, M.E., 'A Tudor Magnate and the Tudor State: Henry fifth earl of Northumberland', in M.E. James, *Politics and Culture: Studies in Early Modern England* (Cambridge, 1986), pp. 48–90.
James, M.E., 'Two Tudor funerals', in M.E. James, *Politics and Culture: Studies in Early Modern England* (Cambridge, 1986), pp. 176–87.
Jones, E.T., 'Illicit business: accounting for smuggling in mid- sixteenth-century Bristol', *Economic History Review*, liv (2001), pp. 17–38.
Kaplan, B., *Divided by Faith: Religious Conflict and the Practice of Toleration in Early Modern Europe* (Cambridge, 2007).
Kearney, H., *Strafford in Ireland 1633-41: A Study in Absolutism* (Manchester, 1959).
Kent, J.R., *The English Village Constable, 1580-1642: A Social and Administrative Study* (Oxford, 1986).
Kerridge, E., 'The movement of rent 1540-1640', *Economic History Review*, 2nd series, vi (1953-4), pp. 16–34.
Kesselring, K.J., *The Northern Rebellion of 1569: Faith, Politics, and Protest in Elizabethan England* (Basingstoke, 2007).
Lantschner, P., 'Revolts and the political order of cities in the late middle ages', *Past & Present*, ccxxv (2014), pp. 3–46.
Lehmberg, S.E., *The Later Parliaments of Henry VIII 1536-1547* (Cambridge, 1977).
Lewis, P.S., *Late Medieval France. The Polity* (1968).
Liddy C., and Haemers, J., 'Popular politics in the late Medieval City: York and Bruges', *English Historical Review*, cxxviii (2013), pp. 771–805.
Loach, J., 'Opposition to the crown in parliament, 1553–1558', Univ. of Oxford D. Phil. thesis (1974).
Loach, J., *Parliament and the Crown in the Reign of Mary Tudor* (Oxford, 1986).
Loach, J., *Parliament under the Tudors* (Oxford, 1991).
Loach, J., *Edward VI* (1999).
Lock, P.W., 'Officeholders and officeholding in early Tudor England c.1520-1540', Univ. of Exeter Ph.D. thesis, 1976.
Langdon, J., 'Horse hauling: a revolution in vehicle transport in twelfth and thirteenth-century England', *Past & Present*, ciii (1984), pp. 37–66.
MacCulloch, D.M., *Thomas Cromwell: A Life* (2018).
Macintyre, A., 'Gerald Harriss', in R.E. Archer and S. Walker, eds., *Rulers and Ruled in Late Medieval England* (1995), pp. ix–xvi.
Marshall, P., review of K.J. Kesselring, *The Northern Rebellion of 1569: Faith, Politics, and Protest in Elizabethan England* (Basingstoke, 2007), *English Historical Review*, cxxiv (2009), pp. 414–16.
McFarlane, K.B., *The Nobility of Later Medieval England* (Oxford, 1973).
Maddicott, J.R, *The Origins of the English Parliament, 924–1327* (Oxford, 2010).

Maddicott, J.R., *English Historical Review*, (2009), pp. 195–6.
Mantel, H., *BBC Reith Lectures* (2017).
Marshall, P., 'Crisis of allegiance: George Throckmorton and Henry Tudor', in P. Marshall and G. Scott, eds., *Catholic Gentry in English Society: The Throckmortons of Coughton from Reformation to Emancipation* (Aldershot, 2009), pp. 40–42.
Marshall, P., and Morgan, J., 'Clerical conformity and the Elizabethan settlement revisited', *Historical Journal*, x (2016), pp. 1–22.
MacDonagh, O., 'The nineteenth-century revolution in government: a reappraisal', *Historical Journal*, i (1958), pp. 52–67.
McFarlane, K.B., *Letters to Friends 1940–1966*, ed. G.L. Harriss (Oxford, 1997).
McGovern, J., 'Was Elizabethan England really a monarchical republic?', *Historical Research*, xcii (2019), pp. 515–29.
McIntosh, M.K., *Poor Relief in England, 1350–1600* (Cambridge, 2012).
McLaren, A., review of O. Arnold, *The Third Citizen: Shakespeare's Theater and the Early Modern House of Commons* (Baltimore, 2007), *English Historical Review*, cxxiii (2008), pp. 1028–9.
Middleton, S., review of E. Haefeli, *New Netherland and the Dutch Origins of American Toleration* (2012), *English Historical Review*, cxxx (2015), pp. 192–4.
Mitchell, I., *The Cost of a Reputation* (1997).
Moreton, C.E., 'The Walsingham conspiracy of 1537', *Historical Research* lxiii (1990), pp. 29–43.
Morton, A., review of M.L. Bush, *The Pilgrims' Complaint: A Study of Political Thought in the Early Tudor North*, *English Historical Review*, cxxviii (2013), pp. 672–4.
Murphy, N., 'Henry VIII's first invasion of France: the Gascon Expedition of 1512', *English Historical Review*, cxxx (2015), pp. 25–56.
Murphy, N., 'Violence, colonisation and Henry VIII's conquest of France, 1544–1546', *Past & Present*, ccxxxiii (2016), pp. 13–51.
Nightingale, P., 'The intervention of the crown and the effectiveness of the sheriff in the execution of judicial writs, c. 1355–1530', *English Historical Review*, cxxiii (2008), pp. 1–34.
Oates, R.,'Puritans and the "Monarchical Republic": conformity and conflict in the Elizabethan church', *English Historical Review*, cxxvii (2012), pp. 819–43.
O'Brien, P.K., 'The triumph and denouement of the British fiscal state: taxation for the wars against Revolutionary and Napoleonic France, 1793–1815', in C. Storrs, ed., *The Fiscal-Military State in Eighteenth-Century Europe* (2009), pp. 267–200.
O'Brien, P.K., 'The nature and historical evolution of an exceptional fiscal state and its possible significance for the precocious commercialization and industrialization of the British economy from Cromwell to Nelson', *Economic History Review*, lxiv (2011), pp. 408–46.
Ormrod, W.M., *Women and Parliament in Later Medieval England* (Cham, Switzerland, 2020).
Ormrod, W.M., Dodd, G., and Musson, A., *Medieval Petitions* (York, 2009).
Osborne, T., review of J.E. Archer, E. Goldring, and S. Knight, eds., *The Progresses, Pageants, and Entertainments of Queen Elizabeth* (2014), *English Historical Review*, cxxiv (2009), pp. 155–7.
Palliser, D.M., *Medieval York 600–1540* (Oxford, 2014).
Payling, S.J., review of S. Walker, *Political Culture in Late Medieval England* (Manchester, 2006), *English Historical Review*, cxxiii (2008), pp. 712–4.
Payling, S.J, review of P.R. Cavill, *The English Parliaments of Henry VII 1485–1504* (Oxford, 2007), *English Historical Review*, cxxvi (2011), pp. 424–5.

Payling, S.J., review of S.J. Gunn, *Henry VII's New Men & the Making of Tudor England* (Oxford, 2016), *Parliamentary History*, xxxvi (2017), pp. 393-6.

Powicke, M., review of A.B. White, *Self-Government at the King's Command: A Study in the Beginnings of English Democracy* (Minneapolis, 1933), *History*, xix (Dec. 1934).

Prestwich, M., review of Y.N. Harari, *Special Operations in the Age of Chivalry, 1100-1550*, *English Historical Review*, cxxiii (2008), pp. 1006-7.

Ramm, H.G., McDowell R.W., and E. Mercer, eds., *Shielings and Bastles* (1970).

Robertson, M., '"The art of the possible": Thomas Cromwell's management of West Country government', *Historical Journal*, xxxii (1989), pp. 793-816.

Rosebank, J., 'G.N. Clark and the Oxford School of Modern History: Hidden Origins of *1066 and All That*', *English Historical Review*, cxxxv (2020), pp. 127-56.

Ross, J., '"Contrary to the right and to the order of the lawe": new evidence of Edward Dudley's activities on behalf of Henry VII in 1504', *English Historical Review*, cxxvii (2012), pp. 24-45.

Rowlands, G., *The Financial Decline of a Great Power: War, Influence and Money in Louis XIV's France* (Oxford, 2012).

Roy, I., review of R.B. Manning, *An apprenticeship in arms: the origins of the British army 1585-1702* (Oxford, 2006), *English Historical Review*, cxxiii (2008), pp. 1033-5.

Russell, C., *The Crisis of Parliaments: English History 1509-1660* (Oxford, 1971).

Russell, E., 'Mary Tudor and Mr Jorkins', *Historical Research*, lxiii (2001), pp. 263-76.

Sabapathy, J., *Officers & Accountability in Medieval England 1170-1300* (Oxford, 2014).

Scarisbrick, J.J., *Henry VIII* (1968).

Scarisbrick, J.J., *The Reformation and the English People* (Oxford, 1984).

Sharpe, R., 'Common carriers in medieval England: evidence from Oxford archives', *Oxoniensia*, lxxxi (2016), pp. 27-62.

Slack, P., review of M.K. McIntosh, *Poor Relief in England, 1350-1600* (Cambridge, 2012). *English Historical Review*, cxxx (2015), pp. 437-8.

Smith R.B., *Land and Politics in the England of Henry VIII: The West Riding of Yorkshire, 1530-46* (Oxford, 1970).

Southern, R.W, 'The historical sense', *TLS*, 24 June 1977, reprinted in R.W. Southern, *History and Historians: Selected Papers of R.W. Southern*, ed. R.J. Bartlett (Oxford, 2004), p. 106.

Stacy, W.R., 'Richard Roose and the use of parliamentary attainder in the reign of Henry VIII', *Historical Journal*, xxix (1986), pp. 1-15.

Starkey D.R., 'The king's privy chamber 1485-1547', University of Cambridge Ph.D. thesis, 1973.

Starkey, D.R., 'Representation through intimacy: a study in the symbolism of monarchy and court office in early modern England', in I.M. Lewis, ed., *Symbols and Sentiments* (1977), pp. 187-224.

Starkey, D., 'From feud to faction: English politics, c.1450-1550', *History Today* (Nov. 1982), pp. 16-22.

Starkey, D., *The Reign of Henry VIII: Personalities and Politics* (1985).

Stoyle, M.J., '"Kill all the gentlemen"? (mis)representing the western rebels of 1549', *Historical Researh*, xcii (2019), pp. 50-72.

Stretton, T., *Women waging war in Elizabethan England* (Cambridge, 1998).

Strype, J., *The Life of the Learned Sir Thomas Smith* (1820).

Strong, R., *Holbein and Henry VIII* (1967).

Thompson, C.. *The Framework of the Crisis of the Aristocracy, 1558-1641* (Wivenhoe, 1986).

Thompson. C., *The Counting of Manors: Professor Stone's Reply Confuted* (Wivenhoe, 1990).
Thompson, S., 'The pastoral work of the English and Welsh bishops, 1500-1558', University of Oxford D. Phil. thesis, 1984.
Thrush, A., 'Survey', in A. Thrush and J.P. Ferris, eds., *The House of Commons 1624-1629*, 6 vols. (2010).
Tyacke, N., 'Introduction: locating the "English Revolution"', in N. Tyacke, ed., *The English Revolution c.1590-1720* (Manchester, 2007).
Waddell, B., 'Governing England through the manor courts, c. 1550-1850', *Historical Journal*, lv (2012), pp. 279-315.
Walker, G., *John Skelton and the Politics of the 1520s* (Cambridge, 1988).
Walker, G., 'The 1527 heresy trial of Thomas Bilney reconsidered', in G. Walker, ed., *'Persuasive Fictions': Faction, Faith and Political Culture in the Reign of Henry VIII* (Aldershot, 1996), pp. 143-65.
Walker, G., 'Continuity and change in the royal court in late medieval and renaissance England', in C.D. Baschiera and J. Everson, eds., *Scenes of Change: Studies in Cultural Tradition* (Pisa, 1996), pp. 193-210.
Wall, A., *Power and Protest in England 1525-1640* (2000).
Walsham, A., *Charitable Hatred: Tolerance and Intolerance in England, 1500-1700* (Manchester, 2006).
Walter, J., review of J.M. Gray, *Oaths and the English Reformation* (Cambridge, 2013), *English Historical Review*, cxxix (2014), pp. 1193-4.
Watts, J., *The Making of Polities: Europe, 1300-1500* (Cambridge, 2009).
Watts, J., '"Common weal" and "commonwealth": England's monarchical republic in the making, c.1450-c.1530', in A. Gamberin, J-P. Genet and A. Zorzi, eds., *The Languages of Political Society: Western Europe, 14th-17th Centuries* (2011), pp. 147-63.
Watts, J., 'King, lords and men in renaissance England: the poetry of John Skelton', in S. Boardman and J. Goodare, eds., *Kings, Lords and Men in Scotland and Britain, 1300-1625* (Edinburgh, 2014), pp. 121-35.
Weiss, M., 'A power in the north? The Percies in the fifteenth century', *Historical Journal*, xix (1976), pp. 501-9,
Wernham, R.B., 'The disgrace of William Davison', *English Historical Review*, xlvi (1931), pp. 632-6.
Wernham, R.B., 'Queen Elizabeth and the siege of Rouen, 1591', *Transactions of the Royal Historical Society*, xv (1932), pp. 163-79.
Wernham, R.B., review of G.R. Elton, *The Tudor Revolution in Government: Administrative Changes in the Reign of Henry VIII* (Cambridge, 1953), *English Historical Review*, lxxi (1956), pp. 92-5.
Wernham, R.B., 'Strategic Bombing', *Oxford Magazine*, 17 May 1962, pp. 308-9.
Wernham, R.B., *Before the Armada: The Growth of English Foreign Policy 1485-1588* (1966).
Wernham, R.B., *After the Armada: Elizabethan England and the Struggle for Western Europe* (Oxford, 1984).
Wernham, R.B., *The Return of the Armadas: the last years of the Elizabethan War against Spain, 1595-1603* (Oxford, 1994).
Wernham, R.B. 'G.R. Elton', paper read to the Senior Historians, Cumberlad Lodge, 1990.
White, A.B., *Self-Government at the King's Command: A Study in the Beginnings of English Democracy* (Minneapolis, 1933).
Willen, D., *John Russell First Earl of Bedford: one of the king's men* (1981).

Williams, P., 'A Revolution in Tudor History? Dr Elton's interpretation of the age', *Past & Present*, xxv (1963), pp. 3–8.
Williams, P., 'A revolution in tudor history?: the tudor state', *Past & Present*, xxv (1963), pp. 39–58.
Williams, P., 'A Revolution in Tudor History?', *Past & Present*, xxxi (1965), pp. 94–6.
Williams, P., review of G.R. Elton, *Policy and Police: the enforcement of the reformation in the age of Thomas Cromwell* (1972), *English Historical Review*, lxxxviii (1973), pp. 596–7.
Williams, P., review of W.K. Jordan, *Edward VI: the threshold of power. The dominance of the Duke of Northumberland* (1970) *English Historical Review*, lxxxviii (1973), pp. 597–8.
Williams, P., *The Tudor Regime* (Oxford, 1979).
Wood, A., *The Memory of the People: Custom and Popular Senses of the Past in Early Modern England* (Cambridge, 2013).
Wood, A., 'The deep roots of Albion's fatal tree: the Tudor state and the monopoly of violence', *History*, xcix (2014), pp. 403–17.
Worden, A.B., review of P. Gwyn, *The King's Cardinal: The Rise and Fall of Thomas Wolsey* (1990) in *London Review of Books*, xii (Nov. 1990).
Wrightson, K., *English Society 1580-1680* (1972).
Youings, J.A., ed., *Devon Monastic Lands, Devon and Cornwall Record Society, new series* I (1955).
Younger, N., 'The practice and politics of troop-raising: Robert Devereux, second earl of Essex, and the Elizabethan regime', *English Historical Review*, cxxvii (2012), pp. 566–91.
Younger, N., review of A. Gajda, *The Earl of Essex and late Elizabethan political culture* (2012), *English Historical Review*, cxxviii (2013), pp. 1564–66.
Youngs, D., '"A Besy Woman … and Full of Lawe": female litigants in early Tudor Star Chamber', *Journal of British Studies*, lviii (2019), pp. 735–50.

Index

Abel, Thomas 47
Act of Annates (1532) 82
    opposition in parliament 82
Act of Appeals (1533) 82
Act of Six Articles (1539) 47, 168
Act of Succession (1534) 47
Act of Uniformity (1549) 169
Act of Uniformity (1552) 169
Alcock, John, mayor of Canterbury 73
Amersham, Buckinghamshire 161
Amicable Grant (1525) 93, 95–6, 134, 147–8, 178
Anglo, Sydney 42
Armies, ways of raising 99–103
    experiences of dukes of Norfolk 102
Arthur (d. 1502), Prince, elder son of Henry VII 31
    married to Catherine of Aragon 31
Arundel, Thomas (1353–1414), Archbishop of Canterbury 161
Ashburton, Devon 158
Ashby, William 73
Ashford, Kent 161
Arundel, *see* Fitzalan, William
Aske, Robert 83, 167, 182–3
Aston, Trevor 187
Attlee, Clement, Prime Minister 123

Bacon, Nicholas 146
Baker, Sir John 74
Barnes, Robert 47
Barton, Elizabeth, nun of Kent 164
Batho, Gordon 63
Benenden 161
Bergavenny, George Nevill, fifth Lord (d. 1535) 103–4
Berwick, fortifications 105
Bible, translated into English 43, 168
Bindoff, S.T. 19
Boleyn, Anne 33, 45, 56
Bond of Association (1584) 34, 38
Bonner, Edmund, Bishop of London 169

Bossy, John 3
Bouchiers, earls of Essex 55
Boulonnais 175
Bourchier, John (1491–1560), second earl of Bath 57
Braddick, Michael 145
Brandon, Charles (c 1485–1545), duke of Suffolk 109, 149
Brewer, J.S (1809–1879) 6
Bridges, John, MP 73
Brodie, R.H. 6
Browne, Sir Anthony 74
Browne, Sir Matthew 74
Buckhurst, Thomas (1527–1608), Lord 154
Buckingham 161
Bulmer, Sir William 73
Bush, Michael 148

Calais 90
Camp, Treaty of (1546) 175
Campbell, James 71
Carew, Sir Peter 151
Carlisle 4, 47, 167
Carr, E.H. 1–2
Castillon, French ambassador 45
Catherine de Valois 18
Catherine of Aragon 31, 33, 35, 45
Catholics in reign of Queen Elizabeth 170–1
Cecil, William (1523–1598), Lord Burghley 38, 53, 54, 139
Chaitour, Christopher 45
Chapuys, Eustache, imperial ambassador 68
    and opposition to Henry VIII's divorce and break with Rome 82, 165
Charles I, king of England 38, 63, 67
Charles V, Holy Roman Emperor 32, 80
Charmley, 4
Chaucer, Geoffrey 52

Cheyne, Thomas 74
Cliffords earls of Cumberland 53
Clopton, William 44
Coke, Sir Edward 39
Coleman, Christopher, criticises Elton's *Tudor Revolution in Government* 117
Collinson, Patrick 37
   and 'monarchical republic' 37-8
Compton, Henry, Lord Compton 53
Compton, Sir William (d. 1528) 49, 53, 122, 133
Compton Wynyates 53
Constable, Sir Robert 167
Constables, parish 140, 141, 142, 143
Cook, Hugh, abbot, of Reading 46
Cope, Sir Anthony 84
Cornwall, Julian 61
Cornwall, rising against taxation (1497) 94
Cornwallis, Sir Thomas 33
coronations 43-4
Count of Feria, Spanish ambassador 37
Courtenay, Henry, marquess of Exeter (d. 1539) 54
   criticism of Break with Rome and dissolution of monasteries 54, 59
courts of law 121
Cranmer, Thomas, archbishop of Canterbury 146
Craven, West Riding, Yorkshire 93
Crewe, Ivor 122
Cromwell, Oliver 38
Cromwell, Thomas 6-7, 45, 46, 53, 73, 139, 146, 185
   annuities 128-30
   and corruption 128-30
   Cromwell's fortune in royal service and purchases of land 123, 129, 30
   Elton's exaggeration of Cromwell's role 124
   enforcement of royal supremacy 153, 166
   England as an empire 116
   and fortifications 105
   gifts 128-30
   and lord lieutenancy 102
   on MPs 73-4, 116
   on Norwich 73
   and parliament 116
   and Pilgrimage of Grace 148
   pressure on mayor of Canterbury 73
   and royal supremacy 116, 124
   supposed mastermind of a *Tudor Revolution in Government* 113
crown lands 90-1
Curteys, Richard, bishop of Chichester 140
customs dues 91-2

Dacre, Sir Cristopher 73, 167
Dacre, Thomas Lord 73
Dacre, William Lord 47, 58
Darcy, Thomas (d. 1537), Lord 84, 104, 148, 167
Darknall, Robert, MP 73
Davies, C.S.L. 15, 63
   criticisms of Elton 188
   critique of nobility 22
   critique of 'Tudor' England 18
   education and academic career 19-23
   and Ireland 174-5
   national service 19-20
   and Peter Wentworth 22, 86
   and propaganda 22
   and rebellions 20
   and Welsh history 20
Davies, Kathleen 19
Davies, Professor Rees 117
De La Pole, Edmund (?1472-1513), earl of Suffolk 32
   flight abroad 32
   sent back by Maximilian, executed by Henry VIII 1513 32
De la Pole, John (1442-92), second duke of Suffolk 32
   married to Elizabeth Plantagenet (1444-1503/4) 32
De La Pole, John (1460-87) 32
   earl of Lincoln, died at battle of Stoke 32
De La Pole, Richard, recognised as king by Louis XII, king of France 32
   claimed crown 32
   killed in battle of Pavia, 1525 32
De Vere, John, earl of Oxford 53

Devereux, Robert (1567–1601), second
    earl of Essex   50–1
  and Ireland   175
  and queen Elizabeth   50–1
Disenchantment   44
Dodd, Gwylym   42
Doncaster   55
Doyle, William   64
Dudley, Edmund   44
  accused by William Clopton   44, 146
  criticism of war   146
  and Henry VII's bonds and
      obligations   44
Dudley, Guildford (d. 1554), married to
    Lady Jane Grey   33
Dudley, John, earl of Warwick, duke of
    Northumberland (1500–53)
    33, 53
  and exclusion of Princess Mary   33
Dyer, Christopher   158

Edgecombe, Sir Peter   166
Edward II, king of England,
    deposition   33
Edward VI, king of England (1537–53)
    33, 36
  and exclusion of Mary   33, 36
Egerton, Thomas, Lord Chancellor
    Ellesmere   120
Ehrenberg, Eva   4
Ehrenberg, Ludwig   4
Ehrenberg, Victor   4–5
Elizabeth, queen of England (1533–1603)
    13–14
  accepted criticism over
      monopolies   81
  choice of councillors   39
  concerns over succession   34
  deliberate ambiguity   170
  dislike of theological debate   170
  and earl of Essex   50–1
  ejection of clergy in early years of
      Elizabeth's reign   172
  and foreign policy   13–14
  limited toleration in practice   171
  parsimony   90
  and portraits   42
  pressure from group of MPs over
      religion and succession   66, 171
  and progresses   43
  religious convictions and
      settlement   145, 170
  resisted councillors over foreign
      policy   37, 39
  shrewd ruler   37
  sparing in creation of nobles   60
  tyrant?   51
  and Wyatt's rebellion   33–4
Elizabeth Plantagenet (1444–1503/4),
    sister of Edward IV   32
Elton, Sir Geoffrey (1921–94), family
    background   1, 4
  applied for lecturerships at Liverpool,
      Glasgow and Cambridge   6–7
  appointed Regius Professor   7
  army service   5
  article on Caesar's Gallic
      Proconsulate   5
  asserts Cromwell's enhancement of
      parliament in 1530s, but came
      to question importance of
      parliaments   86
  attempts to secure publication of his
      Ph.D. thesis   8
  career at Cambridge   7
  chamber   114
  changed name from Gottfried
      Ehrenberg   5
  completed thesis   6, 7
  considered writing doctorate on Henry
      VIII's parliaments   5–6
  and corruption   128–30
  and court   132–3
  court of augmentations   114–15
  court of first fruits   114
  court of general surveyors   114–15
  court of wards   114
  defence of Henry VIII's methods   45
  discussions with V.H.H. Galbraith   10
  dismissive of the arts   42
  duchy of Lancaster   114, 118
  and *England under the Tudors*
      (1955)   10
  exchequer   114, 117
  and Hilary Mantel   191–2
  influence of earlier scholars   9–10
  and king's Council   116, 120–21
  King's secretary   115

and Lord Privy Seal   115
marginalised nobility   51, 64
married Sheila Lambert   6
over-estimated novelty of court of
    augmentations   119
parliament as institution   68
and *Practice of History*   7
reasons for lasting influence of Elton's
    Tudor Revolution   186
relationship with Sir John Neale   5
saw Cromwell's years in power as
    pivotal   176
saw late-fifteenth century
    arrangements as the medieval
    norm   118, 119
saw Pilgrimage of Grace as work of
    disaffected noblemen   148
scepticism about biography   191
similarities with claims of 'state
    formation'   117
studied Thomas Cromwell   6, 7
studying at Rydal School   4
studying for external degree,
    University of London   4–5
teaching at Rydal School   4–5
took Christmas Day and Boxing Day
    off   6
and *The Tudor Revolution in
    Government*   7, 8, 9, 19, 113–17
the *Tudor Revolution in Government* as
    historical construct   117
under-estimated administrative
    reforms of 1690s, 1780s and
    mid-nineteenth century
    118–19, 127
under-estimated medieval
    government   118, 127
under-estimated personal nature of
    government   129–30
under-valued amalgamations of
    1554   119–20
Elyot, Thomas   61
enemies to the realm   79, 81
Everett, Michael   8, 129
    and Cromwell and corruption   129

Faction, alleged in reign of Henry
    VIII   132
Fetherstone, Richard   47

Fincham, Kenneth   23
Fisher, H.A.L.   4
Fisher, John, bishop of Rochester   46, 164
Fisher, Robert, MP for Rochester   82
Fitzalan, William (1476–1544), eleventh
    earl of Arundel   82
Fitzgerald, Gerald, ninth earl of
    Kildare   174
Fleming, William   73
Fleurs, William, mayor of Oxford   73
Florence   150
Foister, Susan   41
Forest, John, Observant Franciscan   165
Fortescue, Sir John   39
    and constitutional monarchy   39
Foxe, John   161
Francis I, king of France   36, 42
Frankland, Noble   12
Froude, James Anthony (1818–1894)   9

Gairdner, J (1828–1910)   6
Galbraith, V.H.H. (1889–1976)   9, 10
Gardiner, Stephen, bishop of
    Winchester   74, 85, 166
Garret, Thomas   47
Gaunt, John of   104
General Proscription (1522)   93, 105,
    122, 156
gentry   156
Giffard, George   73
Gloucestershire, commissioners in   125,
    134
Godsalve, John, p   73
Grace à Dieu   109
Gray, J.M.   144, 164
Green, J.R (1837–1883)   9
Greer Evans, M.   9
Grey, Lady Jane   36
Grey, Lord of Wilton   151
    ransom after capture   109
Grey, Richard (d. 1524), third earl of
    Kent   60
Greys, earls of Kent   53
    Elizabeth Grey, Lady Lisle   45
Greys, marquesses of Dorset   55
Grindal, Edmund, archbishop of
    Canterbury   145, 171
gunfounding   106
Gunn, Steven   101, 102, 105

Guy, John 25, 180
Gwyn, Peter
   biography of Wolsey 24–7
   criticism of Elton 189
   discussion with J.J. Scarisbrick 25
   education and career 24
   planned book on partition of India 27
   presentation of Wolsey as activist 27
   Sussex Tapes 25

Hall, Edward, chronicler, impressed by pageantry 25, 42
   taxation 78–9
Hampton Court Palace 89
Hardy, Thomas 15
Harington, Sir John 41
Harris, Ian 3, 7, 8, 9, 10
Harriss, Gerald 16–18, 63, 64, 185
   academic career 17
   challenged claims for introduction of peacetime taxation 94
   criticises Elton's *Tudor Revolution in Government* 187
   studies in financial administration 17–18
   values 17
   war service 16–17
Harvests, poor 154
Harvey, Barbara 158
Hastings, George (d. 1544), first earl of Huntingdon 56
Hastings, William Lord 104
Hawkyard, Alastair 71, 81
Heal, Felicity 117
Henry I 52
Henry III, king of France 15
Henry IV 161
Henry VI, crowned king of France 5
Henry VI, miraculous cures 44
Henry VII, earl of Richmond, king of England (1457–1509) 18
   built Richmond Palace 41
   character 34
   initialled accounts 34
   married children to Spanish and Scottish royal families 31
   and riots in York 150
   tyrant? 44
   won crown at Bosworth Field 31

Henry VIII, king of England (1491–1547) 33
   allegedly influenced by factions 132–3
   and Amicable Grant 134
   and Anne Boleyn 33, 35
   and armed forces 99–100
   Bible in English 43
   building at Hampton Court, St James's, Westminster 41
   and Catherine of Aragon 33, 35, 45
   and chivalry 105
   deliberate ambiguity 168
   and duke of Buckingham 49–50
   foreign policy 35
   and fortifications on south coast 105
   and hybrid church 167
   imposition of oaths 164–5
   influenced by David, Old Testament monarch 109
   initialled accounts 35
   instigator of wars 35
   and Jane Seymour 33
   knowledge of Anglo-French warfare 108
   leaves difficult legacy 35
   and mass 167
   middle way 168
   and Pilgrimage of Grace 55–6, 148–9, 166–7
   and poor law 157–8
   proclamation in April 1539 168
   progresses 43
   and Protestantism 167–8
   refusal to accept Lutheran confession of Augsburg 168
   and Robert Aske 182–3
   and royal supremacy 124
   sales of land 92, 97
   secures legislation enacting the break with Rome 82–3, 85
   shrewd politician 35, 80
   and Sir George Throckmorton 83, 201
   thaumaturgic powers 44
   and Thomas More 183
   tyrant? 44–8
Herbert, Lord, of Cherbury (d. 1648) 133
Herbert, William (1506–1570), first earl of Pembroke 74

Heresy, prosecution of   161
    unwitting creation by church   162
Hindle, Steve   155
Hinton, Charterhouse   49
Hirst, Michael   192
History curriculum, English
    universities   9, 186
Hitler, Elton's skit on   4
Hobbys, sheriff of Kent   73
Hogarth, W.D.   8
Holbein, Hans, the younger   35
    Great Bible frontispiece   43
    portraits of Henry VIII   41
    propaganda   41–43
Hopkins, Matthew   182
Horsey, William, chancellor of the bishop
    of London   41
Houghton, John, prior, London
    Charterhouse   164
House of Lords, royal influence in   77
Howard, Henry (d. 1547), earl of
    Surrey   109
Howard, Sir Edward   109
Howard, Thomas (1443–1524), second
    duke of Norfolk, victor of
    Flodden   109
Howard, Thomas (1473–1554), third duke
    of Norfolk   36, 47, 56, 73, 93,
    109, 149, 151, 181
Howard, Thomas (1536–1572), fourth
    duke of Norfolk   101
Hoyle, Richard   134
Humfrey, Lawrence   61
Hunne, Richard   41
Husee, John   46
Hussey, John (d. 1537), Lord Hussey   55,
    148

injunctions of 1538   168
Ireland   174–5
    surrender and regrant   174
Isle of Wight, fears of French
    invasion   104
Ives, Eric   25

Jack, Sybil   35
James, Mervyn   62, 185–6
James II, king of England   67
Jenkinson, Sir Hilary   13

Jerome, William   47
John, king of England, and Magna
    Carta   39
JPs   139–40, 141, 142, 143, 166

Kerridge, Eric   61
Ket's rebellion   151, 153
King, Anthony   viii, 122
Kishlansky, Mark   64

Lambert, Sheila   6
Lantschner, P.   150
Latimer, Hugh   184
Latton, John   73
Lee, Rowland, bishop of Lichfield   46
Leland, John   46
Levyns, Christopher   7
Lewis, Peter   149
Loach, Jennifer (1945–95)   23–4, 62
    academic career   23–4
    biography of Edward VI   23–24
    criticism of Elton   189
    and parliaments   23–4
London   143
Longland, John, bishop of London   161
Lords lieutenant   102, 103
Louis XIV   67
Lucas, Colin   64
Luther, Martin   160, 162
    book-burnings and
        prohibitions   162–3

MacCulloch, Diarmaid, case for Cromwell
    as radical reformer   210
McFarlane, K.B. (Bruce)   16–18, 63–4
    critique of Elton's *Tudor
        Revolution*   185, 187
McGrath, Patrick   24
Machiavelli   35, 68
Macintyre, Angus   17
Mackenzie, Robert   48
Maddicott, John   74
Magnus, Thomas, archdeacon, East
    Riding, Yorkshire   114
Maidstone, Kent   161
Malkiewicz, Andrew   63
Mantel, Hilary, and Cromwell's
    memoranda   192
maps   53

Margaret, daughter of Henry VII,
  married to James IV, king of
  Scotland 31
Margaret, duchess of Burgundy, sister of
  Edward IV 31
Manners, Thomas (d. 1543), earl of
  Rutland 56
Marshall, Peter 201
Mary, queen of England 33, 36-7
  burnings 169
  defeats Wyatt's rebellion 36
  marries Philip of Spain 34
  religious repression 169-70
  secures outward conformity 169-70
  secures throne 33
  shrewd politician 36-7
Mary, Queen of Scots 34, 38, 58
Melanchthon, Philip 160
Middlemore, Humphrey, Prior, London
  Charterhouse 164
military revolution 106
Mitchell, Ian 27
Molyneux, John 80
monarchy 40
  prerogatives of monarchs 40
monasteries, dissolution of 90, 166-7
  abbots and monks encouraged to
    surrender houses to Henry
    VIII 167
monopolies 80-1, 85
More, Thomas 24, 46, 76, 83, 146, 155,
  168
Morrill, John 64
Morton, John, Lord Chancellor,
  Cardinal and archbishop of
  Canterbury 22
musters 103

Neale, Professor Sir John 5-6
  advice on publication of Elton's PhD
    thesis 8
  neglected role of nobility 62
  supervises R.B. Wernham's
    dissertation 11
negotiation between monarchs and
  subjects 144-6, 148-49
  limits to 151, 156
Nevills earls of Westmoreland 53
Newcastle, King's College 4

Newton, A.P. (1873-1942) 9
nobility, definition 53
  and central government 52
  cultural values 61-2
  declining and supposed financial
    crisis 49-51, 59-60
  defence against Scots 58
  and lord lieutenancy 57
  raising armed forces 56
  and royal court 52-3
Nonsuch Palace, Surrey 89
Northern rising (1569) 58-9

oaths, imposition of 144
ordnance, royal 106-7
Oxford, University of 162
Oxfordshire, opposition to religious
  reforms in 1549 151, 169

Paget, William 39, 85
Palmer, Julius 169
panegyric 42
  double-edged 42
paradoxes of power 36, 48, 49, 50, 87,
  149, 177, 183, 184
Pardons, royal 41
parliaments, early history of 67
  borough franchises 75
  creation of new boroughs 75
  deference towards monarchs 69
  franchise 69
  gentry and parliaments 69
  house of commons and taxation
    77-8
  infrequency of meetings 68
  and legislation 76
  and liberties of church 83
  occasional insistence on redress of
    grievances 80, 86
  opposition to Elizabeth's religious
    policy by organised
    minority 84
  opposition to feudal aids 79
  opposition to religious changes in
    Edward VI's reign 85
  opposition to religious changes in
    Mary's reign 84
  Pilgrims of Grace call for parliament in
    York 166-7

reformation parliament and alleged
    fundamental change   81, 84,
    123–4
resisted primer seisin bill   79
royal nominees   76–8
transformation in late seventeenth
    century   67
Parr, Katherine, queen of England   36
paternalism   154–5
Paulet, William, marquess of
    Winchester   120
Pennington, John   73
Percies, earls of Northumberland   53
Percy, Thomas, (1528–1572), seventh earl
    of Northumberland   58, 60
petitions   87
Peto, William, berated Henry VIII for
    sexual misconduct   201
Philip II, king of Spain   62
    plans for coronation   34
Philipps, Colin   143
Pickthorn, Kenneth   7
Pilgrimage of Grace   35, 36, 54, 55, 69,
    148, 166–7
Plantagenet, Arthur (d. 1542), viscount
    Lisle, Deputy of Calais   45
Plymouth   168
Pole, Sir Geoffrey   46
politicians, attitudes to   1–2
Pope, Sir Thomas   73
'popularity'   178
poverty and poor relief   157–9
Powell, Edward   47
praemunire   45
progresses, royal   43
propaganda   22, 41–3, 76–7
Pym, John   63

Rabb, Theodore K.   42
Radcliffe, Henry (c.1506–1557), second
    earl of Sussex   57
Radcliffe, Robert (c.1483–1542),
    lord Fitzwalter, first earl of
    Sussex   39
Radcliffe, Thomas (c.1525–83), third earl
    of Sussex   59
Radical reformation in reign of Edward
    VI   169
Ralegh, Sir Walter   39

Reed, alderman of London   93–4
Religious divisions, in 1553–1554   33, 37
    generally   159
Renard, Simon, Spanish ambassador   37
retaining   103–4
Reynolds, Susan   71
Rich, Rchard   42
Richard II, king of England,
    deposition   32
Ross, James   42
Russell, Conrad   63, 64
    and *Crisis of Parliaments*   68
Russell, Elizabeth   36–7
Russell, Francis (1587–1641), fourth earl
    of Bedford   63
Russell, Sir John (c.1485–1555),
    Lord Russell, first earl of
    Bedford   53, 54, 55
    crushes rebellion   55, 151
Rydal School, Colwyn Bay   4
Rye, Sussex   168

Sandon, Sir William   148
Scarisbrick, J.J.   25, 27
    discussion with Peter Gwyn   25
    Sussex Tapes   25
Sellar, W.C., and Yeatman, R.J., *1066 and
    All That* (1930)   35
Seymour, Edward, Lord Protector
    (1500–52)   58
    military activities   105, 109
    sympathy for poor commons   150
    toppled 1549   33
Seymour, queen Jane   33, 109
Seymour, Thomas (d. 1549), Lord
    Sudeley   33, 53, 85
Shakespeare, William   36, 72, 146–7
Sharington, Sir William   53
Sharpe, Kevin   64, 85
Sheffield, Lord   109
sheriffs   138
shipbuilding   107–8
Simnel, Lambert, pretender, claiming to
    be Edward, earl of Warwick, son
    of George, duke of Clarence,
    defeated at Stoke   31, 32, 43
Skelton, John, poet   26, 49
Sleaford, Lincolnshire   55, 148
Smith, Ralph. B   62

Smith, Sir Thomas, lawyer   31, 68, 87, 88
Sommer, Siegfried   4
Southern, Sir Richard   35
Southwell, Sir Richard   33
Stafford, Edward   80
Stafford, Edward (d. 1521), third duke of Buckingham   49, 59
Stanhope, Sir Michael   104
Stanley, Thomas (c.1435–1504), first earl of Derby   34
Stanleys, earls of Derby   53
Starkey, David   25
   criticises Elton's *Tudor Revolution in Government*   117, 130
   criticisms of Starkey   131
   emphasises privy chamber   130–2
   location of privy council   131
Starkey, John   73
State formation   176, 184
Stewart, James, duke of Albany   32
Stone, Lawrence   60
Stoyle, Mark   152, 182
Strickland, William   84
Strong, Roy   43
supplies to armed forces   108
Swallowfield   141
Syon, Brigittine nunnery   164

Tacitus   50
Talbot, Francis (1500–60), fifth earl of Shrewsbury   34, 63, 104
Talbot, George (1468–1538), fourth earl of Shrewsbury   55, 56, 109
   and Pilgrimage of Grace   55, 56, 63, 104, 149, 184
Talbot, Gilbert   46
Talbot, Gilbert (1552–1616), seventh earl of Shrewsbury   104, 154
taxation   77, 92–7
   bargaining in parliaments   78
   new principle of peacetime taxation   94–5
   reforms not attempted   120
Tempest, Thomas   70–1
Tempest, Thomas, advisor to rebels in 1536   32
Temse, MP   80, 82
Tenterden, Kent   161

Thatcher, Margaret   25
Thomas Stanley (1509–72), third earl of Derby   56
Throckmorton, Sir George   83, 201
   boasted that he had berated Henry VIII   201
Tolstoy, Nikolai   27
Tournai   1
Tout, T.F. (1855–1929)   9
Treason   40–1, 47, 49, 166
Tuchet, James, Lord Audley   59
Tudor, Edmund, earl of Richmond   18
Tudor, Owen (c.1400–1461)   18
Tuke, Brian   76
Tunstall, Cuthbert, bishop of Durham   162, 166
Tyndale, William   161
Tyranny   44, 47

Valor Ecclesiasticus   156
Vergil, Polydore, papal tax-collector and historian   25, 34
village assemblies   140–1
Vitalis, Orderic   52

Walker, Simon   142
Walsingham, Norfolk   145
Walsingham, Sir Francis   80
war, opposition to   146–7
Warbeck, Perkin, pretender, claiming to be Richard, duke of York, Edward IV's younger son   31
   attracted support   31
   captured and imprisoned   31
Warham, William, archbishop of Canterbury, Lord Chancellor   78, 162
Watts, John   144
Wentworth, Peter (1524–96)   22, 86
Wentworth, Thomas (1525–1584), Lord   33, 57
Wernham, R.B. (Bruce) (1906–1999)   5, 7, 11–15
   and *Analyses*   13
   assessment of Elton as Tudor historian   187
   and Bomber Command   11–14, 15
   and *Calendar of State Papers, Foreign*   11, 13

criticises Elton's *Revolution in Government* 117, 186–7
and monographs on Elizabethan foreign policy 13–15
philosophy of history 15
polemic against C.H. Wilson 13–14
and Public Record Office 11
war service 11–13
Westminster Palace 131–2
Weston, Richard 74
Whitehall Palace 89, 131–2
Whiting, Richard, abbot of Glastonbury 46
Williams, C.H. 7
Williams, Penry (1925–2013) 14, 16, 187–8
   critique of Elton's *Tudor Revolution* 16, 117, 151
Williams, Sir John 33
William the Silent 38
Wilson, C.H. 13–14
witchcraft 181–2
Wolsey 49
   activist 125
   Amicable Grant 93, 133–4, 78
   bargaining over taxation, survey of enclosures 122
   fall 45, 134
   reformer of church, especially monasteries 25
   relationship with Henry VIII 135
   Thomas, Lord Chancellor, Cardinal and Archbishop of York 22, 24
Wolsthrop, Sir Oswald 83
women and 'agency' 179
   petitioning 129
   plaintiffs in court 180–1
Wood, Andy 145, 206
Wren, Christopher 21
Wrightson, Keith, and polarisation of village society 152
Wriothesley, Thomas (1505–1550), earl of Southampton 73
Wyclif (d. 1384) 160–1
   response to 161
Wydvil, Elizabeth, daughter of Edward IV, wife of Henry VII, king of England 18

York 55, 150
Youngs, Deborah 180

Zwingli, Huldrych 162

www.ingramcontent.com/pod-product-compliance
Lightning Source LLC
Chambersburg PA
CBHW062216300426
44115CB00012BA/2088